AS BORDERS BEND

Pacific Formations: Global Relations in Asian and Pacific Perspectives
Series Editor: Arif Dirlik

AS BORDERS BEND

Transnational Spaces on the Pacific Rim

Xiangming Chen

ROWMAN & LITTLEFIELD PUBLISHERS, INC.
Lanham • Boulder • New York • Toronto • Oxford

ROWMAN & LITTLEFIELD PUBLISHERS, INC.

Published in the United States of America
by Rowman & Littlefield Publishers, Inc.
A wholly owned subsidiary of The Rowman & Littlefield Publishing Group, Inc.
4501 Forbes Boulevard, Suite 200, Lanham, MD 20706
www.rowmanlittlefield.com

P.O. Box 317, Oxford OX2 9RU, UK

British Library Cataloguing in Publication Information Available

Library of Congress Cataloging-in-Publication Data

Chen, Xiangming, 1955–
  As borders bend : transnational spaces on the Pacific rim / Xiangming Chen.
    p. cm. — (Pacific formations : global relations in Asian and Pacific perspectives)
  Includes bibliographical references and index.
  ISBN 0-7425-0093-4 (cloth : alk. paper) — ISBN 0-7425-0094-2 (pbk. : alk. paper)
  1. Asia—Boundaries. 2. Pacific Area—Boundaries. 3. Regionalism—Asia. 4.
Regionalism—Pacific Area. 5. Globalization. I. Title. II. Series: Pacific formations
  DS33.3.C535 2005
  909'.09823083—dc22

                                                                           2004018261

Printed in the United States of America

$\otimes$™ The paper used in this publication meets the minimum requirements of American
National Standard for Information Sciences—Permanence of Paper for Printed Library
Materials, ANSI/NISO Z39.48-1992.

To Maomao, Yaya, Lele in Illinois
and my parents in Beijing

Contents

Please see the book's Web site:

www.rowmanlittlefield.com/ISBN/0742500934

for additional materials.

Illustrations

Photos

Maps

Figures

Tables

Appendix Tables

Preface

L ITTLE DID I KNOW SEVERAL YEARS AGO that the book I began to write would be so timely. The terrorist attacks on September 11, 2001, the subsequent U.S. responses to tighten border security, and the spread of SARS (severe acute respiratory syndrome) in 2003 have thrust international borders into the limelight. This renewed importance of borders and border regions struck me in very personal ways while I was crossing a few international boundaries in the Asia-Pacific region while doing the research for this book. These border crossings have taught me real-world lessons about the double-edged role of international boundaries. Borders can be either barriers or bridges. They both separate and connect very different or similar territories. They have both material and symbolic functions. They create both political hurdles and economic opportunities. They can easily isolate border cities and regions or link them directly or indirectly to the global economy.

Borders have fascinated me, leading me to write about the larger comparative significance of my personal experiences and observations at one international frontier that since 1997 has become a "formal" intra-national border—one that is bent and stretched by dynamic flows into a broader transborder space. I first crossed the border between China and Hong Kong from the Chinese city of Shenzhen, in Guangdong province, on my way back to the United States in 1985. Although Shenzhen had already opened to Hong Kong investment as a booming special economic zone (SEZ), it had a tiny and shabby railroad terminal and a poor and inefficient border crossing facility. I dragged my heavy luggage along a lengthy, bumpy walkway to the Luohu (Lowu) checkpoint and, after slowly clearing the mainland passport and visa checks, was detained for one hour by Hong

Kong immigration officials. I had a valid visa and a confirmed plane ticket, but they questioned why a citizen of the People's Republic of China (PRC) would go to the trouble of traveling through Hong Kong to fly to the United States.

I was fortunate enough to catch my flight from Hong Kong on time, but I realized that people's movement across the Hong Kong–Shenzhen border was still tightly controlled, especially for PRC citizens. In several subsequent crossings over the Hong Kong–Shenzhen border by train or boat since the late 1980s on a PRC passport, I have witnessed and experienced increasing convenience in going through the checkpoints on both sides. There are now five crossing points, as opposed to only one when I first crossed that border. Hong Kong businesspeople commute to Shenzhen by train or to the industrial district of Shekou by boat daily or weekly, and some of them move on to other nearby cities in the Pearl River Delta (PRD). Hong Kong residents go to Shenzhen to eat, buy less expensive goods, and sing Karaoke every day, especially over the weekend. According to a 2001 survey on cross-border consumption by Hong Kong residents, eating accounted for 86.2 percent of the total spending, which averaged about US$40–65 per person per day for the majority. These cross-border activities have become more intensive and frequent since 1997, when the border shifted from an international to an intra-national status with the transition of Hong Kong's sovereignty to China. This border has since become an even stronger anchor for the increasingly integrated Greater Southeast China Subregion (GSCS).

While I have personally experienced and observed the increasingly more open and lively Guangdong–Hong Kong border, I am keenly aware of the always possible and rarely predictable shift between the bridging and barrier role of borders that can be initiated by government authorities in response to changing circumstances near or beyond the borderline itself. Take a look at the two photographs reproduced here. The first shows a young man from Hong Kong flashing his travel document after an easy and smooth crossing after 11 p.m. through the Luomazhou (Lok Ma Chau) checkpoint that became open for 24-hour operations in January 2003. This measure, agreed to by both the Guangdong and Hong Kong governments after extended negotiations, was necessary for promoting greater cross-border flows and more convenient border crossings. The second photo, however, shows an officer of Hong Kong's Health Department checking the body temperature of a mainland visitor at the immigration center at the Luohu–Hong Kong border checkpoint on New Year's Day 2004 as a strict preventive measure against SARS, which broke out in Guangdong province in November 2002 and spread to Hong Kong and other Asian countries in 2003. There was a public outcry in Hong Kong over the weakness of the government in communicating with Guangdong and handling the crisis, with some officials and commentators calling for restricting the flow of people across the border if the SARS crisis were to persist. The image in the second photo is one of escalated infection control over border crossers to prevent the return of the virus, but this increased control has slowed down the normal flows through the busiest land border crossing between China and the outside world, especially after a new travel scheme began to encourage more mainland tourists to visit Hong Kong. The two photos place the bridging versus the barrier effect of borders into sharp contrast.

The Guangdong–Hong Kong border is only one part of this book, which is really a comparative study of a number of transborder subregions in the Asia-Pacific context and beyond. It is an examination as well of the numerous subnational territorial areas that make up these transborder subregions, and the concrete places—cities and towns and their hinterlands—that are embedded within them. More importantly, the book attempts to make comparative sense of the varied economic, political, and sociocultural links among these places within the different transborder subregional contexts. Finally, the book places various local units of the transborder subregions in the layered spaces of transnational and intra-regional flows, examining how the units and flows are mediated by national and subnational contexts and policies.

Acknowledgments

A book project of this geographic scope and complexity would be absolutely impossible to undertake without the various forms of help from knowledgeable people and enabling institutions·spread across multiple localities on both sides of the Pacific. I want to begin by thanking the Great Cities Institute of the University of Illinois at Chicago (UIC)—my home institution—for a Great Cities Faculty Scholarship in 1999. This time off from teaching allowed me to draft the first two chapters and to conceive the structure and content of the remaining chapters. Additional support from UIC came through an International Development Seed Fund from the John Nuveen Center for International Affairs. With this grant, I was able to purchase valuable Chinese publications that contained specifically needed statistical information on my cases. Beyond my home institution, I received financial assistance through a research grant on social capital in 1999 from the Pacific Basin Research Center of Soka University of America in California, which at the time was affiliated with the John F. Kennedy School of Government at Harvard University. I am grateful to John Montgomery at Harvard and John Heffron at Soka University of America for their trust in my proposed study of transnational ethnic social capital in the Asia-Pacific context. I think they would be happy to see that what I proposed

A Hong Kong border crosser flashes his travel document after he clears the Luomazhou (Lok Ma Chau) checkpoint, which became a 24-hour border gate in January 2003. (Photo courtesy of the South China Morning Post, *scmp.com)*

A Hong Kong health officer checks the body temperature of a mainland visitor at the immigration counter at the Luohu (Lowu) checkpoint on New Year's Day 2004. (Photo courtesy of the South China Morning Post, *scmp.com)*

to study then has turned out to be a critical part of the analytical framework for the book now. I would also like to thank the then Centre for Advanced Studies at the National University of Singapore, especially its associate director at the time, K. C. Ho, for hosting me as a short-term visiting scholar during June 1999. During my stay I had access to valuable collections at the main library and the library of the Institute of Southeast Asian Studies on campus. While there, I also benefited from talking to several well-informed scholars whose research focused on the growth triangles in Southeast Asia.

Many people of diverse nationalities in multiple places have offered different forms of help to my research and writing for this book. I owe special thanks to Anthony Orum, Joel Smith, Todd Outcalt, and two reviewers for their comments on the prospectus and various drafts of most chapters. I appreciate the feedback from Ted C. Fishman on chapter 1, William Bridges on chapter 3, Dennis Judd and Audie Klotz on chapters 1–3, Kim Won Bae and Gilbert Rozman on chapters 5–6, David Rubinstein, Leslie Sklair, and Alvin Y. So on chapters 1–4, and Peter Brimble on chapter 7. An intensive conversation with my colleague and friend Anthony Orum on a flight from Chicago to Shanghai in May 2002 prompted me to think long and hard about the analytical mileage I would gain by using a version of the book's main title.

I received a variety of published and unpublished material, including valuable documents and keenly needed statistics, from Peter Brimble and Damrong Saengkaweelert in Bangkok; Kim Won Bae, Jung Hong, Lim Jung Keun, and SangWon Lee in Seoul; Kim Dae Dong and Park Hyang Su in Incheon; Chi-sheng Shih in Taiwan; Ted C. Fishman, Judith Larson, and Kim Scipes in Chicago; Jin Zhongfan in Shanghai; Lu Xianguo, Wang Shengjin, and Zhao Rusheng in Changchun in China's Jilin province; Andrew Marton in Singapore; Tang Guohui in Kunming in China's Yunnan province; and Femy Calderon and Tao Zhang in Tokyo. The people who either facilitated my field interviews or took the time to answer my questions include Jin Zhongfan; Yooshik Gong; Hyung-Kook Kim in Seoul; Lee Yune and Oh Joong Keun in Incheon; Wang Shengjin and Zhu Xianping in Changchun; Xu Mingzhe in Yanji, Jilin province; Peng Xizhe and Xu Jin in Shanghai; and Tang Guohui in Kunming in China's Yunnan province.

While the various types and sources of information provided to me were rich and relevant, I could not incorporate everything of value due to space constraint. Readers interested in more details about the diverse cities and places, many of which are located in frontier regions and are understudied, can find additional information and discussion at this book's Web page: www.rowmanlittlefield.com/isbn/0742500934.

I have gained analytical insights and factual knowledge bearing on my cases from conversations or e-mail communications with Gary Gereffi, William

Parish, James Rosenau, Nian Song, Rebekah Sundin, and Stephen Warner in Chicago; Mark Selden from Binghamton; Jeff Broadbent from Minneapolis; Terry McGee from Vancouver; Tae Kyung Sung in Austin; Alvin So in Hong Kong; Liu Hong in Shekou, Guangdong province; Alan Smart in Shanghai and Albany, New York; K. C. Ho, Martin Perry, and Henry Yeung in Singapore; Heike Löschmann, Sedara Kim, Nguyen Hoai Qieng, and Pham Quang Minh in Hanoi; George Abonyi, Heim Yee Leong, Toru Tatara, Christian Wagner, and Tao Zhang in Tokyo; and Anne Haile, Turo-Kimmo Lehtonen and Stephen Rose in Helsinki. Alan Smart's accidental mentioning of *The South China Morning Post* online, to which I ended up subscribing, has kept me abreast of new developments in Taiwan, Hong Kong, and South China. I thank the Korea Economic Institute of America in Washington, D.C., for sending me periodic publications of valuable and up-to-date articles and reports on developments in various bilateral inter-state relations in Northeast Asia. I am indebted to Young Cho, Moon-Hee Choi, SangWon Lee, and Yoosik Youm at UIC for translating some crucial material from Korean into English. I express deep thanks to my former and current undergraduate and graduate students, Robert Anderson, Wei Huang, and Hermann Maiba, for locating the relevant literature. Many thanks go to Jiaming Sun, who was such an able research assistant to this and another project for over three years; he honed his geographic information systems (GIS) skills through numerous modifications of the maps, which Philip Schwartzberg, a wonderful cartographer, has reproduced and enriched to such a high quality and with fine details. I also thank Professor Takeshi Hamashita at the University of Tokyo for allowing me to use his map as map 2.1 in this book. While I am grateful to all the people mentioned above, I am alone responsible for any factual or interpretive errors that may remain in the book.

I have presented related papers and some drafts of these chapters at a number of national and international conferences and workshops. These include the American Sociological Association annual meetings in Chicago in August 1999 and Washington, D.C., in August 2000; international conferences in Hong Kong and Macau in July 1997; an international conference on Taiwan at the University of Illinois at Urbana, Champaign, in September 1997; the 22nd conference of the Political Economy of World System Section of the American Sociological Association at Northwestern University in April 1998; an international conference in Hiroshima, Japan, in December 1998; the Fourth ASEAN Inter-University Seminar in Pattani, Thailand, in June 1999; the 16th Pacific Regional Science Conference in Seoul in July 1999; an invited workshop on social capital at the Kennedy School of Government at Harvard University in August 1999; an international conference on social capital at Aspen Institute Berlin in Berlin in May 2000; an international conference in Hanoi in February 2003; the

Department of Development and International Relations at Aalborg University in Denmark in October 2003; the East Asian and Globalization Workshops at the University of Chicago in November 2003; a workshop on regional cooperation sponsored by the Asian Development Bank Institute in Tokyo in December 2003; and a symposium on "Enclave" sponsored by the School of Architecture at Yale University in March 2004. Feedback and comments from the audience and participants were helpful in clarifying and sharpening many of the arguments and points in this book.

I express deep thanks to Susan McEachern, executive editor at Rowman & Littlefield, and Arif Dirlik at the University of Oregon, the series editor, for their tremendous patience and continued belief in my ability to complete the book, even when I began to doubt it myself at times, especially when other research projects and commitments interfered with my progress and deadlines. I am also grateful to assistant editor Jessica Gribble, production editor Jehanne Schweitzer, and copy editor Eileen Smith at Rowman & Littlefield for guiding the book through the copyediting and production process to publication.

Last but not least, I am grateful to my parents, my wife, Xiaoyan Hua (Maomao), and our two children, Kayla (Yaya) and Byron (Lele), who supported me wholeheartedly during several years of devoting my considerable attention and energy to the research, travel, and writing for the book when I should have spent more time with them. It is to them and my parents that I lovingly dedicate this book.

Abbreviations

ADB	Asian Development Bank
AEC	ASEAN Economic Community
AFTA	ASEAN Free Trade Area
APEC	Asia-Pacific Economic Cooperation
ASA	Association of Southeast Asia (no longer exists)
ASEAN	Association of Southeast Asian Nations
BCCA	Baltic Chambers of Commerce Association
BECZ	Border Economic Cooperation Zone (Hunchun, Jilin province, China)
BEZ	Border Economic Zone (Vietnam)
BIMP-EAGA	Brunei-Indonesia-Malaysia-Philippines East ASEAN Growth Area
BIP	Border Industrialization Program (Mexico)
BTA	Bilateral Trade Agreement
BYSS	Bohai/Yellow Sea Subregion
CBRERA	China Bohai Region Economic Research Association
CBSS	Council of Baltic Sea States
CCAE	Chinese Central Academy of Ethnology
CDRI	Cambodian Development Research Institute
CEAO	West African Economic Community
CEPA	Closer Economic Partnership Agreement (China and Hong Kong)
CMI	Chiang Mai Initiative
CNAC	China National Air Corporation

CPU	Central Processing Unit
DMZ	Demilitarized Zone (between North and South Korea)
DRAM	Dynamic Random Access Memory
DSP	Digital Signal Processor
EABC	East ASEAN Business Council
EAGA	East ASEAN Growth Area
EBRD	European Bank for Reconstruction and Development
ECAFE	United Nations Economic Commission for Asia and the Far East
EDC	Economic Development Board (Singapore)
EIS	Environmental Information System
EPZ	Export Processing Zone
ESCAP	Economic and Social Commission for Asia and the Pacific
ETCNCB	Economic and Trade Cooperation with Neighboring Countries Bureau (China)
EU	European Union
EUREGIO	The first cross-border cooperation program in Europe (between Germany and the Netherlands)
EWEC	East-West Economic Corridor (Greater Mekong Subregion)
FDI	Foreign Direct Investment
FETZ	Free Economic and Trade Zone (Rajin/Sonbong, North Korea)
FEZ	Free Economic Zone (Nakhodka, RFE)
FTA	Free Trade Agreement
FTZ	Free Trade Zone
GDP	Gross Domestic Product
GEF	Global Environmental Facility
GIS	Geographic Information Systems
GMS	Greater Mekong Subregion
GMS-BF	Greater Mekong Subregion Business Forum
GRDP	Gross Regional Domestic Product
GSCS	Greater Southeast China Subregion
GTS	Greater Tumen Subregion
HEPZ	Hunchun Export Processing Zone (Jilin province, China)
HK	Hong Kong
HKTDC	Hong Kong Trade Development Council
IC	Integrated Circuit
IIA	Incheon International Airport
IMF	International Monetary Fund
IMS-GT	Indonesia-Malaysia-Singapore Growth Triangle
IMT-GT	Indonesia-Malaysia-Thailand Growth Triangle

INTERREG	A Cross-Border Cooperation Program of the European Union
IT	Information Technology
ITDC	Industry and Technology Development Council (Hong Kong)
KCRC	Kowloon Canton Railway Corp (Hong Kong)
KEI	Kyushu Economy International (Japan)
KIIPC	Kyushu International Information Promotion Council
KMT	Kuomintang (The Nationalist Party on Taiwan)
KOFTA	Korea Foreign Trade Association
LSI	Large-Scale Integration
MFA	Multi-Fiber Agreement
MITI	Ministry of International Trade and Industry (Japan)
MOFTEC	Ministry of Foreign Trade and Economic Cooperation (China)
MOU	Memorandum of Understanding
MRC	Mekong River Commission
NAFTA	North American Free Trade Agreement
NET	Natural Economic Territory
NGO	Non-Government Organization
NPA	Nature Protection Area
OBM	Original Brand-Name Manufacturing
ODM	Original Design Manufacturing
OEM	Original Equipment Manufacturing
PC	Personal Computer
PCB	Printed Circuit Board
PCME	Program for Mexican Communities Abroad
PRC	People's Republic of China
PRD	Pearl River Delta (Guangdong province, China)
PTA	Preferential Trade Agreement
R&D	Research and Development
RFE	Russian Far East
SAP	Strategic Action Plan
SAR	Special Administrative Region (Hong Kong)
SARS	Severe Acute Respiratory Syndrome
SEAC	State Ethnic Affairs Commission (China)
SEZ	Special Economic Zone
SIJORI-GT	Singapore-Johor-Riau Growth Triangle (later became IMS-GT)
SME	Small and Medium-Sized Enterprise
SSB	State Statistical Bureau (China)

SSIB	Shenzhen Statistical and Information Bureau
TCE	Thomson Consumer Electronics (France)
TDA	Transboundary Diagnostic Analysis
TEU	Twenty-Foot Equivalent Unit (Container)
TRADP	Tumen River Area Development Program
TRBZ	Tumen River Basin Zone
TREZ	Tumen River Economic Zone
TREDA	Tumen River Economic Development Area
UIC	University of Illinois at Chicago
UNDP	United Nations Development Programme
UNOPS	United Nations Office for Project Services
WTO	World Trade Organization
YRD	Yangtze River Delta
YSSR	Yellow Sea Subregion
ZHPH	Zhonghua Publishing House (China)
ZMM-GT	Zambia-Malawi-Mozambique Growth Triangle

I
BENDING BORDERS AND EMERGING
TRANSNATIONAL SPACES

1

Transborder Dynamics in a Global Era

Situating the Asia-Pacific Transborder Subregions

LIKE WARS, NATIONALIST ASPIRATIONS, and the natural rerouting of great rivers, globalization changes the world's borders by bending and stretching them out of shape and thus creating new transnational spaces. State borders, which on maps define political boundaries, no longer draw the line in people's lives they once did. Often, borders are still where states interdict goods, people, and information, legal or otherwise, but they are just as importantly where trade—including the exit and entrance of people, together with their skills and knowledge—is most intense. During times of war, even desolate borders, if not successfully closed, grow hyperactive with the swapping of goods, human beings, intelligence, and creeds. After the 2003 U.S.-led war against Iraq, Iraq's border with Iran, though officially closed for 20 years since the beginning of the Iran-Iraq war, was reopened to religious pilgrims from Iran. But there are also leaky gateways along the border for smugglers and militants. While former Iraqi army officers guide anti-American Afghan veterans into Iraq across the rugged desert, militants disguised as Iranian merchants or religious pilgrims carry illicit drugs, weapons, and explosives into Iraq to fuel the guerrilla campaign.[1] Everywhere, tumultuous forces, sometimes violent, sometimes economic, sometimes both, are blurring state borders, merging economies closer together and rendering them inexorably interdependent. Borders continue to contain self-described national populations and self-described national activity, but the resurgence of myriad ethnic groups and regional cultures is pushing and stretching their limits. New power centers with their own identities are springing out of once politically trivial and economically marginal landscapes. Smaller, peripheral cities and towns near newly active borders are growing into important and prosperous centers.

The pace and scale of changes at the border highlight a central irony of our time. Borders have become the loci of openness rather than its limit. The late twentieth century had more national borders than the previous century. Yet the world was also more open than at any other time in modern history. Compounding the irony is the fact that as the traditional significance of state borders erodes, border regions are reconfiguring the scope of economic, spatial, and sociocultural dynamics both within and across global, regional, and local levels. To add one more layer of contradiction: we all now live in a world where we grow ever more aware of border dynamics, even when those borders manifest themselves at remote, distant frontiers that we will never cross. This is clearly illustrated by the concern of U.S. citizens about border security and the U.S. government's redoubled efforts at border enforcement following the terrorist attacks of September 11, 2001. The concern strikes Americans as local and global at the same time; they must guard against an amorphous global threat to their own communities. America's newly guarded borders are also supremely relevant to any nation in the network of global trade. Ironically, American government policy following September 11 has been to promote international trade as the key to peace, but also to strictly enforce U.S. borders.

As economic flows across borders intensify, they generate serious social and spatial consequences. As Gerald Blake (1994, p. xii) argues, "boundaries create landscapes, and fundamentally affect communications, settlement patterns, and access to resources." Going a step further in this book, I contend that as borders get pushed and pulled by both domestic and global forces, border regions develop their own distinctive transborder (sub)regional character and structure that in turn reorganize broader national and local political and economic spaces into a new transnational space.

Accelerated Global De-bordering and Re-bordering

Over the last 20 years, national borders in every corner of the globe have undergone an unprecedented opening and blurring that can be dubbed a simultaneous *de-bordering* and *re-bordering*. Rather than referring to simple, literal changes of international boundaries, de-bordering and re-bordering describe a broad, complex process in which borders are considered mutating spaces rather than fixed lines and where the sovereignty of people acting on their own plays a more powerful role than a nation acting or struggling to act as a unified whole. If the national slogan of yesterday was "Out of Many, One," a slogan that fits the shifting reality of today's states is "Out of Many, Many More." This reflects the simultaneous processes and outcomes of globalization and localization. In Rosenau's (1997) definition, globalization is a process that compels individuals and their collectives to act similarly and thus broaden boundaries or de-emphasize them, while localization is a process that narrows the horizons of individual and collective actors and heightens the limiting role of boundaries. With more globalization, the flow of transnational capital and the types of transborder transactions have multiplied geometrically. As more national economies are drawn into the global economic system, the total length of borders open to trade and investment has increased. As most countries integrate more with the global economy, more sections of and points on their borders open to more intensive interactions with more powerful forces and actors beyond their control. While these are features and processes of general de-bordering, they may hit the countervailing forces of localization. This encounter or clash is not necessarily zero-sum. Rather, the meeting of two forces can result in re-bordering. If, for example, more porous and open borders bring nasty unintended consequences, such as new cross-border crime or drug trafficking or dangerous political ideas, and states are forced to rethink their borders as a result, both globalization and localization will have had an effect.

De-bordering and re-bordering also occur across spaces of every scale, from local to global. Although bordered nations have become more involved in the global system, some of the strongest transborder activity is local, with global ties that are limited or indirect at best. Since economic and sociospatial characteristics of border regions and localities tend to differ from the traditional or majority characteristics of the nations of which they are part, the effects of globalization on border regions deserve to be examined up close, in their own local and regional contexts. This book demonstrates that the intersection of global, regional, and local forces along and across borders is a major force behind the formation of transborder subregions. It looks primarily, but not exclusively, at lands of the Asia-Pacific, where this trend has been particularly strong over the last 20 years or so. The dynamics of world trade, politics, and security fall increasingly under the influence of the world's border regions. Any consideration of the world's future must count this trend along with those driven by more traditionally bordered regions and states.

The Reconfigured Nation-State and National Boundaries

De-bordering and re-bordering have been going on since humans first drew lines in the sand. State formation is the most common way in which international boundaries have been drawn and redrawn over time. Against the long history of state formation, the pace at which nation-states have been created anew or reorganized from earlier states or other political forms (e.g., empires, colonized territories) has accelerated through the end of the twentieth century. From 660 BCE, when Japan came into political existence, to 1776, when the United States was declared a nation, states came into being on average once every 175 years. State formation before the nineteenth century was extremely slow despite the signing of the Treaty of Westphalia in 1648, which laid the foundation for the sovereign state. The nineteenth century saw the formation of states at an average of one every four years, for a total of 28. In the first half of the twentieth century, one state was formed every 18 months, with 82 states in 1950, while the formation of states quickened to one in every six months in the latter half of the twentieth century. Just after 1990, 23 new states raised their flags, and most of them have joined the United Nations. By 2003, there were 192 official, independent states; 191 of them (except the Vatican City) were formal members of the United Nations.[2] The most dramatic surge of state formation occurred in 1991, when the collapse of the Soviet Union led to the sudden birth of 14 new independent states, while the disintegration of the former Yugoslavia gave rise to several new independent states. This type of state re-formation not only has redefined and reconfigured many national boundaries but also has reshaped the relationship between the central and local governments of both old and new states.

Generally speaking, as the number of states increases, the total number of national borders also increases. In mid-1993, there were roughly 311 land boundaries in the world, and about 160 of them reached a coast, where they were the beginning point for offshore boundaries. However, the precise number of both land and sea boundaries is difficult to establish (Blake, 1994).[3] As more borders are added to the world map, old disputes and new tensions over international boundaries arise. A number of international boundaries in long-standing dispute make the status of land and offshore border territories uncertain and subject to periodic military conflicts. The Spratly Islands in the South China Sea, the site of potential oil and natural gas, have been claimed by China, Taiwan, Vietnam, Malaysia, and the Philippines since Japan gave up its claim in 1951. The continuing dispute has triggered political and military tension between China and the Philippines in recent years. The long-standing dispute between India and Pakistan over Kashmir since 1947, which triggered three border wars through 1999 and claimed 65,000 lives, mostly civilians, flared up again in 2002 during the war against terrorism in Afghanistan. It remains the most divisive issue for the contentious India-Pakistan relationship, despite the recent efforts and progress by both countries and the Kashmiri separatists to resolve the territorial conflict.

Successful resolution of border disputes generally leads to renewed and improved cross-border economic and social ties. Illustrative cases include the growing border trade between China and Vietnam and China and the Russian Far East (RFE) in the 1980s and 1990s. Russia and Kazakhstan, by agreeing to delimit some 7,500 km of their borderline in 2004 to end the border dispute from the 1991 breakup of the Soviet Union, began new cooperation in fighting against terrorism, weapons smuggling, drug trafficking, and illegal migration.

A re-bordering was set in motion by the formation of new states, and the subsequent interface of more borders may be followed by more intensive cross-border interactions on a distinctive transnational regional scale. This type of transborder regional development could be facilitated by revitalized historical, ethnic, and cultural connections across borders. The Caucasus and Caspian Sea region in Central Asia is a case in point. The breakup of the Soviet Union into independent states and autonomous republics, coupled with its being an important part of the old Silk Road between Europe and Asia, brought about growing economic activity and initiatives related to the transportation of abundant oil and other commodities across the new borders. Instead of through Russia, Uzbekistan has been routing more trainloads of cotton along the Caucasus corridor across the Caspian Sea to the Azerbaijani port of Baku and on to the Georgian port of Poti. A new pipeline began to pump oil from Baku to Supsa, near Poti, in 1999. The United States has committed funds to explore the feasibility of building a US$2.5 billion,[4] 1,650-km oil line from the Azerbaijani capital of Baku, through Georgia, to Turkey's deep-water port of Ceyhan on the Mediterranean Sea.[5] These costly transnational infrastructure projects, however, have been slow to start due to continued political instability and ethnic conflict, which exemplifies the kind of complexities involved in the transborder subregions examined in several later chapters.

Formal Regional Integration and Border Transformations

Another driving force behind the accelerated global de-bordering and re-bordering is the formation of formally integrated regional unions or trade blocs such as the European Union (EU) and North American Free Trade Agreement (NAFTA).

Illustrations from the European Union

While the European Union provides an institutionalized supranational cooperative framework and a governance structure, the removal of trade barriers and freer transnational mobility of production factors have had an uneven local impact on the status, identity, and role of border cities and towns and their interactions. The French town of Saverne provides an example. Located in the Alsace region of northeastern France bordering Germany and Switzerland, Saverne and the surrounding area changed to German control four times between 1648 and 1944, when it was last reclaimed by France. This history, coupled with a border location, has imbued its people with neither a French identity nor a German one. In recent years, Saverne has taken on a pro-European appearance and identity, with EU flags flying everywhere, local residents gathering in the Euro Bar next to the Hotel Europe, and the mayor nicknamed "Mr. Europe."[6] (See chapter 8 for a discussion of the trinational Alsace-Baden-Basel border subregion.)

Regional integration has also reinforced or reshaped the structure and scope of border regions or subregions under the overarching supranational system. To promote cross-border cooperation, a number of Dutch and German municipalities created the EUREGIO, one of the oldest border regions in Europe, in the 1950s. In the early 1990s, the EUREGIO comprised 106 municipalities in an area with 1.9 million residents. Under the EU, initiatives for cooperation along the border of Germany and the Netherlands have been increasing. The EU's policy for stimulating development in economically disadvantaged regions has revitalized many of the 40 unevenly developed "Euregions" defined at the end of the 1980s.[7] One such border region that began to seek new economic opportunities is the Euregion Maas-Rhine, located along the Dutch-Belgian-German borders. It is geographically larger than the older EUREGIO and has pursued cross-border cooperation since 1976 (see chapter 8 for a discussion of both cases).

Examples from NAFTA

The North American Free Trade Agreement offers an exemplary context in which the local impact of formal transnational regional integration on border cities and regions has become more visible and intensified. Economic integration over the U.S.-Mexico border has accelerated since the onset of NAFTA in 1994, evidenced by the border-intensive nature of Mexico's rapidly growing importation of U.S. recoverable waste. In El Paso, Texas, hundreds of flatbed trucks, container-haulers, and tankers line up at the border to cross into Mexico each day, carrying waste paper, beverage-container glass, scrap metals, and plastics to be recycled. In San Diego, California, 2,000 tons of glass containers are collected by a U.S. company each month and sent to its plant in the Mexican border city of Mexicali. In Mexicali, 19 tons of plastic waste are gathered each week from foreign-owned maquiladora plants by a local company and shipped to Guadalajara. In 1997, Mexico imported between US$500 million to US$1 billion worth of U.S. recoverable waste, surpassing South Korea to become the second most popular destination for U.S. waste, after Canada. The booming of border manufacturing in Mexico after NAFTA has brought some prosperity to its border cities, which in turn has enlivened the traditional border business of recycling tires. With about 5 million old truck, car, and motorcycle tires littered in the city, four tires for each resident, Mexicali has become a dominant used-tire city in North America. It has created many jobs in the local tire retreading shops and provided a large and nearby market for U.S.-based tire exporters. However, the buildup of used tires in Mexicali poses a threat to California's Imperial Valley—a lush agricultural region just across the border—as tire dumps are likely to turn into tire fires,[8] while other forms of wastes also pose hazards (see Frey, 2003).

Another old problem has haunted the U.S.-Mexico border. For decades, untreated waste from the leaky sewage system in Tijuana has flowed down through the Tijuana River into the U.S. border communities, negatively affecting local residents. This seemingly mundane local problem has become complicated and magnified in the border context as international diplomacy and multitudes of municipal, state, and federal government agencies of both nations have been involved. Some progress has been made. A joint treatment plant was constructed on U.S. soil that captures and partly cleans about 25 million gallons of the overflow waste each day, and US$140 million was spent on projects in Mexico to expand Tijuana's sewer system and plug leaks that send waste to the U.S. side during heavy winter rains. In 1998, a treatment plant north of the border, built and run by the United States with help from Mexico, began operation, which sent treated waste through a huge pipe directly into the ocean. The persistent problem illustrates the complexity of border pollution or any other border-related issue that typically involves binational agreements, cooperation among multiple government agencies at various levels, border community residents, and such non-government organizations (NGOs) as environmentalist groups.[9] Apparently, the formal transnational regional arrangement of NAFTA, which was concerned primarily with such macroeconomic issues as trade and investment, neglected cross-border environmental issues and thus has little binding effect on pollution along the U.S.-Mexico border.

NAFTA has induced change in transborder flows and regulation of the historically very open U.S.-Canada border. First of all, NAFTA allowed Canadians to obtain temporary work visas at the border quickly. This has accelerated the effort of U.S. companies with severe shortages of high-tech workers to recruit Canadian talent with top salaries and other perquisites. A large number of U.S. companies recruit graduates at the University of Waterloo in Kitchener, Ontario, near the border with the United States. The university has a top-ranked computer science department and serves as a major training ground for Canadian computer scientists and engineers. This southbound "brain drain" continues, even though new U.S. immigration regulations in effect since April 1997 have begun to restrict easy entry of Canadian business travelers into the United States. At the border, businesspeople that do not need visas because of NAFTA often get mixed with people who are required to have a visa to work in the United States. One Toronto-based computer consulting firm reported a loss of contracts because its U.S. clients have stopped using Canadian consultants due to the difficulties in getting them across the border.[10] The evidence suggests that even though the 6,440-km U.S.-Canada border, the world's longest land boundary and one of the busiest, has become more open and porous under NAFTA, the latter has complicated the economic, environmental, and travel conditions on both sides of the line. Since

September 11, 2001, the threat of terrorists slipping through this border, most of which is rural and lightly protected, has further complicated control.

Transborder Transactions and Informal Subregional Clustering

While supranational regional integration has created a certain amount of global de-bordering and re-bordering, the latter has been triggered by more extensive transborder links and intensive transactions of a subregional scale, without a formal integration of entire national economies through inter-state treaties or agreements. This phenomenon is represented by the Asia-Pacific transborder subregions that differ from the EU or NAFTA trade blocks in three crucial ways. First, they generally involve multiple subnational territorial units with a more intensive border focus, rather than several entire nation-states. Second, they usually have a smaller spatial scope than the continental size and spread of the EU or NAFTA. Third, they are much less institutionalized and often have an informal governance structure (see chapter 3 for a differentiation between formal and informal subregional integration).

The Asia-Pacific transborder subregions are variably labeled as "Growth Triangles" (see Chia and Lee, 1993; Parsonage, 1992), "Region States" (Ohmae, 1995), or "Natural Economic Territories" (Scalapino, 1995). Since I will describe the transborder subregions in detail in chapter 2, the task here is to merely locate the rough spatial contour of all the Asia-Pacific transborder subregions, which will be subject to in-depth case and comparative studies in later chapters.

Locating the Asia-Pacific Transborder Subregions

From Northeast Asia on the western Pacific Rim, several transborder subregions stretch south and west to include both mainland and maritime Southeast Asia (see map 1.1). In Northeast Asia, a transborder subregion, designated the Greater Tumen Subregion (GTS) in this study, comprises three areas: the southeastern border region of China's Jilin province, centered on the cities of Hunchun and Tumen; the northern border area of North Korea, featuring the port cities of Rajin and Sonbong; and the Khasan region of the Russian Far East (RFE), anchored on the port city of Posyet and the southern Maritime Territory around Vladivostok. This GTS transborder subregion is physically defined by the Tumen River that connects the border areas of the three riparian states—China, North Korea, and Russia (see chapter 6). Spatially contiguous and economically connected with the GTS is a long border zone that closely links China's Heilongjiang province and the RFE. The broad hinterland of the GTS may include transnational links among China's northeast, the RFE, eastern Mongolia, North Korea, South Korea, and Japan's coastal region facing the Sea of Japan.

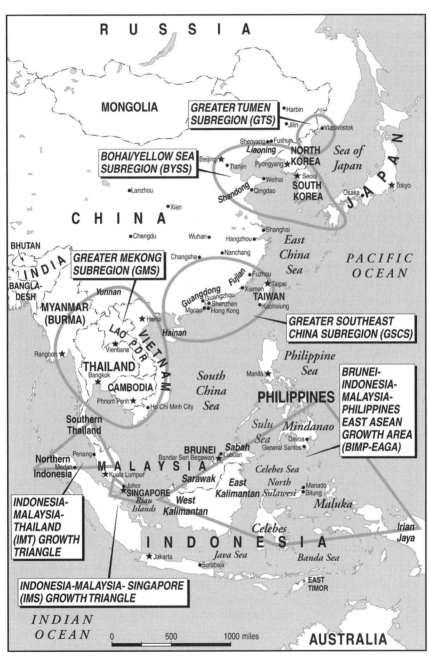

MAP 1.1
Seven Asia-Pacific Transborder Subregions

Farther south and west of the GTS is a transborder subregion that is designated the Bohai/Yellow Sea Subregion (BYSS) in this study. It consists of the coastal zones of China's Liaoning and Shandong provinces plus Beijing and Tianjin, South Korea's west coast, and Japan's Kyushu region. The components of the BYSS, unlike those of the GTS, are internally connected and delimited only by sea borders. The boundaries of the GTS and BYSS, most widely delineated, would make the two transborder subregions almost contiguous and overlapping with some links, thus enveloping much of Northeast Asia. However, the GTS and BYSS are analyzed separately here (in chapters 5 and 6) to focus on subregional and local diversities.

A transborder subregion in East Asia, designated the Greater Southeast China Subregion (GSCS) in this study, covers China's Guangdong and Fujian provinces, Hong Kong, Taiwan, and Macau. (The GSCS is examined in chapter 4.)

To the west of the GSCS, in Southeast Asia, is a transborder subregion designated the Greater Mekong Subregion (GMS) in this study. The GMS extends over China's Yunnan province, Myanmar, Lao People's Democratic Republic (Lao PDR), Thailand, Cambodia, and Vietnam. Unlike the previous subregions, the GMS comprises mainly nation-states; the exception is China's Yunnan province. This subnational unit, coupled with border-specific and intensive interactions among the countries, qualifies the GMS as a transborder subregion rather than a formal regional scheme like the EU. Given its large area and the participation of six countries, the GMS features the longest length and the largest number of national borders, some of which are landlocked. (The GMS is discussed in chapter 7.)

Away from mainland Asia and spread across the entire maritime Southeast Asia are three distinctive transborder subregions or growth triangles, as they are commonly known in the region. The first is the Indonesia-Malaysia-Singapore growth triangle (IMS-GT), which consists of Singapore, the state of Johor in peninsular Malaysia, and the Riau province of Indonesia. The Indonesia-Malaysia-Thailand growth triangle (IMT-GT) encompasses the 14 provinces of southern Thailand, the four states of northwestern Malaysia, and the two Sumatran provinces of western Indonesia. The Brunei-Indonesia-Malaysia-Philippines East ASEAN Growth Area (BIMP-EAGA, hereafter abbreviated as EAGA) includes Brunei Darussalam, southern Mindanao, and the island province of Palawan of the Philippines; North Sulawesi of Indonesia and the two adjacent Indonesian provinces on the island of Borneo (East and West Kalimantan); and the Malaysian territories of Sabah, Sarawak, and Labuan. Unlike the transborder subregions along the edge of mainland Asia, the three maritime Southeast Asian growth triangles are organized, bounded, and crisscrossed largely by sea borders. (These maritime transborder subregions are discussed in chapter 7.)

In terms of geography and demography, the transborder subregions have a collective significance for the entire Asia-Pacific region that cannot be overemphasized. They cover a large block of mainland and maritime Asia and contain a sizeable share of the region's total population. The GSCS, for example, spans 340,000 sq km and has a combined population of 126 million. The more expansive GMS covers 2.3 million sq km and includes a total population of 229 million (see chapter 7). If we measure these subregions by the distance from their dominant centers to their hinterlands, these areas would be even larger. In the BYSS, there are more than 300 million people living within two hours of air travel from Seoul (W. Kim, 1990). In economic terms, the seven transborder subregions encompass mostly subnational parts or all of 16 Asian and other economies that cover the whole spectrum of development levels and stages, from Japan and South Korea at one end and Lao PDR and Cambodia at the other, with Thailand and China somewhere in between. The seven subregions cut across approximately 25 land and offshore boundaries.[11]

Besides including such dominant hubs and gateways as Hong Kong and Singapore that anchor their respective subregions, the transborder subregions have enabled a large number of small border cities and towns to grow from previously peripheral and isolated positions to the development forefront and to connect directly or indirectly with the global economy. One of them, Dongguan, in southeastern China has even risen to the status of world's largest and most concentrated manufacturing location for computer peripherals (see chapter 4).

The Central Argument: From Barriers to Bridges and Back

The comparative analysis of such a diverse set of cases is guided by one central argument: borders are shedding their traditional barrier effects and are playing a more bridging role in the Asia-Pacific area and elsewhere, although this role does lapse back under changed circumstances. The shift from barrier to bridge, and maybe back to barrier, is a more intuitive shorthand for expressing the complex twin concept of de-bordering and re-bordering. Although the barrier-to-bridge shift is not smooth and linear, it is indeed taking place across the previously closed and heavily guarded borders. These borders used to function as political barriers that blocked economic and cultural exchanges to differing degrees. They also existed as military frontiers that received heavy defense spending but little economic assistance. As a result, the zones around these borders became marginalized. Due to changes in a variety of conditions, these borders have begun to bridge separate and isolated local and regional economies. The emerging transnational spaces have provided new opportunities for global-local links, perhaps generating self-sustaining local development that would not be possible without the presence of a transborder subregion.

The bridging role of borders in the transborder subregions is a complex one. Bridging creates a cooperative space between binational or trinational economies. Broadly viewed, bridging generates economic growth and transactions that can spread beyond the immediate border zones to other parts of the transborder subregions. On the other hand, bridging may turn borders and border zones into new contested terrains for illegal migration, drug smuggling, spillover pollution, and other undesirable outcomes. States may respond to these threats by reimposing border control, thus moving back toward the barrier role of borders. This reassertion of state authority was characterized by Andreas (2000a, 2000b) as re-bordering, which he examined at length in the contexts of states controlling and policing illegal drug smuggling and immigration across the U.S.-Mexico border and the EU's emerging eastern boundary. While I share this notion of re-bordering to some extent, my argument about the borders shifting from barriers to bridges and back underscores a broader conceptualization of de-bordering in relation to re-bordering. In contending that the bridging role of borders has become stronger than at anytime before, and that the bridging role is now stronger than the barrier role, I focus on extensive de-bordering in terms of strong links and heavy flows across a large number of international boundaries in several subregional settings. The links and flows in turn usher in a re-bordering process by connecting border cities and their hinterlands into a transnational spatial network that spans multiple boundaries and beyond. This kind of re-bordering is different from and unlikely to be completely reversed by state-initiated re-bordering through enhanced border controls.

Re-bordering After September 11 and SARS:
A Temporary Reversal in a Long-term Trend

The argument about borders changing from barriers to bridges and back has become more salient in light of the terrorist attacks on the United States on September 11, 2001, and the subsequent government response to border security. The terrorists appear to have taken advantage of the very open borders of the United States for visitors and other flows, especially from and through Canada and Mexico. Before September 11, foreign visitors were not carefully checked if they crossed over a land border and could convince an immigration inspector that they were a citizen of Canada or Mexico. In the wake of the terrorist attacks, the United States created the Department of Homeland Security and clamped down on border control, which immediately affected cross-border economic transactions and social life. Tightened inspections at the U.S.-Canada and U.S.-Mexico borders slowed down the normal trucking traffic. Drivers had to wait two or three hours to cross from Ciudad Juárez, Mexico, to El Paso, Texas, which usually takes no more than 45 minutes during peak traffic times. There arose the concern that the slowed flow of commerce would set back efforts to integrate the economies of the United States, Canada, and Mexico under NAFTA (see chapter 8). As Mexicans stopped coming over for shopping due to the long wait through the border crossings, the retail businesses in the Texas border cities and towns of McAllen, Laredo, and Brownsville, which cater heavily to Mexican customers, suffered badly. The heightened security interrupted the traditional ways of life for the Tohono O'odham Indians, a 24,000-member nation whose lands span large parts of northern Mexico and southern Arizona. Many members have stopped crossing the border to visit relatives or to attend traditional religious festivals for fear of being regularly stopped by the Border Patrol.[12] The new fingerprinting procedure at major U.S. air and sea ports, implemented in January 2004, has lengthened the time of entry for 24 million foreign visitors traveling with visas.[13]

The outbreak of SARS in China's Guangdong province and its spread to Hong Kong and beyond in 2003 cast the border between them into international spotlight, this time not for their economic dynamism. It also posed a major challenge to the regional governments on both sides of the porous and "infected" boundary. It was reported that a medical professor from Zhongshan University in Guangzhou infected a group of people during his stay in a Hong Kong hotel, while one of the people in the group spread the disease at the Prince of Wales Hospital (where the mainland professor later died) and then the Amoy Gardens residential complex. One family living there packed up their belongings immediately and returned to their native town in Guangdong. But after they fell sick in Guangdong, they recrossed the border to seek better treatment in Hong Kong. According to official estimates, 10 percent of the people with SARS in Hong Kong had visited the mainland before they got infected. Besides driving down the number of cross-border visits by 40 percent, the crisis raised new issues concerning cross-border integration, such as choice of residence and environmental and public hygiene, which go beyond the more dominant economic and transportation issues regarding the facilitation of growing cross-border investment flows and vehicle traffic. While the immediate, knee-jerk reaction from some in Hong Kong was to propose restrictions on the flow of people across the border, including banning nonessential visits, the SARS crisis has sharpened the sense of common destiny for Guangdong and Hong Kong and both economic and social integration between them. Although the Hong Kong government took some emergency measures, such as checking the temperature of border crossers (see the photo in the preface), it began to seek more extensive cooperation with the Guangdong government to set up a formal mechanism to combat the disease and control its spread[14] and budding recurrence in early 2004. However, it remains to be seen whether this cross-border government cooperation in response to a crisis will sustain itself for the long-term need of guiding deeper and wider integration, given the largely market-driven nature of the cross-border economic links, the laissez-faire tradition of the Hong Kong government, and the difficulty for Hong Kong to fully cooperate with the Guangdong government, which still operates with the constraints of a control-oriented central government in Beijing, as illustrated by the latter's insistence on lab testing for confirming the SARS virus in Beijing in early 2004.

The above developments suggest that the barrier aspect of borders can be resurrected and strengthened by government policy in response to disastrous events, which are illustrated further by the frantic policies of countries to ban imported beef and kill millions of chickens during an isolated incidence of mad cow disease in the United States at the end of 2003 and a limited spread of bird flu in several Asian countries in early 2004. They point to the coexisting and inseparable function of borders as both barriers and bridges. This function of borders may shift back and forth between barrier and bridge depending on different contexts and changing conditions within these contexts. In the Asia-Pacific transborder subregional context, the bridging role of borders has been gaining strength in spite of the existing and emerging barriers created by state policies and the lack of transport infrastructure. The evidence is compelling that broad de-bordering and re-bordering has permeated the Asia-Pacific region in the form of several transborder subregions as contact and cooperative zones. Although this study is sensitive to ways in which borders continue to impede cooperation and even create conflict, it aims at proving that the Asia-Pacific transborder subregions represent a broad and sustainable long-term trend toward cross-border cooperation and integration. This book suggests that despite the kind of re-bordering in terms of escalated security measures at the U.S. borders after September 11, 2001, and infection control and quarantine procedures at the Guangdong–Hong Kong border and other borders across Asian countries after SARS in 2003, they amount to a mere temporary reversal in the inevitable, long-term trend in global de-bordering and re-bordering, as demonstrated by the extensive evidence in this book.

A Conceptual Preview: Multiple Lenses for Integrated Insights

The central argument advanced above raises the crucial analytical question of how to account for the diversity among several transborder subregions in the Asia-Pacific context and elsewhere. As the earlier geographic profile indicates, these transborder subregions comprise three or more subnational border regions or areas across multiple contiguous or adjacent international boundaries. This composition creates several layers and inevitably uneven ties among the differently scaled territorial units. While complex, the composition of the transborder subregions makes them rich cases to interface with theoretical perspectives along multiple dimensions.

Before I provide a foretaste of this interface from the theoretical side, it is important to ask when these transborder subregions emerged and how they really differ from other seemingly similar regional formations. Chapter 2 addresses these questions by offering a long historical view of the economic, cultural, and spatial links among some of the areas involved in the transborder subregions today, as a way of assessing whether the latter had any geographic antecedents. Moving from distant to recent history, chapter 2 also examines why the Cold War era prevented the transborder subregions from emerging until it ended around 1990. The relevance of a geohistorical versus a political economy claim is assessed in anticipation of developing the more comprehensive framework in chapter 3. Having dated the recent timing of the transborder subregions, chapter 2 develops a nuanced conceptualization of the Asia-Pacific transborder subregion by decomposing its constituent units and then refitting them into a nested hierarchy. While this exercise differentiates the transborder subregion from formal supranational schemes such as the EU, it signals the existence of more informal cross-border subregional formations underneath. Ending with an identification of the important characteristics and dimensions of the transborder subregion, chapter 2 paves the way for setting up the analytical framework in chapter 3.

The key to an integrated analytical framework for these cases is to bring together relevant theoretical perspectives and apply them in a coherent and complementary fashion. From the standpoint of the cases, it is highly important to know how to array them and use their attributes as evidence to illuminate significant theoretical debates. Having evaluated what theoretical literatures may be most relevant to the cases, I have settled on organizing the important elements of the literatures into four analytical lenses, examining the economic, political, sociocultural, and spatial dimensions of the cases sequentially and also interactively. Reciprocally, I interpret the comparative evidence on the cases in light of the analytical lenses to produce insights on the debated theoretical issues.

To begin with, I draw selectively from the vast globalization literature to build an economic lens (the global-local nexus) focusing on how the transborder subregions mediate or restructure cross-border links between the world economy and local places. Some of the literature on economic globalization speaks to the strong impact of trade and investment on the interdependence and integration among national economies without paying specific attention to how this impact varies across regional and local areas (see chapter 3). Globalization scholars who deal with specific localities tend to be concerned with how major international metropolises have become global or world cities (see Friedmann, 1986; Sassen, 2001; but see Robinson, 2002, for a recent exception). This omission and bias in the research has left us with both an inflated and limited view of how global economic forces impact or interact with national or local economies. The global-local economic lens reveals that the impact and penetration of the global economy can be mediated or redirected by the varied mixes of comparative advantages and complementarities of the constituent units to yield uneven growth and integration within a transborder subregion. Looking at specific border cities through the global-local economic lens also reveals the extent to which some of them may remain disconnected and thus will not benefit much from the global economy, due to natural endowments and traditional local-local economic ties specific to a transborder subregion. While the GSCS demonstrates the positive mediating effect on global-local economic links (see chapter 4), the GTS may exemplify the constraining influence (see chapter 6). The insight gained from these two and other cases is that to understand the local impact of the global economy and local responses, we must study the mediating role of such in-between structures as the transborder subregions.

One of the other factors bearing crucially on the transborder subregions is the relative role of the state at the central or local level. To capture this role, I have constructed a second analytical lens that looks for different forms of de-centering tendencies and practices of the state that are abundant in the transborder subregional context. Basically, the de-centering state in the transborder subregions manifests itself both institutionally and spatially. In an institutional sense, de-centering takes the primary form of the central state decentralizing flexible policy-making power to border regions and cities in order to rebalance uneven development or target certain areas to take advantage of existing or potential global links. This leads to the rise of local autonomy in varying degrees that facilitates or impedes cross-border cooperation. Institutional de-centering also is reflected in the central states yielding or transferring some policy-making power to the supranational level for the sake of promoting cross-border cooperation. Spatial de-centering of the state, in a related way, takes the form of uneven scattering and diffusion of the authority and influence of the national government from the political center to previously neglected and marginalized border areas (see chapter 3). In the GSCS, the institutional and spatial de-centering has blended into considerable decentralization and effective local autonomy in China's Guangdong and Fujian provinces, thus successfully fostering favorable global-local economic links and the rapid growth and integration of the entire subregion (see chapter 4). On the other hand, the lack of genuine decentralization and local autonomy in the RFE and North Korea, especially the latter, has hampered the growth and integration of the GTS in conjunction with other complicating factors (see chapter 6).

One other cluster of factors that interacts with the economic and political forces in shaping the transborder subregions can be adequately subsumed under the analytical lens of cross-border social capital. To construct this analytical lens, I have pulled together several elements such as historical legacies, ethnic identity, kinship ties, and linguistic similarity and reconfigured them into action-oriented social networks that have uneven presence in the transborder subregions. Through this analytical lens, I intend to show that these cross-border social networks matter a great deal in enabling economic links across the border areas, with the qualifying argument that more extensive and stronger social networks have a more powerful influence. A reasoned employment of this analytical lens is dependent on recognizing that many elements of cross-border social capital lay dormant under closed-border economies and political tension and have only resurfaced recently in the more open and interactive environment of a transborder subregion (see chapter 3). The sharp contrast in the effectiveness of this cross-border social capital is reflected in the GSCS (chapter 4) and the GTS (chapter 6). Viewed from this analytical lens, the cases demonstrate that the concept of social capital, which is typically applied at the individual or group level and has been proven useful for thinking about regional development, sheds considerable light on the aggregate performance of the transborder subregions (see X. Chen, 2000c).

Finally, there needs to be an analytical lens that scans the effects of geographic proximity and cross-border transport infrastructure on the transborder subregions. A key rationale for this lens is that distance, which has lost some friction in a globalizing world, is almost by definition central to the formation of a transborder subregion. In another and perhaps more ironic sense, short distance in terms of geographic contiguity or adjacency is important because it does not necessarily reduce the natural and artificial barrier effects of international boundaries that could impede the growth and integration of a transborder subregion. Besides some location constraints, such as difficult topography and lack of access to sea, the generally less developed cross-border transport links, coupled with the lack of large-scale resources and cross-national cooperation for improving them, negate the advantages of short physical distance between the constituent units of a transborder subregion. Applying the spatial lens to the cases reveals how geographic proximity and cross-border transport links, jointly or independently, facilitate or inhibit the economic, political, and sociocultural factors in determining the formation of the transborder subregions. In the BYSS, the presence of an extensive and still expanding network of air and shipping links has been effective in bridging ocean boundaries (see chapter 5). While it is difficult to link wider distances across a large number of land borders in the expansive GMS due to the shortage of financial resources in the least developed Asian countries involved, the prioritized assistance and financing from the Asian Development Bank (ADB) has alleviated the problem (see chapter 7).

Each of the four analytical lenses draws from a particular body of the literature and is intended to illuminate a distinctive dimension of the transborder subregion. Only in coming together in an integrated framework with cross-references do they work in unison to provide a comprehensive explanation for the similarities and differences among the primary and secondary cases in chapters 4 through 7. The key is to apply these analytical lenses consistently across the cases and be specific about how they complement one another within each case. If this is successfully executed, the cases will shed light on the key theoretical issues that lie behind the analytical lenses. To help stretch the analytical scope of these lenses, I extend the comparative reach to several cases in the U.S.-Mexican and European contexts (see chapter 8). These cases demonstrate how far out the four analytical lenses can see, and they suggest factors that lie beyond the purview of the lenses but nevertheless bear on cross-border subregional dynamics. In the final chapter, I look through the analytical lenses again to highlight the theoretical insights from the set of primary and secondary cases and then turn to the practical challenges posed by these transborder subregions to governance and possible responses to the challenges.

Pushing Beyond What We Have Known

By subjecting a range of cases to a broad comparative analysis within an integrated framework, this book moves beyond the existing literature on the subject, which suffers from three main deficiencies. First of all, there is a lack of a systematic and comprehensive framework that can make overall sense of a fairly large number of discrete case studies and lead to generalizable conclusions. Although several edited volumes have attempted to bring multiple cases together, they either did not devote a balanced attention to all the important dimensions and factors involved or placed major emphasis on policy issues (see Chen and Kwan, 1997; Perkmann and Sum, 2002; Thant, Tang, and Kakazu, 1998). The framework developed here offers a badly need analytical synthesis.

Second, the literature has not provided a balanced and explicitly comparative coverage of all the Asia-Pacific transborder subregions; the overwhelming emphasis has been on the South China–Hong Kong–Taiwan triangle (or the so-called Greater China), with a secondary focus on the Singapore-Johor-Riau triangle. Besides the numerous articles, a number of edited volumes (see

Kwok and So, 1995; Shambaugh, 1995; Naughton, 1997; Drover, Johnson, and Lai Po-wah, 2001; Yeh et al., 2002) have focused on Greater China, especially bilateral links between Guangdong and Hong Kong and between Southeastern China and Taiwan. Studies of the Singapore-Johor-Riau growth triangle have expanded from an early edited book of largely descriptive accounts (Lee, 1991) to a series of more detailed article-length analyses (see Chia and Lee, 1993; Peachey, Perry, and Grundy-Warr, 1998; Grundy-Warr, Peachey, and Perry, 1999). Comparative efforts to bring these two cases together are rare (see Ho and So, 1997). For the first time, this book pulls together seven cases of transborder subregional integration by treating three of them as primary cases and four as secondary cases in an integrated framework.

The third inadequacy in the literature is a shortage of efforts to integrate analyses at different spatial scales (as illustrated in figure 2.1 in chapter 2), with even less attention paid to the nested relations across these levels, especially the highly localized ties between border cities and their direct or indirect links to the global economy. This is truer of the works focusing on the less studied cases such as the Tumen River region and the Greater Mekong Subregion (see Rozman, 1997, 1998a; Valencia, 1995; Asian Development Bank [ADB], 1996a, 1996b, 2002a, 2002b). This book strives to maintain a close scrutiny of the trans-local and global-local ties mediated by higher-order, in-between relations within the transborder subregions, particularly in the three primary cases (chapters 4–6). While chapter 3 introduces the integrated framework with the four analytical lenses, the historical backdrop and conceptual foundation for that framework lie in chapter 2, to which we now turn.

Notes

1. "Porous border a portal for potential terrorists," *Chicago Tribune*, September 15, 2003, p. 6.

2. The total number of states in 1950 (82) was reported by *World Atlas* (DK Publishing, 1997); the total number of states in 2003 (191) was reported in the United Nations' website, www.un.org/overview. Many of the new states formed in the 1990s are successors to the former Soviet Union and Yugoslavia. Future potential new states may emerge from Israel (a Palestinian state), Canada (Quebec), and the two Koreas (through unification).

3. The precise number of land boundaries depends on whether micro-territories are included, and whether boundaries with more than one sector are counted once or twice. Eventually, agreed maritime boundaries will outnumber land boundaries, despite the continued proliferation of new states (see note 2 above). However, maritime delimitation is impossible if there is uncertainty or dispute over the land boundary at the coast (Blake, 1994, p. xiii).

4. Throughout the book, monetary amounts are given in U.S. dollars unless otherwise noted.

5. The information and discussion on Central Asia here has been derived from three articles in the *Wall Street Journal*: "Silk road enjoys new life amid calm in Caucasus," March 3, 1998, p. 14; "Scramble for oil in Central Asia hits roadblocks," March 13, 1998, p. A12; "U.S. pledges Caspian Sea oil funds," June 1, 1998, p. A12.

6. "Europeans search for a shared identity amid dark memories," *Wall Street Journal*, October 19, 1998, pp. A1, A12.

7. "Euregions" (the term combines "European" and "regions") are located along the internal borders of the European Union and involve some form of cross-border cooperation between (semi)public organizations. A "Euregion" can be considered an organized border region (Corvers, Dankbaar, and Hassink, 1996, p. 175).

8. These accounts were taken from two *Wall Street Journal* reports, "Destination Mexico: U.S. scrap enlivens border trade," January 29, 1998, p. A13; "Mexico's 'tire mountain' worries U.S. neighbors," May 17, 1998, pp. B1, B4.

9. Reported in "U.S., Mexico push for solution to border pollution," *Chicago Tribune*, January 3, 2002, p. 9.

10. The accounts were from two *Wall Street Journal* articles, "Canada frets high-tech 'brain drain,'" May 12, 1998, p. A16; "U.S. traps Canadians in a one-size-fits-all border-control policy," June 4, 1998, p. A13.

11. The shared boundary between two states is counted only once. For example, the six participating states in the Greater Mekong Subregion (GMS) have 10 boundaries, instead of 18 if the shared boundaries are counted twice. If a participating area in a transborder subregion joins two other national borders, it is counted twice. For example, Singapore borders Malaysia's Johor state to the north and Indonesia's Riau Islands offshore to the south, whereas Johor and Riau are not joined. Therefore, the Indonesia-Malaysia-Singapore growth triangle (IMS-GT) has only two shared borders (see chapter 7).

12. These examples are from a series of *Chicago Tribune* reports: "High security, long delays," September 12, 2001, p. 17; "Nation's open borders in spotlight," September 26, 2001, p. 9; "Visas add woes in wake of attacks," September 29, 2001, pp. 1, 6; "Mexican trucking debate hits another speed bump," November 5, 2002, p. 7; "Merchants in Texas feeling the pinch," November 2, 2001, p. 13; "Border crackdown vexes tribe," December 30, 2001, p. 14; "Bush seeks more border security funds," January 26, 2002, p. 8.

13. Under the initial procedures, foreign visitors traveling with visas would have two fingerprints scanned by an inkless device and a digital picture taken. The information, stored as part of the visitors' travel records, would be used to verify visitors' identities and to compare the information against a database of known and suspected terrorists and criminals. Future programs and procedures would include phasing in exit procedures at air and sea ports by December 31, 2004, and phasing in entry and exit procedures at the 50 busiest land ports of entry by December 31, 2004, and at all land ports by December 31, 2005. See "Foreign visitors checked," *Chicago Tribune*, January 6, 2004, p. 20.

14. See "The crisis infecting cross-border relations," accessed from the *South China Morning Post*'s website (scmp.com) on May 7, 2003.

2

The Asia-Pacific Transborder Subregions

The Phenomenon, Historical Backdrop, and Conceptualization

The Emergence of the Transborder Subregions

THE PAST TWO DECADES OR SO HAVE SEEN the emergence of several transborder subregions in the Asia-Pacific area. Three features are of note. First, all of these transborder subregions appeared in the 1980s and evolved through the 1990s into the twenty-first century. Generally speaking, this period may be characterized by accelerated economic globalization, the weakening of nation-states, the increasing autonomy of localities (e.g., global cities), and the growing vitality of transnational communities and social spaces. While the relative influence of these forces on the transborder subregions may vary, they have converged at a critical historical conjuncture to shape the transborder subregions being studied in this book.

Second, the emergence of the transborder subregions has been marked by their simultaneous tendencies toward both integration and fragmentation, which have desirable outcomes such as rapid growth, but also undesirable and often unintended consequences, including new spatial inequality and border conflicts. This contradiction stems directly from the make-up of the transborder subregions in as much as it is composed of multiple subnational politicoeconomic and territorial units. This creates a set of complex economic, political, and spatial relations among the units, because they are linked with outside units within countries, among the units within the subregion across borders, and with external units beyond the subregion. Relational change is a constant in this multilayered network. Shifts in the relative positions of the constituent units and the strength of the ties among the latter may lead to strong integration at one level (within a transborder subregion) and potential fragmentation at another (between intra-national areas that are part of a transborder subregion and areas that are not).

Third, the Asia-Pacific transborder subregions have evolved in an uneven manner. Some have achieved growth and collective benefits for the constituent units; others have encountered serious barriers to growth and the internal distribution of potential gains; still others have stagnated after a promising start. The diverse fortunes of the transborder subregions over time reflect both the general impact of large-scale supranational or transnational processes and of conditions and factors specific to individual subregions. These factors include the global economy, economic complementarity, functional specialization, center-local state relations, cross-border social networks, transport infrastructure, and external ties. Before I explain the recent timing, contradictory tendencies, and diverse growth outcomes of the transborder subregions, it is important to examine some historical conditions as a backdrop.

Are There Historical Antecedents?

Despite the fact that the transborder subregions did not take their current shape until the 1980s, their composition of multiple neighboring and adjacent border areas makes one wonder whether they are built upon past economic and spatial relations that have resurfaced more recently? Tracing out the historical antecedents helps place the transborder subregions in a longer temporal context that facilitates the understanding of their origin, present, and future.

Tracing What Could Be the Geographic Genesis

How far back should we go to locate the possible geographic roots of today's transborder subregions? A chronological series of maps and associated texts in *The Penguin Historical Atlas of the Pacific* (McEvedy, 1998) and recent advances in the study of early modern and modern East Asian, Southeast Asian and world history suggest that we should begin in the early 1400s. A map of the Pacific circa 1415 (McEvedy, 1998, p. 29) shows that the Chinese empire under the early Ming dynasty extended farther than previous regimes. It encompassed an area that ranged from a large portion of Siberia, or the present-day Russian Far East (RFE), to Dai Viet, the forerunner of Vietnam. This expansion enlarged and strengthened the Chinese tributary system that had been in place for three or four centuries. McEvedy's subsequent maps show the frequent de-bordering and re-bordering around the western Pacific Rim with the rise and fall and expansion and shrinking of empires and states, the spatial extension of intra- and inter-regional trade ties, and colonization by various European powers. What remained relatively stable over that period, however, were the cooperative and contentious political and economic relations among the peoples of the contiguous areas.

These links were particularly strong within and around the seas, bays, and straits in Asia's maritime environment. The entire period of 1603–1867 saw sustained trade relations between Satsuma and Ryukyu Islands and between the Japanese island of Tsushima and Korea in the Korean Strait (Hamashita, 1997). The latter two are part of the present-day Bohai/Yellow Sea Subregion (BYSS) that includes the Kyushu region of Japan (see chapter 5). In 1526 the Portuguese chased the sultan of Bintan off the island (part of present-day Indonesia's Riau province near Singapore), but he soon set up shop again in Johor, now a Malaysian state at the tip of the Malay peninsula. In 1699, the sultanate of Johor shifted its base to Bintan once more (McEvedy, 1998). All these localities are key components of the Indonesia-Malaysia-Singapore growth triangle (IMS-GT) in Southeast Asia (see chapter 7). The movement of traded goods and reshuffled regimes between locations of the neighboring states in the past implies an early foundation for some present-day Asia-Pacific transborder subregions. Early political and economic links seem to have survived even after more clearly demarcated and rigidly enforced national boundaries were implanted during modern times.

The Imprint of the China-Centric Tributary System

There is some evidence that the transborder subregions today can be traced back to the China-centric tributary system and the geographic structure of maritime Asia that it helped shape after the early 1400s. The China-centric tributary system was "the external expression of hierarchical domestic relations of control, extending downward and outward from the imperial center" (Hamashita, 1997, p. 114). According to Frank (1998), the economic centrality of China in Asia and the world was sustained by the rapid increase of production, consumption, and population and growing external economic influence after 1400. After withdrawing from the sea in the early 1500s following Cheng Ho's voyages into the Indian Ocean, the Ming dynasty revived international ocean trade in the second half of the sixteenth century, partly through the tributary system (Blunden and Elvin, 1983).

The tributary trading network fanned out from coastal China to cover much of maritime Asia from Northeast Asia to East Asia and then from Southeast Asia to Oceania in the form of a series of seas and surrounding landmasses. While China's government trade and tribute trade with maritime Southeast Asia were active in the early fifteenth century, private sea trade, both legal and illegal, of such commodities as sandalwood, coral, ebony, cloves, and tea became more dominant in the 1600s through 1750 (see Ptak, 1998, 1999). This trade took place within and across a string of different-sized adjacent or overlapping circles corresponding to the seas in the regionwide maritime structure, as depicted by the map in Hamashita (1997, p. 116). If we lay that historical map (see map 2.1) over the map of the transborder subregions in chapter 1 (see map 1.1), we see some overlap or at least some resemblance between the old and new geographic patterns. Hamashita (1997, p. 115) also notes that "the states, regions, and cities located along the periphery of each sea zone were close enough to influence one another but too far apart to be assimilated into a larger entity." This observation captures a similar feature of the present-day transborder subregions. Some of them are adjacent to one another in a larger spatial scheme such as the BYSS relative to the Greater Tumen Subregion (GTS), or the Greater Southeast China Subregion (GSCS) relative to the Greater Mekong Subregion (GMS). They nevertheless cover sufficiently distinctive spaces to avoid being completely interconnected or nested.

Different localities and regions in the international political economy not only depend on their geography and accumulation of assets and liabilities but on their ability to adapt to changing circumstances (Agnew and Corbridge, 1995). Although it is plausible to trace the geographic origin of the transborder subregions in the late twentieth century to the China-centric tributary system and its orbit of maritime zones about 600 years ago, there is little evidence regarding political and economic parallels and continuities between the past and present areas. Whether there was any legacy from the earlier maritime Asia, the spatial configuration of today's transborder subregions is embedded in an entirely different political economy (discussed in the next section).

The similar configurations of the past and present subregions reflect cultural, ethnic, and linguistic ties that have facilitated cross-border interactions. The 50 million or so speakers of the Tai-Kadai language family (including Thai and Lao), one of China and Southeast Asia's four language families, have settled and spread from South China southward into peninsular Thailand and west to Myanmar through a process of linguistic fragmentation that occurred over the last 2,500 years (Diamond, 1999). The settlement of the Zhuang in the present-day Guangxi province of China and northern Vietnam, the Shan in northern Myanmar, the Lao in Lao PDR, and the Thai in Thailand in geographic proximity on mainland Southeast Asia dates back to the beginning of the 1400s or earlier (McEvedy, 1998). The migration of southern Fujianese to Taiwan began as early as the 1700s and persisted through the mid-1900s. Periodically heavy migration from Guangdong to Hong Kong and through Hong Kong to Southeast Asia occurred during roughly the same periods. The continuous presence of ties among these ethnic populations promoted earlier

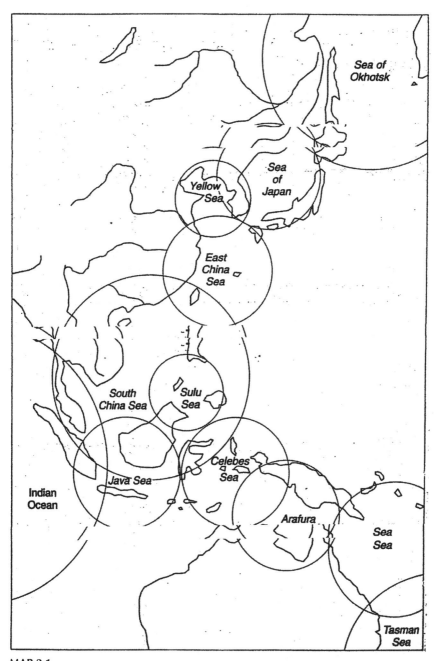

MAP 2.1
Historical Maritime Zones of Asia (Courtesy of Takeshi Hamashita, *China-Centered World Order in Modern Times.* Tokyo: University of Tokyo Press, 1990. Used by permission of the author)

trade and facilitates cross-border economic exchanges in the GMS and the GSCS today, even though they were suppressed by political closure and military conflicts at various points in the recent past. If these ethnic and cultural links that solidified through geographic proximity and cross-border migration were important in earlier history and have resurfaced lately, we need to examine the recent contexts that once suppressed these links and then became favorable to their revival.

The Recent Contexts: How Have Times Changed?

Relative to the geohistorical imprint of earlier Pacific maritime trade on the transborder subregions, the dynamics of the Asian political economy in the twentieth century, especially in its second half, were critical for the timing and form of the transborder subregions. A chain of conditions and events dating back to the early 1900s has had an important role in the uneven cross-border subregional integration in the Asia-Pacific. In an account of Japan's colonization of Korea in 1910 and Manchuria in the 1930s, Cumings (1998) provides evidence about the earlier development of center-hinterland economic links across the Northeast Asian boundaries. By relocating industries to and building transport and communications infrastructures in the contiguous colonies, Japan created a hierarchical production and export structure in a geographically linked subregion that was anchored on Japan as the core and involved Korea and Manchuria as the periphery. This integrated economic space generated cross-border labor mobility. Hundreds of thousands of Koreans migrated to work in the factories and mines in Japan and Manchuria (Cumings, 1998). Although the defeat of Japan in World War II and the effects of the Korean War impeded the development of a Northeast Asian subregion, Japan's colonial efforts left a heavy industrial base in northeastern China that has turned out to be relevant to the GTS in recent years (see chapter 6).

The Cold War Bind

If we could link the emergence of one transborder subregion in Northeast Asia to earlier Japanese colonial expansion, we might attribute the absence of subregional cross-border integration from the end of World War II to the 1980s to the larger Asian political economy shaped by the Cold War. After World War II and the Korean War, East Asia became bifurcated into the capitalist and socialist camps, headed by the United States and China respectively. This bipolar structure was grounded in the strategic and economic relations between the United States and Japan and between the Soviet Union and China until the early 1960s. It also was sustained by the close ties between the smaller capitalist states of South Korea and Taiwan and the United States/Japan on the one hand, and between the smaller communist states of North Korea and North Vietnam and the Soviet Union/China on the other. Although relations between the Soviet Union and China, between the United States and China, and between China and Japan changed drastically in the 1960s and 1970s, the overall political bifurcation continued to define Asia-Pacific regionalism as an aggregation of bilateral state relations into the early 1980s.

According to Katzenstein (1997), these power positions and norms in the regional international system, and their associated development ideologies and strategies, accounted for the absence of formal multilateral regional integration in the Asia-Pacific area. Katzenstein also attributes weak Asian regionalism, with the possible exception of the Association of the Southeast Asian Nations (ASEAN), to the historical and contemporary domestic structures of East and Southeast Asian states. Katzenstein refers them to the legacy of universal empires, regional kingdoms, fragmentary polities, and ritual, rather than legal and effective sovereignty, hierarchical order, and intricate networks.

Although this analysis does not focus squarely on formal regional integration in Asia such as the ASEAN, the absence of a structure like the EU or NAFTA provides insight into the similar absence of cross-border subregional integration until recently. The contentious bipolar geopolitical structure continued to reinforce the sovereignty and security embodied in the national borders of the states on both sides of the ideological divide in Asia. A number of bordering or nearby countries were being divided by the ideological chasm between capitalism and socialism, or by military conflicts. They included China and Taiwan from 1949 to the 1980s, China and the former Soviet Union in Northeast Asia in the late 1960s, China and Vietnam in the late 1970s, and North Korea and South Korea from the early 1950s to the present. These conflicting inter-state relations, reinforced by heavily guarded international boundaries, arrested the role of cross-border geographic proximity and cultural affinity that otherwise might have encouraged cross-national economic cooperation and integration.

Under the constraints of a heavily polarized political economy, neither formal integration at the regional level nor informal cross-border economic integration of a subregional scale could take hold. The ASEAN was an exceptional case. It was formed in 1967 as a political and security response to the Vietnam War (Mattli, 1999) and achieved more political than economic results until its much more recent march to a free trade bloc in the ASEAN Free Trade Area (AFTA). To the extent that there was any regionwide economic integration in the Asia Pacific, Japan held the key to it. Both Katzenstein (1997) and Selden (1997) argue that Japan's effort to regionalize its network-style developmentalism through its economic dominance and outreach is a key factor in creating a network-based integration of the Asia Pacific that is biased in its favor. Hatch and Yamamura (1996) attribute this form of regional integration to the heavy technological dependency of the East and Southeast Asian economies on Japan's embracing transnational production alliance. In addition, there was Japan's intention to create a regional trade bloc anchored to the yen (see Frankel, 1993). Similar to the inhibiting effect of geopolitical bipolarity, this Japan-centric Asian economic network tended to lock the East and Southeast Asian countries into a series of unfavorable bilateral trade and production relationships with the core, further limiting horizontal regional integration of varied forms and scales.

The Favorable Post–Cold War Environment

The geopolitical bipolarity began to disappear with the end of the Cold War. Japan's economic centrality also began to weaken with the opening of China and its integration in the regional economy. The collapse of the bipolar political split created open space and opportunity for Asia-Pacific countries to develop new and more cooperative relationships. The rapid growth of China's coastal region and its heavy involvement in the Asia-Pacific economy (see X. Chen, 1998) began to shift the investment and development focus to a new dynamic corridor along the western Pacific Rim. A number of neighboring economies, first Hong Kong and Japan and then Taiwan and Korea, began to invest heavily in China's contiguous or adjacent border areas. The business community in the Asia-based Chinese diaspora took the lead in reconnecting with China after being cut off from the Chinese mainland by political and military events before and after 1949; these included Japan's takeover of China's coastal regions, the defeat of the Chinese nationalists by the communists, and the U.S. embargo against China during the Cold War (Arrighi, 1998). Selden (1997) argues that the close links with Hong Kong, Taiwan, and Chinese diaspora capital allowed China in the 1990s to challenge Japan's economic and political primacy in East Asia, which turned out to be possible and likely due to a persistent economic depression that has haunted Japan since around 1990.

It is clear by now that the weakening and eventual end of the political bifurcation of capitalism and communism that shaped Asian-Pacific regionalism until recently created a new and favorable context for transborder subregions to develop. The scholars cited above provide a historical and contextual explanation for the lack of formal multilateral integration in the Asia-Pacific region. Convincing as it may be, it does not explain when, why, and how the transborder subregions developed and the roles that they play. Moreover, too much emphasis has been placed on the role of the Chinese diaspora in facilitating cross-border economic networks with China. The diversity of the transborder subregions other than the GSCS has been left largely unexplained. This study moves beyond the relevance of historical and recent contexts to show why the transborder subregion has emerged as a new and useful unit for understanding the increasing significance of regional and local dynamics in the global economy.

Conceptualizing a Distinctive Unit of Regional Analysis

Seeing Through the Reference Cases

What is really distinctive about the transborder subregions? If they had geographic precursors, they are not really new. Their emergence in the 1980s and 1990s makes them a fairly recent phenomenon but does not distinguish them as a unit of regional analysis. To demonstrate the Asia-Pacific transborder subregions as a truly distinctive analytical unit, we need to profile them in comparison with other reference cases of regional integration. In addition, we may appreciate the distinctive features of the Asia-Pacific transborder subregions better by identifying their variants in other continental or regional settings.

Regions and subregions form both within and across national boundaries. By definition, transborder subregions are cross-national. Their most meaningful reference case is the transnational regional integration scheme exemplified by the EU. This form of regional integration involves "the *voluntary* linking in the economic and political domains of two or more formerly independent states to the extent that authority over key areas of national policy is shifted toward the supranational level" (Mattli, 1999, p. 1, italic original). While this definition captures regional integration at its greatest institutional completeness, there are less formal and institutionalized regional integration schemes, oriented primarily toward trade and investment among the member states. These include free trade areas (e.g., NAFTA), custom unions (e.g., the early European Economic Community), and common markets like the Single European Market (X. Chen, 1995). The latter, of course, eventually evolved into the complete economic and even political union of the EU.

Regardless of the variations, all these regional integration projects share a basic principle and structure—independent states brought together as members of a collective union by inter-government negotiations, formal treaties, and some sort of institutionalized supranational governance. In studies of formal regional integration, the level of integration was the most common feature to be explained, while the typical explanatory variables included national goals, size of regional groupings (number of member countries), perceived costs and benefits, and extra-regional factors such as superpower influence

(Axline, 1994). Sovereignty and citizenship issues also have become salient foci of inquiry with the further tightening and deepening of formal regional integration, especially the EU (see Chapman, 1996).

Viewed through the prism of formal regional integration, the transborder subregions are distinctively different. The fundamental differences between the two types of regional integration—inter-state-led and market-state-led—can be summarized through a simple two-by-two matrix as illustrated in figure 2.1. For the sake of conceptual clarity but at the risk of analytical simplicity, figure 2.1 boils down the complexity of regional integration to its governance (vertical) and economic (horizontal) dimensions to highlight the most salient aspects of the transborder subregions. The governance dimension is more important in that it underlies the core difference between the two types of regional integration as inter-state-led (formal) versus market-state-led (informal) integration. Inter-state-led and rule-based, trade blocs and/or political unions are integrated through the use of formal institutional means such as a negotiated treaty or signed agreement among national states or a governance structure in the form of a supranational body. On the other hand, the integration of transborder subregions can be characterized as market-state-led, featuring the more important role of market coordination, social networks, and other non-state actors, while the state, especially the local government, plays a lesser and often complementary part. Although there may be some form and degree of formal links and interactions in transborder subregions at the national state level as in the GTS (chapter 6) and the local level as in the GSCS (see chapter 4), the general difference on the vertical dimension is crucial and carries a number of analytical implications (see chapter 3).

As figure 2.1 suggests, both types of regional integration also vary along the economic integration dimension. Trade blocs generally have strong economic integration and thus locate in cell 1 of the figure, largely because of strong, inter-state-led integration via collective government agreements to remove tariffs and standardize currencies, such as the use of the Euro within much of the EU. Some formal trade blocs, however, may have relatively weak economic integration (cell 3) such as those established in Africa (e.g., the West African Economic Community or CEAO) and Latin America (e.g., the Andean Group) in the 1960s and 1970s (see Axline, 1994). Transborder subregions can vary in the degree of economic integration, as represented by the GSCS (cell 2) versus the GTS (cell 4). This variation is related to the differential degrees of economic complementarity and balance of power among the constituent units of a transborder subregion, as well as the relative weight of the market versus the state on the vertical dimension.

Governance Structure

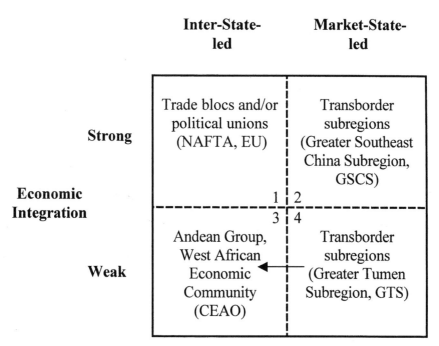

	Inter-State-led	Market-State-led
Strong	Trade blocs and/or political unions (NAFTA, EU)	Transborder subregions (Greater Southeast China Subregion, GSCS)
	1	2
	3	4
Weak	Andean Group, West African Economic Community (CEAO)	Transborder subregions (Greater Tumen Subregion, GTS)

Economic Integration

FIGURE 2.1
A Simple Classification of Cross-National (Sub)Regional Integration

Mixing Units Across Levels

While transborder subregions differ significantly from formal regional integration schemes along both the governance and economic dimensions, they are regions nevertheless and, as such, must be examined in terms of their composition. Regions within national boundaries tend to be homogeneous economic entities, whereas transnational regions such as trade blocs are by definition more heterogeneous because of their multiple national units and cross-national ties. The transborder subregion has an even more complex composition that needs to be deconstructed hierarchically and then reconstituted schematically (see figure 2.2).

As figure 2.2 indicates, the transborder subregion cuts across a nested hierarchy of five levels of analysis that span global-national-local spaces. These multiple spaces are connected and penetrated by transnational flows of capital, goods, and people (migration). The two levels of subregional integration straddle the three layers of economic and political spaces. It is crucial to note that a transborder subregion, which intersects the global-national space, contains multiple intra-national regions or subnational units on or near national borders. Furthermore, the multiple intra-national regions of a transborder region contain a hierarchical network of cities or towns and their hinterlands on and adjacent to both land and sea borders. The agglomeration of several intra- and subnational areas into a transborder subregion highlights its distinctive geo-economic composition and its position that spans the interfaces of global, national, and local spaces.

Figure 2.2 is intended to sharpen the somewhat elusive connections between the transborder subregion and other aggregated units in a totalizing system in which the forms of connections are spatially extended but still bounded (Cooper, 2001). Theoretically speaking, the nation-state has a sovereign and a territorial dimension, which are interconnected, interdependent, and mutually aligned. On one hand, state authority based on sovereignty is demarcated by and confined to a territory (Spruyt, 1994). Territorial boundaries, on the other hand, are not only a necessary basis of national autonomy and political unity (Gilpin, 1987), but define both the inside and outside of nation-states and leave no empty space between them in the global political space (Jarvis and Paolini, 1995). Even as spatial differentiation becomes more intensive and extensive, it nevertheless occurs within the parameters of territorially defined, fixed, and mutually exclusive nation-states (see Ruggie, 1993).

The image and emergent reality portrayed in figure 2.2 are that the transborder subregion renders the border of the nation-state more porous and its political and economic space more curtailed. A transborder region wedges new economic and social spaces between the borders of three or more states and weakens the constraints of political borders that may interfere with the development of what might otherwise be natural economic regions (Lösch, 1954). Methodologically, the formation of a globalized subregional transborder economic space offers a distinctive alternative to the nation-state as the accepted unit for studying the relationship between global economic interdependence and national political change (see chapter 3 for a further discussion).

Globalization by way of rapid and widespread flows of capital, goods, information, and people (labor migration and tourism) has penetrated national borders and impinged on local political economies. Links with the global economy have created both indirect (through the national state) and increasingly more direct opportunities and constraints on local states (governments) in terms of inter-local competition for such resources as investment, technology, and access to markets. If global economic forces weaken the nation-state, as many have claimed (e.g., Strange, 1997), more autonomous local govern-

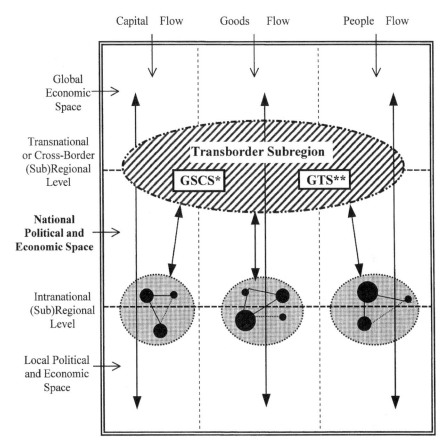

Capital Flow   Goods Flow   People Flow

Global Economic Space

Transnational or Cross-Border (Sub)Regional Level

Transborder Subregion

GSCS*   GTS**

National Political and Economic Space

Intranational (Sub)Regional Level

Local Political and Economic Space

*GSCS stands for the Greater Southeast China Subregion, which includes China's Guangdong and Fujian Provinces, Hong Kong, and Taiwan.
**GTS stands for the Greater Tumen Subregion. which covers the border region of China's Jilin Province, part of the Russian Far East, and North Korea's border area.
Note: The black dots in the circles denote different-sized cities and towns. The arrows denote interactions that have either a harmonious or incompatible influence on the formation and consequences of a transborder subregion.

FIGURE 2.2
The Transborder Subregion Embedded in a Multilevel Nested Hierarchy

ments accentuate its erosion. While the national (central) state has lost power by implementing a variety of administrative and fiscal decentralization policies, local states (governments) have become more assertive in forging global links, often bypassing the political center. The nation-state has been "squeezed from above" by globalization's integrating impact and "pushed from below" by localization's fragmentation. The transborder subregion has intensified this squeezing effect on the nation-state by reconfiguring its multiple subnational units in a more complex manner.

Toward an Inclusive Definition of the Transborder Subregion

The scheme in figure 2.2 provides the conceptual canvas for drawing out a meaningful definition of the transborder subregion. General definitions of regions have varied considerably. Sabel (1994, p. 101) characterizes region until the mid-nineteenth century simply as "a natural unit of economic activity and analysis." To Scalapino, transborder subregions are natural economic territories (NETs), which are "economic entities cutting across political boundaries that combine natural resources, manpower, managerial skills, capital, and technology, depending on the private sector for survival and growth, and varying greatly in size, shape, and number of parties involved, without a formal institutional structure" (Scalapino, 1995, p. 101). Duchacek (1986, p. 17) defines transborder regionalism as "the sum of the various informal and formal networks of communications and problem-solving mechanisms which bring contiguous subnational territorial communities into decisional dyads or triads." What comes closer to the transborder subregion may be Hansen's definition of borderlands as "subnational areas whose economic and social life is directly and significantly affected by proximity to an international boundary" (cited in Asiwaju, 1994, p. 58).

These general or more specific definitions do not appear to capture the multiple dimensions and full complexity of the transborder subregion. As noted, the transborder subregion not only occupies an intermediate status and space between the global economy and the national political economy, but it also involves intra-national (border) regions that lie between the national and local levels. This striking geo-economic composition should be the building block of a useful, broad definition. This definition needs to take into account the hierarchy of cities and their hinterlands that fill out the transnational space of a transborder subregion. Including a realigned center-hinterland structure over international borders in a definition of the transborder subregion is critical to a more comprehensive understanding of this phenomenon. In a related vein, unlike conventional borderlands, which tend to be geographically confined to contiguous border areas of two neighboring countries, transborder subregions, especially those in the Asia Pacific, encompass multiple "borderlands" that lie beyond three or more national boundaries (see chapter 9 for a further distinction after the extended comparative analysis).

By noting both the in-between position of the transborder subregion across interconnected levels of analysis and its reorganized city-hinterland ties, we emphasize the multiple external links between a transborder subregion and the Asia-Pacific regional economy at one level and the world economy at a higher level. These links are rooted in, stem from, and extend beyond a newly restructured production system within a transborder subregional economic space. A broad definition of the transborder subregion must address whether and how this transnational production system is linked to the regional or global economy, because the presence or absence of external ties has analytical implications for understanding the varied outcomes of transborder subregional formation.

Another important dimension of the transborder subregion, as discussed earlier, is the squeezing of the national state by the combined and mutually reinforcing effect of globalization and localization (see Rosenau's 1997 definition in chapter 1). Unlike the EU, in which much state power has shifted to the supranational level, the involvement of border regions and localities in a transborder subregion undermines central state power, thus limiting the role of the national government in affecting cross-border transactions. A broad definition must heed the relatively strong role of local governments.

On still another dimension, the resurgence of regional cultural and ethnic identities has permeated the shared border areas historically (see Fuller, 1997). Suppressed until recently by the lack of economic ties across contentious political borders, this renewed space-bound identity has reactivated latent cross-border social networks that now facilitate economic transactions. This is clearly illustrated by the ethnic Chinese business networks in the GSCS and the ethnic Chinese-Korean ties in the BYSS and the GTS. In these transborder subregions, the boundaries that had either connected or divided ethnic subpopulation groups were artificially and forcefully redrawn at different times by dynastic expansion, Western colonialism, and communist rule. The de-bordering and re-bordering process driving the transborder subregions reflects the impact of the resurgent ethnic identity and social networks, which must be carefully considered.

Given its multiple dimensions mentioned above, the transborder subregion could be broadly defined as a relatively large transnational spatial-economic entity that combines the following elements:

1. The participation and integration of contiguous and/or adjacent subnational border areas of multiple countries.
2. A hierarchy or cluster of cities with or without a central node or gateway nested in hinterlands of varied sizes.

3. A transnational economic system with uneven ties to the local, regional, and global economies and markets.
4. Strong autonomy and role at the local state level with varying forms and degrees of state intervention from the national or supranational level.
5. The presence and influence of cross-border historical connections, migration ties, ethnic affinity, and subcultural identity.

Despite being somewhat cumbersome, this more inclusive definition covers the complexity and multidimensionality of the transborder subregion. It will be sharpened through the development of an integrated analytical framework in the next chapter.

3

From Different Perspectives
to an Integrated Framework

A Synthetic Explanation

Mediating and Restructuring the Global-Local Nexus

DEFINING THE TRANSBORDER SUBREGION broadly prepares us to develop an integrated explanation for the emergence and outcome dimensions of the Asia-Pacific transborder subregions. Starting from the top layer of the nested hierarchy shown in figure 2.1 in chapter 2, we first must account for how globalization both affects and is affected by transborder subregions. While the recognition and intensive use of globalization as a significant social science concept and discourse has coincided with the emergence of the Asia-Pacific transborder subregions over the last two decades, the analysis of economic globalization needs to be made specifically relevant to these cases.

The Global Versus the Local

To a degree, globalization facilitates the formation of transborder subregions, because the border areas and cities that make up these subregions are linked to global dynamics in some fashion. The relationship between the global and the local[1] is strongly mediated by the in-between status and role of transborder subregions (see figure 2.1). Although the literature tends to emphasize the integrating and homogenizing impact of globalization on nations and localities, there are two more balanced and nuanced perspectives on the global-local nexus. The first is Rosenau's (1997) view that globalization and localization are coexisting and interdependent processes (see chapter 1 for his definition of globalization versus localization). Rosenau argues that the integrating force of globalization and fragmenting impact of localization blend into *fragmegrative* (his original usage) processes that produce either complementary or contradictory outcomes. Kloos (2000) has reinforced this perspective by arguing that the twin processes of globalization and localization have a double face: making transnational dynamics and local identities go hand in hand.

This view raises the question of how to conceptualize the global-local nexus in a transborder subregional context. Globalization may reach or even penetrate a border city previously shielded by a national boundary. But whether that border city is directly integrated into the global economy may depend on how it is tied with other localities, especially through or near a central node in a transborder subregion. The latter could strengthen the integrating effect of globalization by creating direct links between the global and local economies. However, a transborder subregion may weaken the integrating effect of globalization by rendering the global-local economic ties less direct and more territorially confined. In this scenario, a transborder subregion may produce some local fragmentation relative to global processes.

The second perspective challenges the thesis that globalization homogenizes by emphasizing persistent local diversity. Amin and Thrift (1994) argue:

> One distinctive characteristic, as in the past, is the uneven distribution of tasks in the international division of labor to different locations offering specific attributes for capital accumulation. Another is the spatially differentiated assimilation and inflection of global imperatives, as the latter encounter places with distinctive, historically layered, socioeconomic structures and traditions. Globalization, therefore, does not imply a sameness between places, but a continuation of the significance of territorial diversity and difference (p. 6).

McMichael (1996) uses the term "local cosmopolitanism" for this local diversity in the global order. Why does local territorial and socioeconomic diversity persist against the impact of globalization? What does resilient localism mean in the context of a transborder subregion? Amin and Thrift (1994, p. 15) attribute lasting local diversity to local "institutional thickness," which includes inter-institutional interaction and synergy, collective representation by many bodies, a common industrial purpose, and shared cultural norms and values. This explanation attaches primary importance to the particular combination of institutional factors across localities that differentiate their development. It both competes with and complements the conventional functionalist and territorial approaches that stress location and infrastructure factors (such as transportation) in determining local economic development (see Christaller, 1972; Hoover, 1968; Weber, 1929).

The transborder subregion provides a timely context for reevaluating the relative role of spatial and institutional dynamics in shaping local-global ties.

In a transborder subregional space, border cities and their immediate hinterlands are more likely to be both local and global at the same time, and subject to the influence of multiple central and local governments as well. Economic transactions between cities on both sides of a border will remain localized if they are facilitated by short distance and the favorable condition of shared cultural identity, but they may be hampered by the lack of access to a broader transport network and the global market. These trans-local economic ties, however, can be elevated directly to the regional level and linked indirectly to the global economy when national and local governments remove or reduce border controls and tariffs and build cross-border transport links.

The importance of the local is also stressed by Patricia Wilson (1996), who expounds an endogenous approach to local economic development that emphasizes the unique factors of the spatial milieu in which economic activity occurs, while recognizing the external impact of the larger structure. The transborder subregion lends itself to identifying these unique factors that are often present in border localities. An isolated and remote location, which limits physical access, can lock a border city out of the global economy, even though it possesses other features that may stimulate external links. A border city with favorable transport links to adjacent cities may experience isolation from the global economy if it lacks economic complementarity with other cities. If these two types of border cities dominate a transborder subregion, the capacity to bridge them with the global economy will be severely curtailed to a set of fragmented local-to-local ties. This spatial structure may force endogenous local development, even if it is not desirable. A different mix of localities in another transborder subregion, however, may create more balanced economic development sustained by both local and global factors.

Local Nodes in Global and Regional Economic Networks

The above perspectives have focused on the dialectics between globalization and localization, with particular attention to why and how localities could continue to pursue endogenous development under global constraints. In the transborder context, localities are nested in multilayered spatial and functional hierarchies. To illustrate the consequences of this structure, I differentiate between the *place-based* versus the *network-based* perspective.

Saskia Sassen's work is an excellent representation of the place-based perspective on the impact of globalization. Sassen (2001) shows that economic globalization has created a new geography of power, which is disproportionately concentrated in global cities such as New York, London, and Tokyo. These cities exert a dominant financial influence as the central nodes of the global economic hierarchy. Sassen (1994) demonstrates that other major international centers, such as Miami, Toronto, and Sydney, could develop certain global-city functions (e.g., banking) without becoming actual global cities. Although Sassen has focused on a small, special set of large international centers, she has brought needed analytical attention to the varied positions and roles of individual localities in the global economy.

If we apply Sassen's perspective to the Asia-Pacific transborder subregions, we find that certain dominant cities—Hong Kong and Singapore, for example—play strategic roles in linking the global and national economies within a transnational space. They are central nodes for the transborder subregions, which are defined in chapter 2 to have such a spatial dimension. However, an emerging transborder urban hierarchy is more complex. Subregional integration across national boundaries reconfigures traditional center-hinterland ties. Uneven spatial clustering at the sectoral or industry level in an open and interactive transborder environment may strengthen some existing centers, downgrade others, elevate a select few to potential world cities, and upgrade the status and functions of previously secondary centers in peripheral locations. The areas being absorbed into a transborder urban system may become more detached from the rest of the national space. This could fragment established intra-national urban systems on various sides of the international boundaries within a transborder subregion. By focusing on understudied border cities, some of which are small and marginal places, this study will contribute fresh evidence and insights to the place-based perspective on globalization beyond the relatively narrow span of research on global cities.

The network-based perspective on the global-local nexus also offers guidance for the study of transborder subregions. This perspective is typically represented by studies that focus on transnational production systems and global commodity chains. A production system involves a functional division of labor through a network of input-output linkages set in a context of power and decision-making (Scott, 1995, p. 52; Storper and Harrison, 1991, p. 411). A production system in a transborder subregion is more complicated because its span over national boundaries involves input-output links among localities embedded in different national and subnational economies. Gereffi (1994) has extended the network-based analysis to include the connected, albeit varied, roles of retailers, trading companies, and marketers, in addition to suppliers and manufacturers, in shaping a commodity chain. He argues that the process of industrial upgrading occurs through a "shift from bilateral, asymmetrical, inter-regional trade flows to a more fully developed intra-regional division of labor incorporating all phases of the commodity chain from raw material supply, through production, distribution, and consumption" (1999, p. 52).

Global commodity chains cut through transborder subregions, but they vary in where and how they enter, reside, and exit. In one transborder subregion, global commodity chains may encompass more cities and their hinterlands than in another transborder subregion. From a local perspective, cities in one transborder subregion may spread more evenly along different segments of a global commodity chain, whereas localities in another transborder subregion may cluster around one distinctive segment of the chain (e.g., raw material supply or manufacturing). The uneven involvement and functions of cities as local nodes in global commodity chains depend on the size and scope of industry and firm networks specific to a transborder subregion. This mediating effect is dynamic; the evolution of the economic base and sectoral mix of transborder subregions could facilitate localities to shift along global or regional commodity chains, with important development consequences. Useful as it is, the network-based perspective through its focus on commodity chains must be contextualized in transborder subregions to account for how specific local nodes are nested in the complex, overlapping divisions of labor across global, national, and regional scales. In other words, the transborder subregions provide ideal cases for an integrated analysis of both places and networks across spatial scales, as advocated by Dicken, Kelly, Olds, and Yeung (2001).

The De-centering of the State

A strong focus on the global-local nexus should not obscure the important role of the nation-state in transborder subregions. On the contrary, the pressure of global and local forces on the state, discussed in chapter 2, raises the question of how the state is adjusting its functions in the transborder subregional environment. This way of looking at the state differs considerably from the state-centric theorizing and debate over the autonomy and power of the state versus the market in shaping national economic development.[2] Instead, I turn to the scholarship on the restructuring of the state's territoriality and regulatory capacity in response to economic globalization for analytical insights.

What happens to the state when it is deeply penetrated by economic globalization from outside and strongly pressured by rising economic regionalism and ethnic power from inside? In one important respect, the state has begun to experience simultaneous de-bordering and re-bordering, as described in chapter 1. In another crucial sense, the state and its space of autonomy and power are being squeezed from above and below, as portrayed in figure 2.1 of chapter 2. Here, the concept of the state's de-centering provides an analytical lens for clarifying the murky political dimension of the transborder subregion.

Blurred Boundaries, Eroded Sovereignty, and Weakened Capacity

The de-centering of the state may be brought about by shifts in its boundary, sovereignty, and capacity. To begin with, we should realize that political boundaries, many of which have been arbitrarily drawn and redrawn, rarely coincide with cultural and ethnic borders. Political boundaries have been characterized as constituting "the cartographic illusion" (Ohmae, 1995), while the nation-state based on these boundaries has been labeled a "myth" (Lewis and Wigen, 1997). Ohmae (1990, 1995) has gone as far as to argue that as the world economy becomes truly borderless, the nation-state is obsolete. In a more realistic and sophisticated account of the state under economic globalization, Sassen has elaborated on how the state and its territorial space are becoming partially denationalized due to the rapid growth of advanced information industries, the embedding of global dynamics in domestic local places, especially in such global cities as New York and London, and the relocation of some components of national state sovereignty onto supranational authorities and privatized corporate systems (Sassen, 1996, 1997).

If state sovereignty can be defined generally as "*supreme legitimate authority within a territory*" (Philpott, 1995, p. 357, italics original), then how do open flows of capital, goods, and people in a transborder subregion affect state sovereignty? This may depend on what aspect of state sovereignty is in question. Differentiating sovereignty into four distinctive types, Krasner (1999) suggests that globalization has a greater impact on *independence sovereignty*—the ability of a government to actually control activities within and across its borders (p. 35)—than on the other three types of sovereignty, which concern the domestic organization, the exclusion of external authority, and the formal international status of the state.[3] Since state sovereignty is partly based on the state's ability to make policy decisions regarding border activities generally, the intensive flows across the already blurred multiple boundaries in a transborder subregion provide a more direct test of how the state may respond. Capital mobility, however, does not constrain states absolutely, as states can ignore markets, especially in a crisis situation (Pauly, 1995), as illustrated by the re-bordering policies of some countries against terrorism and SARS. In this sense, the transborder subregion becomes a realistic context for examining the restructuring of the state under the dual pressure to maintain sovereignty against dealing with a multitude of subnational governments and transnational actors.

The Rise of the Local State

Generally speaking, important decisions regarding border control, customs regulations, trade and investment, taxation, infrastructure development, and tourism in and between neighboring countries reside with the central state. As a transborder subregion takes shape through the growth of closer trade and investment ties between border cities and their hinterlands, the demand for more subnational and local policy-making tends to rise. This downward shift of economic action and associated policy-making raises stakes for both provincial and municipal governments, because their decisions and choices have a stronger and more direct influence on the economic benefit or loss for their jurisdictions. Moreover, since market-driven activity tends to be the main driver of economic transactions in transborder subregions (see figure 2.1), central government interference may have a distorting or inhibiting effect. The pressure of economic globalization on the nation-state to be more market conforming in policy-making, reinforced by the bottom-up pressure from cross-border private sector activities, has shifted decision-making power from the central to the local government and altered the type of policy-making at the central level (see Orum and Chen, 2003). Brimble and Oldfield (1999) suggest that the role of government is to provide a necessary legal and regulatory framework that includes the provision of locationally targeted investment incentives, the control of the tariff and customs schedules, and the development of an initial infrastructure of transportation facilities. Jordan and Khanna (1995) argue that, if central governments could tap into and build on locally driven initiatives and links, this would create positive economic outcomes at the local level.

Despite this shifting relationship between the central and local state that tends to strengthen the latter, how autonomously the local state acts remains constrained by varied national political contexts and is subject to the growing influence of private firms. In some African countries where the central states are weak for lacking governing legitimacy and administrative capacity, local-level authorities, which often are run by warlords, assert a strong measure of autonomy and power in striking business deals with multinational investors in their localities (Reno, 2001). In the Chinese context, while the central state is strong, it has delegated growing decision-making power to provincial and local governments since the early 1980s, which in turn has weakened the central government and strengthened its provincial and local counterparts as loyal but flexible agents and committed stakeholders. More specifically, the enhanced autonomy of local governments in China has stemmed from a clientelist and mutually dependent relationship between officials and entrepreneurs. While the former support the latter through providing access to profits and protection, localized entrepreneurs, both domestic and overseas, influence officials through offering payoffs, employment opportunities, and business partnerships (Wank, 1995, 1999). This symbiotic, utility-maximizing relationship further elevates the stakes and potential benefits for local governments and officials, who in turn have become more willing and flexible in implementing policies to attract overseas private capital to finance economic development. The variation in this relationship can be captured by a comparison across the transborder subregions that involve different border cities of China (see chapters 4–7).

The Dual Dimensions of State De-centering

If we view the above discussion of both the denationalization and decentralization in the sovereign and territorial state in the context of the transborder subregion, we see the crystallization and crossover of these two dimensions into a de-centering process of the state, which in essence refers to both the institutional and spatial scattering of the central state's regulatory capacity. While denationalization through the central state's loss of power in transborder subregions may not be as severe as in a few global cities, it leads to an increasing inability of the central state to control global processes that have entered a larger number of border cities located on the margins of multinational political spaces. Uneven decentralization in a transborder subregion results in differential local autonomy across multiple border cities, which realigns center-local relations in favor of local governments as stakeholders in different ways in different countries.

Both aspects of state de-centering beg specific questions. How does the central state reposition itself to better manage globalized local spaces across national boundaries? How much of the local government's gain is the central government's loss? Is there now a clear differentiation between the scope and format of policy-making of the central and the local government in relation to the private sector? What are the consequences of the de-centered state for the economic and social fortunes of a transborder subregion? The empirical cases examined in later chapters shed comparative light on the de-centering of the state as a complicated form of state restructuring under the "sandwiching" pressure of globalization and the domestic challenge of local autonomy.

Cross-Border Social Capital

Although the Asia-Pacific transborder subregions appear as a striking geoeconomic phenomenon with a distinctive center-local political dimension, they are embedded in a layered sociocultural milieu, which must be examined as an important focus in itself and in conjunction with the other dimensions. Cross-border social capital provides an analytical lens for dissecting this milieu into observable social and cultural conditions that matter to the transborder subregions.

What Is Cross-Border Social Capital?

How do we conceptualize cross-border social capital? Social capital is generally defined and analyzed at the individual or group level. The contemporary analysis of social capital began with Pierre Bourdieu, who defined the concept as "the aggregate of the actual or potential resources which are linked to possession of a durable network of more or less institutionalized relationships of mutual acquaintance or recognition" (cited in Portes, 1998, p. 3). James Coleman (1988, 1990) defines social capital as bridging the combined effects of a social context of norms and mores and of a self-interested principle of utility maximization on an individual's social behavior. Similarly, Nan Lin (2001, p. 19) defines social capital as "investment in social relations with expected returns in the marketplace."

The first attempt to elevate social capital from an individual level to an aggregate feature of communities was made by Robert Putnam, who defines social capital as "the norms and networks of civil society that lubricate cooperative action among both citizens and their institutions" (1998, p. v). Montgomery (2000, p. 1) refers social capital to "the stable pattern of behavioral cooperation that already exists in the society" that can and often is used by governments as a policy or political resource. In a more inclusive fashion, Turner (2000, p. 95) defines social capital as "those forces that increase the potential for economic development in a society by creating and sustaining social relations and patterns of social organization." These scholars have opened up an avenue for studying social capital as an aggregate of assets, ties, and resources that exert broader and presumably positive influence on large-scale and relational structures as embodied by a transborder subregion.

To understand the important role of cross-border social capital in transborder subregions, I conceptualize it broadly to encompass several interrelated elements lodged in a transborder regional social space. First of all, as all social capital is path dependent on centuries of entrenched history and culture (Woolcock, 1998), transnational cultural and ethnic ties through a common history and tradition constitute the basic building block of social capital. These ties in the Asia-Pacific region were severed or weakened by competing political ideologies, military conflicts, and absent economic relations between China and Taiwan, China and South Korea, China and the former Soviet Union, and China and Vietnam at various times. They have revived and been expanding over the past decade or so, however. Secondly, kinship and ancestral networks created and sustained by past and present migration circuits, coupled with shared regional dialects, add to the stock of social capital in the open and highly interactive border environment. Thirdly, cross-border social capital contains a strong native-place identity based on geographic affiliations, which are only reinforced by the spatial proximity that characterizes transborder subregions. Finally, the above elements could nurture an intimate knowledge of local and subregional economic and political practices. The key to conceptualizing cross-border social capital is historically grounded ethnicity and culture that binds people separated by political boundaries. Most importantly, the integrating effect of a shared transborder ethnicity and culture varies by the actual social networks that are created and modified by shifting ethnic and cultural ties over time.

Just as the local economy and state in the transborder context interacts with global processes in complex ways, cross-border social capital could either foster or impede globalization at the local level due to its complex and contingent nature. It not only resides in but also shifts with changes in local development situations and territorially based political institutions such as the local government. Under these concrete conditions, cross-border social capital does not simply exist and cumulate in a normative state but is capable of having a practical influence on border-spanning economic activities.

Social Capital in Practice

The role of cross-border social capital in shaping transborder subregions manifests itself through several mechanisms. Wank (1998) suggests that the three distinctive social networks characterized by kinship, friendship, and ancestry, which involve Chinese emigration to Hong Kong, Taiwan, and Southeast Asia during different historical periods, channel overseas Chinese investment into China differently. *Kinship* networks, rooted in Chinese emigration to Southeast Asia in the nineteenth and early twentieth century, tend to bring overseas Chinese investment back to rural areas in ancestral villages in Fujian and Guangdong provinces, where the support of kin is critical. *Friendship* networks tend to draw investment capital largely to urban areas from new, post-1973 Chinese emigrants who use their personal connections to strike favorable deals with city government officials. *Ancestral* networks involve mostly Taiwanese investors whose ancestors began to emigrate from southern Fujian in the seventeenth century and who return to invest in the entire home region on the basis of linguistic and subcultural familiarity. These social networks often become intertwined in fostering capital mobility and economic production.

Leung (1993) defined *kinship* factories in the Pearl River Delta (PRD) as those that have connections with or are owned by the mainland relatives or close friends of the respective Hong Kong investors/contractors. These factories provide investment confidence and exchange reliability based on the mutual trust established by the kinship or close social relations between Hong Kong investors and their mainland subcontractors. These ties do not automatically lead to business deals, but they are cultivated or activated by both material and non-material gift exchanges such as clothes, banquets, color TV sets, crucial information, and key introduction (see Smart and Smart, 1991).

In my view, cross-border social capital has a twofold role in gluing and lubricating the Asia-Pacific transborder subregions, albeit to differential degrees. *Gluing* involves bringing multiple actors on different sides of a border together in some sort of economic cooperation through mutual investment and joint production. Just bringing economic actors across borders together is not sufficient, as their cooperation may be hampered by frictions of different systems. *Lubricating* refers to ways and tendencies by which ethnic social capital smoothes out cross-border economic cooperation. Without lubrication, the glued seams of economic ties may strain and even come apart under the competing pressures of incompatible systems. The lubricating role of social capital makes cross-border economic cooperation more sustainable (see X. Chen, 2000c).

In fulfilling both gluing and lubricating roles, cross-border social capital also interacts with other conditions and thus mediates their impact on transborder subregional outcomes. First, cross-border social capital grows from and feeds back on simultaneous globalization and localization. As a globalizing economy extends the commercial and business networks of the Chinese diaspora, especially in East and Southeast Asia (see Yeung, 2000), the socially mediated spatial concentration of overseas Chinese investment in China's southeastern coastal areas has created distinctive local economies with extensive export-based global links. Cross-border social capital also is capable of magnifying the effect of geographic proximity on the transborder subregions (see below). Cross-border kinship and ancestral ties facilitate more frequent visits to relatives and hometowns across borders. Much of the early Hong Kong and Taiwanese investment in China's southeastern coastal areas occurred through tourists and relatives visiting local towns and villages.

With state policies favoring greater local autonomy, Taiwanese investors' strategy of cultivating interpersonal relationships (*guanxi*) with local government officials has been very effective in strengthening economic ties across the Taiwan Strait (Hsing, 1997, 1998). Social capital may also foster more effective governance in terms of new or improved government institutions. Local governments of China's southeastern coastal cities have become more market-oriented and efficient in policy-making through their experience in dealing with the large number of small and flexible Taiwanese and Hong Kong investors. While social capital crosses borders, it does not reach all localities on different sides of borders evenly. The kinship- and nativity-based social network ties that connect Taiwanese investors and local government officials in Fujian may or may not work in cities like Dongguan in Guangdong, where Taiwanese investors can't draw upon kinship/friendship ties and don't speak the dialect. Even if social capital could facilitate and sustain business ventures, it may not work as well in helping solve practical problems that may haunt the day-to-day operations, such as low worker productivity and abuses by local officials.[4]

Using the concept of cross-border social capital as an analytical lens, in conjunction with the de-centering state lens, reveals how varied economic ties over multiple spatial boundaries in the heterogeneous Asia-Pacific region are mediated by the evolution of historically concrete and place-specific social, cultural, and political relations (see Dirlik, 1998). More specifically, the social capital lens is used to assess the argument that the transborder subregions endowed with richer cross-border social capital tend to exhibit more positive outcomes, such as faster growth and stronger integration. To avoid circular reasoning that the more successful transborder subregions must be stocked with more social capital, I have defined cross-border social capital as separate from its possible influence on transborder subregions. Three primary and several secondary cases help demonstrate the presence/absence and strength of cross-border social capital prior to the emergence of transborder subregions, and that its presumed influence is contingent on other factors identified before and below.

Geographic Proximity, Transport Links, and Transborder Transactions

Why Does Distance Still Matter?

Geographic contiguity/proximity is a salient feature of the Asia-Pacific transborder subregions. Without geographic proximity there are no transborder subregions to speak of. However, to understand the formation of transborder subregions, we must be clear about why and how geographic proximity is critical. Then we must clarify how geographic proximity interacts with border effects in influencing transborder subregions.

Geographic proximity means a small physical distance between two localities. Short distance in turn means less travel time and lower transportation cost between them. In the classical location literature, least cost theory emphasizes transportation cost and access to raw materials and markets for finished products. Alfred Weber (1929) differentiated between ubiquitous materials, which are found at similar cost everywhere, and localized materials, which are found at specific locations. Gross localized materials draw industries to their sources, making them *material oriented*, whereas the heavy use of ubiquitous materials may lead to *market oriented* locations (Chapman and Walker, 1987, p. 33, italics original). In either case, the ideal location or point of least cost is geared toward shortening the distance of transportation and thus reducing its costs. This logic is a basic element of classical theorizing of intra-regional integration and development. Both central place theory (Christaller, 1972) and the growth pole model (Perroux, 1950) contain explicit assumptions about the roles of market access and distance in the formation of regional urban hierarchies and the diffusion of development benefits.

With increasing transnational capital mobility and division of labor, especially in the financial sector through the extensive use of information technologies, the general importance of geographic distance and physical access to markets has diminished. Some scholars (e.g., O'Brien, 1992) have gone as far as to proclaim the end of geography. In a way, the "end of geography" argument parallels the logic of the "dying of the state" proposition in that neither distance nor sovereignty based on state boundaries matter very much in a globalized economy. Although the emergence of electronic space in global finance renders distance much less relevant, geographic proximity remains a salient factor in some intra- and transnational regional contexts. Glasmeier (1994) and Piore and Sabel (1984) linked the continued vitality and competitiveness of a number of European industrial districts with the spatial clustering of decentralized and vertically disintegrated small and medium-sized manufacturers and suppliers.

Geographic contiguity and proximity are as important in the Asia-Pacific region as they are in Europe, or perhaps even more so, for two reasons. First, the lack of well-developed transportation networks within and across borders, especially road and rail lines, increases the importance for being close to raw materials for efficient production, and if possible to seaports for convenient transportation. Second, geographic contiguity or proximity can weaken the barrier effect and enhance the opportunity effect of national borders.

The Barrier Versus the Opportunity Effect of Borders

The effect of borders is a key to explaining the positive or negative outcomes of transborder subregions. Borders can either block or bridge the development and integration of areas on different sides. Understanding this barrier or opportunity effect of borders hinges on how we conceptualize borders and their functions. The two dominant and commonly accepted views are that a border is either a dividing line or a contact zone. From the "dividing line" perspective, a border represents a frontier territorial edge that sets the legal limit of the state. It tends to separate rather than unite border regions of two states through demarcated jurisdictions, control over crossings, and enforced customs rights. The competing perspective, however, sees a border as a contact zone or filter factor that creates a functioning membrane space for transboundary economic exchanges and social interactions and their diffusion beyond the border (see Ratti, 1993). Gallusser (1994) notes a conceptual shift from the narrow, linear view of borders to the view that borders form a widened socioeconomic landscape in the spatial integration of Western Europe.

A fairly broad conceptualization of borders can also be found in the literature on borderlands such as those that join the United States and Canada and the United States and Mexico. Konrad (1991, p. viii) suggests that:

> The borderlands of the United States and Canada are distinctive regions of mitigating landscapes fading from the common edges of the boundary. Between

Canada and the United States, borderlands regions have emerged, more or less, among peoples with common characteristics, in spite of the political boundary between them. In an extreme sense, borderlands exist when shared characteristics set a region apart from the countries that contain it, and residents have more in common with each other than with members of their respective national cultures.

Martínez (1994, pp. 2–5) developed a conceptual typology of different borderlands: (1) alienated, (2) co-existent, (3) interdependent, and (4) integrated. In the direction of 1 to 4, the borderland changes from high tension, functional closure, and no interaction to increasing stability, more opening, and frequent interaction until it becomes fully integrated, with largely unrestricted movement of people and goods across the boundary. Martínez cited the Israel-Lebanon borderland as alienated, the Israel-Jordan borderland as co-existent, and the U.S.-Mexico borderland as interdependent, while providing no example of the integrated borderland. A number of borderland-like regions in the EU such as the Maas-Rhine region along the Dutch-Belgian-German borders may approximate full integration (see chapter 8).

Borders, however, have multiple barrier effects beyond the rigid legal demarcation of separate states. Rietveld (1993, p. 49) identified four border-related barriers: (1) weak or expensive infrastructure services in transport and communication for international links; (2) consumer preference for domestic rather than foreign products and destinations; (3) government interventions; and (4) lack of information on foreign countries. International road or rail links across borders are generally less developed than domestic links on either side of borders. This creates higher detour costs for transportation between border cities that has to be routed through other domestic cities. Government interventions that increase borders' barrier effects include rigid visa requirements, high tax levies, tight currency exchange controls, and complex registration and certification procedures for border trading companies and border-crossing products (Rietveld, 1993). Overcoming these obstacles helps transform segmented border-area economies into open transborder subregional economies, which in turn facilitates more integration of border cities and hinterlands. To remove the hindrance of transport infrastructure requires building more border-crossing road and rail links and increasing the frequency of bus and train services between border cities.

As discussed above, geographic contiguity/proximity and border effects have both reinforcing and mitigating effects on each other. Short distances between international border cities ameliorate the barrier effects of borders under conditions of border openness, decent cross-border transport infrastructures, and limited government interventions. Severe border obstacles, on the other hand, can neutralize or defeat the comparative advantages of geographic contiguity or proximity in border regions. The Asia-Pacific transborder subregions are spatially more expansive and compositionally more complex than conventional border zones or "natural" borderlands. Unlike the narrow belt of cross-border activity along binational boundaries,[5] the transborder subregions involve large flows across major centers and broad hinterlands within and between three or more national boundaries. Therefore, they require a correspondingly broader scope of spatial analysis.

Pertaining to one Asia-Pacific transborder subregion, Macleod and McGee (1995) characterized Singapore expanding its economic activity and leisure needs into the adjacent regions of the Riau Archipelago (Indonesia) and Johor state (Malaysia) as an expanding city-state model. Chia (1993, p. 3) labeled this process "a metropolitan spillover into the hinterland" (see the case involving Singapore in chapter 7). Some Asia-Pacific transborder subregions have even become an intricate part of the large international urban networks that have benefited from the growth of within-country mega-urban regions, the expansion of selected port cities and other coastal locations, and more frequent and intensive transborder transactions (Douglass, 1995). Stretching and strengthening these development networks are the rapid expansion of air, container shipping, and fiber-optic telecommunications links across national boundaries (Rimmer, 1996). These technological and infrastructural developments tend to make international borders in the Asia-Pacific region more of an opportunity for cooperation than a barrier.

The Power of an Analytical Synthesis

I have discussed four sets of perspectives that pertain to the economic, political, sociocultural, and spatial-infrastructure dimensions of the Asia-Pacific transborder subregions. The next step is to crystallize these perspectives into analytical lenses to make a synthetic framework. In figure 3.1 each of the four quadrants is anchored by an analytical lens derived from the above theoretical discussions that illuminate a set of important factors in shaping a major dimension of a transborder subregion. Together they make more transparent the underlying complexities and contingencies involved in the different cases. The global-local nexus lens emphasizes the interactions between the global and local economies, rather than the one-way structuring impact of globalization, by pointing to the conjunctural importance of economic complementarity, functional specialization, and market size. The political/institutional lens on the state de-centering sensitizes the analysis to the increasingly uneven roles and specific policies of the central versus the differential autonomy of regional and/or local governments in influencing the transborder subregions. The sociocultural lens highlights the role of social networks based on historical continuity, cultural and ethnic ties, and linguistic similarity in shaping the transborder subregions. Finally, the spatio-infrastructure lens sheds light on the relative and interactive effects of geographic proximity, physical distance, border type, and transport networks on the transborder subregions.

A Harmonious Hypothesis as the Analytical Key

Underlying this synthetic framework is a harmonious hypothesis: if the main factors suggested by each analytical lens not only are favorable but also complement one another across the four dimensions, they will induce generally beneficial outcomes for a transborder subregion, such as rapid growth

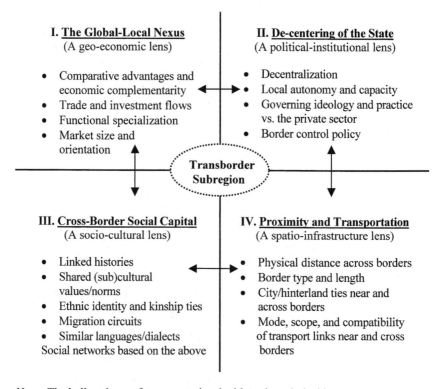

Note: The bullets denote factors associated with each analytical lens.

◄──► Interactions that have either a harmonious or incompatible influence on the formation and consequences of a transborder subregion.

FIGURE 3.1
An Integrated Framework with Four Analytical Lenses and Associated Factors

and close integration. Conversely, if some factors are unfavorable and lack mutual harmony, they will create less desirable consequences, such as slow growth and inter-unit inequality.[6] This harmonious hypothesis suggests not that these factors must and always will work well together, but that the extent to which they do helps explain the differences and similarities across the cases. The ultimate objective of this synthetic explanation is to shed light on the central argument about the changing role of borders in bridging previously isolated border areas into the linked transborder subregions versus the remaining or recurring barrier effect of borders on these transborder subregions (see chapter 1). While none of the four lenses carries necessary or sufficient conditions by itself, the economic lens is closer to highlighting necessary conditions than the other three lenses and thus is treated as the entry point of analysis. Once we have passed this point, we start looking for how economic conditions interact with factors to account for differences and similarities.

In light of this framework and the key hypothesis, it follows that even if a transborder subregion enjoys a high level of economic complementarity among its constituent units and thus attracts substantial foreign investment, the subregion is only successful as a whole if the favorable economic conditions are matched with such favorable political and sociocultural factors as strong local autonomy and rich cross-border social capital. This harmonization is dependent on how the direct and indirect participation of border cities in the global economy is influenced by the policy-making power of local governments relative to the centers and political relations between the central and local governments of different countries involved in a transborder subregion. In a different scenario, the presence of cross-border social capital and extensive transport links within a transborder subregion could not generate positive outcomes when economic complementarity is absent and local autonomy is highly circumscribed. In sum, the harmonious hypothesis calls for a close examination of how the factors work individually and collectively through each analytical lens and how well they coalesce as different sets.

Methodological and Data Issues

This study not only brings forth a synthetic explanation for the transborder subregions through an integrated framework, but it also features a research design and methodology that improve upon the approaches and information used to study this phenomenon. First, the seven chosen Asia-Pacific transborder subregions cover the full permutations of this phenomenon in the region and thus represent a sort of universe. The diversity among the cases, however, has guided me to treat them differentially to achieve a balance between depth and breath and between particularities and generalities. To gain analytical depth, I focus on three primary cases, each of which takes up the space of an entire chapter (chapters 4–6). The three primary cases are sufficiently diverse to be examined individually in great detail and compared as a subset. This part of the empirical analysis focuses on fleshing out the rich details of the specific contexts to reveal the more subtle interactions among the full sets of factors associated with the analytical lenses. Moving beyond the specificities of the primary cases for some generalization, chapter 7 examines four transborder subregions in Southeast Asia as secondary cases. In this more restricted comparative analysis, I look for broad similarities and differences against the primary cases. Finally, chapter 8 moves beyond the Asia-Pacific context to incorporate cases from the North American and European settings. This extended comparison aims at drawing further parallels among the cases to maximize the generalizability about transborder subregional integration.

The second methodological feature of this study is dealing with nested units of analysis that differ considerably from the nation-state as a conventional macro unit of study. While each transborder subregion is treated as a single, holistic case, it actually exists as a place-based, multilayered network that comprises territorial units of varied geographic scales (see chapter 2). Since it is necessary to examine all these constituent units in order to understand the totality of a transborder subregion, it is crucial to regard them as being nested or embedded into one another, rather than existing discretely or independently. That a transborder subregion contains units such as border cities from different national systems complicates the unit of analysis further, as the units may not be compatible in terms of both physical size and administrative status. Therefore, the methodological challenge is twofold. In one respect, the analysis needs to be sensitive to the varied existential and functional attributes of units or places. In a more important sense, it is imperative to focus on the relational aspects of these units or places. The analytical strategy is to simultaneously unbundle the units of a transborder subregion and examine how they are reconfigured as a whole. This study both isolates the features of certain border cities and looks at how they are connected with each other and with higher-order spatial and administrative units such as regions, provinces (or states), or nations across multiple international borders.

The broad coverage of cases, coupled with handling nested units of analysis within cases has made data collection very difficult. A related, albeit tougher, challenge was to obtain information at the subregional and local levels across countries at which data are not regularly and systematically compiled and, if they are, may not be compatible across cases. To partially overcome these constraints, I rely on some national-level statistics (most of which are presented in the appendix to this book) to show how economic relations among higher-order units may influence ties among subnational and local units across borders. To be faithful to the most important units of analysis—border cities within the subregions—I have pieced together from various indigenous sources extensive statistical data on the economic and transport links among border cities within the three transborder subregions that are the primary cases. To capture some of the local dynamics not reflected in the statistical data, I have conducted field interviews with local informants in various border cities, even though this fieldwork was uneven across the cases due to budgetary and travel restrictions. To supplement these data, I have included extensive secondary material from such sources as published studies, government documents, Internet-based information, reports by organizations such as the Asian Development Bank (ADB), and newspapers.

It is important to note the uneven temporal coverage of the time-series data on the cases. The information on trade and investment ties among the countries/economies involved in the transborder subregions includes much of the 1980s and the entire 1990s, which largely bracket the emergence and evolution of the transborder subregions (see chapter 2). Unfortunately, data presented in the tabular form on the subnational and local units are more truncated to different beginning and ending years in the 1990s due to the tremendous difficulty in collecting them. Nevertheless, these data reflect a period of growth and change, including the dramatic event of the Asian financial crisis in 1997–1998, which affected the transborder subregions. In addition, I have managed to bring these cases up to date by piecing together scattered yet much more recent information from various sources. Regardless of these data limitations, integrating different types and sources of information provides a broad empirical foundation on which to launch the series of in-depth case analyses that begin with the next chapter.

Notes

1. The definition of what is the local and what is the global may not be precise, just as it is difficult to pin down the physical boundaries between the local and the global. While generally using the term *local* to mean localities such as cities and regions rather than nations, and the term *global* to signify worldwide processes, Amin and Thrift (1994, p. 6) choose to leave both terms more or less ambiguous. They highlight the more varied use of the *local*, which might refer to a small area such as the rural industrial districts of Italy or a large agglomeration such as Silicon Valley as a player in the world economy. In this book, I use *local* to refer to the border cities or areas that are the basic building blocks of transborder subregions and are actual or potential players in the global economy. This allows me to examine explicitly the role of transborder subregions in mediating the economic relations between border cities or areas and the global economy.

2. The role of the state in economic development, especially in the East Asian context, has drawn sustained scholarly attention and debates, stimulated partly by the publication of *Bringing the State Back In* (Evans, Rueschemeyer, and Skocpol, 1985; also see Block, 1987). While the

literature is too extensive to summarize here, the controversy has shifted from disagreement between the neoclassical economics view and the developmental state perspective to a debate between the latter and an institutional approach and interpretation. Representing the developmental state school, Amsden (1989) and Wade (1990) suggest that the state has guided and directed the market with a heavy hand through such policies as picking winners and losers and protecting domestic firms. For an extended summary of these policies, see Henderson and Appelbaum (1992, pp. 21–22). On the other hand, Kuo (1995) challenges the developmental state model by pointing to evidently important roles of business associations and firms in a changing clientelist or corporatist relationship with the state in Taiwan and the Philippines. Evans (1995) demonstrates that the South Korean state only became developmental when it was embedded in social networks and cooperated with important actors in civil society. Kim and Suh (1999, p. 5) argue convincingly that the successful attainment of economic development, the growth of the private sector, and the international pressure for a "free market" have weakened the dominance of the developmental state and forced it into a symbiotic relationship with businesses in which it must transform itself. This critique of the developmental state perspective provides a nice transition to my focus on the de-centered state in the context of transborder subregions.

3. The three other types of sovereignty are domestic, Westphalian, and international legal. *Domestic sovereignty* refers to the organization of authority within a given polity; *Westphalian sovereignty* refers to the exclusion of external authority, that is, the right of a government to be independent of external authority structures; *international legal sovereignty* refers to the recognition of one state by another, which is associated with diplomatic immunity and the right to sign treaties and join international organizations (Krasner, 1999, p. 35, italics original).

4. I am grateful to Alvin Y. So for alerting me to these limits of cross-border social capital.

5. In more established borderlands or border regions straddling a binational boundary, cross-border activities and movement tend to be territorially confined to a rather narrow belt on either side of the border. Bufon (1994, p. 24) found that 80 percent of the cross-border activities such as shopping and visiting relatives around the twin towns of Gorizia and Nova Gorica on the Italian-Slovene border occurred in a 5 km border belt, except for work commuting, which exceeded this territorial limit.

6. I would like to thank Alvin Y. So for suggesting the term and notion of "harmonious hypothesis" as a parsimonious way of positing the complex interactions among the four sets of factors.

II

DIVERSITY AMONG THREE
EAST ASIAN CASES

4

Binding Porous Borders

The Greater Southeast China Subregion

THE FIRST OF THE THREE PRIMARY CASES in this study, the Greater Southeast China Subregion[1] (GSCS), is a distinctive transborder subregion that consists of Hong Kong, Taiwan, Macau, and China's Guangdong and Fujian provinces (see map 4.1). It conforms to the generic composition of a transborder subregion because at least one of the participating parties is a subnational (provincial) unit adjacent to an international border. Although the China–Hong Kong border became "intra-national" in a formal, legalistic sense with the return of the former British colony to Chinese sovereignty in 1997, that border has remained functionally "international" due to continued, albeit gradually relaxed, restrictions on crossings. The distinctive and administrative status of Hong Kong as a special administrative region (SAR) tends to reinforce these restrictions. The political separation and tension between China and Taiwan has kept the ocean boundary between them officially international and largely closed. While I refer to Guangdong and Fujian provinces specifically as subnational units of China relative to Hong Kong and Taiwan in the GSCS, I use China or mainland China interchangeably, depending on both the reference cases and temporal conditions (before or after 1997) at the aggregate, contextual level of analysis below.

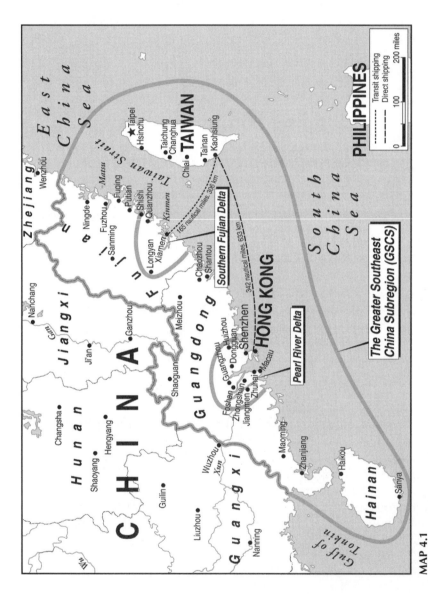

MAP 4.1
The Greater Southeast China Subregion (GSCS)

Subregionalized Global-Local Economic Links

Following the sequential and logical connections among the analytical lenses in the integrated framework in the preceding chapter, I begin by examining how global-local economic links manifest themselves within the GSCS and how the latter mediates these links and their influence on subregional and local development. Looking through the geo-economic lens (see figure 3.1 in chapter 3), the analysis focuses specifically on trade and investment flows, economic complementarities, cross-border production networks, global-local commodity chains, local functional specialization and clustering, and restructured urban hierarchies in the GSCS.

Evolving Trade Ties

Aggregate trade growth among China, Hong Kong, and Taiwan facilitated the eventual formation of the GSCS. Prior to 1970, Hong Kong, still under British rule, was the largest market for exports from China. Hong Kong had a trade deficit with China that accounted for one-fifth of China's total exports at that time (Sung, 1997). In the 1970s, China and Taiwan started light indirect trade through their respective trading companies in Hong Kong. During 1970–1978, cumulative China-Taiwan indirect trade via Hong Kong was estimated at US$121 million, with Taiwan's exports accounting for a minuscule 0.6 percent (Long, 1998).

China-Taiwan indirect trade grew rapidly in the early 1980s in spite of Taiwan's resistance to trade with China until 1985, when it permitted indirect trade. China-Taiwan indirect trade through Hong Kong rose further in the late 1980s as a result of the Taiwanese government loosening foreign exchange control and permitting Taiwanese residents to visit the mainland in 1987. By 1991, trade among China, Hong Kong, and Taiwan accounted for 30 percent of their total external trade, up from 10 percent in 1978 (Shieh, 1997).

China's exports to Taiwan expanded from US$1.1 billion in 1991 to US$8 billion in 2002, while Taiwan's exports to China soared to US$29 billion (see figure 4.1), which accounted for one-quarter of its total exports.[2] In 2003, the mainland became Taiwan's top trading partner, leapfrogging the United States and Japan. Trade through direct or indirect channels among the three Chinese economies has solidified the macroeconomic foundation for the GSCS. (See table 4.A in the appendix for more detailed information on trade between China and Taiwan through Hong Kong.)

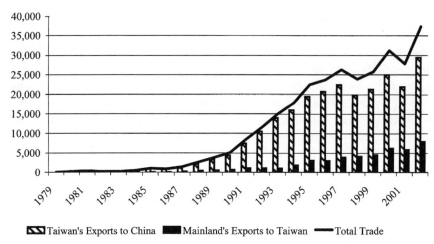

 KNN Taiwan's Exports to China ■■■ Mainland's Exports to Taiwan ━━━Total Trade

FIGURE 4.1
Trade Between Mainland China and Taiwan Through Hong Kong, 1979–2002

Networked Production Links

Trade ties within the GSCS are grounded in cross-border production links, which are based on comparative advantages and complementarities among the three Chinese economies. Since the GSCS's networked production consists of the China–Hong Kong and China-Taiwan dyads, I examine each separately within the larger triangular structure.

The China–Hong Kong Manufacturing Nexus

The production system straddling the China–Hong Kong border began to form in 1979 when the establishment of four special economic zones (SEZs) in southeastern China triggered the initial movement of Hong Kong's labor-intensive processing and assembly operations over the border. Two decades later, a massive (re)division of labor between Hong Kong and southern China has been firmly entrenched and was figuratively described as "Hong Kong as the shop window and China as the factory floor" (Overholt, 1993, p. 183). Hong Kong's manufacturing employment declined from a peak of about 1 million in 1980, 46 percent of the active labor force (Berger and Lester, 1997, p. 9), to approximately 250,000 in 1998, only 8 percent of the labor force (Martin, 2000, p. 18). With the continued exodus of manufacturing over the border, worsened by the economic depression in the wake of the 1997–1998 Asian financial crisis, Hong Kong's manufacturing employment fell below 200,000 in 2002, down to only 5.4 percent of the active labor force.[3] By the end of 2003, close to 10 million jobs were created by 53,000 Hong Kong–invested factories in Guangdong province, accounting for 90 percent of all Hong Kong–invested factories in China.[4]

Industry-level change provides more concrete evidence on the scale and features of the production system linking China and Hong Kong, as illustrated by the electronics industry. Hong Kong electronics firms have moved most of the assembly of consumer electronics to Guangdong province, which offers low-cost labor capable of making quality products, some raw materials at a reasonable price and quality, and easy geographic access for the timely delivery and transportation of products. In 1994, the electronics industry accounted for 10.5 percent of all Hong Kong manufacturing labor, 19 percent of Hong Kong's total industrial output, and 26.2 percent of Hong Kong's total domestic exports (Reif and Sodini, 1997), while exporting roughly 90 percent of its own output (Enright, Scott, and Dodwell, 1997). This high export dependency on mature consumer products with thin profit margins has been sustained through an extensive cross-border reorganization of the industry.

According to Reif and Sodini (1997), four Hong Kong electronics companies making original equipment manufacturing (OEM) products employed an average of 5,400 workers in their manufacturing facilities in the Pearl River Delta (PRD), compared to an average of 540 Hong Kong–based employees (a 10:1 ratio) who focus on such activities as technology innovation, product design, quality control, marketing, and distribution.[5] Hong Kong's electronics firms that made more technology-intensive electronic components, including high-end printed circuit boards (PCBs) and semiconductor devices, some of which are original brand-name manufactures (OBM), had zero employment in China, because they require low labor input, high automation, and quality infrastructure, which are only available in Hong Kong proper (Reif and Sodini, 1997).[6]

The electronics industry illustrates the constraints and opportunities associated with a simultaneous process of downloading and upgrading in Hong Kong's manufacturing sector. Downloading—moving labor-intensive production to China—creates growing competition for this export market. Upgrading to high-tech manufacturing has been constrained by the lack of product/technology innovation and of initial public and private (bank) capital for new start-ups, except limited family financing (Reif and Sodini, 1997). Changes have occurred recently, however. Endorsed and promoted by the Industry and Technology Development Council (ITDC), Hong Kong built and opened its first ever science park in 2001, which provides a focal point for both larger companies and small fledgling high-tech ventures in IT, engineering materials, and drugs-based genetic research.

The production link between China and Hong Kong is by no means a one-way flow of manufacturing investment from Hong Kong into China. Often overlooked is China's growing investment in Hong Kong. As of June 1, 1996, China had poured about US$20 billion into Hong Kong's manufacturing sector, accounting for 7 percent of the total foreign manufacturing investment, behind only Japan's 39 percent and the United States' 28 percent (Hong Kong Trade Development Council [HKTDC], 1997). Mainland China has channeled considerably more investment into Hong Kong since the 1997 handover, and a bulk of this investment has bought up equity stakes in properties, shopping malls, and banks.

The China-Taiwan Manufacturing Nexus

Networked production spanning the Taiwan Strait must be placed in the context of accelerated Taiwanese investment in China through Hong Kong since the late 1980s. According to China's government statistics, contracted cumulative Taiwanese investment in China by 2001 amounted to US$52 billion in approximately 50,000 ventures. While the estimate by the Taiwanese sources was lower, they finally acknowledged that cumulative investment on the mainland had surpassed US$50 billion in over 50,000 ventures by September 2002 and might even approach US$100 billion (Shapiro, 2002).[7] Of Taiwan's manufacturing investment, electrical and electronics (30 percent), food and beverages (17 percent), plastics and rubber (15 percent), and metal making (14 percent) ranked as the top four industries (see X. Chen, 1996). In the late 1990s, Taiwanese manufacturing investment in China, especially in such high-tech sectors as integrated circuits (ICs), began to flow heavily into Shanghai and Jiangsu province, which accounted for nearly half of all Taiwanese investment in China in 2000, surpassing the combined total of Guangdong and Fujian (Lawrance, 2002). However, the five Guangdong and Fujian cities (Shenzhen, Dongguan, Guangzhou, Xiamen, Fuzhou) have continued to rank as the most popular locations for Taiwan-invested factories. The capitalization of Taiwanese investment per project rose from US$735,000 in 1991 to US$2.4 million by the late 1990s (Mainland Affairs Council, 2000, p. 24),[8] indicating an increase in the capital intensity and the technological content of the investment flow.

As table 4.1 shows, a larger proportion of firms in the more capital-intensive industry cluster (e.g., electrical equipment) maintained production after investing in China than did firms in the two more labor-intensive industry clusters (footwear and textiles/garments). On average, the mainland-based factories substituted the Taiwan-based factories in finishing generally labor-intensive products, whereas two-thirds of the surveyed firms kept higher-value-added production in Taiwan (3c). One-third of the firms in all industry clusters finished identical products (3e), suggesting a certain degree of substitutable production across the Taiwan Strait. Table 4.1 also shows that 92 percent of the firms kept order receiving in Taiwan (4a), while only 27.8 percent of the firms shifted order receiving, manufacturing, and exporting to their

TABLE 4.1.
Division of Labor Between Taiwanese Companies and Their Mainland Factories, by Industry Cluster

Division of Labor	Total Sample	Industry Cluster			
		Electrical Equipment, Vehicles, and Metals	Footwear, Daily Necessities, Bamboo and Paper Products	Textiles, Garments, Toys, Plastic and Leather Products	Other Industries
1. Number of firms surveyed	140	33	25	44	38
2. Continuing production in Taiwan after setting up factories in China (%)	69.1	86.2	61.9	55.0	75.8
3. If continuing production in Taiwan:					
a. Taiwan factories make parts or semiprocess; mainland factories assemble and/or finish (%)	25.8	26.9	22.2	23.1	29.6
b. Mainland factories make parts or semiprocess; Taiwan factories assemble and/or finish (%)	29.9	34.6	44.4	26.9	18.5
c. Both factories finish products, but Taiwan factories make higher-value-added ones (%)	67.0	69.2	72.2	61.5	66.7

(continued)

TABLE 4.1 (*continued*)

Division of Labor	Total Sample	Industry Cluster			
		Electrical Equipment, Vehicles, and Metals	Footwear, Daily Necessities, Bamboo and Paper Products	Textiles, Garments, Toys, Plastic and Leather Products	Other Industries
d. Both factories finish products, but mainland factories make higher-value-added ones (%)	7.2	3.8	5.6	3.8	14.8
e. Both factories finish identical products (%)	33.0	30.8	33.3	34.6	33.3
f. Both factories finish unrelated products (%)	17.5	23.1	11.1	15.4	18.5
4. Marketing and exportation of products:					
a. Taiwan receives orders; mainland manufactures and exports (%)	**92.1**	**92.9**	**90.9**	**97.7**	**84.4**
b. Mainland receives orders; mainland manufactures and exports (%)	27.8	21.4	22.7	22.7	43.7
c. Taiwan receives orders; mainland makes parts and semiprocesses; Taiwan finishes and exports (%)	16.7	28.6	13.6	9.1	18.6

Source: Adapted from Kao et al. (1995, pp. 177–178).

mainland factories (4b). By keeping the well-established function of order receiving in Taiwan, Taiwanese firms maintain control and manipulate the distribution of profits, while the mainland factories benefit mainly from labor input during manufacturing. Some Taiwanese firms shifted order receiving to the mainland (4b) to achieve profitability in a different way.[9]

As the manufacturing ties between China and Taiwan became stronger, the Taiwanese government, in 1992, articulated a vision for the cross-strait division of labor strictly based on comparative advantages and vertical integration. In principle, the mainland would specialize in labor-intensive industries, while Taiwan would focus on capital- and technology-intensive manufacturing. Taiwan would concentrate on the upstream activity of developing new components, whereas China would engage in downstream manufacturing and assembly. This vision was also characterized as "keeping the roots planted" in Taiwan and "letting the branches and leaves grow out" in China (X. Chen, 2000a). This reorganized cross-strait production system, coupled with the production nexus across the China–Hong Kong border, has created global-local economic links in a subregionalized environment.

The Variety and Dynamics of Subregionalized Global Commodity Chains

The role of the GSCS in restructuring global-local economic links manifests itself in the formation of global commodity chains that span Taiwan, Hong Kong, and cities in Guangdong and Fujian. Commodity chains consist of flows between the nodes, the relations of production, the dominant organization of production, the geographic loci of production, and other backward and forward linkages (Hopkins and Wallerstein, 1986; Gereffi, 1994). Figure 4.2 displays the complementary inputs from and the functional links between the four geographic nodes of exemplary commodity chains between the GSCS and the global economy.

With regard to the chain of athletic shoes, multinationals such as Nike and Reebok used to order the bulk of shoes from their subsidiaries or subcontractors in Taiwan, which began to move their factories to such cities as Dongguan in Guangdong and Putian in Fujian. Most of the raw materials were shipped from Taiwan through Hong Kong to the mainland sites, at least initially, before they could be increasingly sourced locally. Each of the shoe factories used a few Taiwanese resident managers who had been in the shoe business for years and might also speak the local dialect. Hong Kong–based staff of companies such as Nike continue to handle accounting and designs, make sure the sample and raw materials reach the factories on time, and transport the finished shoes out of China through Hong Kong toward their destined markets. The chain of toys is similarly structured: toys

FIGURE 4.2
Subregionalized Global-Local Economic Links Embedded in Cross-Border Production and Commodity Chains in and out of the Greater Southeast China Subregion (GSCS)

are designed in Hong Kong, assembled in Guangdong, often with a Taiwan-made chip for talking dolls, and finally packaged in and shipped from Hong Kong to world markets.[10]

As global commodity chains become more subregionalized, they have begun to encompass newer and more sophisticated industries such as computers and chips, within the GSCS and beyond (see figure 4.2). Although Taiwan became the world's third-largest PC maker in 1995, after the United States and Japan, it has continued to rely heavily on OEM and, to a less degree, on original design manufacturing (ODM) of PC peripherals and assembly for global computer giants. Since an average 60 percent of their products are exported to the fiercely competitive international markets, Taiwanese PC makers face constant pressure to lower production costs by moving more or all segments of production to China. By 1993, China had already accounted for 34.6 percent of Taiwan's offshore production of PC hardware, including almost half of Taiwan's offshore production of motherboards and more than 50 percent of its offshore production of monitors (Chung, 1997). Major monitor makers Kuo Feng and Shamrock Technology moved two-thirds of their monthly production of monitors to China in 1999. With IBM increasing its purchase of OEM products from Taiwan by 50 percent in 1997, more production of PC peripherals in nearby mainland, especially around the city of Dongguan in Guangdong (see the section below) by Taiwanese suppliers for major U.S. computer companies could ensure lower manufacturing costs and fast delivery of components (X. Chen, 1999a).

Since the mid-1990s, two trends have begun to reshape the commodity chains for certain industries within and beyond the GSCS. First, as more U.S. and Japanese companies, especially IT manufacturers, have moved production and sourcing to China, key Taiwanese suppliers and assemblers have followed suit by shifting entire production lines to Guangdong and increasingly to Shanghai and the Jiangsu province (F. Wang, 2003). Hon Hai Precision Electronics, which was founded by Terry Ho, Taiwan's richest high-tech entrepreneur, has built an entire manufacturing segment of a supply chain on the mainland, with factories concentrated heavily in Guangdong that make everything in a PC except key components such as the microprocessor. In 2002, nearly half of Taiwan's IT hardware output was expected to come from mainland China (Lawrance, 2002). The second trend features increasing competition between Chinese high-tech companies and Taiwanese and Hong Kong firms. It has occurred because the mainland has cheaper and well-educated engineers, technicians, and scientists, who have raised their competence level, and some large high-tech companies, which have lured more and more higher-value-added or high-tech investments from both Taiwan and Hong Kong. A number of high-tech or science parks have cropped up in and around Guangzhou and Shenzhen in Guangdong. This trend breeds a higher level of cooperative synergy, as strong R&D capacity, rich venture capital, and mature enterprise management in Taiwan, coupled with Hong Kong's knowledge in finance, logistics, and marketing for IT industries and networking in international markets, could help mainland high-tech companies turn their inventions into marketable products.[11]

Local Functional Specialization and Economic Development

The preceding commodity chain analysis has revealed both the cooperative and competitive aspects of industry-level inter-firm ties across mainland China, Hong Kong, and Taiwan. The broad distribution of benefits for the different nodes of a given chain varies according to their relative position on and contribution to its overall value. Generally speaking, multinational companies are most profitable by controlling marketing and retail. Hong Kong and Taiwanese firms control the less profitable segments of order receiving and manufacturing services, while mainland-based factories profit the least by occupying the middle segment of manufacturing (see X. Chen, 1994a). Since cities are a distinctive local focus of the study, it is instructive to examine how the cities in southeastern China have benefited from subregionalized global commodity chains.

The most illustrative cases are cities located in the PRD, which has been the fastest-growing region of the fastest-growing province in the fastest-growing large economy in the world over the past two decades. By 2001, the PRD accounted for about 3.3 percent of China's population, but 8.7 percent of the GDP, 24.6 percent of foreign investment, and 34.1 percent of exports.[12] The PRD accounts for disproportionately large shares of China's important exports of electric and electronics products: 88.2 percent of fans, 78.8 percent of telephones, 43.6 percent of video recorders, 34.8 percent of color TVs, and 19.1 percent of mobile phones[13] (see maps on the book's Web page), with 10 percent of its total exports ending up on Wal-Mart's shelves.[14]

The city of Dongguan in the PRD has become the most heavily favored location for Taiwanese computer manufacturers to supply global computer giants. Nearly half of the 5,000 Taiwan-owned enterprises registered in Dongguan belong to the PC-related industry. As Taiwanese firms have shifted more manufacturing of computer components (switch power supply units, motherboards) and peripherals (monitors, keyboards) to the mainland, upstream suppliers of plastics, resistors, and printed circuit boards (PCBs) have followed suit. As a result, a newly indigenized supply and production chain has been formed in Dongguan. This allows a PC to be assembled and shipped within 15 days within an area of 50 sq km in which specialized suppliers of such peripherals as monitors and keyboards cluster with motherboard manufacturers and final assemblers. Within Dongguan, there is further specialization in the manufacturing of PC peripherals and other products. The town of Qingxi, with only 30,000 residents, hosts several large-scale manufacturing facilities of seven large Taiwanese PC companies traded on Taiwan's stock market. The town turns out 2 million monitors, 700,000 keyboards, and 13 million PC boxes (20 percent of the world's total) a year.[15] Today Dongguan is the world's largest supplier of computer peripherals, and IBM and Compaq have set up purchasing centers there. The case illustrates the significant role of externally linked, highly specialized local clusters in certain networked and globalized industries (see Porter, 2000).

The heavy concentration of Taiwanese manufacturing investment in Dongguan also has had a highly favorable impact on local development. Formerly a rural township surrounded by rice fields and known for growing litchis, Dongguan has exploded over just one decade into a large urban, industrial center that covers 2,520 sq km and has over 4 million people, the majority of whom are among the approximately 20 million migrant workers cycled through Guangdong province every year. The Taiwan-invested factories in Dongguan have created 600,000 jobs. In 1998, Dongguan's economy grew 26 percent, and Dongguan became China's third-ranked city in exports and foreign exchange earnings, behind only Shanghai and Shenzhen. Not surprisingly, the export of PC-related products reached US$6.7 billion and accounted for over 40 percent of Dongguan's total exports.[16] The city has planned to build several science and technology parks focusing on the computer-related industries. With large revenues from leasing increasingly valuable land for building Taiwan-invested factories, the local government is capable of funding the entire span of primary and secondary education at no cost to residents and of experimenting with completely free health insurance and old-age pensions in some towns. At the household level, the level of wealth in Dongguan is reflected in a 20 percent ownership of private cars, the highest of all cities in Guangdong province and one of the highest in China.[17]

The Downside of Rapid Local Development: A View from the Ground Up

While Dongguan typifies the rapid growth and rising prosperity of many previously small and poor cities and towns in Guangdong, it tends to mask some serious and undesirable social consequences. This downside of development becomes visible if we pierce through the formal structure of the athletic shoe commodity chain to look at the shop floor of shoe factories in the PRD, which as the heart of China's shoe manufacturing industry had about 3,000 factories employing over 200,000 workers as of the mid-1990s, representing another regional-level industry cluster. In 1994, these factories produced 1 billion pairs of shoes with an export value of US$2.5 billion, accounting for half of the value of China's total shoe exports. Nearly 1,000 factories in the PRD ran on Taiwanese and Hong Kong investments and made huge quantities of brand-name athletic shoes such as Reebok and Nike (Asia Monitor Resource Center, 1995, pp. 2–3). Case studies conducted in the mid-1990s revealed a lot about these shoe factories. One of the cases was Yue Yuen Industrial Holdings Co. Ltd., which was established in Dongguan in 1989 by the Taiwanese shoe company of Pao Chen Cooperative, the world's largest sport shoe producer. Yue Yuen employed 50,000–60,000 workers, 80 percent of whom were women between the ages of 18 and 22. These workers worked 60–84 hours a week usually, which was at least 20 hours over the limit set by China's labor law. Half of the workers were paid piece rate for overtime work instead of the overtime pay of 150 percent required by the labor law. The factory did not provide social security benefits, health care, child care, and bereavement leave. It also had problems with noise pollution, air pollution, and fumes, which caused skin irritations, dizziness, and headaches for some workers (Asia Monitor Resource Center, 1997).

In addition to unfavorable working conditions, some workers have suffered losing their arms or hands to the machines in the factories in Shenzhen owned by Taiwanese and Hong Kong companies, with the latter accounting for about one-third of all Hong Kong–invested factories in China. A few injured workers have secured compensation from their former employers with the help of stubborn lawyers. One complaint is that the local government protected the interests of overseas investors rather than the interests of local workers.[18] It is ironic that factory workers have experienced this lack of decency and protection in a dynamic and prosperous city such as Shenzhen, which has the highest GDP per capita of all Chinese cities at over US$5,000. The view from the factory floor reveals a hidden contradiction between the aggregate success of local development and the individual costs and sufferings incurred by that success. Across the subregional, local, industry, and individual levels, the rapid growth and some of its undesirable consequences in the PRD not only have a lot to do with the extensive and dense global-local economic links, but also have been heavily influenced by the strong role of local governments. It is time to shift to the political/institutional lens through which a key dimension of the de-centering Chinese state—local autonomy—can be examined.

The Rise and Role of the Local State

The transborder subregion's global economic ties, coupled with its open geographic position, tend to pull the local governments outward and away from the political gravity of the center, reflecting the de-centering of the state. Pushing the local governments toward a more autonomous position, ironically, are often central government policies in response to the impact of economic globalization. The GSCS is an excellent case for examining the pull-push forces in enhancing the autonomous role of the local government.

From Decentralization to Local Autonomy

Two types of decentralization of power in China after 1978 had a strong influence on the emergence of Guangdong and Fujian provinces and their cities as subnational units in the GSCS. The first involved the decentralization of administrative policy-making power to subnational (provincial) and local governments, allowing the latter to redesign the direction and model of regional and local economic development. Second, as the national government decentralized specific decision-making powers concerning revenues, investment priorities, and foreign trade, provincial and local governments began to control more financial resources for economic development. Moreover, decentralization in China since 1978 has been highly selective and uneven across regions and localities, favoring some cities in Guangdong and Fujian to become key territorial units in the GSCS, such as Shenzhen and Dongguan.

During the initial round of decentralization in the late 1970s and the early 1980s, the central government granted a set of favorable policies and rights exclusively to Guangdong and Fujian provinces. They were allowed to levy lower enterprise taxes, enjoy more fiscal freedom, and retain greater foreign exchange earnings. Guangdong and Fujian were the first to establish profit remittance contracts with Beijing. Guangdong remitted a fixed annual amount of US$125 million to Beijing from 1979 to 1988, even when the province's revenue tripled annually during the period (Hsing, 1998). Guangdong and Fujian also were allowed to approve investment projects capitalized up to US$30 million, as opposed to lower caps for other coastal provinces. The three special economic zones (Shenzhen, Zhuhai, Shantou) in Guangdong and one (Xiamen) in Fujian were given even greater autonomy than other localities. Income tax on foreign ventures in Shenzhen was levied at a considerably reduced rate of 15 percent, as opposed to 33 percent elsewhere. Shenzhen also was allowed to keep 100 percent of its foreign exchange earnings, which was an exceptional perk in light of China's tightly controlled and centralized foreign trade regime at that time. By privileging Guangdong and Fujian provinces and a selected number of their border cities, the central government provided the initial trigger to the subsequent development of a transborder subregion.

In the early 1980s, the central government also shifted from a heavy industry-oriented strategy to one based on more diversified industries, with a growing emphasis on the light consumer goods industry. This policy adjustment immediately favored Guangdong and Fujian by boosting their strong but long suppressed light industries. Toward the end of the 1980s, the central government adopted a series of favorable policies specifically to induce Taiwanese investment, including more generous tax incentives, opening a wider range of industries, and the establishment of Taiwanese investment zones in Fuzhou and

Xiamen. These targeted policies reinforced the "first-mover advantages" of Guangdong and Fujian.[19] The reversion of Hong Kong to Chinese sovereignty as a SAR in 1997 created a different kind of subnational unit with supposedly complete autonomy from Beijing. In addition, what has transpired in cross-strait relations since 2000 have made select Taiwanese local governments actors with certain de facto autonomy from Taipei.

Decentralization is a generally top-down, push process that tends to de-center the governance structure of the state in favor of local governments. In a transborder subregion like the GSCS, however, what local governments do with the decentralized power becomes a bottom-up force behind local development through fostering links with international economic actors. The expected dual outcome is increasing trans-local integration and shifting center-local relations toward local autonomy and action.

From Local Autonomy to Local Action

Local governments in Guangdong and Fujian provinces have played a twofold role in the GSCS. At the institutional level, they have become effective *generators* and willing *providers* of financial resources and policy incentives that reinforce the positive impact of overseas Chinese capital on local economic growth and cross-border integration. As a result of fiscal reforms, which defined localities' share of the tax revenues, local governments have the right to keep the fiscal surplus (Oi, 1995). The more growth and revenues that could be generated, the more surplus revenues local governments could keep after turning in their share of the tax. Thus, local governments have become more motivated to make economic development the top priority. In cities of Guangdong and Fujian, investing surplus revenues heavily in physical infrastructure has become a common strategy for spurring more growth. In Shenzhen, which lacked the physical infrastructure for being a newly created special economic zone in 1979, the local government poured massive investment of its surplus from earlier growth into the construction of roads, factories, and power and telecommunications facilities (X. Chen, 1993). This upgrade and expansion of physical infrastructure in turn has contributed to sustained economic growth.

Local autonomy in Guangdong also has translated into other flexible policy actions. In the city of Dongguan, both municipal and township governments are particularly willing to offer financial incentives such as reduced land prices, factory leases, and utilities charges to Taiwanese investors. The Taiwan Affairs Office of Dongguan provides special services to Taiwanese investors in processing entry and exit travel documents, clearing traded goods, settling economic disputes, maintaining public order, and arranging for child education. These favorable policies and practices have helped make Dongguan the most popular and concentrated locality in China for Taiwanese companies to set up factories, which account for over one-third of all Taiwan-invested factories in Guangdong province, more than Shenzhen. Not coincidentally, Dongguan also hosts more Hong Kong–invested factories than the bigger and better known Shenzhen bordering on Hong Kong (see map on the book's Web page).

Compared to more autonomous local governments in Guangdong, the Hong Kong SAR government has since 1997 played more assertive roles vis-à-vis the neighboring Guangdong provincial and local governments. Unlike its laissez-faire colonial predecessor, which avoided taking any official initiative, the SAR government has been more involved and even interventionist in promoting physical infrastructure and dealing with local and transborder economic issues. Under the lobbying pressure of the tourist industry and small and medium-sized enterprises (SMEs), which were left to fend for themselves in the competitive global marketplace under the colonial government, the SAR government supported the building of a bridge to link Hong Kong with the western PRD to boost tourism and the survival of SMEs, which would be able to reduce their transport costs. In trying to stem the money outflow to prosperous Guangdong, which has contributed to the worsening of Hong Kong's economy after the Asian financial crisis in 1997–1998, the SAR government has contemplated such irrational measures as making border crossings difficult, offering special incentives for mainlanders to purchase properties in Hong Kong, and even possibly reducing mainland immigration to Hong Kong to slow down labor force growth.

On the other hand, under the pressure and advocacy by both the private sector and the Beijing government, the SAR government has belatedly recognized the crucial importance of fully integrating with the PRD economy and has begun to plan steps to achieve that goal, such as organizing manufacturers in the PRD to showcase their products in Hong Kong and staging large-scale promotions of Hong Kong as the head of the PRD. The most ardent advocates of Hong Kong's full integration with the PRD considered the SAR government indecisive and inactive, and trying to use "one country, two systems" as an excuse not to be more proactive in promoting cross-border integration.[20] During the SARS crisis in 2003, the Hong Kong government also was criticized for being ineffective and tardy in communicating with the Guangdong government and for not taking a more aggressive stance in waging a public campaign to explain real risks, advise sensible precautions, and reassure people that the government was managing the crisis decisively.[21] Facing strong public pressure for government action, the chief executive of Hong Kong, Tung Chee-hwa, met with the governor of Guangdong in May 2003 and discussed cooperative strategies to fight SARS.[22] It took a crisis of such magnitude for the Hong Kong government to realize that the socioeconomic well-being of the territories and people on both sides of the border are so intertwined that close inter-government cooperation is needed.

Taking advantage of recent changes in cross-border relations introduced by the Taiwanese central government, local authorities have taken autonomous, bold actions. Since the opening of three "mini-links" (of trade, transportation, and post) between Taiwan's small islands and mainland China in January 2001, the local governments of the Kinmen and Matsu islands off the mainland coast have become active in promoting trade and tourism with the cities of Xiamen and Fuzhou in Fujian province (Hannon, 2002). In January 2003, the county government on Kinmen hosted the largest trade fair after the mini-links, featuring products and commodities from 42 mainland and Taiwanese companies. The county magistrate of Kinmen went out of his way to emphasize the ancient ties, linguistic similarity, and shared customs between Kinmen and Xiamen as the solid foundation for close and strong trade relations.[23] (The influence of historical and cultural ties on economic transactions will be treated in greater detail later.) Despite the local activism of the small islands' governments, the control over the directness of real cross-strait economic ties rests strictly with the Taipei government, which is continuing to wrestle with the dilemma of allowing economic exchange across the Taiwan Strait without letting it endanger Taiwan's security (see Chu, 1997).

Comparative evidence suggests that the open and increasingly integrated economic environment of the GSCS has fostered decentralization and local autonomy either intentionally or as a secondary or delayed effect. This stronger local autonomy has manifested in some assertive and aggressive government policies with beneficial outcomes, and has induced more complex relations between the central and local state and between local authorities and other important actors and interests, as illustrated by the changing orientation and behavior of local government officials.

Party Heads Wearing Entrepreneurial Hats

While administrative and fiscal decentralization has provided the institutional basis for the autonomous action of the Chinese local state in the GSCS, there is also a personalized manifestation of this action. Top and key local government officials become direct participants in promoting economic growth and important partners in working with overseas Chinese investors. In addition to the expectedly strong drive of mayors and directors of foreign investment commissions, party secretaries of cities and towns have played a front and central role. In the city of Shishi in Fujian, the party secretary, in his late 30s, took the lead in implementing a variety of policies to make Shishi a manufacturing center of textiles and garments for Taiwanese companies. He made sure that Taiwanese investors would receive lower prices for land development and assistance in marketing their products in other Chinese cities. Under the party secretary's personal attention, the annual expo for clothing fashions has become a central attraction to Taiwanese investors and traders. With the top municipal officials pushing for targeted industrial development, Shishi has emerged as a major location for textile and garment manufacturing by Taiwanese companies, with 70 percent of the municipal GDP coming from this sector. The manufacturing strength recently prompted Taiwanese companies to jointly establish a clothing design center in the city.[24] The case reflects the influence of an active local party-state leader on functional specialization and development.

The new party secretary of Shantou in Guangdong has been the lead person in selling the unique asset of the city—the 3 million overseas relatives of its 4 million residents—to overseas Chinese investors. He has done so by emphasizing and strengthening the strong traditional value of a good education and quality labor force. This business-oriented political leadership, reinforced by Shantou's cumulative early advantage as a special economic zone, has drawn approximately 10,000 overseas Chinese companies and heavy financing from overseas Chinese for its secondary and higher educational institutions. Built with US$225 million donated by Li Ka-shing (a Hong Kong tycoon who is a native of Shantou), Shantou University today is the largest and one of the best private universities in China.[25]

By leading the charge in generating economic growth and cross-border business ties, top local party and government officials in Guangdong and Fujian have shifted from the role of regulators to that of advocates in a clientelist relationship with businesspeople (Oi, 1995) or bureaucratic entrepreneurs (Hsing, 1998). They have benefited from fiscal decentralization that created a favorable local environment, and from more economic resources such as land, raw materials, and foreign exchange at their disposal. The rational thinking and conduct of local party and government leaders have altered the traditional orientation and governing competence of these bureaucracies. Local governments in Guangdong have earned a reputation among foreign investors for being more straightforward and sophisticated than those elsewhere in China in approving and regulating investment projects (Liao, 1999). It has been reported that a larger proportion of foreign investors in the PRD make more money than those elsewhere in China.[26]

The more flexible and pragmatic leadership of local governments in Guangdong and Fujian personalizes the type and strength of local autonomy that has evolved as part of the de-centering of the state. It has developed from the early opening and market orientation of this Chinese region, whose rapid growth and prosperity could be partly attributed to the combined institutional and individual aspects of local autonomy. This phenomenon, in more ways than one, reflects some elements of urban entrepreneurialism or the "entrepreneurial city," such as officials aggressively promoting local places through entrepreneurial strategies (see Wu, 2003). It also reflects a convergence of interests between local governments and entrepreneurs. While local governments have enhanced their power in jurisdictions by pursuing commercial interests, entrepreneurs have gained power to develop their enterprises by managing their dependence on the local state (Wank, 1999). On the other hand, strategies such as wooing investors with incentives and straying from formal policies make local officials vulnerable to corruption and abuses of power, especially when formal rules are not clear and transparent and competition gets very tough. This has generated its fair share of complaints from Hong Kong and Taiwanese businesspeople.[27] At the same time, taking advantage of the slack cut by local officials, some Hong Kong and Taiwanese managers have engaged in despotic factory practices such as unpaid overtime, cursing, and lack of medical and industrial accident insurance (So, 2003). Asking why these somewhat contradictory situations have emerged leads naturally to continuing the analysis through the sociocultural lens.

Cross-Border Social Capital: Permeating the GSCS

As the preceding section has argued, in a transborder subregion such as the GSCS, the local governments have become more active in pursuing outward-oriented economic development, while the central state has retreated after providing the initial trigger. This creates more space for cross-border social capital to interact with specific central and local government policy initiatives. If local government has a strong role in social capital construction, as Warner (1999) has suggested, the extent of decentralized policy-making in a transborder subregion will influence how cross-border social capital exerts itself. In the GSCS, cross-border social capital refers essentially to boundary-spanning ethnic Chinese social networks that foster local development and transborder subregional integration.

The Origin and Resurgence of Ethnic Chinese Social Capital

Cross-border ethnic Chinese capital has a deep root, a strong resurgence, and an intensive interaction with policy dynamics, and exerts a strong impact on local economic growth and cross-border cooperation in the GSCS. The seed of cross-border ethnic Chinese social capital in the GSCS today was sown as far back as the seventeenth century, when the modern Chinese diaspora began. Driven by poverty, war, and political turmoil, the outflow of Chinese migrants to Hong Kong, Taiwan, and Southeast Asia accelerated during the eighteenth through the mid-twentieth centuries. A large proportion of these emigrants originated in areas around the first treaty ports opened to Western countries, such as Fuzhou, Xiamen, Shantou, and Guangzhou. Some towns in the dynamic PRD today also were the historical sources for many emigrants who later settled heavily in Hong Kong (see Chan, 1995). Besides these distinctive places of origin, local customs, surnames, dialects, eating habits, and other cultural practices distinguish the diasporic Chinese communities beyond the Chinese mainland.

Before these historically rooted elements of social capital resurfaced in the late twentieth century, they were used by the imperial Qing government for a nationalistic agenda at the end of the nineteenth and beginning of the twentieth centuries. In order to seek financial support and technical skills from the overseas Chinese to increase national strength, the imperial state removed its ban on emigration and established consulates in Southeast Asia (Duara, 1997). To attract abundant overseas Chinese capital to modernize China, the communist government, a century later, adopted favorable policies and financial incentives toward Hong Kong and Taiwanese investors. The historical irony aside, this is consistent evidence of the opportunistic use of social capital regardless of political regimes. However, social capital ingrained in ethnic and cultural ties is subject to political suppression. Just as the Qing state executed repatriated emigrants to deter potential travelers from leaving the empire (Duara, 1997), the communist state persecuted many returned overseas Chinese in the late 1950s and PRC citizens with overseas connections during the Cultural Revolution (1966–1976). Social capital possesses such latent power that despite a period of dormancy enforced by repressive policies, it has reappeared under the more open political and economic environment in China since the early 1980s.

The resurgence of cross-border social capital in the GSCS manifests itself through a complex set of socially imbedded and mediated cross-border economic relations. This manifestation takes the form of a variety of social networks based on overlapped kinship, friendship, ancestry, native-place identity, and dialectic similarity that collectively mediate economic activities and transactions.

Cross-Border Social Capital in Action

The kinship-based social network has become an effective mechanism for tuning the economic engine that has driven wealth creation and prosperity in the GSCS. The process often begins with Hong Kong and Taiwanese residents returning to visit the villages and towns of their ancestral origin. These visits provide occasions for initiating business deals that include making philanthropic donations and setting up factories, sometimes using the former to realize the latter. By Leung's definition (1993, p. 281), kinship factories in the PRD are those that have connections with or are owned by mainland relatives or close friends of the respective Hong Kong investors. These factories provide investment confidence and reliable exchange based on the mutual trust established through kinship or close social ties between Hong Kong investors and their mainland subcontractors. Mellor (1993) refers to this kind of cross-border investment as "investment of feeling." To demonstrate their feelings for specific places of origin and ancestry in Guangdong and Fujian as a way of facilitating business deals, some wealthy overseas Chinese have funded large-scale infrastructure projects such as highways, hospitals, and educational institutions that have both local and extra-local significance.

While kinship-based social networks have something to do with the concentration of thousands of small and medium-sized factories in Guangdong and Fujian, specific locations of factories depend heavily on a combination of knowing individual local government officials and understanding location advantages. A Hong Kong company chose to build a plant in the town of Xixiang because it had social connections with one local official. In addition, Xixiang, just outside Shenzhen, not only is close to Hong Kong but also lies beyond Shenzhen's bureaucratic regulations that tend to be heavier than its surrounding areas (Lee, 1998).

At the firm level, kinship has facilitated the recruitment and management of badly needed workers for labor-intensive manufacturing. At a shoe factory located in Guangdong, the Hong Kong owner focused on hiring children of his and his wife's relatives through a closely maintained relationship with his native village that involved frequent visits and sponsoring local causes. He considered it an obligation to look after his kin through his business venture in southern China (Smart and Smart, 1993). Another factory encouraged current workers to recruit a small number of relatives and others from their hometowns. The rationale was that the mutual trust between the recruiter and new employees would ensure the latter's confidence in factory management and thus good performance.[28] With or without kinship ties, Taiwanese managers at some shoe factories in southern China manipulated social capital by invoking the family metaphor in labor-management relations as a strategy for maintaining the paternal authority of the male managers as father figures or elder brothers in disciplining young female workers (Hsing, 1998).

Beyond Kinship and Native Ties: The Farther Reach of Social Capital

However extensive and place-specific they might be, the kinship and native ties of Hong Kong and Taiwanese investors in Guangdong and Fujian cannot fully account for both the spatial dispersal and certain degree of clustering of their investment, especially in cities like Dongguan. A fuller explanation may stem from how local autonomy and social capital reinforce each other, given the latter's broader enabling influence beyond kinship and native ties.

The growing autonomy in Guangdong and Fujian has allowed local officials to be flexible in approving investment projects. This flexibility, however, implies a personalized and arbitrary approach to decision-making, especially under less developed and transparent legal conditions. While local autonomy creates a lot of room for cross-border social capital to be active, social capital in terms of kinship or native ties does not automatically lead to business deals; even if it happens, the terms of deals could vary considerably. Therefore, Hong Kong and Taiwanese investors try to cultivate relations (*guanxi*) with local power-holders through material or non-material gift exchanges such as clothes, banquets, color TVs, crucial information, and key introductions (Smart and Smart, 1991). Some Taiwanese investors have mastered the art of gift exchange by maintaining the balance between offering material favors and expressing friendship and loyalty to each other as the basis of mutual trust. They also use gifts to convey underlying important messages regarding mutual trust and reciprocity (Hsing, 1997, pp. 152–153).[29] These practices of social capital are particularly important if there are no kinship or native ties to draw on. Since mutual trust within former communist societies was compromised by political control (Neace, 1999), the relaxation of political control from the center makes the practical use of ethnic Chinese social capital effective in facilitating business relations with or without kinship or native ties. The investment strategies of Hong Kong and Taiwanese companies also contribute to the evolution of local autonomy by generating resources that are not available within the local official hierarchy (Smart, 2000) but could improve the fortune of localities.

The city of Dongguan illustrates a distinctive way in which cross-border social capital has worked beyond kinship ties and gift exchange under autonomous local policy-making. Many Taiwanese investors rely heavily on the business and social networks that they have transferred from Taiwan or established within Dongguan. With the supplier-manufacturer-assembler network firmly in place for the PC industry, Taiwanese managers can use deep trust among one another to conduct business. A quick telephone call can get the supplier to deliver component parts quickly. Telephone calls replace time-consuming legal contracts that otherwise will have to be signed with multiple first- and second-tier suppliers. This socially mediated production chain shortens the assembly of PCs in Dongguan to just 15 days, as opposed to a much longer turnaround time elsewhere. Time spent together on golf courses and in karaoke bars provides opportunities for Taiwanese businesspeople to strengthen friendship ties and mutual trust, which in turn sustain the closely linked business networks (Zang, 1999).

Local government officials in Dongguan are flexible in interpreting standard policies and in offering special incentives for land use and tax collection. They often go the extra mile in lowering factory rents and electricity charges for Taiwanese investors, which also is consistent with the national government's political agenda for promoting unification with Taiwan through economic union. These favorable government practices reflect a cooperative relationship with the local Taiwanese business association. Of the 5,000 or so Taiwanese firms in Dongguan, over 80 percent are members. For the total of 32 towns and districts under the municipal government of Dongguan, there are 29 branch Taiwanese business associations. Besides having the largest, most organized, and most effective Taiwanese business association in China, Dongguan also boasts the only Taiwanese businesswomen's friendship association in China, involving the wives of the businessmen living in the city (S. Chen, 2000). In 2003, with the approval of Dongguan's government, the Taiwan business association unveiled a plan to build the first hospital in mainland China exclusively for Taiwanese businesspeople and their families in Dongguan, which number about 100,000; about 40,000 of them live there permanently.[30] These organizations not only strengthen the social networks based on interpersonal and inter-firm relationships but also deliver services to meet the practical needs of a large and localized Taiwanese community.

By utilizing social capital effectively to gain favors from local officials, Taiwanese and Hong Kong investors in southeastern China are successful in circumventing some bureaucratic rules and obstacles and in seeking rents from business ventures and activities with limited access. This evidence supports Smart's argument that behaviors directed toward creating and capturing rents may make important contributions to economic efficiency in circumstances where the societal and legal infrastructure for market capitalism are underdeveloped (Smart, 1993, p. 16).

When a Valuable Resource Goes Only So Far:
The Limits and Downside of Social Capital

While cross-border ethnic Chinese social capital has helped sustain the heavy concentration of Hong Kong and Taiwanese capital in Guangdong and Fujian provinces, more recent investment, especially from Taiwan, has flowed to other regions, especially Shanghai and Jiangsu, which absorbed 47.2 percent of all Taiwanese investment in 2002, as opposed to 24.3 percent for Guangdong and 11.2 percent for Fujian.[31] Besides Shanghai and Jiangsu's attraction for Taiwanese investment in high-tech industries, its spread beyond southeastern China may signal the latter's eroded lure based on kinship ties, native place identity, and similar subcultures and dialects.

If all forms of social capital have a potential downside (Portes, 1998) or the possibility of backlashes (Montgomery, 2000), cross-border ethnic Chinese social capital is no exception. The practice of hiring relatives and sticking with them even if they are not productive sustains a moral and social obligation, but it is economically inefficient and may lead to failing factory operations (Smart and Smart, 1993). Preferring to hire people from certain places in Guangdong province, some Taiwanese employers tend to discriminate against workers from the poor neighboring province of Hunan based on their stereotyped personality (Zang, 1999). Gift exchange may build up interpersonal trust and reciprocity between overseas Chinese investors and local officials, but it has a tendency to slip into bribery and corruption, which led to the prosecution and execution of a number of party and government officials and customs officers in Guangdong in recent years. The favorable treatment of overseas Chinese investors by China's central and local governments may have disadvantaged some state-owned investment projects by creating unfair competition. There is a delicate balance between using cross-border social capital to generate economic benefits and not letting it induce undesirable behaviors and practices.

To minimize the downside of social capital in the GSCS context may require modifying or shifting the form and functions of this resource as it evolves. Powerful as social networks or informal associations are in fostering economic development, they may and should be gradually replaced by formal administrative structures and impersonal market mechanisms. The latter may be more efficient than social networks for selecting the *best* buyer or seller, who may not be part of a network (Serageldin and Grootaert, 2000). Although this shift toward more formal institutions of law, market, and governance may weaken or deplete existing social capital, it eventually leads to a new type of social capital that is embedded in the economic system, rather than the other way around (Stiglitz, 2000). The dynamic aspect of social capital, ironically, points to its inherent limitations. The important role of social capital may not be sustainable beyond a particular model and stage of successful development, unless it becomes more subordinate to a truly market-based economic system.

Social capital's limit also is reflected in the seemingly irreconcilable relationship between Chinese ethnic and national identity, inter-government politics, and practical individual economic considerations as experienced intensively by Taiwanese investors in southern China. Having spent most of the past eight years in Guangdong managing her family's speaker manufacturing factory, a Taiwanese businesswoman was closing the family's remaining business in Taiwan and going to move permanently to Guangdong with her family. However, she insisted that "China is not a home to me. It is a place to manufacture a product and make money. Economically the two sides should unite, but politically Taiwan can't become part of China. I can't even stand people calling me a Chinese."[32] To the extent that this sentiment may be prevalent among Taiwanese businesspeople in southern China, it shows their aggressive and often successful pursuit of economic opportunities by resorting to different elements of ethnic Chinese social capital under major political differences and yet increasingly close physical links across the Taiwan Strait.

Border Effects, Transport Links, and Spatial Integration

Cross-border ethnic Chinese social capital has helped bridge the political distance between Guangdong and Fujian on the one side and Hong Kong and Taiwan on the other and fostered extensive and lasting economic ties across their boundaries. The spatial distance between the four units of the GSCS is limited thanks to geographic contiguity and proximity, which should promote frequent movement of people, goods, and services under uniformly open borders. However, the borders between mainland China and Hong Kong versus Taiwan are uneven in openness, connectivity, and control. This calls for using the spatial/infrastructural lens to examine relations between distance, border effects, and the spatial integration of the GSCS.

So Close and So Closely Integrated:
The Porous Mainland–Hong Kong Border

Hong Kong is physically connected to Guangdong and borders on the city of Shenzhen (see map 4.1). The symbiotic historical and contemporary relations between Hong Kong and Guangdong have earned the metaphoric description of "as close as lips are to teeth" or "when Hong Kong sneezes, Guangdong catches a cold." Back in the 1950s and 1960s, however, the Shenzhen–Hong Kong border, while heavily guarded, provided an outlet for mainland residents to sneak illegally into Hong Kong, with or without success. Even in the mid-1980s, legally crossing the lone Luohu (Lowu) checkpoint, as I describe in the preface to this book, could be frustrating and time consuming. Since then, especially after 1997, the Guangdong–Hong Kong border has become one of the world's most open and yet still heavily guarded borders.

The opening and blurring of the Guangdong–Hong Kong border have been intimately linked with the miraculous growth of Shenzhen from a tiny border farming and fishing town to a large modern metropolis over the past two decades. Shenzhen and Hong Kong have literally grown into each other and formed an extensive cross-border metropolitan region. Today huge volumes of people and goods flow through the four rail and road checkpoints along the Shenzhen–Hong Kong border.[33] The Luohu crossing point has become China's busiest land port for human traffic. The number of person crossings rose from 56 million in 1997 to 94 million in 2002, with a daily average of over 250,000 person crossings and significantly more on holidays. This massive human flow has far exceeded and strained the handling capacity for 4 million annual crossings at the checkpoint built in the early 1980s.[34] The Huanggang-Luomazhou crossing point is China's busiest land port for trucked cargo and goods, seeing close to 70 percent of the daily flow of 33,000 trucks between Hong Kong and the PRD.[35] According to official statistics (Shenzhen Statistical and Information Bureau [SSIB], 2000), during 1998–2000, human crossings through Shenzhen's border checkpoints accounted for over 50 percent of the national total, while the traffic of cars, trucks, and boats through Shenzhen's crossing points accounted for over 70 percent of the national total.

Reversal of Fortune? Making Money in Hong Kong and Spending It in Shenzhen

The aggregate statistics on human and vehicular flows across the Hong Kong–Shenzhen border mask a variety of activities of Hong Kong residents on Shenzhen's side of the border. On weekends and holidays, thousands of Hong Kong residents ride the train and then walk through the crossing points to shop, dine, and enjoy entertainment, such as listening to Cantonese opera and signing Karaoke in Shenzhen, where food, goods, and entertainment are cheaper than in Hong Kong. While fans of the Cantonese opera, young and old, come over to sing it with local bands, many cruise the department stores, variety shops, and food markets to pick up a whole range of merchandise, and most would not leave without indulging in nice, yet inexpensive meals. It is not surprising that food consumption, which is what Hong Kong people cherish, accounts for 86.2 percent of the total spending by border crossers (averaging US$40–64 per day), followed by the purchase of such items as clothing, health products, books, cosmetics, and shoes. In 2001 alone, Hong Kong people spent a total of US$3.5 billion across the border.[36]

This pattern is beginning to reverse the flow of money and wealth in the old days, when Hong Kong residents would bring over consumer goods such as household electronics and daily necessities to their relatives and friends north of the border. It has reportedly contributed to declining profits for Hong Kong's restaurant, retailing, and entertainment businesses. Just as budget-conscious Hong Kong consumers spend more money in Shenzhen and end up spending less, the increasingly wealthy mainland consumers, especially from Shenzhen, have begun to spend more in Hong Kong. In the first seven months of 2002, mainland tourists, mostly from the PRD, spent a total of US$3 billion in Hong Kong. To accommodate this new trend, 17 financial institutions in Shenzhen launched a new scheme at the beginning of 2003 by issuing 2.5 million debit cards to allow mainlanders to withdraw cash and pay for purchases in Hong Kong.[37]

If the movement of people, goods, and money has made the Hong Kong–Shenzhen border more porous, the concentrated development and mutual purchase of residential properties on either side of the border has blurred its spatial distinction and separation. Despite their geographic contiguity, Hong Kong and Shenzhen remained a world apart in land and housing prices when new housing in Hong Kong cost 10 times as much as new housing in Shenzhen. Even housing in the less expensive New Territories would cost six to eight times more than comparable housing across the border. This large price differential made properties north of the border very appealing to Hong Kong residents. In 1996, of the 20 million square meters of newly completed commercial housing stock, 10 percent was sold to Hong Kong residents. Even with Shenzhen's home prices doubling over the past decade and Hong Kong's home values dropping by 60 percent during a five-year slump, property prices in Hong Kong remain two to three times those of Shenzhen, thus sustaining Hong Kong residents' buying of Shenzhen's properties. In 2001, Hong Kong residents bought 40 percent of the new commercial housing in Shenzhen, especially near the Luohu crossing point. Based on sales during the first three quarters, about 20,000 property units in Shenzhen were projected to be snapped up by Hong Kong residents in 2002, a 14 percent rise from 2001. As Hong Kong developers such as Sun Hung Kai Properties and Henderson Land lost money by writing down the value of their holdings, others such as Hutchison Whampoa are developing residential properties in Shenzhen, near the Luohu and Luomazhou border posts. To offset slumping mortgage business at home, Hong Kong lenders such as Bank of East Asia have offered incentive packages to Hong Kong residents buying property across the border.[38]

It was reported that about 90 percent of the Hong Kong buyers of Shenzhen properties would not sell their residences in Hong Kong. They tend to use their homes in Shenzhen for weekend trips or for extended vacations. Today approximately 300,000 Hong Kongers (nearly 5 percent of Hong Kong's total population) live in Shenzhen on a regular basis. It was projected that close to 1 million Hong Kongers (one-seventh of the total population), including more retirees, may set up either short- or long-term residence in Shenzhen in the next 10 years.[39] And Hong Kong residents have been buying properties in other PRD cities, especially Guangzhou and Dongguan. Many of these buyers are Hong Kong businesspeople who make regular, extended trips to the PRD or are managers and supervisors in the factories in the region and beyond. In

2003, Hong Kong residents working north of the border totaled 238,000, 90 percent of whom are in and around the PRD cities in Guangdong, up from 198,000 in 2002 and just 64,000 in 1992.[40] The property units they have bought provide a home away from home where they can stay for weeks at a time. Both short and longer distance commutes have helped weaken the barrier effects of the distance/border between Hong Kong and Guangdong.

The Declining Friction of Distance and an Impeded Out-stretched Border Zone

Although the rise of Shenzhen is perceived as a potential threat to Hong Kong,[41] the GSCS is still anchored and centered on Hong Kong. Proximity to or distance from the center can lead to broader spatial integration or lack of it in a center-hinterland context. From 1984 to 1990, the number of foreign investment projects and foreign investment per capita in Guangdong's cities decreased as their distance from Hong Kong increased. However, the effect of distance and population potential became weaker over time.[42] With land and labor costs in the main border cities rising since the early 1990s, investments from and through Hong Kong have spread farther north among other PRD cities, where almost 70 percent of all foreign-invested enterprises in Guangdong province are located (Duan, 1999).

In the late 1990s, the cross-border relocation of Hong Kong's low-cost manufacturing slowed down, as there was little labor-intensive manufacturing left to move. In the meantime, Guangdong's workers became more educated and skilled while continuing to earn about one-seventh of their counterparts in Hong Kong. The combination of these conditions prompted Hong Kong to shift some producer service operations and even the central offices of manufacturing companies over the border to further reduce labor cost with little loss of quality and productivity. With distance being an important factor still, Shenzhen is most attractive to this wave of service investment. Standard Chartered, a top Hong Kong banking institution, has recently decided to expand its back-office processing functions in Shenzhen and is planning to set up a call center there to support its global call-center operations in India and Malaysia.[43] However, distance matters less to the kind of back-office business services relocated from Hong Kong, as they rely more on the Internet than frequent human contact. Hong Kong companies invested nearly US$15 billion in Guangdong's service industry during 1994–1999, and a bulk of this investment went to Guangzhou (Mitchell, 2000). Despite its location at the northern end of the PRD (see map 4.1), Guangzhou's good infrastructure and more educated labor force have attracted the data processing and logistics support offices of Hong Kong–based Cathay Pacific Airways and the Hong Kong and

Shanghai Bank. The rising wealth and purchasing power in the PRD also have drawn Hong Kong banks and retailers, large or small, to expand their presence in and beyond Shenzhen (see the book's Web page). The enlarged regional economic space is accommodating a broader and more varied redistribution of linked activities in southern China.

While the declining importance of distance from Hong Kong has accelerated the spatial integration of the GSCS, the second border, which cordons off Shenzhen from the rest of Guangdong and the mainland, functions as a remaining physical barrier to the spread of development and further integration (see the book's Web page). It is somewhat ironic that even as the barrier effect of the more policed Hong Kong–Shenzhen border has waned and thus enlarged the border zone, the latter has a limited diffusion effect due to an internal border that was built 20 years ago to protect the unique status of Shenzhen as a fledgling special economic zone. While becoming largely obsolete, Shenzhen's second border tests the political will of the Chinese central and local state to balance between more even regional economic development and local political and social control and stability. This internal border illustrates the entrenched tendency toward re-bordering even as de-bordering occurs.

Curbing the Tide or Facilitating the Flow

A stronger challenge to government regarding border control involves how to deal with the heavy flow between Hong Kong and Guangdong, primarily Shenzhen. After 1997, China's central and local government began to push for a more open border to facilitate commerce and eventually proposed to keep the border open 24 hours rather than closing it at 11:30 p.m. This was intended to enhance the PRD's economic gains from further spatial integration with Hong Kong. The Hong Kong SAR government, however, was for some time more concerned with an economic recession, rising unemployment, net capital outflow (to the mainland), negative equity, and weak consumption, which were triggered by the Asian financial crisis in 1997 and worsened afterward. The SAR government also faced a dilemma over whether it should integrate with the PRD more deeply. Further integration would call for lifting boundary control, which would lead to more capital flow and consumer spending over the border. Avoiding further integration would imply maintaining strict border control, thus losing the opportunity for Hong Kong to benefit from the dynamic PRD as a source of recovery and continued growth.[44]

Eventually, the SAR government chose the further integration route by agreeing to extend the open hours at the Luohu checkpoint to midnight as of December 1, 2001. On the first day of the extended border opening, 300,700 people entered and exited the checkpoint, with about 5,000 people passing through in the last half hour.[45] Border control was relaxed further on January 27, 2003, when the Luomazhou crossing began to open 24 hours. Although the event did not have any immediate impact, as 80 percent of passenger traffic still moves through Luohu, freight forwarders began to benefit from the added hours to get through each day, and queues and delivery times were shortened. In the wake of opening Luomazhou around the clock, some pro-Beijing SAR government officials began to call for making Luohu the same 24-hour crossing and opening the restricted buffer zone in the northern New Territories, which was set up in the colonial era to deter illegal immigrants from the mainland, to boost economic integration with the PRD.[46] This further opening of the border was derailed by the outbreak of SARS in Guangdong and its spread to Hong Kong in 2003, with mixed consequences for both sides (see the book's Web page).

The extent and rigor of controlling the Hong Kong–Shenzhen border reflect the complex challenges facing states at different levels as they struggle to balance between keeping the legal cross-border economic flows and curbing the illegal or illicit transboundary transactions, such as illegal immigration and drug trafficking, that are often simultaneous and intertwined (Friman and Andreas, 1999). Border guards on both sides of the Hong Kong–Guangdong divide regularly check under border-crossing trucks for hidden illegals from the Chinese mainland (Edwards, 1997). The number of illegal mainland workers arrested rose sharply from 2,917 in 1996 to 6,552 in 2001. With the SAR government raising the quota of mainland tour-group visitors at the beginning of 2002, the number of illegal mainlanders caught by Hong Kong police jumped again, with 5,538 arrests by July of 2002.[47]

Regarding the short- and long-term impact of 24-hour crossing at the Luomazhou checkpoint, mainland China's press has emphasized the potential positive outcomes, such as reducing the artificial distortions of prices by the border and attracting the wealthy mainland residents in the PRD to "go south" to purchase lower-priced properties in Hong Kong.[48] Easier border crossing, however, could induce more Hong Kong residents, especially those living in the New Territories, to spend money north of the border. The planned expansion of such popular theme parks as Jurassic Park in Shenzhen will draw more Hong Kong and overseas tourists, before and even after the opening of Hong Kong's new US$2.8 billion Disneyland in 2005–2006. The increasing openness of this border, coupled with unpredictable state responses to the uncertain consequences, continues to reshape opportunities and life chances on either side.

So Close and Still Partially Closed: Indirect Cross-Strait Links

Mainland China and Taiwan do not border each other by land; they face each other across a 140-km-wide ocean strait. Taiwan-held Dadan Island sits

2 km away from Xiamen. Xiamenese can use binoculars to observe their kin-folk on Dadan Island, with whom they have traditionally intermarried (Mel-lor, 1993). The bigger Taiwanese islands of Kinmen and Matsu are only 6 km away from the Fujian coast (see map 4.1). But the strait separating Taiwan and China's southeastern coast remains one of the world's more tension-filled mil-itary divides. The Taiwanese government has officially banned direct trade, transport, and postal links since 1949. Since the mid-1980s the Chinese main-land and Taiwan have become linked by one of the most frequently, albeit in-directly, crossed economic boundaries in the world.

Officially sanctioned links across the Taiwan Strait did not exist prior to Oc-tober 1987, when the Taiwanese government permitted Taiwanese citizens to visit mainland relatives and the Taiwan Red Cross Society began processing ap-plications for mainland visits. In 1988, some 431,000 Taiwanese residents ap-plied for mainland China traveling visas, with an estimated 200,000 crossing the strait through Hong Kong. In 1989, about 540,000 Taiwanese tourists visited the mainland (Silk, 1990). In those early years, Taiwanese visitors flocked heavily to the cities of Xiamen and Fuzhou, which share a common dialect, a long trade history, and strong family ties with Taiwan. In 1989, 67 percent of all Taiwanese visitors to the mainland ended up in the coastal cities of Fujian (State Statistical Bureau [SSB], 1991). Some of these earlier visitors used the trip to scout for business opportunities, especially in their places of origin, striking many small-scale business deals. The initial cross-strait contact set the pattern of the main-land-Taiwan economic relations, which began to evolve in the mid-1990s.

While the number of Taiwanese visitors to the mainland via Hong Kong av-eraged well over 1 million annually from 1998 to 2001,[49] the Taiwan Strait re-mained closed to any direct links. Indirect links, however, multiplied dramat-ically in the 1990s. Since 1990, when Taiwan's Central Bank began recording statistics on indirect individual remittance to mainland China, the money flow increased substantially in frequency and volume. The average amount of remittance, which included donations and transfer payments (excluding trav-eling expenditures), rose from US$1,195 per transaction in 1990 to US$4,005 in 2002. Indirect business remittance from Taiwan grew even faster and ex-ceeded the volume of individual remittance by greater margins from the late 1990s. Indirect business remittance refers to funds that Taiwanese companies received after exporting from their mainland-based factories and then sent back there as reinvestment or for covering operational expenses. The in-creased remittance reflects the rapid growth of Taiwanese investors' exports and profits from the mainland, some of which they are willing to reinvest back there. That Taiwanese investors began to make more money is confirmed by their indirect remittance from the mainland surpassing their indirect business remittance from Taiwan after 1999 (see appendix table 4.B).

Telecommunication across the Taiwan Strait also increased in frequency, as indicated by the number of telephone calls in both directions (see figure 4.3). Cross-strait transport links, however, have evolved more slowly through a series of developments.[50] From April 1997 to December 2002, the Offshore Transshipment Center at Kaohsiung Harbor received a total of 4,719 vessels, each of which carried 470 TEUs (20-foot equivalent units) on average for a total of about 2.2 million TEUs (Mainland Affairs Council, 2002). While these numbers were not insignificant, the regulatory and logistic difficulties limited the transshipping system's carrying capacity to less than 5 percent of the total cargo volume coming into Kaohsiung Harbor yearly, forcing up to 15 million tons of bilateral trade cargo to be transshipped via third ports each year (X. Chen, 1999a).

Taiwan's ban on direct air links forces flights bound for the mainland to fly through Hong Kong and Macau. The vast majority of the over 2 million trips from Taiwan to mainland China (see appendix table 4.C) are made through Hong Kong, making the Taiwan–Hong Kong corridor one of the busiest stretches of sky in the world. Taipei–Hong Kong flights are 85 percent full despite a frequency increase to 170 a week from about 120 before July 2001.[51] Since 1995, cross-strait air traffic also has been flowing through Macau on two Taiwanese air carriers (TransAsia Airways and Eva Air) and Air Macau.[52] About 90 percent of the traffic into Macau's new international airport is

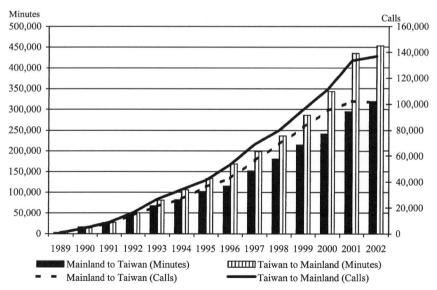

FIGURE 4.3
Telephone Calls Between Mainland China and Taiwan, 1989–2002

transfer flights from Taiwan to various mainland cities. Approximately 80 percent of the passengers on TransAsia alone, which has six flights to Macau daily, transfer on to Fuzhou and Xiamen (Matich, 2000a). Although remittances, telecommunication, shipping, and air travel occur indirectly, they constitute a set of diverse and extensive cross-strait links that matter greatly to mainland-Taiwan relations and the broader integration of the GSCS.

However, indirect cross-strait links incur tremendous costs. Between 1989 and 1995, Taiwanese residents paid a total of US$59 million (1.9 billion New Taiwan dollars) in connecting fees for calling the mainland through third-party telephone exchanges in Hong Kong, Singapore, and Japan. The connecting fee was as high as one-third of the call rate.[53] A round trip through Hong Kong stretches 800–1,000 nautical miles and takes three full days to complete, whereas a straight sail from Taiwan to Xiamen covers less than 200 nautical miles and takes only 8–10 hours. Shipping a TEU container through Hong Kong costs roughly over US$1,000. Direct cross-strait shipping would yield an annual savings of US$248 million based on the 620,000 TEUs that crossed the Taiwan Strait in 1996 and a savings of US$400 per container (X. Chen, 1999a). With direct flights, the travel time from Taipei or Kaohsiung to Xiamen will be reduced from four hours through Macau (including the stopover) to barely 20 minutes. With direct flights, Taiwanese travelers could save roughly US$375 million annually from airfare and time of travel for the Taipei-Shanghai route, while the full-day trip from Taipei to Shanghai would be trimmed to a two-hour flight (see the book's Web page). If direct remittance were possible and accounts settled in Taiwan, instead of paying it to a third-party bank in Hong Kong, Taiwanese banks could generate US$22 million in revenue annually for handling cross-strait remittance.[54]

From Indirect Links to Direct Mini-links: Cosmetic or Real Improvement?

Under pressure from Taiwan's business community and public opinion, the Chen Shui-bian government approved direct crossing and shipping between the islands of Matsu and Kinmen and Xiamen and Fuzhou on January 2, 2001. On June 8, 2001, the first passenger liner, carrying 363 travelers, sailed directly from Kaohsiung to Xiamen with a stopover at Kinmen. This marked the beginning of de facto passenger shipping between Taiwan and the mainland. Between January 2001 and November 2003, both sides ran a total of 1,931 boat trips that carried 116,820 passengers (person trips) in both directions. Altogether 1,245 Taiwanese passenger and freight boats sailed from Kinmen to Xiamen and from Matsu to Fuzhou, while only 686 mainland boats crossed from Xiamen to Kinmen and from Fuzhou to Matsu. There were 111,184 Taiwanese visitors (person trips) from Kinmen and Matsu versus only 5,636 mainland visitors (person trips) to the two Taiwanese islands, a ratio of almost 20 to 1 (Mainland Affairs Council, 2004). This traffic flow is very lopsided in Taiwan's favor because of the much larger number of Taiwanese businesspeople and tourists from Kinmen and Matsu visiting the mainland, and the small number of mainlanders visiting the two small islands.

These unbalanced mini-links, unprecedented as they may be since 1949, are far from enough to meet the growing demands for direct cross-strait shipping of people and goods, especially since both China and Taiwan have joined the World Trade Organization (WTO). The Chinese government characterized the mini-links as mere cosmetic changes introduced by the Taiwanese government to placate the growing popular desire for direct links. The Taiwanese government, on the other hand, saw the mini-links as an experiment to test the management of small-scale cross-strait links before the establishment of real links (Matich, 2000b). Nevertheless, the mini-links paved the way for further steps from both sides to facilitate cross-strait travel.

Beyond the Mini-links: What Next?

Following almost two years of experiment, the Taiwanese government in August 2002 relaxed regulations about travel to mainland China by allowing businesspeople from the Taiwan island to sail directly to Fujian province from Kinmen and Matsu. These business travelers must have government-approved investments or business ventures in Fujian and must get official permission before departure, and their family members also are allowed to apply for such trips. While this new initiative moved beyond the mini-links and came closer to lifting the 50-year ban on direct cross-strait travel, a larger-scale and more significant development occurred in January 2003 when both governments approved 16 chartered flights by several Taiwanese airlines to ferry Taiwanese businesspeople and their families from Shanghai to Taipei and Kaohsiung for the traditional Chinese New Year Festival. Although these special flights had to stop for an hour or so in either Hong Kong or Macau, the passengers did not have to change planes (see the book's Web page). Some Taiwanese officials hailed this as a "historic event," which might lead to the possibility of further flights for the Dragon Boat Festival in June and the Autumn Moon Festival in September.

Business executives who had taken the first chartered flight saw this as the natural result of increasing economic and cultural exchanges between the two sides. The Chinese government was more flexible and pragmatic in negotiating for these chartered flights, forgoing the involvement of mainland carriers, and eliminating the time-consuming stopovers in Hong Kong and Macau (estimated at US$30,000 for both stopovers during the round trip between

Shanghai and Taipei via Hong Kong or Macau), whereas the Taiwanese government was more reluctant and defensive, worrying about security.[55] Given the re-election of the Chen Shui-bian government in March 2004, the prospect of direct cross-strait shipping and air links under a scenario of a Kuomintang (KMT) government has dimmed.

No matter whether or how soon the chartered flight may lead to real direct flights, businesses have already begun to assess the economic implications of the growing commercial and spatial links across the Taiwan Strait. Well before the chartered flight experiment, the exodus of businesses to mainland China had already taken a toll in Taiwan. Taiwan's property market slumped as more and more people began to buy homes on the mainland. Business club memberships, restaurant businesses, and car sales also declined.[56] In comparison, the impact of direct cross-strait links on Hong Kong was more mixed. While 97 percent of the surveyed Taiwanese companies in Hong Kong would not close their offices in the HKSAR, 62.1 percent of the Taiwanese companies in Shenzhen and Dongguan expected their demand for Hong Kong's passenger transit services to drop, versus 74.3 percent of the respondents in Shanghai, Suzhou, and Kunshan of Jiangsu province. Also, 33.8 percent of the surveyed Taiwanese companies in Shenzhen and Dongguan expected their demand for Hong Kong services to drop, versus 56.7 percent in Shanghai, Suzhou, and Kunshan.[57] While Hong Kong may lose some of its lucrative role as a transit hub, Taiwan could gain from direct air links, especially its high-tech companies, since they depend heavily on air cargo services, which will become cheaper with direct flights, and they will improve their time-to-market capability. The present absence of direct cross-strait links is reinforced by extensive indirect connections via Hong Kong, so that Hong Kong currently sustains its role as the transit node in the GSCS. This also is true of Macau, albeit to a much lesser extent. Their varied roles highlight the central importance of the transport infrastructure for the integration of the GSCS.

Making Close Closer: The Development of Cross-Border Transport Infrastructure

Convenient crossing over the Hong Kong–Guangdong border is a crucial factor in the deep economic integration between Taiwan and southeastern China. This integration has been fostered by the rapid development of cross-border transport infrastructure.

After the six-lane superhighway built by Gordon Wu (a Hong Kong tycoon) was completed in 1995, what used to be a two-day, bumper-to-bumper round trip from Hong Kong's port to factories in Guangzhou became a morning's drive. Many two-lane highways have been constructed to connect the booming industrial cities and towns in the PRD and the Hong Kong–Guangzhou super-highway. The formerly two-day trip between Guangzhou and Zhuhai, with six transfers and a boat ride, is reduced to 90 minutes on a new multilane highway. The fairly new superhighway between Guangzhou and the Shantou SEZ in southeastern Guangdong has shortened the previous day-long trip to less than four hours. The coupling of these two superhighways not only provides the crucial north-south transport corridor between Hong Kong and the PRD but also creates a badly needed east-west corridor that can help spread the development impulse from the PRD to the less prosperous eastern Guangdong.

In the mid-1990s, the Yantian port at Shenzhen, the first deep-water port in southern China, was opened. With phase two of its development completed in 1996, Yantian began to handle an annual capacity of 1.7 million standard containers and has become China's second largest container port, behind Shanghai. Yantian played a crucial role in boosting Pearl River trade with Hong Kong from 9.3 million tons in 1990 to more than 30 million in 1998 (HKTDC, 1999). In 2001, Shenzhen's Chiwan, Shekou, and Yantian ports collectively handled 5.1 million TEUs, pushing Shenzhen's ranking in throughput from eleventh of all container ports in the world for 2000 to eighth place in 2001, sixth place in 2002, and was projected to rise to fourth place in 2003 (*China Shipping Gazette*, 2003). This rapid growth was fueled by sustained high growth in the PRD and rising exports to the U.S. market.[58]

In the GSCS, five new or considerably upgraded airports in Hong Kong, Macau, Shenzhen, Zhuhai, and Xiamen went into operation in the 1990s, with the new and improved Baiyun International Airport opening in 2004. In April 2002, two Hong Kong aviation service companies launched helicopter flights from Hong Kong and Macau to Shenzhen. Passengers, mostly business executives and managers working in the PRD, can board from a helicopter pad on the Hong Kong Island for a quick hop across the border. A privately owned Taiwanese bus company started operating at Hong Kong's new Chek Lap Kok Airport in 1998 to take business travelers from Taiwan directly to Dongguan. With only four daily departures at the beginning, the bus company has since increased its scheduled departures to 27 every day, carrying about 20,000 Taiwanese managers and their family members between Hong Kong's airport and Dongguan every month (S. Chen, 2000). Beginning with the implementation of a policy on mutual recognition of driving qualifications between Hong Kong and the mainland in 2004, Hong Kong residents with cars registered on the mainland are allowed to drive over the border without having to obtain a mainland driving license.[59] While this cross-border driving will be facilitated by a new bridge between Yuen Long of Hong Kong and Shenzhen—the so-called Western Corridor—which is designed to carry 80,000 vehicles a day and to be opened in 2006, it remains to be seen whether, or more realistically when, Hong Kong will switch to driving on the right side of the road to make cross-border traffic integration easier and safer.

The More the Better? Balancing Supply with Demand

Besides the expanded transport infrastructure, the ongoing and planned new transport projects on both sides of the Hong Kong–Guangdong border are intended to induce a broader scope of and greater efficiency in economic and spatial integration (see the book's Web page). Is there sufficient future demand to justify this massive buildup of transport infrastructure on both sides of the border? Is oversupply looming on the horizon?

The economic downturn that has haunted Hong Kong in the last few years has already put a damper on the various ambitious projects. Although the PRD has been booming, there are already signs that some overcapacity has either developed or may be in the offing. Zhuhai International Airport is an unfortunate victim of oversupply and less favorable geography as one of five major airports in a 200 km radius with about one hour's drive among them. First, intense competition from Hong Kong International Airport, the new Macau International Airport (less than 30 km away), and other PRD airports absorb almost all passenger and cargo traffic from the PRD. Second, Zhuhai was never able to acquire international flights and become a gateway. Third, though linked by hovercraft and ferry to Hong Kong (about a 60-minute trip), Zhuhai was considered too distant from other primary cities and production centers in the PRD, mainly Guangzhou and Shenzhen. Fourth, the central government became disenchanted with Zhuhai's expensive "build it and they will come" high-risk approach and eventually withdrew their support. The result was a costly, grossly underutilized airport with a magnificent terminal, the longest runway in China, and well-designed surface transport links, but only limited domestic traffic and no international traffic (Kasarda, forthcoming). In 2001, only 630,000 passengers passed through Zhuhai International Airport; the initial projection was for 730,000 passengers in 1996, growing to 11.2 million by 2011.[60]

The wasteful and underutilized Zhuhai airport suggests two lessons for the development of cross-border transport infrastructure. One is that too much emphasis and resources have been placed on building up the "hardware" infrastructure without sufficient attention to improving the "software" for making the transport system operate efficiently, such as regular maintenance, toll management, and highway safety.[61] A broader understanding of improving the "software" might include making the regional government more forthcoming and accountable in sharing information about all critical issues affecting both sides of the border. During the SARS crisis of spring 2003, critics faulted the Guangdong government for clamping down on reporting the disease early and not taking immediate precautions to protect doctors and nurses in hospitals, but focusing on building more bridges and 24-hour border crossings.[62] The other lesson is that the various regional and local governments need coordinated planning to develop a more integrated transport system. When it comes to building large-scale transport projects that require huge capital outlays, strong local autonomy may be less effective. Nevertheless, the rapid economic growth and spatial integration of the GSCS has created the great need for an extensive boundary-spanning transport infrastructure, which is critical to overcoming the remaining distance and border barriers in achieving greater subregional prosperity.

A Prototypical Transborder Subregion?

Of the Asia-Pacific transborder subregions under study, the GSCS is not only the most mature and successful in growth and integration, but also the most ideal case with regard to the analytical power of the synthetic framework. Both the success of the GSCS and its being a prototypical transborder subregion definitely can be attributed to the presence of and complementarity among the studied factors associated with the four analytical lenses. A brief recount below serves to illustrate how the framework has worked for the GSCS and its analytical value for the other Asia-Pacific transborder subregions.

First of all, the global-local economic nexus lens has illuminated how the comparative advantages of the four main units of the GSCS (Hong Kong, Taiwan, Guangdong, and Fujian) have created a powerful synergy for rapid growth and integration. Economic complementarity among the GSCS's constituent units has created direct and strong links between the global and local economies via investment flows and commodity chains. These flows and links allow cities in Guangdong and Fujian to become differentially specialized centers of manufacturing activity, as exemplified by Dongguan's clustered computer peripherals assembly. However, with growth and wealth being heavily concentrated in the PRD,[63] uneven development is part of the success story, which also is accompanied by undesirable labor practices and working conditions on the factory floor. A stronger and more competitive PRD, coupled with the lingering impact of the Asian financial crisis and recent economic slowdowns in Hong Kong and Taiwan, challenges the latters' relative positions in the GSCS. Deeper cross-border integration, facilitated by the implementation of the Closer Economic Partnership Agreement (CEPA) between mainland China and Hong Kong on January 1, 2004, could introduce both greater cooperation and competition and thus uncertainty into the economic links in the GSCS (see the book's Web page).

Second, through the lens of the de-centering state, we have seen that rapid local economic growth and transformation in Guangdong and Fujian would not have occurred without the autonomous and developmentally minded local government agencies and officials. Compared with government officials elsewhere, Guangdong's local officials are more amenable to investors making a handsome return of 20 percent and approve projects much faster (Edwards, 1997). When local party heads put on the "entrepreneurial hat" and take the lead in attracting investment and pushing for growth, their actions tend to induce a favorable reaction from Hong Kong and Taiwanese investors and strong support from the local population. This pragmatism and flexibility helped bridge the systemic political and economic differences between Hong Kong/Taiwan and Guangdong/Fujian, highlighting the more important role of the local state, even though the central Chinese state provided the initial triggering policy. As cross-border economic, social, and spatial integration widens and deepens, it remains to be seen whether the more autonomous local governments in the PRD are capable of governing more efficiently and transparently in the future (see the book's Web page).

Third, the cross-border social capital lens sheds light on how kinship ties and other forms of social networks between Hong Kong, Taiwan, Guangdong, and Fujian bind the GSCS by accentuating economic complementarity, global-local ties, and local autonomy. The combined presence of historical links, kinship ties, native identity, and dialectic similarity has fostered the differential concentration of Hong Kong capital in Guangdong and Taiwanese capital in Fujian. The over 6,000 Taiwan-invested enterprises in Fujian, especially in Xiamen and Fuzhou, involve larger investors and more capital than Hong Kong firms. As Xiamenese often point out, they have more in common with Taiwanese than they do with people of neighboring Guangdong (Mellor, 1993). In Dongguan, where so many Taiwanese businesspeople do not have kinship ties or speak Cantonese, they resort to transplanted business-based social networks from Taiwan to coordinate local supply and production of products for the global market.

Finally, the spatial/infrastructural lens has provided clarity on the positive effects of geographic contiguity and proximity, porous borders, and transport infrastructure on the growth and integration of the GSCS. They have strengthened cross-border social networks by making travel to Guangdong and Fujian quite easy for Hong Kong and Taiwanese businesspeople, even without direct cross-strait water and air links. Close economic interdependence across the Hong Kong–Guangdong border has reduced the friction of distance and thus contributed to some diffusion of both manufacturing and service activities over an extended border zone covering the PRD. This process has narrowed the previous economic and social gaps created by the distortion of the more restricted border. It also has begun to pressure regional and local governments to relax border control with 24-hour crossing points. In terms of the central argument for the book, the states on both sides of the border have adapted to its bridging role and largely avoided reinforcing its barrier effect even when the border flows have begun to favor Guangdong at some expense of Hong Kong.

The GSCS reflects the complementary reinforcement of four sets of largely favorable factors, thus supporting the harmonious hypothesis stated in chapter 3. This case also proves that it is necessary to assess how these factors interact to influence the formation and evolution of a transborder subregion. In addition, the GSCS provides a prototypical case against which we can examine the comparative evidence regarding other Asia-Pacific transborder subregions. We proceed with the Bohai/Yellow Sea Subregion (BYSS) in the next chapter.

Notes

1. There have been many labels for the integration of the People's Republic of China, Hong Kong, and Taiwan economies into a dynamic transnational regional economic system with global economic impact. The three Chinese economies' combined share of the world's total exports rose from 4.8 percent in 1985 to 8.9 percent in 1997, ranking third behind the United States' 12.6 percent and Germany's 9.4 percent, and ahead of Japan's 7.7 percent (Mainland Affairs Council, 1998, p. 54). The most popular and commonly used label is "Greater China." According to Harding (1993, p. 662), "Greater China" was originally used in the 1930s to refer to the combination of "China Proper" (the areas directly controlled by the central government) and "Outer China" (the remote and border areas largely populated by minorities). While the contemporary use of "Greater China" did not appear until the mid-1980s, Hong Kong scholar Zhi-Lian Huang (1993, pp. 7–8) identifies about 30 terms or labels coined between 1980 and 1992 to describe the same phenomenon, and the overwhelming majority of them appeared in Chinese-language publications. Naughton (1997b, pp. 5–6) defines the "China Circle" as comprising three concentric circles that extend outward from (1) the smallest and most inner circle of the greater Hong Kong metropolitan area to (2) the next larger circle of Hong Kong, Taiwan, and Guangdong and Fujian provinces, and to (3) the entire China, Hong Kong, and Taiwan economies. I use the GSCS, which has the same scope as (2) of Naughton's China Circle, to conform to the general definition of the transborder subregion in chapter 2. While Macau also is included in the GSCS as an important transit stop for indirect mainland to Taiwan air travel, I treat it sparingly in the analysis, given its smallest economic weight.

2. Reported in *Renmin Ribao* (The People's Daily), overseas edition, January 22, 2003, p. 1.

3. Derived from online data released by the Census and Statistics Department of Hong Kong, accessed from www.info.gov.hk/censtatd/eng/hkstat/fas/labour/employment/labour4index .html, March 13, 2003.

4. This most recent figure was taken from the report "Down in the Delta," on the *South China Morning Post* website, scmp.com, accessed on December 19, 2003. The *South China Morning Post* is Hong Kong's most influential English newspaper.

5. A simple product (e.g., transistor radio) may involve creating little kits—plastic bags filled with all the components needed to build a radio—in Hong Kong, shipping the kits to China for assembly, and bringing the assembled products back to Hong Kong for final testing and inspection before distribution (X. Chen, 1999b).

6. An illustrative case involves the start-up of Compass Technology Co., a high-tech manufacturing venture, in northern Hong Kong. Compass makes flexible substrates, a thin, film-like component on which semiconductor chips are mounted. The two founders of Compass cited capital raising, skilled labor, product quality, and precision in manufacturing and shipping as reasons for locating their facility in Hong Kong. They did not anticipate moving into China or to another low-cost location for several years (HKTDC, 1998).

7. The Taiwanese government's figure was cited in Georgie Anne Geyer, "Flow of capital to Beijing drains Taiwan's strength," *Chicago Tribune*, June 15, 2001, p. 29. The magazine *Asiaweek* reported that Taiwanese investment in China could be close to US$100 billion, which is at the high end of the estimated range, depending on the source of information (see Lawrance, 2002, p. 17).

8. Although the Taiwanese government began to restrict large-scale projects after the cross-strait political crisis in 1996, halting a US$3.2 billion deal for the Formosa Plastics Group to build a power plant in Zhangzhou, Fujian province, Taiwanese investment continued to flow into China, up 20 percent in 1997 when it slowed in Southeast Asia. Some large companies have broken large projects into smaller installments and sequential stages, aiming to create vertically integrated production over time (X. Chen, 1999b). Although the Taiwanese government lifted the ban on direct investment in China in 2002, it has continued to control substantial investments by requiring companies that have accumulated investments exceeding US$20 million to submit a report annually to the Ministry of Economic Affairs.

9. Although the unit price for exports would be 10–15 percent lower for using mainland facilities to receive orders, manufacture, and export, Taiwanese firms could achieve a 10–15 percent higher net profit than doing it from Taiwan because the production cost on the mainland would be 25–30 percent lower (Kao, Lee, and Lin, 1992).

10. In the early 1980s, children's dolls were designed in Hong Kong and their molds produced in Hong Kong, where sophisticated machinery was available. Then the molds were shipped to China, where workers formed the plastic, assembled the dolls, painted the figures, and made the dolls' clothing. Then the dolls were brought back to Hong Kong for final testing, inspection, and packaging, which could not be done up to quality in China. Finally, they were distributed from Hong Kong. (Interview with Victor Fung, in Magretta, 1998, p. 105.) Nowadays, though the dolls may still be contracted to and designed by a Hong Kong firm, the manufacturing process through packaging is normally completed in China, which shifts "Made by Hong Kong" to "Made by China." Hong Kong, however, still controls the front (design) and back (distribution) ends of the process. In this sense, "Made by Hong Kong" has shifted to "Made in Hong Kong but Made by China" (see Berger and Lester, 1997).

11. This emerging scenario was suggested by the report "HK firms wary of mainland competition," scmp.com, accessed on October 14, 2002.

12. According to the 1987 officially delineated boundary of the Pearl River Delta (PRD) Open Economic Zone and the 1990 statistical definition, the PRD included Guangzhou, Shenzhen, Zhuhai, and seven other prefectural level cities, and 21 of their administered counties and cities at the county level. This region covers an area of 47,430 sq km and about 20 million people. For the names of all the cities and counties in the PRD, see Lin (1997, p. 17, note 3) and Loo (1997). From 1980 to 2000, the PRD's economy grew at a rate of 16.9 percent annually; the growth rate was 13.8 percent for Guangdong province, and 9.6 percent for China as a whole. Information from "Boom times on our doorstep," accessed at scmp.com on November 27, 2002.

13. Figures from *Guangdong Statistical Yearbook 2001*, Guangdong Statistical Bureau, Guangzhou, 2001.

14. "China's coast as factory of the world," *Christian Science Monitor*, December 16, 2003, p. 1.

15. Reported in *Renmin Ribao* (The People's Daily), overseas edition, June 10, 1998, p. 5.

16. *Renmin Ribao* (The People's Daily), overseas edition, June 10, 1998, p. 5.

17. Reported in *Renmin Ribao* (The People's Daily), overseas edition, July 9, 2002, p. 4.

18. Reported in "The dark side of Shenzhen's bright future," scmp.com, accessed on October 21, 2002.

19. For more detailed discussions of the policies and outcomes of decentralization, see Hsing (1998, chap. 5); Oi (1995); Shirk (1993); and Wong (1991).

20. See "Battling deltas: The regional fight for preeminence," "Will Hong Kong take the lead in the delta's development?" and "Academic challenges delta barriers," scmp.com, accessed on December 5, 2002, January 10, 2003, and April 14, 2003, respectively.

21. "Stay strong and live long, Hong Kong," scmp.com, accessed on April 7, 2003.

22. See "The crisis infecting cross-border relations," scmp.com, accessed on May 7, 2003.

23. Reported in *Renmin Ribao* (The People's Daily), overseas edition, January 17, 2003, p. 5.

24. An interview with the party secretary of the Shishi municipality, Fujian province, on the program *Haixia Liangan* (Both Sides of the Taiwan Strait), China Central Television International Channel (CCTV-4), August 7, 2000.

25. An interview with the party secretary of the Shantou municipality, Guangdong province, on the program *Zhongguo Baodao* (China Report), China Central Television International Channel (CCTV-4), August 23, 2000.

26. "Why you shouldn't bet against the Pearl River Delta region," scmp.com, accessed on December 12, 2002.

27. I am thankful to Alvin So for suggesting this side of the argument that autonomous local officials are all good for business relations and performance.

28. The author's interview with several managers and workers in Guangzhou, August 1998.

29. In one case, a Taiwanese investor gave a box of rare and special Chinese herbal medicine to the deputy director of the local land bureau for the latter's mother, who needed exactly this particular medicine. The gift carried great significance because it showed the Taiwanese investor caring for the director's family, something closest to the heart of the Chinese people (Hsing, 1997, p. 153).

30. The hospital would cost US$35 million to build, and the Taiwan business association in Dongguan would foot most of the bill, with a hospital in Taiwan participating in the design and construction. The hospital would have a total of 500 beds, with the first phase of the construction yielding 250 beds. The hospital's staff could come from Taiwan or any other countries. See *Renmin Ribao* (The People's Daily), overseas edition, August 27, 2003, p. 5.

31. Reported in Taiwan's Mainland Affairs Council website, www.chinabiz.org.tw/maz/Eco-Month/124-2002-12/menu.htm.

32. This quote was taken from an article entitled "Taiwan's brain drain to China," scmp.com, accessed on August 15, 2003.

33. Besides the oldest rail crossing point of Luohu (Lowu), the three other land crossings are Wenjingdu (Man Kam To), Shatoujiao (Sha Tou Kok), and Huanggang (Wong Gong)-Luomazhou (Lok Ma Chau).

34. The overwhelming majority of the people crossing the Luohu checkpoint are Hong Kong and Macau residents, who accounted for 84 million of the 94 million crossings in 2002. Growing cross-border tourism, which involved over 900,000 tourists in 7,300 groups crossing the Luohu border in 2002, also has fueled the rapid increase in border crossings. On May 1 (the Labor Day holiday), 2002, over 31,000 people in 1,379 tourist groups from Hong Kong and

Macau cleared through the checkpoint. *Renmin Ribao* (The People's Daily), overseas edition, June 7, 2001, p. 1; January 3, 2003, p. 5.

35. Figures cited in *Renmin Ribao* (The People's Daily), overseas edition, January 18, 2003, p. 4.

36. Reported in *Renmin Ribao* (The People's Daily), overseas edition, October 9, 2002, p. 5; December 6, 2002, p. 8.

37. In fact, this experiment started at the end of 2002 when five Shenzhen financial institutions provided convenience to about 2 million Shenzhen customers and SAR merchants through a wider use of electronic fund transfers. "Shenzhen-issued debit cards to be formatted for SAR for next year," scmp.com, accessed on December 24, 2002.

38. See "Hong Kong buyers snap up mainland properties," and "Commuters drive up Shenzhen house prices," scmp.com, accessed on October 23, 2002 and December 30, 2002.

39. These statistics were reported in *Renmin Ribao* (The People's Daily), overseas edition, April 19, 1997, p. 2; October 7, 2000, p. 3; January 9, 2002, p. 8.

40. "20pc rise in the residents working across the border," scmp.com, accessed on December 30, 2003.

41. Shenzhen already has the fourth largest GDP and the highest GDP per capita of all Chinese cities at US$5,400. Shenzhen has over 4 million people, against Hong Kong's 7 million. Shenzhen has the advantage over Hong Kong in closer ties with the entire Chinese economy without formal boundary restrictions. Shenzhen boasts lower labor cost, about one-quarter of Hong Kong's. "Shenzhen the greater threat, analyst warns," scmp.com, accessed on October 8, 2002.

42. Using data for 1984, 1987, and 1990, I computed the correlations between the number of foreign investment projects and foreign investment per capita in all Guangdong cities with their distance to Hong Kong and the population potential of Hong Kong as the "center" in a spatially defined region—Guangdong province. To compute the potential of population measure (see Duncan, Cuzzort, and Duncan, 1961, pp. 52–53), I used the formula:

Population Potential of Hong Kong = $P_{HK} \div D_i^2$; where

P_{HK} = The population of Hong Kong
D_i^2 = The distance of Hong Kong from a given Guangdong city (squared)
The squared term is used, as the effect of gravitation from a center on other areal units may be nonlinear.

43. "Standard Chartered eyes Shenzhen expansion," scmp.com, accessed on November 9, 2002.

44. "Cross-border flows hit SAR," scmp.com, accessed on September 16, 2002; "Shenzhen the greater threat, analyst warns," scmp.com, accessed on October 8, 2002; "Battling deltas: The regional fight for preeminence," scmp.com, accessed on December 5, 2002; "Will Hong Kong take the lead in the delta's development," scmp.com, accessed on January 10, 2003.

45. The mainland and Hong Kong governments also agreed to open the Huanggang border crossing half an hour earlier in the morning and close it two hours later, which added more people and vehicular traffic through the Hong Kong–Shenzhen border. Reported in *Renmin Ribao* (The People's Daily), overseas edition, December 3, 2001, p. 1.

46. "Critics say time is right to open up buffer zone," and "Easier border crossing welcome; now for Lowu," scmp.com, accessed on January 27, 2003.

47. Most of those arrested were on two-way permits issued by mainland officials, who were often bribed to give three-month permits when only one-month permits were allowed. Some of the illegal mainlanders have become scavengers who sell rubbish for recycling. Unlike local scavengers who are elderly, many of the scavengers from mainland China were unemployed, while others were farmers, taxi drivers, carpenters, even sales managers back home in rural areas of Fu-

jian, Guangdong, Sichuan, Shandong, Anhui, and Jiangsu provinces. They have come to Hong Kong through the use of cross-border social networks. In one case, the relatives of a neighborhood shoemaker came to visit and stayed on to scavenge. They were joined by friends and then friends of friends. They tend to live with five or six people crammed into one room in subdivided cubicles in old apartment buildings. Although illegal workers could face a maximum penalty of HK$50,000 (HK$7.70=US$1) in fines and imprisonment for up to two years, they have continued to come to scavenge and account for about 30 percent of all scavengers in Hong Kong, up from 10 percent a few years ago. See "It's a dirty job," scmp.com, accessed on September 16, 2002.

48. See *Renmin Ribao* (The People's Daily), overseas edition, January 18, 2003, p. 4.

49. "Taiwan companies will stick with SAR, survey says," scmp.com, accessed on November 1, 2002.

50. In January 1986, Taiwan's Ministry of Transportation issued regulations that enabled Hong Kong transshipment and third-port customs clearance for ships carrying bulk cargo across the Taiwan Strait. In 1988, Taiwanese authorities allowed both foreign freight and passenger ships traveling between Hong Kong and Okinawa to ply the strait. In 1995, Taiwan unveiled an "offshore transshipment center" plan in Kaohsiung and allowed mainland containers to enter Taiwan on foreign ships, lowering the transport costs for Taiwanese companies operating in China. On April 19, 1997, the so-called point-to-point cargo transportation link across the Taiwan Strait formally began, with only Kaohsiung, Xiamen, and Fuzhou being the points of departure and destination (see map 4.1). Under this arrangement, foreign-registered mainland and Taiwanese vessels may travel directly between Kaohsiung and Xiamen or Fuzhou, but their cargoes may not pass through Taiwan's customs or enter Taiwan's markets. Instead, the cargo must be offloaded at a third port, which is primarily Hong Kong. In addition, Xiamen and Fuzhou's locations make access from them to other parts of China limited. Three Taiwanese shippers and five mainland carriers have been approved to ship across the Taiwan Strait, but only if they carry "transshipment goods," which means that mainland-made or Taiwan-made cargo transported this way cannot be offloaded across the strait (Underwood, 2000). However, some vessels would just detour slightly to pass by the Japanese port of Ishigaki in the southern Ryukyus, 270 km from Taiwan (Shapiro, 2002).

51. "Cross-strait exodus taking toll on travel and housing," scmp.com, accessed on September 2, 2002.

52. A special agreement with China's Xiamen Airlines allows TransAsia's passengers to book flights to Fuzhou via Macau while in Taiwan. Under this agreement, TransAsia also has complete control over the route's marketing. A Taiwanese resident who wants to fly to Xiamen on Taiwan's EVA Air can book the entire flight from Taiwan but must transfer to one of its three mainland partner airlines (CNAC, China Northern, and China Northwest) in Macau. In contrast, the Air Macau flights from Taiwan can fly directly to a number of major mainland cities after a brief stopover in Macau. While there, the passengers get off for about 45 minutes as the flights change their numbers. Then the crew and passengers get back on the plane to fly into China (Y. Chen, 1997).

53. True direct dialing, without going through a third party, not only will reduce the cost for cross-strait calling but also will improve the voice quality. *Renmin Ribao* (The People's Daily), overseas edition, January 3, 1996, p. 5.

54. Figures from *Renmin Ribao* (The People's Daily), overseas edition, January 21, 1997, p. 5; November 15, 2001, p. 2.

55. "Spring Festival landing marks historic moment," scmp.com, accessed on January 20, 2003; "A day of milestones for integration," and "Stopovers cost time and money," scmp.com, accessed on January 27, 2003.

56. "Cross-strait exodus taking toll on travel and housing," scmp.com, accessed on September 2, 2002.

57. "Taiwan companies will stick with SAR, survey says," scmp.com, accessed on November 1, 2002.

58. *Renmin Ribao* (The People's Daily), overseas edition, February 2, 2002, p. 1; "Shenzhen container trade up nearly 50pc," scmp.com, accessed on November 5, 2002; "Shenzhen cargo soars as ports and economy improve," scmp.com, accessed on December 4, 2002.

59. Hong Kong motorists simply have to present their Hong Kong licenses at the mainland's Public Security Bureau and fill out a few forms, as well as pass a simple medical test. Similarly, mainland drivers are able to obtain a Hong Kong driving license from the Transport Department easily. However, as of 2004, the cross-border driving privilege is enjoyed by only about 10,000 Hong Kong motorists whose cars have mainland registration, as they meet property ownership or investment requirements imposed by mainland authorities. See "Driving over the border: Drivers on road to cross-border integration," scmp.com, accessed on December 28, 2003.

60. "Driving over the border," scmp.com.

61. On two separate bus rides along the Shenzhen-Guangzhou highway during a research trip in the late 1990s, I noticed several poorly maintained stretches of the highway and experienced a serious traffic accident when the bus I was on ran over a Mercedes sedan that was illegally crossing the median. Then it took a very long time for the traffic police to arrive at the scene. Fortunately, the driver and the front passenger of the sedan were only slightly injured.

62. See "Stay strong and live long, Hong Kong," scmp.com, accessed on April 7, 2003.

63. While the PRD occupies only 23 percent of Guangdong's territory, it accounts for about 80 percent of its GDP and tax revenue and close to 90 percent of its total foreign direct investment. *Renmin Ribao* (The People's Daily), overseas edition, April 2, 2003, p. 5.

5

Bridging Ocean Boundaries

The Bohai/Yellow Sea Subregion

IF THE PROSPERITY OF THE GSCS has earned it the deserving reputation of the gold coast on China's southeastern shore, the emergence of the Bohai/Yellow Sea Subregion (BYSS) has created another gold coast on China's northern seaboard facing South Korea and Japan (see map 5.1). Although the BYSS lags somewhat behind the GSCS in growth, integration, regional importance, and global impact, it is similar to the GSCS in several important aspects that make the BYSS enlightening for understanding the complex dimensions and broader implications of the Asia-Pacific transborder subregions.

Before looking at the BYSS closely through the four analytical lenses, it is important to recognize the composition of the BYSS as a typical transborder subregion in terms of multiple geographically contiguous or adjacent subnational units. The BYSS consists of China's Bohai region,[1] especially the Liaoning and Shandong provinces, South Korea (mostly its west coastal region), and the southwestern (Kyushu) region of Japan, while North Korea is much less involved, with limited northern border trade and tourism ties with China.[2]

Like the GSCS, the BYSS involves two differentially advanced economies (Japan and South Korea) and a coastal region of China, with the possible involvement of a part of North Korea, with complementarities among them. It is logical to begin by analyzing how this composition mediates global-local and trans-local economic links in ways that are similar to or different from the GSCS.

MAP 5.1
The Bohai/Yellow Sea Subregion (BYSS)

Subregional Economic Integration with Global and Local Ties

The extent to which global and local economies are linked through transborder subregions varies from case to case. Unlike the GSCS, the BYSS does not
contain a fully subregionalized global-local economic nexus. Instead, the
BYSS features extensive and partially overlapped global-local, trans-local, and
national-local economic ties.

Rapidly Growing Bilateral Trade

As with the GSCS, the emergence of the BYSS must be placed in the broader context of bilateral trade between each pair of the three main national economies involved, excluding North Korea, which figures more prominently in the next chapter. Trade between China and South Korea was very limited from the late 1970s to the mid-1980s. In fact, China had more trade with North Korea than with South Korea until 1985, when the latter surpassed North Korea in trade with China (H. Lee, 1995). However, earlier China–South Korea trade paled in comparison to trade between China and Japan and between Japan and South Korea. Trade between China and South Korea grew rapidly in the late 1980s and early 1990s, but it was conducted mostly through Hong Kong, very similar to China-Taiwan trade. Since the establishment of diplomatic relations between China and South Korea in 1992, trade between them has surged in absolute volume, even though it still trailed behind trade between the other two dyads in the economic triangle (see appendix table 5.A).

It is worth noting that as shares of China–South Korea trade in their total trade rose after 1992, both the weight of China's trade with Japan and of South Korea's trade with Japan relative to China and South Korea's total trade declined (see figure 5.1). Of the three trading dyads, China–South Korea trade, relative to China-Japan trade or Japan–South Korea trade, has been more important to the formation of the BYSS. The rapid growth of South Korea's exports to China was instrumental in helping its faster than expected economic recovery from the Asian financial crisis in 1998. Between 1996 and 2002, South Korea's exports to

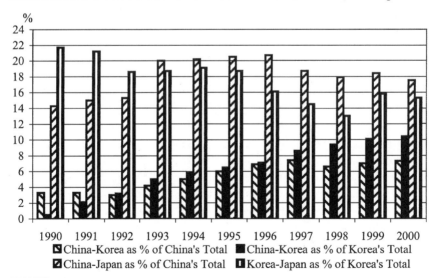

FIGURE 5.1
Trade Shares Among China, Japan, and South Korea, 1990–2000

China doubled to around US$40 billion, as China passed Japan and the United States to become South Korea's top trade partner in 2002.[3]

Given their respective natural endowments and levels of development, China and South Korea have a complementary but evolving trade relationship. China's exports to South Korea consist of mostly raw materials (e.g., coal and nonferrous metals), agricultural products (e.g., corn and animal foods), and textile raw materials (e.g., silk and cotton fibers). As a result of more large South Korean companies setting up manufacturing facilities in China, China began to export some semi- or completely manufactured products to South Korea, including consumer electronics and automotive parts (see next section). In the other direction, through the mid-1990s, South Korea's exports consisted mostly of second-rate consumer goods at low prices. From the late 1990s, large Korean *chaebols* like Samsung and Lucky Goldstar (LG) began to export pricier, stylish, and hard-to-copy goods to the China market, where some increasingly affluent consumers began to demand and could afford brand-name products. At the same time, South Korea has continued to sell a lot of industrial goods to China.

Direct Investment and Cross-Border Production

As chapter 4 has shown, trade and direct investment have been intertwined in the GSCS through various global commodity chains. To what extent is this also true of the BYSS? Given the comparative advantages in labor cost and geographic proximity, investment should flow from Japan and South Korea to China, especially to its Bohai and Yellow Sea coastal region, just as Hong Kong and Taiwan investments have flown heavily to China's southeast coastal region.

At the national level, as table 5.1 shows, Japan and South Korea's direct investments in China have constituted the two largest flows among the three pairs. South Korea's investment foray into China began as early as 1985, when an overseas subsidiary of a South Korean firm established a factory in the form of a Hong Kong company to make stuffed toys in China (S. Kim, 1995). This also was the time when Taiwanese firms had just begun to invest on the mainland through Hong Kong. Although much of the earlier, indirect South Korean investment in China involved small and medium-sized firms, the *chaebols*, or large conglomerates, began to make inroads into China using their political clout, financial resources, and foreign subsidiaries. Through a Hong Kong subsidiary in 1988, Daewoo Corporation sank US$12.5 million into a 48 percent stake in a refrigerator plant in Fuzhou, Fujian province (Yun, 1989).

As South Korean investment in China picked up its pace in the 1990s, the number of larger and more heavily capitalized projects increased rapidly, with investment projects capitalized at US$10 million or more reaching 41 in 1997 (see table 5.2). This shift was reflected in South Korean investment spreading across a variety of Chinese industries, including more capital-intensive industries such as metal making and automotive manufacturing (see the book's Web page).

TABLE 5.1

Direct Investment Between China, South Korea, and Japan, 1988–1999 (millions of U.S. dollars in current price)

Year	S. Korea's Investment in China: Cases[a] (1)	S. Korea's Investment in China: Amount[b] (2)	Japan's Investment in China: Amount[b] (3)	Japan's Investment in S. Korea: Amount (4)	S. Korea's Investment in Japan: Amount (5)	China's Investment in S. Korea: Amount (6)
1988	2	3	371	—	—	—
1989	12	10	515	—	—	—
1990	38	55	478	—	—	—
1991	112	85	886	265	12	1
1992	**269**	**222**	748	230	28	3
1993	**629 (6)**	**622**	1,361	260	6	2
1994	**1,051 (6)**	**809**	2,086	411	58	2
1995	**883 (15)**	**1,016**	7,592	460	105	7
1996	**797 (16)**	**1,374**	5,131	430	81	3
1997	**853 (41)**	**1,380**	3,401	449	64	3
1998	—	1,803	3,400	296	23	3
1999	—	1,275	2,973	—	48	13
Cumulative Total	**4,646**	**8,654**	**28,942**	**2,801**	**425**	**37**

Sources: Adapted from Kim (2000), table 2.4, p. 11, and SSB (1992, 1996, 1999, 2000), various tables.
[a]The numbers in parentheses for 1993–1997 refer to projects capitalized at US$10 million or more.
[b]The data for 1998 and 1999 are from Kim (2000), table 2.4, p. 11, whereas earlier time-series data are from the other sources identified.

TABLE 5.2

Geographic Distribution of South Korean Investment in China, Pre-1992 to 1997

(millions of U.S. dollars, percentages in parentheses)

Province, Region	Cumulative to 1992	1993	1994	1995	1996	Cumulative for 1988–1997[a]
Liaoning	66.7 (18.4)	59.7 (9.6)	118.5 (14.4)	121.6 (9.9)	155.2 (19.2)	522
Shandong	126.7 (35.0)	254.9 (41.0)	206.9 (25.2)	326.7 (26.5)	123.7 (15.3)	1,039
Tianjin	25.3 (7.0)	94.6 (15.2)	112.3 (13.7)	162.6 (13.2)	78.7 (9.7)	474
Beijing	37.3 (10.4)	24.6 (4.0)	62.5 (7.6)	135.5 (11.0)	89.3 (11.0)	349
China's Bohai/Yellow Sea Region	256.0 (73.1)	433.8 (69.8)	500.2 (60.9)	746.4 (60.6)	447 (55.2)	3,224 (57.8)
Jilin	11.3 (3.1)	35.6 (5.7)	50.6 (6.2)	42.4 (3.4)	23.3 (2.9)	163
Heilongjiang	31.9 (8.8)	56.1 (9.0)	22.4 (2.7)	36.3 (2.9)	3.7 (—)	150

Northeastern China (Jilin and Heilongjiang)	**43.2** (11.9)	**91.7** (14.7)	**73.0** (8.9)	**78.7** (6.3)	**26.0** (2.9)	**729** (13.1)
Shanghai	7.5 (2.1)	11.2 (1.8)	47.5 (5.8)	134.1 (10.9)	144.7 (17.9)	345
Jiangsu	9.1 (2.5)	35.1 (5.6)	67.4 (8.2)	179.5 (14.6)	94.0 (11.6)	385
The Yangtze River Region	**16.6** (6.2)	**46.3** (7.4)	**114.9** (14.0)	**313.6** (25.5)	**238.7** (29.5)	**1,241** (22.3)
Southeastern China (Fujian, Guangdong, Guangxi, Hainan)	**31.9** (8.7)	—	—	—	—	**248** (4.4)
China's Inland Region	**0.5** (0.1)	—	—	—	—	**134** (2.4)

Sources: Adapted from S. Kim (1995), p. 207; Kim and Kwon (1998), various tables; Ministry of Finance and Economy (1998), various tables.

Note: Not all percentages in the columns add up to 100.0 due to the exclusion of other provinces.

[a]The provincial cumulative totals do not include the figures for 1997. The regional total for 1988–1997 for China's Bohai and Yellow Sea region also includes Hebei province. The cumulative total for the Yangtze River region also includes Zhejiang province.

With approximately 90 percent of their investment in China in the manufacturing sector, which is even higher than the corresponding shares of Hong Kong and Taiwanese investments in China, South Korean firms are primarily attracted to China's abundant low-cost labor. This is why South Korean manufacturing investment has concentrated most heavily in several typical labor-intensive industries such as toys, footwear, and garments. Kim and Kwon (1998) showed that South Korean investors in China ranked cheap labor as the most important motivating factor (27.9 percent), followed by the reduction of other costs (24.4 percent), access to raw materials (15.1 percent), and market expansion (14.8 percent). Another salient characteristic of South Korean investment in China has been its striking geographic concentration.

Clustering Around China's Bohai and Yellow Sea Coast

Trade and investment flows across the Yellow Sea, especially between China and South Korea, have had a direct integrating impact on the emergence of the BYSS. As table 5.2 shows, almost two-thirds of South Korean cumulative investment in China through 1997 was concentrated in China's Bohai and Yellow Sea region. Within this favored zone for South Korean investment, Liaoning and Shandong provinces, especially the latter, stood out as the most attractive destinations. Until the early 1990s, Liaoning and Shandong accounted for about half of the total South Korean investment in China. The combined share of Liaoning and Shandong dropped only slightly through the mid-1990s. The larger influx of South Korean investment into Shandong province raised the latter's share of China's total foreign investment from 1.7 percent during 1986–1990 to 6.9 percent during 1991–1995 (Kim and Kwon, 1998). Reflecting the particularly strong economic link between South Korea and Shandong, South Korea edged out Japan to become Shandong's largest trading partner in 2002, accounting for 21.9 percent of the province's total trade against Japan's 21.7 percent.[4]

The appeal of China's two most northeastern provinces (Jilin and Heilongjiang) to South Korean investment reflects the economic ties of an adjacent transborder subregion (see chapter 6). While South Korean investment shifted toward China's Yangtze River region, especially to Shanghai over time, its heavy clustering in the Bohai and Yellow Sea region facilitated increasing local agglomeration and functional specialization. This resembles the continued geographic concentration of Hong Kong and Taiwanese investments in Guangdong and Fujian against a most recent shift toward Shanghai and Jiangsu province.

Despite the concentration of South Korean investment in China's Bohai and Yellow Sea region, it has been unevenly distributed among a number of cities. The few major port centers (Dalian, Tianjin, Qingdao, Yantai; see map 5.1) have accounted for the lion's share of the total South Korean investment in the region from the outset (see the book's Web page). The heavy South Korean investment in the major coastal cities of Shandong indicates that their industrial structure has a special appeal to and complementarity with South Korean firms. Despite having a large agricultural sector, Shandong province has developed a large and fairly balanced base of both heavy and light industries. The more substantial and competitive industries include electronics, petrochemicals, heavy machinery, automotives, textiles, and foodstuffs, which are located fairly evenly in the major coastal cities. Textiles, electronics, machinery, and foodstuffs all ranked in the top five industries in Qingdao, Yantai, and Weifang, a medium-sized city not far from the coast (Liu and Hou, 1994). Since the appreciation of the Korean won and rising wages began to dampen the growth and competitiveness of South Korea's export-oriented electronics industry in the mid-1980s, South Korean firms have relocated some manufacturing operations to such Chinese coastal cities as Qingdao and Weihai, a large industrial port closest to South Korea (see map 5.1).

The Geographic Origin of South Korean Investment

Just as the Chinese destinations for South Korean investment are along the coast of the Shandong peninsula, the geographic origins of South Korean investment are primarily along the country's west coast, primarily Seoul, Incheon, and the vicinity. As of 1997, 77.1 percent of the South Korean investment in Shandong province came from firms located on South Korean's west coast, with 73.7 percent coming from Seoul, Incheon, and the vicinity. For the cities of Qingdao, Yantai, and Weihai, the respective percentages were 72.5 percent and 70 percent, 80 percent and 80 percent, and 82.5 percent and 81.5 percent, while less than 20 percent came from the southeast and other regions of South Korea (Kim and Kwon, 1998; Park, 1998). The geographic sources of South Korean investment in Shandong's coastal region reflect the historical regional differences and recent shift of regional development policy within South Korea. Given the historical and continued concentration of manufacturing activity in the region surrounding Seoul, Incheon, and Suwon, its much larger share of outward investment in Shandong is largely expected.

Outside the Seoul-Incheon region, South Korea's west coast, especially Cholla-Namdo (or Chonnam province) has been much less developed, especially compared with the southeast region around Pusan. In the late 1980s, the South Korean government unveiled the "west coast development plan" for improving the transport infrastructure and constructing new industrial parks along the Incheon-Mokpo axis (see the next section for a more detailed discussion of this plan in the context of the changing South Korean state and successive presidents).

The "west coast development plan" also was motivated and has been sustained by conducting more trade and business with China, especially with Shandong province. With the South Korean *chaebols* building new capital- and technology-intensive manufacturing facilities on the west coast in the 1990s, they have relocated more labor-intensive operations to Shandong across the Yellow Sea. The concentrated investment in specific Chinese cities has created a certain degree of subregionalized global-local economic integration that is akin to the commodity chains that link China with Hong Kong and China with Taiwan in and out the GSCS.

The China–South Korean Manufacturing Nexus: From Local Production to National and Global Markets

As the previous chapter has shown, the GSCS features spatially integrated global-local economic links embedded in specific commodity chains. In comparison, the China–South Korean manufacturing nexus in the BYSS involves less extensive links between the various segments of certain commodity chains. Nevertheless, there are established links of cross-border production between China and South Korea that generate exports from China-based manufacturing to other markets.

The intra-organizational ties between South Korean companies and their China-based factories by functions are similar to those across the Taiwan Strait (see table 4.1). According to survey results reported in Kim and Kwon (1998, table 3.13), 90.2 percent and 94.6 percent of the South Korean–invested factories in China received technology transfer and parts supplies from their mother companies in South Korea. Regarding somewhat less connected functions, 83.1 percent and 79.1 percent of the South Korean–invested factories in China used equipment from the mother country and were allowed by the latter to conduct some R&D. In contrast, only 55.9 percent and 40.4 percent of the factories were engaged in order receiving/marketing and training. By keeping order-receiving and marketing functions at home, South Korean firms with manufacturing operations in China can control the lucrative front and back ends of the exports. China-based factories depend heavily on parts and equipment from South Korea, just as Taiwan-invested factories in southeastern China did earlier. The cutting and sewing machines at one Chinese–South Korean joint venture factory were imported exclusively from South Korea (K. Lee, 1995).

Like Guangdong and Fujian provinces for Hong Kong and Taiwanese firms, the coastal areas of Shandong province have become distinctive export platforms for South Korean companies with local manufacturing facilities. As Kim and Kwon (1998, table 3.9) have shown, 81 percent of the South Korean companies that set up factories in Shandong's coastal region were exporters by 1996. While the proportion of firms exporting to all markets dropped from 79.4 percent initially to 61.8 percent in 1996, the share of firms exporting back to South Korea rose from 43.6 percent to 56.3 percent. The evidence suggests that as South Korean companies in China began to export less and sold more in China, they sent more semi- or largely completed products to the home market for finishing, consumption, or re-export. This practice is similar to what some Taiwanese companies do from their factories in Guangdong and Fujian.

According to data by export destination and industry (Kim and Kwon, 1998, table 3.11), there is considerable inter-industry variation in South Korean firms' exports to different markets from Shandong's coastal region. For garments, 63 percent of the South Korean firms exported to Japan, followed by South Korea (25 percent) and North America (12 percent). For electronics, 89 percent of the South Korean firms exported to South Korea, while only 11 percent exported to North America, with no other markets involved. These data reveal important differences between the BYSS and GSCS with regard to the export markets for products manufactured in different regions of China. South Korean garment manufacturers in China export the majority of their products, like China-based Taiwanese and Hong Kong manufacturers. However, much of the South Korean exports from China go to Japan due to geographic proximity, as opposed to the large exports of Taiwanese and Hong Kong garments from China to the United States. Second, the dominant share of electronics exports back to South Korea reflects the high demand for economically produced small parts such as monitors, transformers, switches, and automotive components, which are used for final assembly and then re-exported from South Korea. This differs somewhat from Taiwanese and Hong Kong manufacturers in Guangdong and Fujian, from where they export locally assembled and labor-intensive electronic products.

Beyond Labor-Intensive Manufacturing: Kyushu's Growing Economic Links to South Korea and China

While the China (Shandong)–South Korea (west coast) manufacturing nexus and export outlet constitute a labor-intensive, low-tech dyad of the BYSS economic triangle, the Japan (Kyushu)–South Korea dyad contains more technology-intensive production links to the Asia-Pacific regional and global economy. The Kyushu region's involvement, coupled with the shrinking gap between some Japanese and South Korean industries, has introduced relational dynamics involving China that differ from the heavy dominance of low-end assembly and manufacturing in the GSCS.

A proper context for looking at Kyushu's links to South Korea and China at the industry level is provided by some figures on Kyushu's increasingly closer links with Asia in general and South Korea and China in particular. First of all, Kyushu's exports to Asia as a share of its total exports increased from 44.6 percent in 1991 to 52 percent in 2001, while the corresponding import figures rose more sharply, from 36.6 percent to 48.7 percent. The proportion of all companies in Kyushu with operations in Asia grew from 64.2 percent to 75.3 percent over that decade. While the volume of Kyushu's trade with South Korea nearly doubled from 1991 to 2001, the value of Kyushu-China trade quadrupled over the same time span. In 2001, 16.7 percent of Kyushu's exports went to South Korea, as opposed to only 6.3 percent from Japan as a whole (Kyushu Economy International [KEI], 2002a). From 1995 to 2000, the numbers of Japanese departing Kyushu for China and South Korea rose 74.2 percent and 50.8 percent respectively, versus 20.7 percent for all destinations. The numbers of Chinese and South Korean nationals visiting Kyushu during 1995–2001 grew 46.8 percent and 35.7 percent relative to 29.6 percent from Asia and 32.2 percent from all origins (KEI, 2002b). Future Kyushu–South Korea economic links also will get a boost from a new bilateral investment treaty between Japan and South Korea signed in 2002 and the prospect of a free trade agreement (FTA) between the two countries (Ahn, 2003).

High-tech and Not So High-tech Industry Links

At the industry level, Kyushu's companies have been developing various ties with South Korea and China, as well as other Asian economies. The semiconductor industry provides a high-tech example of the organizational and spatial aspects of these ties. As its traditional large, materials-producing industries have declined, contributing to a process of deindustrialization, the Kyushu region has undergone a steady transition toward high-tech manufacturing and assembly industries, especially the semiconductor/integrated circuit (IC) industry, earning the reputation as an emerging "Silicon Island" (W. Kim, 2000). The growth of Kyushu's semiconductor industry has benefited from established connections with its strong South Korean counterpart, while the peripheral sector of Kyushu's semiconductor industry has begun to forge links with China. As a 2001 survey of Kyushu's semiconductor companies showed, 43.5 percent of the respondents preferred to maintain the status quo regarding their operations in South Korea, 34.8 percent planned to expand, and 21.7 percent viewed South Korea as a new frontier. Regarding the China market, the percentages were 3.7 percent, 44.4 percent, and 51.9 percent, respectively (KEI, 2002b, p. 3). A cautious attitude toward China as an emerging investment destination is evident, compared to a more balanced approach to a mature market such as South Korea.

Inter-firm ties vary between semiconductor device manufacturers and semiconductor manufacturing equipment/testing equipment manufacturers. A Kyushu-based parent device manufacturer would typically send silicon wafer and other raw materials to a 100 percent subsidiary manufacturer either in Japan or South Korea, which then produces high value and sophisticated products such as small/thin semiconductors and sends them back to the parent company. Both the parent company and the subsidiary may jointly invest in an overseas company (primarily in Southeast Asia but gradually shifting to China), which engages in large-scale production of lower value semiconductor devices to be shipped to audio and mobile phone assembly factories locally and in neighboring countries. A semiconductor manufacturing equipment/testing equipment manufacturer in Kyushu tends to outsource parts manufacturing or export products directly to a joint venture partner in Taiwan. The joint venture company in Taiwan then subcontracts the manufacturing to a local company, which in turn makes printed circuit boards (PCBs) and other products for the parent company. The parent company in Kyushu then sends them to a major equipment manufacturer in Japan or South Korea to make manufacturing equipment for export to markets such as the United States. While some companies in Kyushu are beginning to connect with companies in China for parts manufacturing or direct sales of finished products, they export high-tech manufacturing/testing equipment and other semiconductor products to South Korea (KEI, 2002b).

Kyushu's export of semiconductor products to South Korea, especially bipolar integrated circuits (ICs), flash memory, and digital signal processors (DSPs), has increased recently. In 2001, 21.9 percent of Kyushu's export of semiconductor and other electronic parts went to South Korea, far exceeding the 10.8 percent of the national share of these exports to South Korea (KEI, 2002b, p. 4). These semiconductor products are critical inputs for the assembly of cellular phones, personal computers, appliances, and VCRs by South Korean firms for domestic sales or exports to international markets. In the other direction, Kyushu has been importing more dynamic random access memory (DRAM) from South Korea as Kyushu's semiconductor factories have gradually shifted away from DRAM production toward logic ICs (e.g., system large-scale integration [LSI], central processing units [CPUs]). The imported DRAM is used in car navigation systems, FAX boards, and printers in Kyushu, where some DRAM wafers also are cut and affixed to the lead-frame for final export to such countries as the United States (Kyushu International Information Promotion Council [KIIPC], 2000).

Toward the lower end of the technology spectrum, the declining heavy industry of iron and steel in Kyushu has experienced a revival through exporting scrap metal to China and South Korea. The clustering of such heavy industries as machinery and automotives in Liaoning and Shandong provinces has fueled a large demand for Kyushu's scrap metal. In 2001, China became the most popular destination for Kyushu's scrap metal, absorbing 47.1 of its exports, while South Korea was a close second by taking in 43.8 percent. In comparison, the China and South Korea shares of Japan's entire scrap metal export were 44.1 percent and 28.8 percent, respectively. China also absorbed 19.7 percent of Kyushu's export of used paper, behind only Thailand and Taiwan (KEI, 2002b, p. 5).

From Closer Links to Emerging Competition

The increasing links with South Korea and China, especially China, may alleviate the pain of deindustrialization in Kyushu, but they have created growing competition and uncertainty in this economic triangle. The low labor cost in China (about one-twentieth that of Kyushu), the cheap and abundant parts production capacity, and the purchasing capacity lure Kyushu companies to shift production there. The concentration of Chinese companies with improved technological capability and the expansion of the consumer durables and non-durables markets in the coastal region also spur the tendency of Kyushu companies to cross the Yellow Sea. On the other hand, Kyushu companies are concerned about Chinese companies' rapidly surging production capacity accompanied by technological catch-up, as well as their price competitiveness (KEI, 2002b). In the meantime, South Korea has begun to worry about China as an emerging competitor as it is trying to catch up with Japan in technological competition. According to a recent survey of 245 South Korean companies by the Federation of Korean Industries, the respondents expected to lose competitiveness to China in some key industries, including automobile and auto parts, and to run a neck-and-neck race in electronics and the information and technology sectors, in about four years, while looking to close their gap with Japan in about the same amount of time.[5]

The emerging competition among the three national or subnational economies is not unexpected, given their close and deepening ties across a variety of industries. These ties differ between the largely labor-intensive manufacturing nexus between Shandong province and South Korea's west coast and Kyushu's more high-tech manufacturing links with both South Korea and increasingly with China. Although these ties do not exhibit the degree of distinctive local concentration and functional specialization found in the GSCS, they link both light and heavy industries in and across a group of major coastal cities around the Bohai and Yellow Sea Rim into an increasingly integrated subregional economic network. While not as globally linked as the GSCS, the BYSS has developed a more balanced, simultaneous orientation toward global, national, and local markets. This transborder subregional formation, like the GSCS, would not have occurred without the national and local states playing different and shifting roles.

Convergence Toward Decentralization with Uneven Local Autonomy

Viewed from the political/institutional lens, state de-centering has occurred in the BYSS through a rough convergence toward decentralization. Decentralization in the GSCS context has translated into genuine local autonomy in southeastern China, which in turn has complemented market-oriented activity of large numbers of small- and medium-sized enterprises from Taiwan and Hong Kong. In comparison, the convergence toward decentralization in the BYSS not only has taken different forms in the three countries but also has happened at different times. Moreover, the expected outcome of decentralization—local autonomy—has been uneven due to the mediating influence of the varied historical and contemporary political contexts.

China Favoring the Bohai Rim: A Later Start but a Step Ahead

Opening and decentralization came to China's Bohai coast later than to its southeast coastal region. However, it could be argued that the participation of China's Bohai rim in the BYSS began as early as 1984, when the central government designated 14 coastal cities as favored open localities for foreign investment. Five of these cities were Tianjin, Dalian, Qinhuangdao, Yantai, and Qingdao (see map 5.1), which have since become the key Chinese nodes in the BYSS. Although these Chinese cities were not groomed specifically as part of a transborder subregion in 1984, the favorable administrative and financial incentives to local governments (e.g., local approval of investment projects, lower taxes) distinguished these cities as appealing, nearby Chinese localities for South Korean and Japanese investments. In the second half of the 1980s, China's coastal development strategy reflected a growing shift to the Bohai region. In 1987, 15 cities around Bohai Bay (including Dalian, Tianjin, Qingdao, and Yantai) established a loose inter-city alliance—the Joint Conference on Economic Cooperation Around the Bohai Region—that would link the Liaoning and Shandong peninsulas through the anchoring city of Tianjin (SSB, 1994). Shandong province established eight export processing zones in such major coastal and inland cities as Qingdao, Yantai, Weihai, and Jinan (Yun, 1989). The different waves of decentralization created incremental local autonomy for these cities to compete for foreign investment and choose their own development priorities. Thus, they became more appealing beyond geographic proximity to South Korean investment.

While some central and provincial government policies during the 1980s were not necessarily designed to target South Korean investment, others were adopted to foster trade with and investment from South Korea. Beginning in 1983, both China and South Korea relaxed restrictions on travel in both directions, leading to reciprocal visits of businesspeople, economic officials, scholars, and ships' crews. Between 1988–1991, 3,580 South Korean business groups with 8,600 people visited Shandong province (X. Chen, 1998). China also permitted South Korean ships to carry goods directly to China, as long as the ships were registered with a third country and would not fly the South Korean flag (Yun, 1989). To avoid angering North Korea, China's conciliatory stance toward South Korea focused on provincial-level initiatives. Shandong province was permitted to send delegations to South Korea and open a trade promotion office in Seoul through Hong Kong. Liaoning province quickly followed suit. Six major coastal cities in Shandong were allowed to set up special trading companies to deal with South Korean businesses.

In the 1990s, especially after establishing diplomatic relations with South Korea in 1992, Shandong province implemented a series of more favorable and more regionally and locally oriented measures to attract South Korean investors. The Shandong government focused on developing the peninsula into the primary location for South Korean manufacturing and the primary outlet for exporting to South Korea. The cities of Qingdao, Yantai, and Weihai began to develop special industrial districts for South Korean companies to build factories, in order to achieve local agglomeration and more efficient administration. As a further example, the coastal strip of the city of Weihai gradually developed a heavy clustering of processing and assembly operations set up by small- and medium-sized South Korean firms (Peng and Yan, 1994). The provincial and local initiatives have played a critical role in making the major cities around the Bohai rim, especially those on the Shandong peninsula, important economic players and contributors that are a step ahead of the South Korean cities in local autonomy.

South Korea "Going West and Local": A Practical Shift with a Personal Touch

Decentralization in South Korea that facilitated the BYSS must have occurred against a strong tradition of political and administrative centralization like that of China. In premodern times, Confucianism, which originated in China and later spread to Korea and Japan, strengthened administrative centralization by creating a heavy bureaucracy in the large national capitals to control the country. However, the Confucian emphasis on the family and community, in conjunction with the very scale of China, prevented centralization from becoming excessive through most dynasties. The Korean urban system favored the capital of Seoul, where Confucianism was more dominant, as a primate city[6] (which was disproportionally larger than any other Korean city), while the much smaller scale created a stronger version of centralization than in China (Rozman, 2002). In modern times, while China's adoption of Soviet-style socialism had perpetuated high administrative centralization before 1980, South Korea created and sustained a centralized developmental state that drove rapid industrialization with top-down initiatives from the 1960s and well into the 1980s.

Since the mid-1980s, South Korea has implemented different decentralization measures that have an important bearing on the BYSS. Similar to what has happened in China, the South Korean state has introduced a series of regional and local development policies that have enhanced the level and capacity of participation of certain South Korean localities in the BYSS. Back in 1986, the South Korean government unveiled a large-scale plan of shifting the gravity of economic construction and development to the west coast, which has been known as the "west coast development plan." While this plan was intended to reduce the development gap between eastern and western South Korea, it also was a goal to improve economic relations with China's Bohai rim. The timing of this plan was by no means coincidental, given China's launch of its Bohai rim initiative at that time. Nevertheless, there were serious domestic economic and political reasons for implementing the "west coast development plan" in the late 1980s.

Having endured a long neglect by the central government, South Korea's west coast, especially the southwest region, fell behind the rest of the nation in industrial investment and infrastructure development.[7] GNP per capita for the west coast was only 70 percent of the national average in the late 1980s (Li and Jin, 1999). The regional bias against the southwest had a lot to do with the background and policies of South Korea's authoritarian leaders from Park Chung Hee through Chun Doo Hwan to Roh Tae Woo, all of whom were from Kyongsang-Bukdo (Kyongbuk province) in the southeastern region of the country, especially Pusan. The "Kwangju massacre" unleashed by the Chun Doo Hwan regime contributed to the "emotional split" between the east and west regions. As a result, in the 1987 presidential election, Roh Tae Woo got only 7 percent and 13 percent of the total votes in Cholla-Bugdo and Cholla-Namdo in the southwest, respectively (F. Li, 1996). By channeling heavy investment to the west coast, the Roh regime attempted to narrow the regional disparities and thus ameliorate their associated domestic tension. Although he also was from the southeast, Kim Young Sam won the election and in 1993 became the first non-military president in 30 years. A supporter of the "west coast development plan" from his opposition leader days in 1987, Kim Young Sam carried on the plan during his presidency through 1998, with continued buildup of large-scale transport infrastructure and industrial projects on the west coast.

In 1998, Kim Young Sam lost the presidency to his rival Kim Dae Jung, who not only was a native of Cholla-Namdo (South Cholla province) in the southwest but also represented the Democratic Liberal Party based in the southwest. Following the tradition of playing regional politics in South Korea, Kim Dae Jung continued to favor and implement the "west coast development plan." Despite being from Pusan, the current president, Roh Moo Hyun, who took office in 2003, came from Kim Dae Jung's Democratic Liberal Party. He appears to continue supporting the development of the west coast for the practical reason of close economic exchange with China, if not for traditional party politics.[8]

With the transition to civilian rule, the Kim Young Sam government also ushered in a new era of decentralizing authority and using financial resources highlighted by the election for chief executive officers in local areas. These policies began to reverse a long-standing authoritarian tradition of suppressing local autonomy. The popular election of local assemblies after 1952 was discontinued by the military coup led by Park Chung Hee in 1961. Although a subsequent constitutional amendment of South Korea emphasized local autonomy that had existed before independence, in practice the authoritarian developmental state adopted a more top-down approach, which severely limited local autonomy. Following the resumption of directly elected local assemblies in 1995, administrative decentralization in 1996–1997 allowed local governments to formulate their own development plans instead of having to follow that of the central government. Specifically, local governments were authorized to reduce or increase up to 50 percent acquisition, registration, and property taxes as a means of securing funds for economic development in their jurisdictions. Local governments also were allowed to contact foreign central and local governments and business enterprises for various forms of cooperation without consulting the central government (Korea Foreign Trade Association [KOFTA], 1997). These policies were similar to those granted by the Chinese central government to authorities of selected coastal cities, including those on the Bohai rim.

The outcomes of these decentralization initiatives are mixed. On one hand, local governments and bureaucrats couldn't shake off their dependency on the central government and developed little initiative or sense of responsibility. They misused central funds, looked away from corruption, and spurred little grassroots entrepreneurship (Rozman, 2002). On the bright side, the pragmatic "west coast development plan," which was partly designed to strengthen economic ties with China's Bohai region, paid off in the 1990s, during which South Korea's west coast cities became important economic partners with Chinese cities across the Yellow Sea.

Decentralization in Japan: Late but with Regionalist Tendencies

While serious decentralization in South Korea started almost a decade behind China, Japan initiated its own decentralization and regionalist policies in the 1990s. Like South Korea, Japan was long entrenched in political and administrative centralization characterized by the concentration of power in the capital city. In early times, while there was some sort of center-local balance in Japan, the dominance of castle cities over their hinterlands and of lords over the townspeople allowed the gradual rise of and excessive centralization in Edo (Tokyo) as a primate center, which also became the world's largest city around 1800. Later, Japan's drive toward modernization as an imperial power not only was facilitated by centralized, top-down governance but also ended up strengthening it (see Rozman, 2002). This history left a strong inertia for the modern Japanese state to overcome in its decentralization efforts.

The wave of decentralization in Japan in the 1990s was more of a response to domestic concerns since the 1970s. Earlier on, the Japanese developmental state was successful in pushing through effective policies, as illustrated by the role of the Ministry of International Trade and Industry (MITI) in industrial planning (Johnson, 1982). However, there were emerging concerns that the central government had too much control over financial resources, ignored local issues regarding social welfare and environmental protection, and channeled disproportionate investment into the Tokyo metropolitan region. Many placed the blame for the economic troubles since 1990 on a lack of decentralization (Rozman, 1999, 2002).

The pressure for decentralization came to a head in 1993–1994 when the Morihiro government began to consider proposals from a subcommittee on decentralization. In May 1995, the cabinet of Tomiichi passed a decentralization law. In July 1995, the Ryutaro government established seven "regional power promotion commissions" in light of the decentralization law. The goals were to (1) enlarge the scope of power for regional and local authorities; (2) increase the flow of resources to regional and local authorities; and (3) disperse human resources to various regions (Li and Jin, 1999). In March 1998, the central government unveiled plans to reduce concentration in Tokyo, for example by creating four new axes of development around the country. These decentralization initiatives stimulated regionalist tendencies in autonomous development and external link-ups. The prefectures along the Sea of Japan from Tottori in southwestern Honshu to Hokkaido began to seek direct international opportunities in Northeast Asia based on their diverse regional and local strengths (Rozman, 1999).

Given its geographic proximity to South Korea and China's Bohai region, the Kyushu region is in a natural position to become an integral part of the BYSS. The two primary cities on the northern tip of the Kyushu Island—Fukuoka and Kitakyushu—have both claimed to be and served as the gateway to East Asia, with their extensive historical, commercial, and cultural ties to China and South Korea. Fukuoka has focused on developing inter-city cooperation in Northeast Asia by holding the first Asia-Pacific City Summit in 1994. In 1991, Kitakyushu proposed the idea of the East Asian City Conference, which included all the major cities in the BYSS (W. Kim, 2000). More recently, the prefectures and major cities of Kyushu have intensified their efforts to promote business ties with China and South Korea, highlighting the concentrated strength of the region's semiconductor industry, by organizing regular international trade fairs. This effort has been spearheaded by the Kyushu International Information Promotion Council (KIIPC), which is organized by and represents all local governments, trade associations, and businesses in Kyushu. The joint government-business effort was strengthened further in 2001, when the Kyushu Economy International (KEI) was established to promote the internationalization of Kyushu and its autonomous development through economic exchange with foreign countries, especially East Asian economies such as those of South Korea and China.[9] The two major cities of Fukuoka and Kitakyushu, which may be direct competitors for the title of largest city and for the dominant position in the region, agreed to be equal partners as formal members of KEI.

From Decentralization to Local Autonomy to Cross-Border Cooperation

The waves of decentralization hit the shores of all the subnational areas of the three countries involved in the BYSS during the 1980s and 1990s. Although decentralization in China's Bohai region has gone farther than South Korea and Japan, it has yielded less local autonomy than in the southeast coastal region. Decentralization in South Korea and Japan has engendered relatively little local autonomy, as local governments in both countries continue to depend on the central government and ministries for most of local budgets. This problem was more serious in South Korea, where people tend not to trust local governments and bureaucrats (Rozman, 2002). Without true local autonomy, decentralization lacks a crucial mechanism to transmit its positive effect on cross-border integration around the Yellow Sea.

As a solution, Rozman (2002) has called for decentralization to be combined with measures to take advantage of regionalism and globalization, such as conforming to the WTO environment, making borders more open to integrate with neighboring urban systems, and unleashing more local vitality through greater democratization. Although there is a clear need to move beyond just general decentralization principles and policies, the convergence toward decentralization, uneven and unsynchronized as it is, in China, South Korea, and Japan from the 1980s through 1990s has had some cumulative and complementary influence on the formation of the BYSS. The loosening of central government control has fostered some regionalist and local initiatives to promote trade and investment across the Yellow Sea. Whether inspired by these initiatives or not, the autarchic North Korea, with its west coast sitting on the Yellow Sea, and bordering China's Liaoning province to the north and South Korea to the south, announced in 2002 that it would establish a new special administrative region (SAR) at Sinujiu, opposite the Chinese border city of Dandong in Liaoning. While this attempt was in the spirit of decentralization, it has largely failed, for a variety of reasons, before it could become a node of the BYSS (see the book's Web page for a detailed account and analysis of the case).

Cross-Border Social Capital: Limited but Working

As cross-border social capital has been shown to be a strong force behind the success of the GSCS, the ways in which it manifests itself in other Asia-Pacific transborder subregions will provide comparative evidence on how much social capital really matters. We now subject the BYSS to the sociocultural lens to see whether the role of cross-border social capital is similar to or different from the GSCS.

Historical Links, Immigration Streams, and Citizenship Struggle

Just as historical Chinese emigration laid down the root of cross-border social capital in the GSCS, the economic and sociocultural ties between the cities in the BYSS today can be traced back many centuries. Beginning around 400 BCE, Korean farmers expanded into southwestern Japan, specifically the Kyushu region, and then advanced northeast up the Japanese archipelago (Diamond, 1999). During China's Tang Dynasty (618–907 CE), the United Shilla Period in Korea (668–935 CE), and Japan's imperial eras of Yamato (starting in the fifth century), Nara (710–794 CE), and Heian (794–1185 CE),[10] there was very active coastal trade and cultural ties among the three countries. The ancient port city of Hakata, now part of the city of Fukuoka in northern Kyushu, prospered as a free trade port, especially for trade with Korea across the Korea Strait through the sixteenth century (W. Kim, 2000). As the crossroads between Japan and China, Fukuoka was the place where Buddhism and tea were introduced from China to Japan. Shofuku-ji in Fukuoka, founded in 1195 by Eisai after years of study in China, is the oldest Zen temple in Japan. Korean captives were brought back to Fukuoka and responsible for starting up an important pottery industry, which is still around today.

The early migration of people across the Yellow Sea may date as far back as the Shang Dynasty (around the sixteenth to eleventh centuries BCE) when a small number of Chinese settled on the Korean peninsula. With continued Chinese migration over time, the number of Chinese living in Korea peaked at over 60,000 at one point. Just before the Communists' victory in China in 1949, there was another wave of emigrants, many of whom were affiliated with the Nationalist army, to Korea. About 95 percent of the Chinese immigrants to Korea trace their roots to Shandong province, especially the major cities of Yantai, Qingdao, and Weihai on the peninsula. During the Japanese occupation of Korea (1910–1945) and subsequent Korean regimes, the Chinese suffered discrimination, which forced many to return to China, while a large number left Korea for the United States, Taiwan, and Japan. While accounting for almost 10 percent of the total population of Incheon at the end of the nineteenth century, the local Chinese community shrunk considerably.[11]

The early Chinese immigrants who stayed and are still in Korea today, numbering approximately 30,000, are heavily concentrated in the port city of Incheon, which faces the Shandong peninsula. They have faced discriminatory attitudes and practices for a long time, especially under the past authoritarian regimes. The tax levied on the Chinese businesses was twice as high as that on Korean businesses. Even worse, the Chinese faced an almost insurmountable barrier in receiving Korean citizenship, which could be more easily obtained by those with a lot of money. Otherwise, the Chinese had to possess an advanced education and a high income, speak Korean, and have made contributions to Korean society. Any Chinese person who meets the above criteria for Korean citizenship would have to be recommended by two low-level civil servants and wait through a one-year probation period. Only after South Korea and China established diplomatic relations in 1992 did the South Korean government relax the criteria for Chinese to become citizens, but would only grant citizenship to Chinese born in Korea and reaching age 18. Despite this improved climate, it remains difficult for the older Chinese born in China to become citizens and thus receive equal treatment as Koreans. As a result, a number of them and their families in Incheon left for Taiwan and the United States.[12]

From the Old to the New:
The Revival of the Chinese Community in South Korea

Since 1992 the Chinese community in South Korea, small as it is, has experienced a revival for both internal and external reasons. After 1992, ethnic Chinese in South Korea were allowed to visit China directly instead of having to go through a third party. In the late 1990s, the Incheon municipal government decided to rebuild and expand its Chinatown, the only distinctive Chinese community left anywhere in South Korea today.[13] A documentary was produced on the mistreatment of ethnic Chinese, while a drama reminded

Koreans of the once prosperous Chinatown. These initiatives reflected the national and local governments' efforts to reverse the poor treatment of ethnic Chinese in South Korea in the past and to attract more tourists from China. The World Cup held in South Korea in 2002 provided another boost to a number of new construction projects for improving the Chinatown in Incheon, which drew a large number of Chinese soccer fans visiting as tourists.

The revival of the Chinese community in South Korea also has been fueled by the influx of new Chinese arrivals over the last few years. Numbering over 100,000, most of these Chinese, many of whom are ethnic Koreans in China, have come to take on various kinds of jobs in South Korean companies and factories through open advertising and hiring, with an increasing number taking up permanent residence. However, it is important to note that about half of these new Chinese have a college degree. This larger number of newly arrived Chinese has renewed the bond with the older Chinese in South Korea. Together they have started new social organizations and associations and strengthened existing ones. Through a collective effort and with strong support from the South Korean government in 2002, Chinese in South Korea were successful in winning the bid to hold the Eighth World Congress of Chinese Entrepreneurs in Seoul in 2005.[14]

The revival of the Chinese community in South Korea, especially its core in Incheon, has become an important catalyst in revitalizing historically based ethnic ties and native attachment across the Yellow Sea under more open and favorable political relations between China and South Korea.

Back to Native Places in China

Given the critically important role of ethnic Chinese ties in the GSCS, one wonders whether the more limited ethnic ties between China and South Korea make any difference to the BYSS. Like Hong Kong and Taiwanese investors in southeastern China, ethnic Chinese businesspeople in South Korea have shown a strong desire to return to their native places in coastal Shandong to do business. Their approaches to business opportunities reveal the specific constraints of a very small number of Chinese investors: for example, their highly limited financial resources and relatively little leverage in China. On the other hand, they demonstrate a common tendency among all overseas Chinese entrepreneurs in using important elements of cross-border social capital such as Chinese identity and a sense of attachment to native places to achieve business goals.

First of all, a number of ethnic Chinese in South Korea were among the earliest South Korean investors in China in the late 1980s. Mostly from the port city of Incheon, these Chinese tended to set up small-scale investment projects in the coastal cities of Shandong, just like the predominantly small and medium-sized South Korean firms. Although these small-scale Chinese investors had the advantage over their South Korean counterparts in understanding Chinese culture at the local level, they had a hard time running a successful business due to a lack of operating capital, limited economy of scale, and Chinese bureaucratic interference.[15]

The second approach of ethnic Chinese in South Korea in doing business in China is to become facilitators for small and medium-sized South Korean companies. These companies constitute the bulk of the total number of South Korean investment projects in China, as the average Korean investment project was just US$900,000 during the 1990s, a third the size of the average Korean investment in other countries.[16] While this is similar to the typically small investment ventures set up by Taiwanese and Hong Kong firms in southeastern China (see chapter 4), the difference is that the small and medium-sized Korean firms knew very little about the Chinese system and culture, which created a valuable opportunity for the ethnic Chinese living in South Korea. Some of the ethnic Chinese businesspeople originally came from the coastal cities and towns of Shandong and Liaoning provinces; because they knew the local customs and spoke the dialect, they became the needed contact and facilitator for negotiating and setting up investment projects for small and medium-sized South Korean companies. One of my informants in Incheon, whose Chinese roots go back to a coastal area of Shandong, gained some access to the then mayor of Dalian, who recognized his strong Shandong accent. With this kind of personal contact with municipal government officials and through convenient travel between Incheon and China's Bohai rim cities, he traveled back and forth frequently across the Yellow Sea and succeeded in helping a number of small and medium-sized South Korean companies establish investment projects in China.[17]

More ethnic Chinese were involved in this facilitator role, which is less risky and more flexible than the entrepreneurial type who would bring their limited capital from South Korea to invest in China. This facilitator role also involves some ethnic Chinese from South Korea serving as mid-level managers in Korean-run factories in China and being effective in bridging the cultural and communications gap between Chinese workers and senior Korean managers.[18] In a similar way but on a different scale, Japanese companies, both large and small, have preferred to invest in northeastern China, especially in the port city of Dalian, where a disproportionally large share of earlier Japanese capital was concentrated. This location preference reflects Japan's historical affinity with that region of China during the 1930s, despite the negative colonial rule of that period. There was even a special place attachment to the city of Dalian for some Japanese businesspeople.[19] This use of some elements of cross-border social capital by ethnic Chinese from South Korea and even

Japanese investors bears some resemblance to Taiwanese and Hong Kong businesspeople in Guangdong and Fujian provinces in the GSCS.

The Severe Limits of Social Capital: Small Numbers and Less Favorable Politics

The otherwise positive role of ethnic Chinese ties across the Yellow Sea is severely limited due to two factors. First of all, the population and capital bases of ethnic Chinese in South Korea are too small. With only 30,000 people, they don't come close to the scope of business interests from the millions of ethnic Chinese in Hong Kong and Taiwan. Since most of the ethnic Chinese in South Korea are relatively uneducated and operate small businesses such as restaurants and shops, they have too few resources to make as real an economic difference as the Hong Kong and Taiwanese investors. Even their limited strengths—local cultural knowledge, speaking the Chinese language with an appealing indigenous accent, and a sense of native places—have attenuated over time as large *chaebols* such as Samsung and Daewoo, which depend more on the merits of the projects (e.g., larger capitalization and more advanced technology) than on personal and social relations, began to invest heavily in China (X. Chen, 1998).

Second, because of their small numbers and limited economic influence, the national government and local authorities of Shandong have not implemented nearly the range of targeted, favorable policies for ethnic Chinese investors from South Korea as did the central state and the provincial and municipal governments in Guangdong and Fujian. Even though ethnic Chinese in South Korea may be pushed to invest in China for being treated unfavorably by the South Korean government, they find the heavy bureaucracy and lack of legal transparency in China difficult to deal with. They may only go so far in using their social and local connections without crossing the ambiguous and potentially dangerous borderline of resorting to gift-giving and even bribes. In contrast, Hong Kong and Taiwanese investors may get away with such tactics because they tend to deal with more market-oriented and flexible local officials and are capable of delivering bigger and more attractive business projects (see chapter 4). However, more recently, as South Korean businesses have become more agglomerated in Shandong's coastal cities, some of these municipal governments have begun to create special incentives and conveniences for all South Korean businesspeople and their families regardless of whether they are ethnic Chinese or not. These favors range from offering local TV news in Korean with a hired native Korean broadcaster to waiving tolls for South Korean businesspeople driving on inter-local highways, as well as waiving fees for schools and doctor visits for the family members of the South Korean investors with long-term local residence.[20] This bears resemblance to what some local governments in Guangdong (e.g., Dongguan) have done for the large number of Taiwanese businesspeople and their families (see chapter 4).

The evidence on the BYSS confirms the insight from the GSCS that cross-border social capital based on resilient ethnic and local place ties can play an important role in facilitating economic exchanges between incompatible political systems. However, it also demonstrates the limitations of these ties in the presence of other factors, which include the important role of cross-border transport infrastructure in overcoming the barrier effect of ocean boundaries in the BYSS.

Spanning the Bohai and Yellow Sea

Unlike the GSCS, which is joined by both sea and land borders, the BYSS's constituent units do not share land boundaries, except the two currently less important sections of land borders between the west coasts of South Korea and North Korea and between North Korea and the coastal region of Liaoning province. Therefore, trans-local sea links, which have multiplied rapidly, have played a stronger role thus far than air and land links in bridging economic interactions within the BYSS.

Cross-Border Sea Links: Direct and Extensive

As recently as the late 1980s, there were hardly any true transport links among the main regional and local units of the BYSS, especially between China and South Korea. China did not permit South Korean ships and crews to ship goods directly to China until 1988, but only ships that were registered with a third country and did not fly the South Korean flag (Yun, 1989). The onset of the 1990s, however, saw an accelerated growth of sea transport links between the major port cities in the BYSS, especially between key Chinese and South Korean cities.

The first China–South Korea passenger/cargo liner route began in 1990 between South Korea's second largest trading port of Incheon and the Chinese port city of Weihai on the tip of Shandong peninsula. This route marks the shortest distance between any pair of major Chinese and South Korean cities; it takes only 14 hours for a passenger or cargo liner to cover the 238 nautical miles between Incheon and Weihai. After inception, the Incheon-Weihai route carried a steadily growing number of passengers annually during 1992–1998 and remains the busiest of all the China–South Korea inter-city routes (see figure 5.2). By the late 1990s, a total of nine sea transport routes between Chinese and South Korean port cities were opened, with six of them involving Incheon (see appendix table 5.B). Some of these routes (e.g., Incheon-Tianjin) are more cargo than passengers oriented. Between 1995 and 1998, container shipments (both local and feeder) from South Korea to China on all the routes rose from 252,031 to 337,519 TEUs, a rise of 34 percent, while the shipments on all the China–South Korea routes grew less rapidly, from 317,258 to 392,711 TEUs (Ahn, 2003, p. 25). Given the increasing shipping flows between China and South Korea and the latter's continuing improvement of the infrastructure facilities on its west coast, smaller ports like Kunsan and Mokpo (see map 5.1) may grow faster than the traditionally dominant southeastern port of Pusan, which depends heavily on cargo and passenger links with Japan (see figure 5.2).

The emergence and expansion of these sea transport links have greatly facilitated passenger and cargo transport between the Chinese and South Korean west coast cities, among which the port city of Incheon has stood out as the central hub for China-related travel and trade (see the book's Web page). The Chinese city of Qingdao benefited very early from opening both sea and air links to South Korea. Qingdao's exports to South Korea soared from US$440,000 in 1990 to US$169 million in 1993 and topped US$1 billion in 1996 when South Korea surpassed Japan to become the city's largest export market (W. Kim, 2000, p. 37). The fast trade growth between specific Chinese and South Korean cities in the 1990s had a lot to do with the normalization of diplomatic relations in 1992 and the subsequent surge of South Korean investment in China's Bohai rim. However, the important carrying capacity of sea transport for the traded goods could not be ignored.

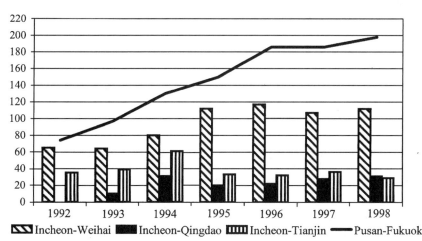

FIGURE 5.2
Passenger Liner Traffic Between Major Cities in the BYSS, 1992–1998

Compared to the China–South Korea sea links, China's Bohai rim has developed less extensive connections with Kyushu. The city of Qingdao in Shandong is linked with the port city of Shimonoseki on the southern tip of Honshu by a weekly ferry service, which carries cargo back and forth and brings a growing number of Chinese tourists to economically depressed Japan. This is borne out by the earlier figures on the rapid increase in the total number of Chinese nationals visiting Kyushu during 1995–2001. To accommodate this growing traffic from China, the Kagoshima prefectural government of Kyushu sent a Shibushi Port sales mission and a tourist mission to both Dalian and Shanghai in October 2001 to further promote the use of Shibushi Port, where ships from Dalian and Shanghai call (see map 5.1). The longer distance and thus higher transport cost only partly explains the somewhat slower growth of cross-sea links between China's Bohai rim and the Kyushu region, which indirectly reflects the much faster growth of China–South Korean trade and investment and tourism during that period of time.

Air and Land Links Across and Within Borders

Given the spatial composition of the BYSS, air links are almost as important as sea links in fostering cross-border subregional economic and human interactions, while the role of land links is much more limited. The network of air routes among the constituent units of the BYSS is more balanced than in the GSCS, in which direct air links between mainland China and Taiwan do not yet exist (see chapter 4). However, international routes in the BYSS are unevenly distributed among the major cities. While few cities are connected with frequent flights, other major cities are not yet linked. According to statistics compiled by Kim (2000, p. 76), there are 28 flights per week between Fukuoka and Seoul, the most of any routes. The Seoul-Beijing route follows with 21 flights per week, whereas the Seoul-Qingdao route is third with 14 flights. While there are only four flights between Fukuoka and Qingdao, the least frequent of the international routes, such major Chinese cities as Tianjin were not yet connected with either Seoul or Fukuoka.

If the GSCS is a reference case, the integration and growth of a transborder subregion may depend on the construction of major new airports with large and modern facilities that can accommodate heavy cross-border passenger flows. This critical component of cross-border transport infrastructure has taken shape in the BYSS through the construction of Incheon International Airport, which opened in March 2001. Costing US$5.5 billion, this airport was the largest infrastructure project ever undertaken in South Korea (see the book's Web page).

Despite its accelerated growth after 1992, the number of air passengers on the South Korea–China route was about 1.1 million and about 6.1 million on the South Korea–Japan route in 1998 (Ahn, 2003). By the peak travel season of summer 2002, however, China had surpassed Japan to receive the largest number of flights from the Incheon airport. There were 2,285 flights from Incheon to Chinese cities between July 19 and August 11, 2002, up 281 flights from the same period of the preceding year, while there were 2,124 flights to Japanese cities, down from 2,186. The number of South Korean air travelers from Incheon to China rose 9.3 percent to 405,127 during the summer peak season, whereas the number flying to Japan declined 9.2 percent to 433,204 (Incheon International Airport [IIA], 2002). This recent growth, especially in air traffic to and from China, may have provided early supporting evidence to the Incheon airport's claim to become Northeast Asia's new air hub in light of South Korea's favorable location.[21] Besides location, the Incheon airport has other comparative advantages against other major airports in Northeast Asia and East Asia (see the book's Web page).

Despite a slower pace, the development of land transport links across and within borders has accompanied the development of the BYSS. Following the June 2000 summit between the two Koreas, the South Korean government broke ground in September 2000 to reconnect the railroad links between South and North Korea. This project began with repairs on the track linking Seoul to Pyongyang and onward to Sinujiu on the border with the Chinese city of Dandong. While this project was delayed due to continued political tension in inter-Korean relations and North Korea's foot-dragging, in September 2002 the two Koreas made renewed efforts to reconnect the rail links by starting to clear land mines inside the Demilitarized Zone (DMZ). When completed, the reopened railroad link could facilitate the opening of the North Korean city of Kaesong as a new special economic zone (see the book's Web page for details), just across the DMZ, to foreign investment and the development of the North Korean port city of Nampo on the Yellow Sea. As an example of the less ambitious within-border land links, South Korea had been building, as part of the "west coast development plan," a new coastal superhighway from Incheon through Kunsan and Mokpo to Sunchon, totaling 505 km (F. Li, 1996). Across the Yellow Sea, the Shandong government has since 1998 invested nearly US$8 billion annually in constructing inter-city superhighways, which exceeded 2,000 km by the end of 2000, ranking first among all the provinces of China.[22]

Uneven Transport Lines, Inter-Modal Links, and Inter-City Competition Versus Cooperation in the BYSS

The development of a transport infrastructure in the BYSS encompasses direct cross-border links and inter-local tie-ups near the international boundaries by the shores, in the air, and on land. The unevenly spaced and distributed links in this transport network are not unusual, as this huge subregion is intersected by large water distances among the territorial units. A more important factor in the integration of the BYSS may be inter-modal transport links and spin-off development projects at and between the key cities, due to their location advantages and existing transport facilities and capacities. As part of South Korea's vision to become the business hub for Northeast Asia, the government has planned to turn Incheon into a logistic hub, given its existing and projected facilities (see the book's Web page).

The rising importance of Incheon as an air and sea passenger/freight hub in East Asia on the Yellow Sea shore does not overshadow similar developments at and between major port cities across the water on China's Bohai rim. Four of China's largest container ports (Tanggu, Tianjin, Dalian, and Qingdao) are clustered here, and three of them have been expanding their berths and cargo handling capacities. The Chinese government has decided to build a rail ferry route as an ocean-land corridor across Bohai Bay, linking Dalian at the southern tip of the Liaoning peninsula with Yantai at the northern end of the Shandong peninsula (see map 5.1). The route over water is about 400 to 1,000 km shorter than existing railway routes, which make a circuitous loop on land through Beijing and Tianjin. Given the shorter distance and cost savings for customers, the Chinese government expected that the project would attract overseas investors to help finance the estimated construction cost of US$370 million.[23] More significantly, the city of Tianjin, with the assistance of the central government, has completed two rail lines that can transport container cargo from its port directly to other parts of China. Mongolia has already switched to using this new sea-rail-land bridge to ship its cargo out through the Tianjin port, while the bulk of container cargo from the United States, South Korea, and Japan for Mongolia has been moved along this route through northern China.[24]

While this simultaneous expansion of more inter-modal transport links around the Bohai/Yellow Sea rim provides better and faster connections between the major coastal cities and their hinterlands, it may have strengthened a competitive tendency among the few largest centers to reach the position and functional influence of the regional hub. To be successful, Incheon has already adopted specific strategies, such as offering lower landing fees, in order to capture more of the transit cargo from China. However, the Chinese city of Tianjin remains a top competitor for hub status because of its larger size, well-established port, and growing connectivity through inter-modal transportation to China's vast interior market. Fukuoka also has been strengthening its historical position as Japan's "gateway" to China and South Korea through coordinated government-business initiatives (discussed earlier).

As this competition has heated up, "cool heads" have advocated more cross-border and trans-local cooperation among the major cities in the subregion.

Based on its more central location between Japan and China, the Seoul-Incheon region should and could play a more active role in facilitating regional cooperation (W. Kim, forthcoming). Given the heavy clustering of large and important coastal cities with extensive port, air, and land transport facilities and links, trans-local competition and cooperation appear as inevitably co-existing and mutually reinforcing trends. How to balance and manage them by national and local governments is key to the long-term growth and integration of the BYSS.

A Dynamic Transborder Subregion in the Making

If the GSCS is already a fully integrated transborder subregion, particularly in economic and spatial terms, the BYSS is not far from becoming one, because both share a few fundamental similarities despite some important differences. The three main portions of the BYSS involve subnational regional or local units of China, South Korea, and Japan, as opposed to the only subnational region (China's Guangdong and Fujian provinces) in the GSCS. Just as Macau is a much less important fourth member of the GSCS, except for its air transit position between mainland China and Taiwan, the west coast of North Korea is marginal at best, at least for the time being. Yet it is worth noting that traffic between Incheon and the North Korean port of Nampo has increased following improved relations between the two Koreas over the last few years.

The first analytical lens has revealed that the BYSS has created and sustains the kind, if not the scope, of economic complementarity and synergy that permeate the GSCS. The relative positions of China, South Korea, and Japan lend clarity to three overlapped levels and nexuses of cross-border economic links. At one level, the surplus capital from both South Korea and Japan has flown heavily into the geographically adjacent Bohai region of China for low-cost production. At another level, the BYSS features the spatial concentration of South Korean manufacturing investment on the Shandong peninsula. The third level of connections involves the manufacturing and trade of such high-tech products as semiconductors between the Kyushu region and South Korea that have begun to incorporate China. The cross-border production links in the BYSS, even the China–South Korean nexus, are less oriented to the global market than the GSCS. Nevertheless, the BYSS has grown rapidly through a blend of comparative economic advantages and varied links among national, regional, and global markets.

Viewed from the de-centering state lens, economic growth and integration of the BYSS have been strongly facilitated by the common tendency toward decentralization with uneven local autonomy in all three countries over time.

Although varying in the mechanism of decentralization and the resulting degree of regional and local autonomy, the regional and local governments of China, and Japan and South Korea to a lesser extent, have become more actively and directly involved in initiating and implementing some locally oriented development strategies. This domestic policy shift, belated and more limited in South Korea than in China and Japan, has contributed to cross-border, trans-local economic cooperation across the BYSS.

From the lens of cross-border social capital, the BYSS is a much less convincing case than the GSCS. Despite close historical ties and geographic proximity among the three countries across the Yellow Sea, the much limited immigration and weaker ethnic Chinese ties between China and South Korea, coupled with colonial legacy and discriminatory domestic politics, have restricted the role of social capital in cross-border economic interactions. However, the way in which ethnic Chinese ties have mattered to China–South Korean trade and investment resembles that phenomenon in the GSCS. Taking advantage of their native-place origin in Shandong's coastal region and being able to speak Mandarin Chinese with a Shandong accent, some ethnic Chinese from South Korea secured personal access to local Chinese government officials and thus facilitated business negotiation and approval for small and medium-sized South Korean investors. In this sense, the BYSS has reinforced the GSCS in supporting the argument that cross-border social capital is capable of bridging business transactions between politically incompatible systems that are spatially parts of the same transborder subregion.

Finally, the BYSS provides as equally striking an illustration as the GSCS of the critical function of a cross-border, inter-city transport infrastructure for the integration of a transborder subregion. The BYSS is tied together through almost exclusively ocean boundaries across a larger number of more populous cities over wider geographic distances than those in the GSCS. These natural barriers, however, have largely fallen, due to the development of extensive sea and air links among most of the major cities, especially nodal cities like Incheon and Tianjin, which are free of the kind of official ban on transport links across the Taiwan Strait. As the BYSS illustrates, if a large-scale cross-border transport network can cover multiple subnational territories of geographic contiguity or adjacency, it facilitates frequent and efficient border-crossing economic interactions and people movements that are essential to a transborder subregion.

In the BYSS context, the overall configuration and relative importance of the factors revealed through the four analytical lenses lend support to the harmonious hypothesis in chapter 3, albeit in a different way from the GSCS. In the BYSS, local autonomy and cross-border social capital add only favorable political and cultural stimuli to the powerful economic and infrastructure links for the BYSS. Economic synergy in the BYSS is weaker than in the GSCS, partly because the tight spatial integration over the Hong Kong–Guangdong boundary and Hong Kong's gateway role have compensated for the lack of direct sea and air links across the Taiwan Strait. Local autonomy and cross-border social capital in the BYSS also carry less weight in facilitating economic and spatial integration than in the GSCS. Intrigued by how these factors interact and intersect in another context, I now turn to the Greater Tumen Subregion in the next chapter.

Notes

1. China's Bohai region has both a narrower and a broader spatial boundary. The narrower or inner area includes Beijing and Tianjin and about 30 municipalities and their immediate hinterlands within Liaoning, Hebei, and Shandong provinces (see Wang, Zhang, and Yang, 1995, p. 15, for the names of the cities). This area, which I label the "Bohai Belt," wraps around the Bohai Sea rim like a big letter "C" or a necklace. It encompasses about 172,600 sq km and about 68 million people. The broader region, which I label the "Greater Bohai," is bounded by Liaoning, Hebei, and Shandong provinces plus Beijing and Tianjin. The Greater Bohai covers 520,000 sq km, approximately 100 cities of varied sizes, and a combined population of 198 million (China Bohai Region Economic Research Association [CBRERA], 1991).

2. What I have delineated as the BYSS is similar to the Yellow Sea Subregion (YSSR) defined by Won Bae Kim (2000), which includes China's Bohai region, the western part of the Korean peninsula (including North Korea), and the southwestern part of Japan. I differ somewhat from Kim regarding the constituent units in that I focus more specifically on the links between China's Bohai Belt and South Korea's west coast, while giving less attention to the China-Japan and Korea-Japan dyads. This approach is analytically analogous to my focus on the dyadic ties between Hong Kong and Guangdong/Fujian and Taiwan and Fujian/Guangdong in chapter 4.

3. "The China market: How Korean firms found a gold mine on the mainland," accessed from the *South China Morning Post* website, scmp.com, on March 24, 2003.

4. Reported in *Renmin Ribao* (The People's Daily), overseas edition, February 20, 2003, p. 3.

5. "China to overtake Korea in tech competitiveness within four years," *Korean Times*, January 29, 2003, accessed on April 10, 2003, at the paper's website, times.hankooki.com/lpage/tech/.

6. According to the rank-size distribution, or "Zipf's Law," after George Kingsley Zipf (Zipf, 1941), there is a remarkable regularity in the distribution of city sizes over the world. This distribution exhibits itself graphically through a smooth slope based on a log-linear relationship between city rank and city size (measured in number of people) if one calculates the natural logarithm of the rank and of the city size and plots the resulting data in a diagram. If the largest city or top-ranked city is disproportionally larger than the second largest or ranked city and other cities below it in a city system, the largest city is labeled a "primate city" and the city system may be characterized as immature and by the cities other than the largest one falling below the log-normal line (see X. Chen, 1991, for different applications of the rank-size rule to China's city system).

7. South Korea's west coast includes Kyonggi-man, Chungchong-Namdo (Chungnam), Cholla-Bugdo (Chonbuk), and part of Cholla-Namdo (Chonnam). The west coast, especially Cholla-Namdo, was long neglected by the central-government-driven development policy. In the mid-1980s, per capita income for Cholla-Namdo in the southwest ranked third from the

bottom among the nine provinces and five major cities in South Korea, earning Cholla-Namdo the nickname of the "neglected corner" (F. Li, 1996). For some detailed statistics on the uneven geographic distribution of industrial output and employment across the provinces and cities of South Korea through the mid-1980s, see Wessel (1997).

8. I am thankful to SangWon Lee for sharing this information and observation with me.

9. Some of the formal members of KEI are six prefectures (including Fukuoka, Nagasaki, and Oita), the cities of Fukuoka and Kitakyushu, and 10 other quasi-government agencies such as the Japan Tourist Association Kyushu Branch and Fukuoka Convention and Visitor Bureau. KEI also includes eight supporting organizations such as the Development Bank of Japan Kyushu Branch and Japan National Tourist Organization. The two advisors to KEI are the Kyushu Bureau of Economy, Trade, and Industry and the Kyushu Bureau of Transport (KEI, 2002a).

10. I thank Jeffrey Broadbent and Young Cho for helping me identify the specific years covered by these periods in ancient Korea and Japan.

11. Extracted from an in-depth report on the ethnic Chinese in South Korea, *Renmin Ribao* (The People's Daily), overseas edition, October 31, 2002, p. 4.

12. A noticeable sign of the declining Chinatown in Incheon is the size of the graduating class of the local Chinese high school, which shrunk from about 150 students 20 years ago to only 40–50 students recently. More and more high school graduates now go to Taiwan and the United States for college rather than staying in South Korea. A Chinese high school in Seoul has experienced a similar decline in enrollment. The author's interview with an informant in Incheon, July 1999.

13. For example, the old "China Street" in Pusan, which was reinaugurated on October 2, 2002, has lost much of its Chinese character. While a few old-generation Chinese were still operating restaurants, almost all the younger residents could not find adequate jobs and have left. Now 80–90 percent of the businesses on the "China Street" in downtown Pusan are owned and run by foreigners, many of whom are Russians from Vladivostok. There are Russian waitresses in the karaoke bars, and the menus in the Chinese restaurants include Russian translations. Reported by *Renmin Ribao* (The People's Daily), November 7, 2002, p. 5.

14. Reported in *Renmin Ribao* (The People's Daily), overseas edition, February 12, 2002, p. 15; May 5, 2003, p. 5.

15. For example, the father of an informant in Incheon started a small furniture business in the coastal city of Yantai in 1989, but the operation struggled financially and thus failed to realize the presumed advantage of being an ethnic Chinese venture. The author's interview in Incheon, July 1999.

16. "The China market," scmp.com, accessed on March 24, 2003.

17. The author's telephone interview with an ethnic Chinese businessman who spoke with a heavy Shandong accent in Incheon, July 1999.

18. My thanks to Dr. Kim Won Bae in Seoul for supplying this example.

19. When Japan controlled China's three northeastern provinces of Heilongjiang, Jilin, and Liaoning as Manchuria, it designated the city of Dalian as a separate and special Japanese prefecture that was somewhat independent from Manchuria and much closer to Japan. Some middle-aged Japanese businessmen who either were born in Dalian and its vicinity or whose fathers were stationed there have returned to do business and also to renew their roots by visiting their old houses. My thanks to Nian Song (a native of Dalian) for this information.

20. The municipal government of Rushan City, near the city of Weihai, in Shandong, has adopted this range of practices to accommodate the interests and needs of the over 1,000 South Koreans living locally, a group that includes factory owners, schoolteachers, and translators (mostly ethnic Chinese from South Korea). Reported in *Renmin Ribao* (The People's Daily), overseas edition, August 30, 2003, p. 8.

21. South Korea is located between Japan—the center of the "Pacific Ocean economy"—and China, which is the center of the newly emerging "continental economy." Given this location, the South Korean government unveiled a blueprint in 2002 to make South Korea a business hub for Northeast Asia to serve as a bridge between the Pacific Ocean economy and the continental economy (Ahn, 2003). Incheon in turn is specifically located at the intersection of the trunk routes between North America and China, with more than 30 cities of a population in excess of one million within one and a half hours' flying time.

22. Figures from *Renmin Ribao* (The People's Daily), overseas edition, November 9, 2000, p. 2.

23. Reported in "Ocean corridor on the cards," *Business Weekly*, May 14–20, 2002, p. 9.

24. Reported in *Renmin Ribao* (The People's Daily), overseas edition, December 19, 2002, p. 2.

6

Spanning Socialist and Post-Socialist Borders

The Greater Tumen Subregion and Beyond

ESPITE SOME IMPORTANT DIFFERENCES between the Greater Southeast China
Subregion (GSCS) and the Bohai/Yellow Sea Subregion (BYSS), the similar features and success of both have gone some way toward validating the
synthetic explanation based on the interaction among the factors associated
with the four analytical lenses. This chapter focuses the lenses on the Greater
Tumen Subregion (GTS) to show how important differences in the key factors
have shaped the GTS into a very different transborder subregion. The goal is
to demonstrate, through the four lenses, that the main variations among the
three primary cases can be accounted for by how the factors of the framework
interact temporally.

Compared with either the GSCS or the BYSS, the GTS is more difficult and arbitrary to define in that it could include several concentric spatial, economic, and
political boundaries. At the innermost core is a small triangle anchored on the
border city of Hunchun in China's Jilin province, the border port city of Sonbong
of North Korea, and the port city of Posyet in the Khasan region of the Russian
Far East (RFE), all located within a radius of 40–50 km from the estuary of the
Tumen River. This zone of 1,000 sq km was originally labeled the Tumen River
Economic Zone (TREZ) when the United Nations Development Programme
(UNDP) began its involvement in the Tumen River development project in the
early 1990s. It was enlarged into a bigger triangular region called the Tumen River
Economic Development Area (TREDA) in 1994.[1] Covering approximately 10,000
sq km, the TREDA is bounded at its apexes by the Chinese border city of Yanji,
the North Korean port city of Chongjin, and Vladivostok and Nakhodka in the
RFE, located within 80–120 km of the estuary of the Tumen River (see map 6.1).

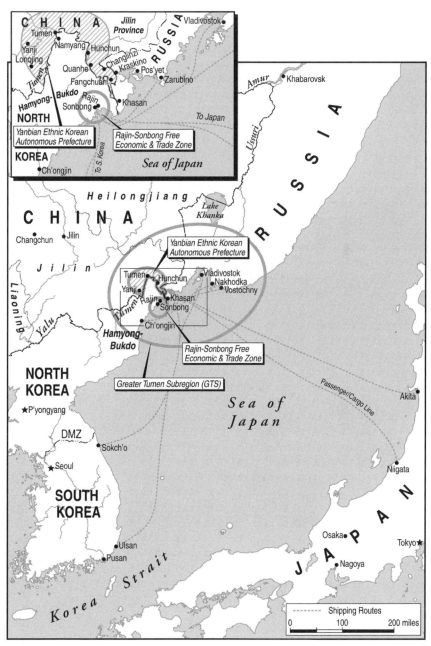

MAP 6.1
The Greater Tumen Subregion (GTS) and Beyond

The hinterlands of the TREDA would envelope the bulk of China's Jilin and Heilongjiang provinces, the entire Hamgyong-Bukdo of North Korea (a provincial-level administrative unit bordering Jilin province), and the southern portions of Primorskii Krai (Maritime Territory), Khabarovsk Krai, and Amurskaia Oblast (all provincial administrative units) within the RFE. On a still larger scale, the TREDA and its hinterlands constitute the spatial core of economic cooperation in Northeast Asia among northeastern China, North Korea, South Korea, the RFE, Mongolia (especially its eastern part), and Japan along the Sea of Japan (see Fukagawa, 1997; Marton, McGee, and Paterson, 1995).

By using the term Greater Tumen Subregion, I focus primarily on the transborder delta space spanning the riparian parts of China, North Korea, and the RFE covered by the Tumen River,[2] as well as some portions of its hinterlands as defined above. As it is, the GTS covers roughly 37,200 sq km and 3–4 million people (Ding, 1993).[3] As with the GSCS and the BYSS, I begin by examining the GTS through the global-local economic nexus lens.

Socialist Interactions in the Capitalist World Economy

Compared with the GSCS and the BYSS, the GTS is much less connected with the global economy, primarily because it comprises mainly the border and hence peripheral areas of three socialist and post-socialist countries: China, Russia, and North Korea. To gauge the extent to which the parts of these countries in the GTS are linked to the global economy, we first examine trade among China, Russia, and North Korea as they have evolved from closed and planned economies through reforms toward more open and market oriented economies.

No More Camaraderie Trade?

Since the early 1980s, trade between China, Russia, and North Korea has exhibited trajectories that parallel major changes in their political and economic relations. Trade between China and the former Soviet Union from the late 1970s to the early 1980s was limited, which reflected the political conflict and military tension between the two communist countries at the time. Bilateral trade rose rapidly after 1982 when the two countries resumed normal relations. Despite a drop after 1993, China-Russian trade remained the largest volume of the three trading dyads at a steady level (see appendix table 6.A).

Trade between China and North Korea mirrors the fairly steady political relationship between the two countries and China's continued support for North Korea even after China began to deviate from the orthodox socialist path and distance itself somewhat from its socialist neighbor around 1980. Historically,

China was North Korea's second largest patron after the former Soviet Union, delivering nearly US$900 million in assistance to North Korea between 1948 and 1984. Since the early 1990s when North Korea–Russian relations began to decline, China has supplied about one-third of North Korea's imports, especially oil and grains. Moreover, China provided a certain portion of the oil and grains on a concessional or "friendly prices" basis (Noland, 1996). However, China began to abolish some friendly prices for its trade with North Korea in the early 1990s (Goto, 1999), signaling that the era of camaraderie trade between two "socialist brethren" was coming to an end. This change in the terms of trade contributed to the worsening of China–North Korean trade in the second half of the 1990s. However, realizing that North Korea would be unable or unwilling to meet hard currency cash payments, China waived North Korea's debt in friendly prices for oil and food and has remained the leader in humanitarian assistance and the largest trading partner for North Korea (see Kim and Lee, 2002).

Camaraderie trade between North Korea and the former Soviet Union came to a more abrupt end in 1991 when the latter disintegrated. Historically, the former Soviet Union was North Korea's principal patron and largest trading partner ahead of China. Between 1948 and 1984, the former Soviet Union provided North Korea with US$2.2 billion in aid and credits. Like China, the former Soviet Union sold oil to North Korea at below world market prices but stopped doing so after 1990. In the mid-1980s, the former Soviet Union also demanded that North Korea repay the accumulated credits until the entire debt was paid off (Noland, 1996). The political collapse of the Soviet Union and the ensuing economic crisis in Russia in the early 1990s led to a significant decline in North Korea–Russian trade and its share in North Korea's total trade (see appendix table 6.A). The Yeltsin administration then also ended transfers of military equipment and technology to Pyongyang and ceased economic and scientific cooperation, and even direct flights, while in response Pyongyang refused to pay a 4 billion ruble loan (Wishnick, 2002).

Aside from the domestic political change and economic reforms in China and Russia, the increasing participation of these two countries in the global economy and its competitive pressure has contributed to their varied withdrawal of support for and trade with North Korea. As the three countries stopped trading with one another as "close comrades" at the national level, they became closer trading partners as territorial neighbors across their joint borders in Northeast Asia.

Jilin's Border Trade with North Korea

Border trade between China's Jilin province and North Korea sheds light on the opportunities and constraints facing the GTS, as this trade flows between a number of important Chinese and North Korean border cities on both sides of the Tumen River. As table 6.1 shows, trade between Jilin province and North Korea grew rapidly from a small base in 1982. During 1954–1970, trade between Jilin and North Korea was largely confined to small-scale bartering between the Yanbian Korean Autonomous Prefecture (which is over 40 percent ethnic Korean) of Jilin province and the Hamgyong-Bukdo of North Korea. Due to China's Cultural Revolution, this trade was suspended from 1970 until 1982, when Jilin province resumed both border trade and local barter trade with North Korea. Between 1982 and 1990, border and barter trade was conducted in Swiss francs, and Jilin exported mostly lumber, rice, rubber, steel, and metal products, while North Korea's exports included seafood products, fruits, steel, and fertilizer (Shi and Yu, 1995).

The period 1991–1994 saw the most rapid growth of Jilin–North Korean trade, now conducted in U.S. dollars (see table 6.1). The number of traded items went from eight in 1982 to 217 in 1987 and to 230 in 1994. The number of Chinese and North Korean companies involved in trade rose from 20 in 1991 to over 110 in 1994. The volume of trade between Yanbian and North Korea surged from US$75 million in 1991 to US$310 million in 1993. The latter figure accounted for nearly 70 percent of Yanbian's total foreign trade (Lawrence, 1999) and about 60 percent of Jilin's total trade with North Korea that year (Shi and Yu, 1995).

Trade between North Korea and Jilin, especially Yanbian, began to contract in the second half of 1994 and dropped sharply in 1995 (see table 6.1). The floods in North Korea, coupled with economic mismanagement, severely reduced the short list of commodities (e.g., rice) that could be exported to Jilin. The problem of North Korean trading companies being late in payments for Chinese exports got worse due to a severe shortage of cash. The proportion of North Korean traders who could deliver goods and cash contractually dropped below 20 percent. The Chinese central government withdrew the favorable policy of the 50 percent tax on imports through local barter trade, which led Jilin province to reduce its trade with North Korea. The unstable markets for steel and automobiles in China also contributed to the slowdown in Jilin's import of North Korean steel and cars that were made in Russia and Poland and transshipped through North Korea (Shi and Yu, 1995). By 1996, trade between North Korea and Yanbian declined to US$27 million and rose only slightly to US$32 million in 1998 (Lawrence, 1999).

To jump-start the sluggish border trade, the Chinese government introduced new incentives for small-quantity border trade in 1996. In 1997, Jilin and North Korean border authorities agreed to establish a free market in a North Korean town on the border to facilitate barter trade. Opening once a week, the free market yielded transactions worth about US$63,000 on most trading days (Chen and Ding, 1999). By allowing private economic transactions in the

TABLE 6.1

Jilin Province's Trade with North Korea and the Soviet Union (Russia), 1982–1995

Year	North Korea[a]			Russia[b]		
	Total Trade	Export	Import	Total Trade	Export	Import
1982	103	52	51	—	—	—
1983	1,199	664	535	—	—	—
1984	4,445	2,110	2,335	—	—	—
1985	10,987	5,758	5,229	—	—	—
1986	8,656	4,472	4,184	—	—	—
1987	12,772	6,726	6,046	—	—	—
1988	**15,796**	**7,870**	**7,926**	**1,210**	**687**	**532**
	(15.5)	**(10.4)**	**(31.5)**	**(1.2)**	**(0.9)**	**(2.1)**
1989	22,856	11,175	11,681	8,221	5,988	2,233
1990	14,802	8,152	6,650	11,124	5,368	5,756
1991	**9,271**	**4,843**	**4,428**	**11,478**	**5,890**	**5,588**
	(6.9[c])	**(4.7)**	**(11.7)**	**(8.2)**	**(5.7)**	**(14.7)**
1992	23,400	11,200	12,200	16,400	1,700	14,700
		(8.6)	(19.1)		(12.9)	(22.9)
1993	47,126	22,960	24,165	—	—	—
	(15.8)					
1994	45,500	25,300	20,200	55,600	31,300	24,300
1995	11,000	7,300	3,700	—	8,000	—

Sources: Compiled from Fu (1998), pp. 410–411; Fukagawa (1997), table 3.5; Li, Zhu, and He (1997), p. 37; Liu and Liao (1993), tables 3 and 4; and Shi and Yu (1995), table 1.

[a]The figures prior to 1991 are in 10,000 Swiss francs, which had a roughly 1:1 exchange rate with the U.S. dollar. The figures for 1991 through 1994 are in 10,000 U.S. dollars.

[b]Data before 1991 pertain to the former Soviet Union.

[c]The figures in parentheses for 1988 and 1991 are percentages of the province's total foreign trade.

border area against North Korea's mounting debt and the bankruptcy of some Chinese companies from North Korean defaults on debts, China ended up subsidizing border trade with North Korea (Kim and Lee, 2002). While China–North Korean border trade reached US$24 million in the first half of 1997, rising nine times over the same period of 1996 (Fu, 1998), the heyday of border trade across the Jilin–North Korea border appears to have passed.

Border Trade with the RFE

Border trade between China and the RFE constitutes another critical economic nexus of regional and local development and trans-local economic cooperation within the GTS and even beyond. Unlike China–North Korean border trade, China-RFE border trade occurs more heavily across the long boundary between China's Heilongjiang province and the RFE. While most Heilongjiang-RFE border trade takes place between border cities located either near or far away from the Tumen River, it has a great economic influence on the hinterlands of the GTS.

As table 6.2 indicates, China was by far the most important trading partner with the RFE between 1988 and 1992, with Japan as the close second. The

TABLE 6.2
Percentage Barter and Border Trade Between the
Russian Far East (RFE) and China and Japan, 1988–1992

	Year				
Country	1988	1989	1990	1991	1992
1. Total	100.0%	100.0%	100.0%	100.0%	100.0%
China	56.8	87.8	78.3	86.6	58.0
Japan	42.5	5.4	7.6	11.9	26.6
Other countries	0.7	6.8	14.1	1.5	15.4
2. Barter trade					
(of total above)	21.2	92.4	95.2	97.6	93.3
China	21.2	85.5	77.7	86.5	58.0
Japan	—	—	3.5	9.8	20.1
Other countries	—	6.6	14.0	1.3	15.2
3. Coastal (border) trade					
(of total above)	77.8	7.6	4.8	2.4	6.7
China	35.6	2.0	0.6	0.1	0.0
Japan	42.5	5.4	4.1	2.1	6.5
Other countries	0.7%	0.2%	0.1%	0.2%	0.2%

Source: Adapted from Liu (1995), table 16.
Note: The total (1) was broken down into barter trade (2) and coastal (border) trade (3).

overwhelming proportion of the RFE's trade involved barter trade after 1988, and China accounted for the bulk of that barter trade. Although the gap between China and Japan in barter trade with the RFE began to narrow in 1992, China, especially Heilongjiang, remained the most dominant partner in cross-border barter trade with the RFE through most of the 1990s.

After the normalization of China-Soviet political and economic relations in 1982, cross-border trade rose from about US$16 million in 1983 to US$720 million in 1990. The collapse of the former Soviet Union in 1991 and its subsequent economic crisis, especially the severe shortage of daily necessities, pushed up demand for Chinese goods. Rapid growth of the Chinese economy, coupled with a further loosening of border trade policies, enhanced exports. In 1993, Heilongjiang's border trade with the RFE reached US$2 billion, which accounted for one-third of China's trade with Russia. In 1993, Heilongjiang's border trade with the RFE rose to 57 percent of China's total border trade with Russia, from 21 percent in 1987 (J. Wang, 1999, p. 170).

The end of 1993 saw the beginning of the slide in border trade that lasted through 1997. By year-end 1997, trade at and through all border crossings along the Heilongjiang-RFE boundary had halved from its peak in 1993 (Chen and Ding, 1999). There were several reasons for this negative turn. From the Chinese side, the macroeconomic control, greatly curtailed credits, and weakened real estate sector reduced demand for raw materials such as the Russian steel for construction. The RFE, on the other hand, began to raise prices for Chinese consumer goods, which made local exports from and re-exports through Heilongjiang less profitable. The risk of bartering in cross-border trade tended to lower mutual trust between Chinese and Russian traders. Finally, based on the perception that the large number of Chinese traders crossing the border posed a threat and that certain Chinese products were inferior,[4] local authorities in the RFE tightened border control by introducing more stringent visa requirements for Chinese traders (J. Wang, 1999, also see Rozman, 1998a, 1998b).

The third economic dyad of the GTS, the fairly active border trade between the RFE and North Korea, dwindled in the late 1980s and early 1990s, paralleling the decline in bilateral economic and political relations. By the mid-1990s, however, regional leaders in the RFE refocused on improving economic cooperation with North Korea. This policy turn helped sustain the trade of Primorskii Krai in the RFE, which borders on North Korea, with the latter at a slightly fluctuating annual level of US$2–3 million through the 1990s. While North Korea depended on the exports of food products and timber from the RFE, the regions of Amur Oblast, Sakhalin Oblast, and Primorskii Krai recently have hired 5,000 North Korean farm workers on contracts to lower local food prices by stepping up farm production.[5] Some joint ventures between North Korea and Primorskii Krai in seaweed processing also developed, but large projects were more difficult due to a lack of financing (Wishnick, 2002).

From Border Cities to Frontier Growth Centers and Beyond

A salient economic feature of a less integrated and developed transborder subregion is the rise of marginal and sleepy border towns to the status of frontier trade and growth centers. During this process, they may become (1) nodes in a cross-border regional economic network with potential global ties, and (2) gateways for channeling cross-border economic flows into the respective hinterlands of within-country border regions. We examine three selected cities in the GTS as illustrative cases below.

The Chinese City of Hunchun: A Potential Central Node for the GTS?

The border city of Hunchun in China's Jilin province is arguably the most important city in the GTS, primarily because of its uniquely favorable geographic location. Centrally situated at the trilateral borders of China, North Korea, and the RFE, Hunchun has the closest and most convenient access to the railroad and road terminuses near the North Korean and RFE borders and through them to all major North Korean and RFE ports.[6] Thanks to its location advantages, particularly its previous access to the sea, Hunchun had a long history as a frontier center for trade with Japan, Korea, and Russia.[7] This prosperous ocean trade ended in 1938 when Japan unilaterally imposed a blockade on shipping on the Tumen River from Hunchun to the Sea of Japan.

From 1949 to the mid-1980s, at the time a rural county, Hunchun remained an officially classified important border post and was largely cordoned off from domestic entry unless one had a special permit. Buildings of two stories or taller were banned, and the area became economically marginalized. Hunchun entered a new era of opening and rapid economic growth in 1985 when its border crossing with the RFE was (re)opened. In 1988, Hunchun was administratively upgraded from a county to a municipality and allowed by Jilin province to build a special economic zone. Following the onset of the UNDP-sponsored Tumen River development in 1992, Hunchun was chosen by the central government to be among the first group of officially designated open border cities and allowed to set up China's first border economic cooperation zone (BECZ). Bounded for 88 sq km and planned for 24 sq km, the Hunchun BECZ received infrastructure investment totaling US$150 million from the state. In April 2000, the national government approved the establishment of the Hunchun Export Processing Zone (HEPZ), one of only 15 in China. In February 2001, the national government approved the Hunchun China-Russia Free Market and Trade Zone. Along with a huge indoor market hall, the zone offered financial incentives and procedural conveniences, including visa-free entry for Russian traders and duty-free exodus of Russian goods taken out of the zone by Chinese traders.[8]

In just 10 years, Hunchun rose from a peripheral, backward outpost to a booming industrial city on China's northeastern frontier. In 1992, Hunchun had a population of approximately 175,000, which grew to 250,000 by the end of the decade. Its industrial output, however, more than tripled, from US$46 million in 1992 to US$150 million in 1999. Its GDP in 2001 tripled that of 1995. Since 1995, Hunchun's foreign trade has been growing almost 100 percent annually, while its GDP has been up between 16–20 percent a year. Passenger and cargo flows through Hunchun's overland ports with North Korea and the RFE have been rising over 30 percent per annum.[9] About 80 percent of the industrial enterprises in Hunchun have received some direct foreign investment, most of which came from Hong Kong, South Korea, and Japan. The two largest foreign-owned companies, which involved a combined US$100 million, were a Japanese steel producer and a South Korean textiles/garment factory. The Japanese-invested mill produced high-quality steel pipes, while the South Korean-invested textiles/garment factory turned out a well-known thick sweater for export. Although the Asian financial crisis in 1997–1998 dealt a heavy blow to both manufacturers,[10] Hunchun made a relatively quick recovery by attracting 33 foreign-invested enterprises into the BECZ that involved contracted capitalization of US$127 million by the end of 2000.[11]

The RFE Port City of Nakhodka: A Struggling Free Economic Zone

If Hunchun constitutes the Chinese anchor for the triangular GTS, Nakhodka, with Vladivostok, forms the RFE pole, even though Nakhodka is located about 300 km away from the Tumen River on the south coast of Primorskii Krai (see map 6.1). More appropriate than Vladivostok for comparison with Hunchun, Nakhodka was designated as a free economic zone (FEZ) in 1990, slightly before the Chinese city was given a similar status. Unlike Hunchun, Nakhodka becoming a FEZ had little to do with the initiation of the Tumen River regional development project. It instead reflected growing decentralization during Gorbachev's reform program (perestroika), the tendency of independence of the RFE from Moscow, and Russia's effort to promote trade and economic cooperation with its Pacific Rim neighbors in the late 1980s and early 1990s (Manezhev, 1993). Since then, Nakhodka has been linked with the discussion and development of the GTS in terms of geographic proximity and commercial ties.

Long Russia's major gateway to the Pacific Rim, Nakhodka was one of the busiest and most important commercial ports during tsarist Russia. During the era of the former Soviet Union, Nakhodka took on some military functions, albeit less so than Vladivostok, which served as the headquarters for the Soviet Pacific fleet. Since the early 1990s, Nakhodka may have been busier than the better-known Vladivostok 100 km to the west.[12] As the cargo terminus of the Trans-Siberian Railway, the Nakhodka station handled 20 million tons of freight annually. Together with its sister port of Vostochny, Nakhodka handled 65 percent of the RFE's port trade (Paisley and Lilley, 1993) and about one-quarter of Russia's overland freight in the first half of 1996 (A. Wilson, 1996). Imports and exports accounted for 90.7 percent of the total cargo through Nakhodka, higher than 86.5 percent for Vladivostok (Liu, 1995). Its location on the Sea of Japan and relatively close proximity to China and North Korea, coupled with its attractive FEZ status, could make Nakhodka a more important shipping and business center.

Foreign investment and economic development in the Nakhodka FEZ, however, has lagged behind the growth of the city's port activity. By mid-1996, 383 foreign companies had committed US$500 million to the FEZ of 4.6 sq km, which was much smaller than the Hunchun zone. Half of the committed capital came from Chinese companies and entrepreneurs who were involved primarily in small-scale trade and shipping operations. Western companies targeted their investment at infrastructure development. The U.S. container operator Sea-Land advised the city on how to develop an integrated transport system. Britain's Cable and Wireless bought a stake in a local telecommunications company, while the European Bank for Reconstruction and Development (EBRD) financed the construction of a US$50 million grain terminal at Vostochny, part of the Nakhodka FEZ (Paisley and Lilley, 1993). Japanese and South Korean companies were behind the Chinese investors, as their combined investment accounted for just over 10 percent of the total foreign capital in the FEZ. However, South Korea was beginning to build a 3.3 sq km industrial park between Nakhodka and Vostochny to accommodate 100 manufacturers in the future (A. Wilson, 1996). Major manufacturing investment projects have been rare and often stalled due to the continued bureaucratic influence from the central government in Moscow and lack of local autonomy (discussed below). The Nakhodka FEZ in the post-socialist RFE has been struggling to become a frontier economic center and a real player in the Northeast Asian regional economy.

Rajin-Sonbong of North Korea: Capitalist Enclave in a Socialist State

Setting up a special economic zone to attract capitalist investors still appears an unthinkable policy for the secluded socialist kingdom of North Korea today. Yet this actually took place as early as 1991, when the North Korean government established a free economic and trade zone (FETZ) involving some areas of the city of Rajin and Sonbong Kun (county).[13] Covering 642 sq km with about 150,000 residents, the Rajin-Sonbong FETZ borders on China to the north and faces the RFE and the Sea of Japan to the east. About 100 km south of the Rajin-Sonbong FETZ is the port city of Chongjin, which was designated as a "free trade port" in 1991. In 1995, the Rajin-Sonbong FETZ was enlarged to 746 sq km to absorb a border area that included the bridge connecting with the Chinese border crossing point near Hunchun (S. Zhang, 1997).

The favorable border location aside, the Rajin-Sonbong FETZ and the surrounding region are endowed with such valuable natural resources as coal and iron ore. Once favored for socialist industrialization as an important frontier region,[14] the Rajin-Sonbong FETZ and its vicinity have a cluster of heavy industries. While North Korea's largest steel mill is located in Chongjin to the south, Sonbong Kun is home to the country's largest oil refinery, which processes petroleum imported primarily from the RFE. The region's industries also include fishing, seafood processing, lumber, and tourism for its natural beauty. As the Rajin-Sonbong FETZ provided a small yet precious opening for badly needed foreign investment, it has been accorded a top national priority and an ambitious plan for development. The three-phase plan for 1993–2010 envisioned (1) developing 10 industrial parks; (2) considerably upgrading the transport infrastructure, including expanded capacities at the Rajin and Sonbong ports and more extended and connected border rail and road networks with northeastern China and the RFE; and (3) the development of tourism (Y. Zhang, 1994).

However, foreign capital, which would drive this plan, was slow to roll in. Until mid-1996, the Rajin-Sonbong FETZ had attracted only US$34 million in foreign investment, most of which came from neighboring China. The barriers included bad physical infrastructure (e.g., tardiness in improving roads) and heavy government control despite the promulgation of several laws on foreign investment after 1992. After September 1996, when an international trade and investment forum was held in Rajin-Sonbong, foreign investment gained some momentum. The forum itself led to US$840 million in contracts and commitments, including a seaside luxury hotel and casino valued at US$180 million to be built by the Emperor Group, a property developer and investor based in Hong Kong, and a US$400 million oil refinery to be developed by a Hong Kong company

(Glain, 1996). By 1998, a total of 150 foreign companies—most of them Chinese—opened offices or factories in the Rajin-Sonbong FETZ with US$88 million in direct investment and economic ties reaching beyond the zone. A Jilin-based Chinese shipping company, together with a South Korean partner, began to operate a shipping route for container cargo between Rajin and the South Korean port of Pusan every 10 days. The service carried 6,000 containers in 1998 and made its first profit (Lawrence, 1999). While few sizeable investment projects have materialized in the zone, the Emperor Hotel and Casino in Rajin built by the Hong Kong developer was finally opened with a grand ceremony in October 2000, following construction delays, insufficient water and electricity supply, and a shortage of local labor (Ying, 2001).

The growth of the Rajin-Sonbong FETZ has been impeded by the lack of foreign investment in the manufacturing sector, in spite of the very low land and labor costs.[15] The Asian financial crisis in 1997–1998 also halted the development of the major commercial projects in the zone, including the Emperor Hotel and Casino.[16] For these internal and external reasons, the capitalist enclave of the Rajin-Sonbong FETZ has been trapped in North Korea's centrally planned system.

An Impeded Outreach to the Global Economy

Through the opening of important border cities such as the three FEZ cities above, the GTS has been trying to reach out to the global economy from a geopolitically important part of Asia that has been politically unstable and economically underdeveloped. This outreach has benefited from the UNDP's boost from the outside and the geostrategic advantages of the GTS itself, but it has barely touched the global economy or created the kind of beneficial local-global economic links found in the GSCS. A disadvantage may be the concentration of extractive industries in the GTS, as natural and mineral resources for extraction are fixed in space and physical isolation (see Bunker, 1989). What has connected is growing, albeit fluctuating, border trade within the GTS that has fostered some trans-local commercial ties within the transborder subregion. The relatively limited foreign investment in the GTS has been unevenly distributed, favoring the Yanbian prefecture of Jilin province and the Primorskii Territory of the RFE over the Rajin-Sonbong zone of North Korea (see figure 6.1). Nevertheless, some geo-economically confined links have begun to extend beyond the GTS, such as the container cargo shipping route that involves both Chinese and South Korean investments and runs between North Korea's Rajin port and the South Korean port of Pusan (see map 6.1).

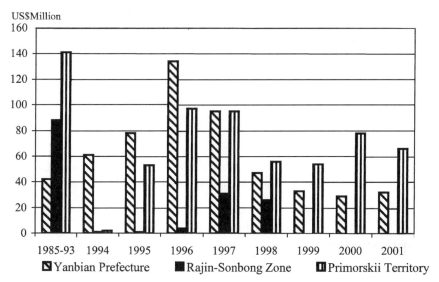

FIGURE 6.1
Foreign Direct Investment in the Chinese, North Korean, and Russian Areas of the
Greater Tumen Subregion, 1985–2001

Despite its natural beauty and relatively easy access,[17] the Rajin-Sonbong zone has attracted a fairly small number of international tourists. After rising from 43,000 in 1996 to 111,5000 in 1997, the number of international tourists dropped sharply in 1998 due to the Asian financial crisis. It rebounded to 102,087 in 1999 and 121,120 in 2000. The majority of them, however, were business travelers. The share of visitors that were Chinese declined from almost 100 percent in the early 1990s to 79 percent in 1999 and 67 percent in 2000 (UNDP, 2001–2003). Some of the Chinese visitors were wealthy businessmen from neighboring northeastern China coming over to gamble in the Emperor Hotel and Casino in Rajin. The tourist industry in the Rajin-Sonbong zone created only limited links to the global economy that might bring in more revenue.

The major barrier to creating global-local economic links for the GTS is the lack of economic complementarity among its three constituent units, compared with the GSCS and the BYSS. This barrier is difficult to overcome because the GTS consists of the poorer and more peripheral regions of the three countries. It has severely limited the kind and scale of foreign manufacturing investment that has turned out competitive exports from the key locations in the GSCS and the BYSS. With their special financial incentives and favorable locations, the three FEZs of Hunchun, Nakhodka, and Rajin-Sonbong have done better to varying degrees in attracting foreign investment than other localities in the GTS. However, none of the three cities, perhaps not even Hunchun, can serve as a powerful node for the GTS in achieving agglomeration in manufacturing, services, and transportation. They are unlikely to come remotely close to those of Hong Kong or Shenzhen in the GSCS and Tianjin or Incheon in the BYSS.

As we are through with the first analytical lens, we again should be looking for interactions between global-local economic links or lack thereof and the political, sociocultural, and spatial/infrastructure conditions in the GTS context. These interactions arise from the restructuring of center-local state relations during the uneven reforms in the three socialist and post-socialist countries.

Beyond External Facilitation and Between
Central Power and Local Autonomy

From the UNDP's Initial Boost to Internal Center-Local Dynamics

Unlike the GSCS or the BYSS, the GTS would not have emerged without the initial strong role of the UNDP in launching the Tumen River Area Development Program (TRADP) back in 1991. The TRADP represented a predominantly inter-governmental effort to foster economic cooperation and development in Northeast Asia, which is often characterized by stagnating economies, border conflicts, and political instability. On the other hand, Northeast Asia has certain location advantages (deep sea ports, access to the Trans-Siberian Railway, and the vast East Asian markets) and some complementarities of Japanese and South Korean capital and know-how, low-cost Chinese and North Korean labor, and rich natural resources in Mongolia and the RFE. The UNDP saw the potential to create successful economic development and cooperation based on these favorable conditions. By the end of the 1990s, the UNDP's vision faded as its efforts to facilitate inter-governmental cooperation had yielded little success. As an outside institutional actor trying to be a facilitator, the UNDP was in no position to overcome such difficult barriers to economic cooperation as the pain of converting planned economies, core-periphery governance conflicts, and the continued salience of borders. As a result, the UNDP not only settled into a lesser role but also helped turn the more formal multilateral framework of TRADP into a more informal and locally targeted approach to fostering foreign investment and economic development (see Hunter, 1998).

While the UNDP's facilitating role has helped shape the larger context in which the GTS is located, it matters less as an institutional force to the GTS than the domestic politics and policy-making of the three countries whose border areas make up the GTS. In this sense, the GTS is a market-state-led transborder subregion rather than a formal regional structure created purely by inter-state agreements (see figure 2.1). This conceptual distinction makes it imperative to look beneath the UNDP-fostered inter-state structure for the more important influence of varied center-local political dynamics.

China and Russia have experienced different degrees of internal pains in their transition toward an open and market-oriented economy, while North Korea has been mired in dealing with domestic natural and economic disasters and holding on to an outdated political ideology. These problems have limited the ability of the three countries to adopt a consistent and coordinated policy toward the GTS. Given that the direct involvement of border localities in a transborder subregion calls for more local autonomy, as argued in chapter 3, the role of the main local governments in the GTS relative to that of the respective national governments has become a key factor. Unlike the GSCS or the BYSS, which feature some changing center-local relations in democratic systems with the exception of China, all three center-local relations in the GTS have been evolving along a transitional socialist path.

In socialist countries, border regions and cities tend to have the ironic status of being militarily strategic and economically marginal at the same time. As both national security outposts and economic backwaters, they are under close central control and receive considerable outlays for military buildup, but they get little policy leeway and financial assistance for local economic development. While decentralization of power generally characterizes transition toward market economics in China and Russia, its manifestation and impact on the countries' border areas in the GTS vary due to the political and geographic differences between the two transitional economies.

When It Was the Turn for Northeast China and the Tumen Region

While China's open policy of favoring the southeast coast in the late 1970s and early 1980s gave the GSCS a head start, its subsequent policy of targeting the Bohai rim, especially the Shandong and Liaoning peninsulas in the mid- and late 1980s, boosted the BYSS. Ranking lower among the priorities for regional development, the northeast region of China fell farther behind the two distinctive segments of the booming coastal belt. In the early 1990s, however, the central government began to shift the open policy and development focus to the more isolated and backward inland border regions by offering them financial incentives that had been granted exclusively to the coastal areas. This policy adjustment was intended to narrow growing regional disparities and appease leaders of the inland areas who believed they had been mistreated. Provincial and local leaders of Northeast China complained about unequal exchange as the main products from the region—oil, coal, lumber, and grain—were sold at low state-set prices (Rozman, 1998a). Northeast China finally got its turn to catch up in opening and development.

The central government singled out specific border areas of Jilin province along the Tumen River for more favorable policy treatment, which also was stimulated by the UNDP-sponsored Tumen River development initiatives in the early 1990s. The State Council of China established a special office and a research and development team with the State Science and Technology Commission as the leading unit to handle issues concerning Tumen River development, while the State Development and Planning Commission incorporated the Tumen River project into the ninth Five-Year Plan.[18] The central government handed out the largest favor in 1992 by designating the city of Hunchun a top-level open border city. This gave Hunchun the privilege of implementing all the favorable policies that had been granted to the coastal cities. It also allowed Hunchun to set up one of China's first and few border economic cooperation zones.

Following the central government's initiative, the governments of Jilin province, Yanbian prefecture, and Hunchun municipality formed leaders' groups and special offices in charge of developing the Tumen region. The Jilin provincial government immediately adopted favorable policies to spur the growth of cities like Yanji and Hunchun. In 1992, the Jilin government shifted 10 provincial-level rights of approval in border economic cooperation and trade down to the municipal government of Hunchun and granted the latter over 20 other favorable policies. From the mid-1980s through 1993, the national and provincial governments doled out a cumulative total of US$140 million to build up the infrastructure in Hunchun's energy, transportation, and telecommunications sectors (G. Yu, 1994). With the support of the UNDP and China's Ministry of Foreign Trade and Economic Cooperation, the prefectural and municipal governments successfully staged a Tumen River Area International Investment Trade Fair in 1995 and 1998 and attracted considerable foreign investment. As happened to the key Chinese cities in the GSCS and the BYSS, the central government's combined strategy of granting favorable policies, decentralizing administrative power, and capital outlays, coupled with proactive local responses, elevated the status and role of Hunchun in the place hierarchy of the GTS.

Despite the weakened central control and stronger central support, local governments in Northeast China, particularly in the Tumen region, have been constrained from taking full advantage of these favorable conditions. Given their border locations in China's primary region of state-owned extractive and heavy industries, cities such as Hunchun became heavily dependent on subsidies from both central and provincial governments. Although these local governments were permitted to provide financial incentives to foreign investors and to create and keep revenues through exports, the lack of exportable light consumer goods limited their opportunities. The government of Hunchun, for example, was not in a position to achieve fast growth and generate wealth in the way that a city like Dongguan in Guangdong has done (see chapter 4). The shift of favorable policy and the decentralization of power to border regions in general and to key border cities in particular since the early 1990s have coincided with a growing trend toward local internationalism in Asia and elsewhere. "Local internationalism" refers to governments of localities actively seeking cross-border economic cooperation, often without central government involvement. Rather than creating simple bilateral ties between border cities of two neighboring countries, this cooperation generally takes the form of inter-city networks that may involve triangular relations among multiple border cities (B. Yu, 1998), as illustrated by the key cities in the BYSS. In comparison, Chinese border cities such as Hunchun have developed fewer and weaker economic ties with the RFE and North Korean cities, even though they are adjacent to one another. This has a lot to do with the still limited autonomy of localities in the RFE and North Korea involved in the GTS.

So Far Away and Yet Still Close to Moscow's Influence

The Chinese saying "the mountains are high and the emperor is far away" aptly captures the autonomous sentiment and behavior of local government officials of China's southeastern coastal cities in the GSCS. Local officials in the RFE ought to enjoy greater autonomy since they are 10,000 km and six time zones away from Moscow. Yet the long shadow of Russia's political center has remained cast over the RFE.[19] In spite of the breakup of the former Soviet Union and a politically more open Russia subsequently, decentralization has proceeded more slowly than in China. According to Rozman (1997, p. 543), "hesitation in decentralization resulted from a power struggle involving two forces. On the one hand, local elites grabbed assets for personal gain instead of fostering development. On the other, the center refused to approve development opportunities and transfer control over necessary assets for fear that it would lose control or that they would be squandered." This contentious relationship between Moscow and the RFE was shaped during the Soviet period when the RFE remained a resource periphery versus the economic core of European Russia. While milking the RFE for natural resources, Moscow provided some economic assistance because of the region's geostrategic significance but neglected its long-term economic viability (Bradshaw, 1999). In the early 1990s, Russian President Boris Yeltsin continued to struggle in striking a constitutional deal for allowing localities to keep more of their wealth (Paisley and Lilley, 1993). The RFE found itself in the difficult position of trying to balance between continued influence and some independence from Moscow.

This delicate balance is typically reflected in how local political leaders and governments struggle to gain and sustain a more favorable policy from Moscow. For example, despite the shift of power from a reform-minded governor of Primorskii Krai to a more conservative successor in 1993,[20] the new governor, Yevgeny Nazdratenko, pressed to maintain the right to export 30 percent of coal and timber without federal licenses. He threatened to keep more revenues locally by creating his own tax service as he scorned Moscow bureaucrats for making people at the center rich (Lilley, 1993b). He later also fought with Moscow over fuel prices and subsidies.[21] Having privatized port facilities in the Nakhodka FEZ, its chairman was proud that Moscow no longer had direct control over this important trade artery (Kohan, 1993). Russian entrepreneurs in the zone, however, became victims of Moscow's differential and unfair policy. In 1996, the State Customs Committee suddenly raised duties on imported components, followed by federal authorities removing the meager tax benefits for Russian-foreign joint ventures in the Nakhodka FEZ. As a result, a local printer assembler lost big business to a large Moscow-based organization that was virtually exempt from taxes (A. Wilson, 1996). As these examples indicate, the political and economic fortunes have remained tied up with the long leash from the Moscow end.

While the evolving center-local relations in China have led to more local autonomy, the frictions in the interaction between Moscow and the RFE are associated with persistent economic problems that have plagued the region's natural resource-based industrial structure. During 1990–1995, industrial production in both Primorskii and Khabarovskii Krais, where 51 percent of the RFE's population resided, experienced the steepest decline among the region's 10 administrative units. The primary reason was the rapidly increased prices of resources to world levels, which led to the physical volume of production declining much faster than the value of production. Local governments often misused the funds provided by the federal government to solve the local problems (Bradshaw, 1999). Primorskii Territory, for example, despite having received more federal monies than any other region in the RFE thanks to its populist governor, has not been able to relieve its economic and energy crises.[22] The corruptive and rent-seeking practices reduce the incentive for the center to release control. In the meantime, local RFE governments continue to struggle with the double constraint of Moscow's political interference and the shortage of local financial resources for development.

A Small Local Opening Under an All-Mighty Center

The different restructuring of center-local state relations in China and Russia has had a varied influence on the involvement of their border cities in the

GTS. The Rajin-Sonbong FETZ in North Korea provides another case for understanding how the within-country relationship between the central and local government can affect both global-local and trans-local ties in a transborder subregion.

Like China in the late 1970s and the former Soviet Union in the late 1980s, North Korea, the world's most reclusive regime, in 1991 began to flirt with capitalism by setting up the Rajin-Sonbong FETZ in the country's northeastern corner bordering China and the RFE. Like the Hunchun and Nakhodka FEZs, the Rajin-Sonbong FETZ offered a host of financial incentives to foreign investors. While foreign investors in other parts of North Korea are required to pay a 25 percent income tax, they pay only 14 percent in the zone (Shiode, 1994), which is more attractive than the 15 percent tax rate in China's special economic zones. The North Korean government marketed the zone aggressively to foreign investors by sending the official in charge to visit Hong Kong in 1993[23] and by holding an international investment forum in Rajin-Sonbong in 1996. The forum drew over 500 government trade officials, Western corporate executives, and traders from 26 countries, which was unprecedented for North Korea. The North Korean government also co-sponsored two sessions of the Rajin-Sonbong International Investment and Trade Fair with international organizations. By year-end 1995, about 200 delegations from some 30 countries had visited and inspected the Rajin-Sonbong FETZ. By making the Rajin-Sonbong FETZ a national initiative, the North Korean government has committed its limited resources to a large-scale buildup and improvement of the transportation and telecommunications infrastructure in the area and to link it to Chinese border cities. It managed to maintain an annual investment of US$150 million through 1998. By 1998, the Rajin-Sonbong zone had attracted more than 70 foreign investment projects, with a total contracted capitalization of US$350 million, of which US$150 million was realized (Jiang, 1999; S. Zhang, 1997). These could be regarded as promising results of a localized opening of a long closed economic system.

The political and economic realities, however, were much less rosy. Politically, as the Rajin-Sonbong FETZ was the personal pet project of the then supreme leader Kim Il Sung and his son successor Kim Jong Il, it would continue to be only a token of a more "open" North Korean official policy (Clifford, 1993). On the other hand, the zone's direct vertical relationship to North Korea's supreme leader was clear evidence of tight central control of any opening to the outside. The head of the Rajin-Sonbong FETZ was quoted as saying, "What we like, we will swallow; what we don't, we will spit it out," right after the international investment promotion forum held in the zone in 1996 (Glain, 1996, p. 1). Economically, the North Korean central government didn't have sufficient capital to back up its grand plan for the Rajin-Sonbong FETZ, whose underdeveloped infrastructure has remained a major barrier to large foreign investment inflows. The contracted investment in the Rajin-Sonbong zone, much of which has not been committed, is a drop in the bucket of North Korea's annual trade deficit of US$500 million and total foreign debt of US$12 billion (Winder, 2000). Much of the realized investment in the zone came from China and some from Mongolia, both of which were motivated by their practical interest in accessing the Rajin port for exporting from their land-locked regions (Babson, 2002).

Unsatisfied with the slow progress of the Rajin-Sonbong zone, the North Korean government has responded to South Korea's "Sunshine Policy" of reconciliation under President Kim Dae Jung by agreeing in the late 1990s to allow Hyundai to develop the Haeju District on North Korea's western coast as another special economic zone.[24] The remote Rajin-Sonbong zone is no longer strategically central to the economic interest of either Korea (Babson, 2002). Without real decentralization of power and local autonomy, the highly selective opening of certain localities, regardless of where they may be, could have only a marginal benefit for the national economy.

The Center Versus the Locality in the GTS

As the above cases indicate, center-local relations in China, Russia, and North Korea have evolved in distinctive ways and thus exerted differential effects on the degree and effectiveness of the important cities of the three countries in the GTS. These differences appear more sharply if viewed specifically from the de-centering state lens.

In the Chinese context, the state de-centering manifests itself in the central government making the border city of Hunchun a focal point for participating in the GTS and granting the provincial and local governments considerable autonomy to achieve that goal. A central government priority led to selective, genuine decentralization of both national and provincial power to the local level, which was translated into more independent and rational decision-making in economic development and external integration. In Russia, the de-centering is much more circumscribed. Although there was de jure decentralization through establishing the Nakhodka FEZ and opening a number of ports such as Vladivostok, Nakhodka, and Zarubino to commercial trade within the GTS, there was little de facto decentralization in terms of either initial financial assistance or real devolution of power from Moscow. As a result, the RFE in general and Nakhodka in particular are left under the severe constraints of their troubled economic past and existing resource shortages. The political problem has offset the favorable conditions such as geographic location and port facilities, which might otherwise facilitate the integration of cities like Nakhodka into the GTS. In North Korea, there is no de-centering to speak of. In contrast, the Rajin-Sonbong FETZ represents a worse case of center-controlled local opening. The center's direct command over the zone through a local official belonging to the Kim Il Sung family, coupled with the lack of domestic resources, greatly restricted autonomous development and external links with the GTS.

Complicating and potentially further disrupting the center-local relations in the GTS context are the divergent and perhaps conflicting objectives that the three central governments have set for the key localities. China pushed the development of Hunchun in order to use its critical location on the Tumen River to (re)gain access to the Sea of Japan. North Korea focused on improving the Rajin-Sonbong and Chongjin ports into major modern transshipment facilities. Russia's plan was to develop a Greater Vladivostok Economic Region to help enliven the coastal economy of southern Siberia. To paraphrase a Chinese saying, these three countries had different dreams, although they all shared the same bed of developing the Tumen River region (Scalapino, 1995, p. 105). In a recent move to bypass the different policy goals, in 2002 the North Korean leader Kim Jong Il made a trip to the RFE by crossing the Khasan checkpoint between the two countries and met Russian President Vladimir Putin in Vladivostok. The secretive trip was reported as North Korea's desperate effort to expand economic ties with the RFE and Russia's reciprocal move to increase its influence in Pacific Asia after their economic relations faltered from the 1980s and especially after 1991.[25]

The three cases reinforce the central point revealed through the political optic: despite the important initial role of the UNDP in facilitating the formation of an inter-state framework through top-down and outside influence, the GTS has featured uneven participation and performance by its constituent units from Northeast China, the RFE, and North Korea, which were heavily influenced by the varied center-local relations in the three countries. Greater decentralization in China has helped put Hunchun ahead in growth and functional influence in the GTS, while the lack of decentralization in Russia and North Korea has impaired the development of cities such as Nakhodka and Rajin-Sonbong and their contributions to the GTS, albeit to different degrees. That all three cities were designated as some sort of special economic zone should not mask the important differences in their local autonomy for choosing development priorities and integrating with one another within the GTS and reaching beyond it. Finally, the divergent objectives of the central governments for the key border regions and cities and their continued top-down direction and influence, especially in Russia and North Korea, have created additional contradictions for autonomous trans-local links.

Does Cross-Border Social Capital Make a Difference?

Since the lack of growth and integration in the GTS can be attributed to the unfavorable economic conditions (shortage of capital, weak global links) and political factors (continued central control and limited local autonomy), can cross-border social capital, which contributed to the prosperity of the GSCS and even the BYSS, make any redeeming difference? In other words, can the bridging role of cross-border ethnic ties help overcome the economic and political barriers to subregional integration? Through the sociocultural lens, we address this question by first examining the historical and contemporary conditions of ethnic Koreans in China.

The Persistence of Cross-Border Ethnic Ties: Historical Root, Critical Mass, and Cultural Adaptation

Just as historical Chinese emigration laid down the root of cross-border social capital in the GSCS, early Korean immigration to China created a similar precondition for the subsequent formation of social capital over international boundaries. While beginning as early as the Yuan dynasty (1271–1368), the main Korean migration to China occurred in the 1860s. The Qing emperors reserved the wild and empty Manchuria as a sort of game park, which attracted Korean poachers and squatters among its early settlers (Kaye, 1992a). Japan's colonization of Korea in the early 1900s led to the migration of some Koreans to Japan. By 1940, hundreds of thousands of Koreans migrated to work in the factories and mines in Japan and Manchuria (Cumings, 1998), a Japanese puppet state that included China's three northeastern provinces. Before 1949, the Chinese Communists treated ethnic Koreans in China favorably by granting land to them. This policy was partly a reward for ethnic Koreans, some of whom fought bravely for the People's Liberation Army, first against the Japanese army and then against the Kuomintang (Nationalist) troops in the 1940s.

Given the historical settlement pattern of Koreans in China, China's 1990 census revealed that 97 percent of the nearly 2 million ethnic Koreans in China lived in the three northeastern provinces, with 1.2 million of them residing in Jilin province. The Yanbian Autonomous Prefecture in Jilin, which administers the key Chinese border cities of Yanji, Hunchun, and Tumen in the GTS (see map 6.1), was home to approximately 900,000 ethnic Koreans, which accounted for 41 percent of Yanbian's total population and 43 percent of the entire ethnic Korean population in China. In the city of Hunchun in 1992, ethnic Koreans accounted for 47.3 percent of the local population (Li and Wu, 1998). The city of Tumen had a population of 140,000, 58.6 percent of which were ethnic Koreans. There are also over 30 townships in Northeast China with predominantly ethnic Korean populations, many near the border with North Korea. Altogether, nearly 1 million Korean Chinese are concentrated along the China–North Korea border (Li and Wu, 1998). Through several centuries of migration between and beyond the China–North Korea border, the ethnic Koreans in China's Tumen River region have developed extensive transnational ancestral and kinship ties with the Korean peninsula, Japan, Russia, and some other countries. Of the 2 million ethnic Koreans in China, 20 percent have such ties. In 1990, 53,637 households, or 23 percent of all households in the Yanbian region, had relatives overseas. Of those households, nearly 50,000 had kinship ties with North Korea, about 3,800 with South Korea, and nearly 2,000 with Japan (Li and Wu, 1998). More importantly, a certain percentage of these overseas kin were wealthy business-people and government officials.[26] As a form of cross-border ethnic social capital, the preexisting transnational kinship ties could facilitate economic links.

Like any other immigrant ethnic group, the ethnic Koreans in Northeast China's border region have blended their Korean background and culture into the Chinese society through assimilation and adaptation. In Yanbian, eating cold noodles, a Korean staple, has been widely accepted by Chinese residents who traditionally emphasized cooked (warm) dishes. Local ethnic Koreans, while maintaining the Korean dietary habit of eating the combination of *kimchi* (the preserved cabbage with red hot pepper), rice, and soup, have adapted to preparing stir-fry dishes. The opening of this region and the growing contact with South Korea since 1992 have brought about a new round of cultural diffusion and adoption. Ethnic Korean Chinese whose accent was similar to that of the border region of North Korea have begun to imitate the more popular and fashionable South Korean accent. Some students of ethnic Korean descent at the local university in the city of Yanji have tried to learn the way South Koreans talk.[27] The "Seoul-style" Korean rhetoric of a young preacher in a Protestant church in downtown Yanji appealed strongly to young Yanbian Koreans (Kaye, 1992b). In the early 1990s, it took six months or longer for new popular South Korean songs to reach the city of Yanji. In 1999, a new popular song from South Korea would become "hot" in Yanji almost simultaneously.[28] With a more open border, cultural adaptation and linguistic similarity also have become valuable ethnic social capital that could foster economic exchanges.

Ethnic Social Capital and Economic Interactions

The geographic concentration of South Korean investment in the Yanbian region validates the connection between the location of social capital and flow of economic capital. Also spurred by the establishment of diplomatic relations between China and South Korea in 1992, South Korean investors flocked to Yanbian to set up factories in garments manufacturing, food processing, chemicals, and construction materials. Particularly, a number of small South Korean food-processing and cold-storage companies began to congregate here to export products back to South Korean supermarkets. The 42 Korean-invested enterprises by the end of 1992 accounted for one-third of all foreign ventures in the prefecture and reached US$16 million in capitalization (Peng and Yan, 1994). In the city of Yanji, the capital of the Yanbian prefecture, 119 (over 50 percent) of the 226 foreign-invested enterprises by 1995 were financed by South Korean capital (Wang and Zhang, 1998). Yanji also hosted a Chinese–South Korean joint venture, which was the largest in China's husbandry industry. South Korean companies also targeted the city of Tumen and the city of Ji'an, which borders North Korea.

The city of Yanji, as the heart of the Chinese Korean region, has remained the most attractive destination in northeastern China for South Korean investment and remittance. According to the local informants in Yanji whom I interviewed in 1999, a heavy influx of remittance from South Koreans boosted the local economy in the mid-1990s, especially in real estate development and the restaurant business. Some of the remittance came from the Korean Chinese working as temporary labor in South Korea. In 1996, for example, remittance from South Korea accounted for half of the real estate investment in Yanji. Remittance helped elevate per capita income for Yanji to the fourth highest of all Chinese cities. A growing number of South Korean tourists came to see Mt. Baiktu in the Changbai Mountain Range (called Baiktu Daegan Mountain Range in Korean), which they have considered a sacred place because they believe that their ancestor came from that mountain (see maps on the book's Web page). Some of them also took time to visit relatives in Yanji. Heavy spending by these tourists also contributed to the boom of the local economy.

The onset of the Asian financial crisis in 1997 dampened Yanji's prosperity. South Korean investors quickly pulled out from their ventures and left behind stockpiles of unsold products waiting to be exported. Since the large majority of the South Korean–invested enterprises were small, collectively owned local firms that offered no guaranteed employment (the so-called iron rice bowl), the withdrawal of South Korean capital (see figure 6.1) left many local workers unemployed. The financial crisis also led to a sharp reduction of South Korean tourists, and even those who came after 1998 engaged largely in window-shopping. Nevertheless, the striking billboard for the South Korean airline, Asiana, dominated at the visibly empty Yanji Airport, despite the fact that it was not yet allowed to fly in. There was little question of the heavy South Korean presence in this Chinese border region heavily populated by ethnic Koreans.

The ethnic ties brought not only South Korean investment into Yanbian but also new types of economic exchanges (besides barter trade) across the China–North Korea border under the favorable policies of the local governments toward North Korea businesses. In Yanbian, North Korea had invested in 25 businesses, mostly restaurants, sauna parlors, karaoke bars, and real estate companies on the Chinese side of the border (X. Chen, 1995; Lawrence, 1999). Young North Korean women illegally in the country worked in some of the karaoke bars in Yanji without being detained, as local informants revealed. Ethnic Korean merchants continued to do business with their North Korean counterparts, even under the unfavorable conditions of not getting paid on time and having few attractive goods to buy. Unlike the South Korean connections discussed earlier, the Korean Chinese kinship-based social networks were used under a more open policy to generate economic exchanges intended to benefit North Koreans on the other side of the border.

Ethnic Korean identity has facilitated economic exchanges across additional national borders within the GTS and beyond. Although South Koreans were allowed to visit the Mt. Kumgang area in southeastern North Korea on group tours in 1998, their contact with North Koreans and the rest of the country has been highly limited. This curiosity of South Koreans for North Korea created a money-making opportunity on the Chinese–North Korea border. Outside the city of Yanji along the Tumen River, South Korean tourists could pay the local Chinese residents for a picture taken against the backdrop of North Korea, just across the water, with the giant portrait of the late leader, Kim Il Sung, looming large (Lawrence, 1999). The pro-North ethnic Korean residents in Japan, known as *Chosen Soren*[29] in Japanese, have made investment in both the Rajin-Sonbong FETZ in North Korea and the Yanbian region in China. Their project of a hospital and a hotel in the Rajin-Sonbong zone was one of the largest in contracted capital (Liu and Yuan, 1997). They built an upscale hotel and restaurant complex in Yanji, which was staffed with North Korean waitresses (Lawrence, 1999). The *Chosen Soren* also played a key role in smuggling used Japanese cars across the Tumen River into China and garnered high profits, which were used to help subsidize North Korea.[30] While network ties across the Korean diaspora communities in Northeast Asia have fostered cross-border economic activity, they appear to have aided, albeit indirectly, the impoverished and closed regime of North Korea.

In addition to fostering economic exchanges across political boundaries, ethnic Korean ties have served to bridge the growing income and living standards across the China–North Korea border. My field interviews with local residents reveal that in the 1960s and 1970s, when North Korea was economically better off than China, some Korean Chinese crossed the border into North Korea, and Chinese residents in the border area depended on North

Korea for electricity supply. After China's economic reforms improved local living conditions, some of those who had left returned home. China began to export daily necessities such as flashlights to North Korea, which has sustained a severe shortage of rural energy (Williams, von Hippel, and Hayes, 2000). Having maintained ties with their relatives in North Korea in the face of the latter's self-imposed closed policy, local Korean Chinese have tried to offer assistance to their less fortunate kin across the border. Through difficult prior arrangements, some Korean Chinese would meet their relatives at the Tumen River crossing and use the occasion to barter for simple goods. Some Korean Chinese would give their North Korean relatives enough Chinese currency for them to buy a year's grain supply.

Searching for Food, Longing for Freedom: Temporary North Korean Migrants

Transboundary ethnic Korean ties play a double-edged role across contentious borders in a larger, complex economic and political context involving multiple local units and national states. This is illustrated no better than by the tragic phenomenon of North Koreans illegally crossing into China and its serious consequences for inter-state relations and human life experience. Since the late 1990s, if not earlier, large numbers of North Koreans, driven by hunger from a devastating famine in the mid-1990s and lack of political and personal freedom, and encouraged by lax border control, have crossed into the Yanbian region. While most of them seek food and temporary work, some attempt to escape the authoritarian regime by making their way to South Korea as political refugees.

The estimated number of North Korean migrants ranged between 100,000 and 400,000 in 1998 and 1999 (Shim, 1999). Most of them originated from North Korea's border region and cities such as Chongjin. The border poses few barriers to this human movement. The border along the shallow portions of the Tumen River, which narrows to just 30 meters at some places and is frozen in winter, is usually lightly guarded. The North Korean border guards, hungry themselves, let the migrants pass for a share of the food and money they bring back. This large human flow constitutes one of the world's most unusual population movements, as some of them return to North Korea after a brief stay or a single meal from an ethnic Korean relative in China's border area, especially in rural villages. Some have tried to make money by working for farmers or by approaching relatives or South Korean visitors. Those working on farms may get paid only in rice. Many of these North Koreans had to leave behind family members, often children, and tried desperately to collect enough money to return to buy rice for the family. Some female migrants could not find proper means to work but resorted to prostitution, while others were sold as brides by human traffickers to places such as Shandong province. Unable to feed their children, some parents had to give them away to be raised in local orphanages. The unlucky boys might end up being sold to childless couples in interior China.[31] To help these desperate Northerners, some members of South Korean charities and churches have come on short-term tourist visas, while others take jobs with South Korean businesses in the Chinese border cities (see Shim, 1999).

The stay of these North Korean migrants and refugees has become increasingly difficult and dangerous since 2001 due to the stepped-up effort of the Chinese border police to arrest and then deport them back to North Korea. While this crackdown was originally intended as a response to such crimes as prostitution and human trafficking, it has become intensified in the wake of illegal North Koreans successfully taking refuge in foreign embassies in Beijing since early 2002. A growing number of North Koreans in China's border areas, who used to visit marketplaces and sleep in cheap inns, have been rounded up and sent back by trucks across the border. Local government authorities and police began to scrutinize the churches where North Korean migrants tended to take refuge. North Korean agents came to the churches posing as ordinary migrants. The number of the deportees, which stood around 8,000 during the first half of 2000, rose rapidly to approach an estimated 20 percent of all illegal North Koreans in China around mid-2002. Fearing being caught and deported, many migrants have gone underground and move from hideout to hideout, which sometimes includes mountain caves. Others have tried to trek long distances to remote places in southwestern China in order to get to South Korea eventually. According to a more recent estimate, the number of North Koreans remaining in China dropped to as low as 20,000 at the beginning of 2003.[32]

In this tragic human ordeal for North Korean migrants in China, cross-border social capital, domestic politics, and inter-state relations are not only closely intertwined but also play out in a contentious manner, which adds even more pain to the people involved. Generally, ethnic Koreans in the border cities and villages have been willing to help the North Koreans by offering meals, money, and even hideouts based on a strong cross-border ethnic identity. However, this willingness to help has dwindled more recently because the local Korean Chinese are concerned about the theft and violence exhibited by some North Korean migrants and the threat posed by the Chinese police. The crackdown by Chinese authorities also has hampered the efforts by South Korean activist groups such as Helping Hands Korea and individuals to help North Koreans with a safe passage out of China to South Korea. A nasty political complication of this tragedy is how to define the status of the North Korean border crossers. While the Chinese government views them as illegal immigrants crossing for economic purposes, many of these North Koreans see themselves as refugees seeking freedom and avoiding political persecution, which has won sympathy and support from the international human rights groups.[33] It's reported that with the possible exception of first-time offenders, the North Koreans sent back across the border tend to be severely punished in labor camps in cities such as Chongjin not far from the border.[34] However, under the mutual repatriation treaty with North Korea, the Chinese authorities have continued to send back North Koreans caught in China. As recent as early 2003, Chinese police rounded up 78 illegal North Koreans in various places, including the port city of Yantai in Shandong, where they were trying to board a ship for South Korea.[35] China is extremely concerned that acknowledging the illegal North Korean migrants as refugees will mean allowing open humanitarian relief and granting political asylum, which may set off a much larger influx of North Koreans over the border.

Cross-Border Ethnic Ties That Are Insufficient and Contentious

As the preceding account and analysis show, cross-border ethnic Korean ties have made a weaker difference in the GTS than the cross-border ethnic Chinese networks in the GSCS. First of all, the GTS has a much smaller stock of social capital in that the population of ethnic Koreans in China is smaller than the Chinese diaspora in Hong Kong, Taiwan, and Southeast Asia. Secondly, ethnic Korean ties in the GTS are less specific to local native places. More importantly, the potential role of cross-border social capital in the GTS is severely restricted by the absence of other economic and political factors that have favored the GSCS or the BYSS. Limited economic complementarity among northeastern China, the RFE, and North Korea has hampered what cross-border ethnic Korean ties can do to facilitate economic cooperation within the GTS. Poor economic conditions and political problems in the RFE and North Korea also have dampened the advantage of cross-border ethnic connections for economic exchange.

Compared with the GSCS or the BYSS, cross-border ethnic ties in the GTS exhibit a more complex and contentious side, due to greater ethnic diversity and a unique set of historical and political circumstances. The breakup of the Soviet Union unleashed the process and prospect for many ethnic Koreans in such Central Asian republics as Uzbekistan and Kazakhstan to return to their original homelands in the RFE decades after a deportation in 1937.[36] The Russian government explored the legal possibility of allowing ethnic Koreans to recover their former lands in the RFE. Many ethnic Koreans were enticed by the opportunity of working for South Korean fish processing and light manufacturing enterprises in the RFE. The Russians of European background in the RFE resented the preferential treatment for Koreans by South Korean companies, even though they didn't speak Korean (Lilley, 1993a). In the 1990s, the RFE's regional and local authorities also faced the challenge of balancing the benefit and cost associated with a steady influx of Chinese workers, traders, and businesspeople from across the border. On one hand, due to a severe shortage of labor, local authorities in the RFE needed to import Chinese contract workers for unskilled work at construction sites and on agricultural fields. On the other hand, they found it difficult to deal with such problems as violent street fights that involved Chinese Koreans and Han Chinese.[37] Given the estimated 250,000–300,000 Chinese already in the RFE and the projected bigger demand for more labor (Zayonchkovskaya, n.d.), the tension between cross-border ethnic groups may rise further as the need for greater economic cooperation among them increases.

Finally and most ironically, the otherwise positive aspect of ethnic Korean ties across the China–North Korea border has produced some tragic consequences from the heavy flow of illegal North Koreans into ethnic Korean cities and villages in the Yanbian region, although these may be unintended. While these ties have provided some temporary relief to hungry and impoverished North Korean migrants, they are not capable of accommodating the strong desire of some North Koreans to flee a repressive regime for freedom under the current interstate political relations. In fact, the very willingness of the ethnic Koreans to help the North Korean migrants has provoked the Chinese state to crack down and thus reinforces the political salience and barrier of the border. Cross-border social capital and its flexible influence at the local level have run into the wall of more powerful and rigid politics at the national and inter-state level.

The Dilemma of Development: Expanding Transport Links Versus Preserving the Natural Environment

If the lack of success for the GTS is a combined outcome of economic and political problems in the RFE and North Korea and restricted cross-border social capital, could geographic proximity, border situations, and cross-border transport infrastructure compensate to make a difference? To answer this question, I turn to the last analytical lens, first presenting an overview of the border crossings and the cross-border transport infrastructure in the GTS.

Lengthy Borders and Multiple Crossings

In the GTS, long and shared borders offer a great potential for cross-border economic links. The China-Russian border runs 4,300 km long, and approximately 3,300 km divide the RFE from China's Heilongjiang and Jilin provinces (Hsuen and Lu, 1999). The Chinese city of Hunchun alone shares 232 km with the Khasan region of Primorskii Krai of the RFE, while the narrow territory of southwestern Primorskii, 10–60 km wide, stretches along the Russia-China border for over 200 km. The China–North Korea border extends 1,404 km, of which 1,204 km straddle the boundary between North Korea and Jilin province. The city of Hunchun shares a border of 140 km with North Korea (G. Yu, 1994). The Chinese cities of Hunchun, Yanji, and Tumen lie on one side of a borderline of over 300 km, with Hamgyong-Bukdo of North Korea and Primorskii Krai of the RFE on the other. Major segments of the China-RFE and China–North Korea borders provide natural geographic advantages for cross-border physical and economic links.

These links exist physically at a number of overland crossings that dot the China-RFE and China–North Korea borders. All the most important border crossings string along the boundary between the Yanbian prefecture and portions of the RFE and North Korea's border areas, the territorial center of the GTS (see appendix table 6.B). Six of these crossings are grade one crossings, which are directly approved by China's State Council and may be administered by either the central government or a provincial or prefectural government. Grade two crossings, approved and set up by a provincial or prefectural government, are less important in that they generally serve local border trade and local residents' crossings. It is worth taking a brief look at three crossings that are important for the GTS (see the book's Web page).

Weak Infrastructure, but Improving Links

The combination of multiple border crossings and both land and rail access to several good and geographically proximate ports has not created the kind of tight cross-border links that would help overcome the economic and political barriers to the integration of the GTS. The primary reason lies in the overall underdevelopment of transport infrastructure. The various border regions and cities in the GTS are remote and peripheral to the economic and political centers of the three countries involved. Because of this status, they have suffered from a cumulative shortage of large-scale investment for improving their transport facilities. The roads and railroads in and between these places were limited, not well connected, and had low grades and carrying capacity. The seaports were poorly equipped with loading and storage facilities and therefore could not perform up to full capacity. For example, while the Chinese side was completing parts of a highway leading to the Quanhe border crossing in 2000, the North Korean side still used a sand and gravel track that would turn into mud in the rain or snow. This poor condition made it difficult for trucks carrying containers to cross the border (Lawrence, 1999). Improving the transport infrastructure in the GTS requires huge resources and sustained large-scale buildup to yield both short- and long-term payoffs.

The short-term benefits are reflected in the completion of several shipping routes, main roads, and railroads leading up to, along, and across the borders in the GTS in recent years. The shipping routes through land crossings include regular container shipping from Hunchun to the Rajin port and on to Pusan in South Korea (mentioned earlier), and from Hunchun to the Posyet port in the RFE and then across the Sea of Japan to Akita in Japan (see map 6.1 and the book's Web page). As part of the renewed cooperation between the RFE and North Korea, Russian engineers have begun to help upgrade the cargo facilities at the Rajin port, which could relieve cargo congestion in Vladivostok and Nakhodka. In addition, Russian workers have begun to build the first highway bridge across the North Korean border and renovate the railroad down to Rajin. On the other hand, the Russian district of Khasan directly bordering North Korea has set up a thriving cargo and passenger ferry service between Vladivostok and Sokcho, a South Korea port below the DMZ (see map 6.1), deliberately bypassing North Korea due to the difficulties in doing business with the latter.[38]

Transport Flows and Uncertain Future Demand

The long-term payoffs from improved transport links are shrouded in uncertain future demand for the cross-border flow of goods, which fluctuated in the mid-1990s (see appendix table 6.C and the book's Web page). Further integration and development of the GTS and greater cross-border trade flows will put more pressure on the still underdeveloped transport system across the border regions of northeastern China, the RFE, and North Korea. While this broad scenario may turn out to be realistic, the specific demand on the various cross-border transport links may be uncertain. It is projected that the volume of China-RFE trade through the Changlingzi crossing could reach 200,000 tons by 2005, while the through volumes of China–North Korean trade at the Quanhe, Shatuozi, and Tumen crossings may approach the same level. The projection is partly based on the steadily growing exports of large quantities of grain and high-heat coal from Yanbian to meet the shortages in North Korea and the RFE and continued demand in Japan and South Korea. In addition, the growth of foreign-invested companies in Yanbian, especially in its strong lumber processing industry, will stimulate greater import of timber and export of processed wood and paper products (C. Chen, 1998).

The projected demand from economic growth and integration for cross-border transport infrastructure may not materialize due the persistent lack of favorable economic and political conditions for growth and cooperation, such as shortage of foreign direct investment and limited local autonomy, particularly in the RFE and North Korea, as examined earlier. Continued growth in Jilin's border region alone is not sufficient to pull the GTS along and create sufficient demand for more transboundary infrastructure. The slower growth in the RFE and no growth in North Korea may sustain a certain level of oversupply in transport facilities and capacities. The RFE, for example, needs more foreign trade to consume the combined capacities of its cluster of deep-water ports, while about 75 percent of the handling capacity of the Rajin port remains unused (Jiang, 1999). This oversupply problem, however, may be easier to overcome with sufficient growth than the greater challenge in the shortage of resources to finance an expansion of cross-border transport infrastructure if demand eventually catches up.

A Price to Pay or a Problem to Solve? Preserving Biodiversity and International Water Resources in the GTS

Just as actual economic growth and cooperation and infrastructure expansion in the GTS have fallen short of the ambitious goals envisioned originally by the UNDP, the transborder subregion has already been facing another significant challenge—protecting the natural environment—which may or may not be compatible with economic development goals and require difficult choices regarding development priorities. This challenge involves dealing with the existing and emerging threats to biodiversity and international water resources for all three countries in the GTS, given their geographic contiguity and shared links to the Tumen River and other natural resources in light of some historical antecedents (see the book's Web page).

The various forms of pollution have begun to affect the important habitats nourished by the Tumen River and its rich forests and wetlands for some significant endangered species, including the Amur tiger, Far-eastern leopard, bears, migratory birds, and certain non-fish species (see the book's Web page). Given the widespread territories of tigers and leopards throughout the forest in the Tumen River region, the cutting of forests and construction of transport facilities can easily destroy their habitats. Destruction of habitat causes isolated species to be in danger of extinction.[39] Aggressive coastal fishing off Primorskii Krai, where the fishing industry accounted for 30 percent of local industrial output in 2001, led to overharvesting of some economically valuable species such as mollusks, sea urchins, holothurians, and shrimps.[40] Contamination originating from areas near Peter the Great Bay, the Sea of Japan's most biologically productive zone, may threaten hundreds of species of marine invertebrates, three species of whales, seals, and over 200,000 water fowls (Hunter, 1998).

To respond to the cross-border nature of these environmental threats under the condition of weak regional cooperation, the UNDP reasserted its role in pushing the development of a multilateral environmental framework through the TRADP (see the book's Web page). This external assistance has coexisted and even conflicted with national and local economic development interests. China has been waging a persistent fight to gain navigation rights it lost in 1938 for the 12 km of the Tumen River from the Chinese border through the shared waters of North Korea and the RFE. Besides opposition by North Korea, which wants China to continue using its Rajin-Sonbong ports for sea access, the UNDP also has opposed China's initiative, because dredging the lower Tumen for shipping would be environmentally disastrous. However, with growing autonomy from the central government from the early 1990s, Jilin province has been fixated on gaining that coastal access and pushing for short-term economic growth to improve its poor status, and in doing so has seen little reason and value in the long-term commitment toward environmental preservation (Hunter, 1998).

In this transborder subregion of low economic development and cooperation and rich but vulnerable biodiversity, the dilemma of growth versus preservation is not only very salient but also deeply entrenched. It is extremely difficult to reconcile in light of the competing or at least inconsistent ideologies and policies of multiple political players, including the international organization of UNDP, strong national states, and some autonomous local governments. In the GTS, the balance between economic development and environmental protection is just as delicate as that between the different spheres of the subregion's biodiversity and ecosystem spanning multiple borders.

The Unrealized Potentials of a Transborder Subregion

Compared with the GSCS and the BYSS, the GTS has lagged much behind in the degree of economic and spatial integration. These lags are somewhat disappointing in light of the GTS's huge potential for development. The GTS is uniquely endowed with abundant natural and mineral resources, such as coal and timber, that can spur and support the growth of both extractive and manufacturing industries. The GTS may also be the only transborder subregion in the world that has received initial financial assistance and sustained institutional backing from the United Nations. Moreover, the key constituent units of the GTS are blessed by favorable locations in terms of convenient access to a cluster of deep-water ports in the RFE and North Korea, the Trans-Siberian Railway, and shipping to the northwestern coast of Japan. The conjuncture of these advantages would seem to favor the conquering of the GTS as the last development frontier on the Pacific Rim and allow it to grow and integrate like the BYSS and the GSCS.

The GTS's great potential for becoming a prosperous transborder subregion is yet to be realized due to a number of unfavorable factors. These become more apparent individually and in interaction if seen through the four analytical lenses of our framework. The low starting level of economic development and the lack of market forces in and economic complementarity among the GTS's three participating units, coupled with extremely limited global ties, form the primary economic barrier. In this economic environment, the dominance of extractive and heavy industries has turned into a liability. It not only offsets the shared asset of low-cost labor, especially over the Chinese and North Korean borders, but also creates serious environmental problems for the subregion's biodiversity and international water resources.

Politically, the GTS has been hampered by tension and instability on the Korean peninsula arising from North Korea's domestic power transition and nuclear threat, which flared up during 2002–2003. The real political hurdle to the GTS lies in the lack of decentralization in Russia and North Korea. The RFE has been trapped in a double bind of continued control by and dependence on Moscow. This has left the RFE with little room and few resources to unleash its strength in and contribution to the GTS. In addition, the RFE has been a somewhat reluctant participant in the GTS from the very outset due to its ecological concerns, the psychological impacts of Russia's decline as a superpower, and the historical border conflicts between Russia and its Asian neighbors (see Hunter, 1998). The very short leash from the totally controlling political center in North Korea has practically eliminated any chance for autonomous development of the Rajin-Sonbong FETZ that would otherwise occur with the status of a special economic zone as in China. In contrast, the de-centering tendencies of the Chinese state have finally created some room for Jilin province to maneuver with some flexible and decentralized policies, particularly targeting the Yanbian Korean prefecture and such cities as Hunchun as dynamic local actors and contributors in the GTS.

The sociocultural conditions in the GTS have been more positive but limited in their impact. Cross-border ethnic Korean ties have served as valuable social capital that has induced some concentration of South Korean investment in the predominantly ethnic Korean region of Yanbian. The ethnic Korean identity and ties, which are not as extensive and strong as the ethnic Chinese social networks in the GSCS, could not entice more South Korean investment and sustain it during the Asian financial crisis. The ethnic Korean ties have facilitated some border trade between Yanbian and North Korea and provided a temporary haven for border-crossing North Koreans in search of food, work, and escape to freedom. But they could not help alleviate the food and energy crises in North Korea and the growing cross-border disparities in economic growth and standard of living. More importantly, they have fallen far short in countering the powerful political and security concerns of the Chinese national and local authorities over the border that have led to crackdowns on the helpless North Korean border crossers.

While the steadily expanding transport links have contributed to the movement of goods across the borders, their further extension and networking have been impeded by the lack of large-scale financing. The latter is unlikely to come from external, international sources without more realized economic potential and greater cross-border stability and cooperation in the GTS. With the exception of China, the national and local governments of the RFE and North Korea are too financially strapped, to different degrees, to invest in cross-border transport projects. As a result, the infrastructure constraints on the GTS are likely to persist for some time. In the meantime, the future demand for cross-border transport infrastructure is uncertain due to limited economic growth and cooperative links among the constituent units of the GTS. What is more certain is the undesirable impact of expanding cross-border transport infrastructure on the ecosystems of the GTS, which imposes another constraint on its future development.

The extensive evidence on the GTS largely contradicts the harmonious hypothesis regarding the sources of transborder subregional formation, growth, and integration. Despite the strong earlier push and continued, albeit gradually less formal, involvement of the UNDP, the four sets of factors suggested by the analytical lenses have not complemented and reinforced one another in a synergistic fashion, as they generally have in the GSCS and the BYSS. This raises the question of whether the GTS is a unique case. To search for broader comparative evidence that may lead to more generalizable conclusions about the Asia-Pacific transborder subregions, I move on to examine several cases in Southeast Asia in the next chapter.

Notes

1. The relatively short history of Tumen River regional development is checkered and complex. The origin of the project could be traced to the First International Conference on Northeast Asian Regional Economic Cooperation held in Changchun, Jilin province, on July 16–18, 1990, and sponsored by the Asia-Pacific Institute of China, the East-West Center in Hawaii, and the United Nations Development Programme (UNDP). At this conference, which marked the beginning of the UNDP's crucial involvement, the original ideas of local Chinese scholars for developing the Tumen River region were discussed for the first time in terms of a general plan that could facilitate economic cooperation in Northeast Asia. Following a subsequent international conference in Ulaanbaatar, Mongolia, on July 6–7, 1991, the UNDP commissioned

a pre-feasibility study to be conducted by a team of three expert consultants. The mission produced a lengthy report that outlined three differentially ambitious plans (see Marton, McGee, and Paterson, 1995, pp. 16–18). The most grandiose of the three was Plan C, which called for the development of a Tumen River Economic Zone (TREZ). The core of the TREZ was a transnational city that would have a population of over 500,000 and grow to 3 million in 20 years. It would develop a diverse industrial structure; extensive cross-border transport infrastructure in terms of networked seaports, airports, roads, and railroads; and financial and transshipping facilities for a total projected cost of US$30 billion. Once completed, it would have similar functions as Rotterdam and Hong Kong (S. Ding, 1992). In 1991, the interstate Tumen River Area Development Program (TRADP) was officially launched, which comprised China, Russia, North Korea, South Korea, and Mongolia and was coordinated by the UNDP. Between 1990 and 1994, a total of 27 international conferences devoted to promoting the TRADP were held in Changchun, Pyongyang, Ulaanbaatar, New York, Seoul, Beijing, Hunchun, Vladivostok, Moscow, and Hong Kong (Ren, 1994). The "Tumen Fever" cooled in 1994 when the TREZ concept was abandoned and replaced by the TREDA as a more expansive but looser plan. In 1995, TRADP members dropped a multilateral framework for a "concerted unilateralism" approach focusing on creating an "enabling environment" for investment in the three riparian countries' individual development plans within the TREDA region (Hunter, 1998, p. 2). The role of the UNDP was reduced to a facilitator through the establishment of the UNDP Tumen Secretariat in Beijing in June 1996. This turn of events marked the beginning of a new phase of the Tumen River development project whose legal and institutional framework was worked out in 1995. It included a Coordination Committee consisting of China, North Korea, and Russia, a Consultative Commission made up of the three members of the Coordination Committee plus South Korea and Mongolia, and other supporting bodies. The phase saw a number of activities such as promoting investment in the TREDA in conjunction with UNIDO and the establishment of the Tumen Trust Fund in 1996. This phase was followed by another one (1997–1999), which focused exclusively on investment promotion (Underdown, 1997).

2. The Tumen River, which originates from the east wing of Changbaishan (Changbai Mountain) in Jilin province, has a total length of 516 km. The 498 km of Tumen River's upper and middle reaches run along the China–North Korea border; for the last 18 km or so, the river divides North Korea from the RFE before it empties into the Sea of Japan. The entire riparian region of the Tumen River covers 33,168 sq km, of which 22,861 sq km are on the Chinese side, approximately 10,000 sq km on the North Korean side, and the remaining 300 km on the RFE's sides (Yu, 1994).

3. The China portion of the GTS covers the eastern portion of Jilin province and includes four cities—Hunchun, Tumen, Yanji, and Longjing, (see map 6.1) and their surrounding rural areas. It spreads over approximately 10,000 sq km and has close to 1 million people. The part of North Korea bounded by the GTS refers to Hamgyong-Bukdo, which spans 12,188 sq km with about 900,000 people. The crucial part of the RFE in the GTS is the Greater Vladivostok region, which refers to the southern part of Primorskii Krai including the main cities of Vladivostok, Nakhodka, and Slavjanka. It covers 15,200 sq km and about 1.2 million people (Ding, 1993).

4. According to some Chinese sources, some Russian border traders called Chinese exports "Chinese garbage," "one-week shoes," and "paper jackets." Some Russian shopkeepers refused to sell Chinese goods (see Rozman, 1998a, p. 9).

5. "Korea: Russia looking to the North," *International Herald Tribune*, February 13, 2003, p. 6.

6. Hunchun features a unique combination of both overland opening and sea access. Its border with Primorskii Krai (Maritime Territory) of the RFE to the southeast covers 232 km. Its overland border crossing is only 32 km from the RFE border town of Kraskino, which is con-

nected to the Trans-Siberian Railway through a spur line. Hunchun is about 46 km from the small RFE port of Posyet and 140 km from the largest and most important port of Vladivostok in the RFE. Hunchun borders Hamgyong-Bukdo of North Korea to the southwest across the Tumen River along 140 km. The Chinese border town of Fangchuan, the easternmost point of China's land border along the Tumen River, is only 2 km from the North Korean border train station at Doo-Man River Lee (an equivalent of a township). The rail and land crossings connect Hunchun conveniently with the three North Korean ports of Rajin (90 km away), Sonbong, and Chongjin. Finally, with the town of Fangchuan only 15 km away from the Sea of Japan, Hunchun marks the closest shipping point from northeastern China to the west coast of Japan, with a distance of 800 km from Niigata (see Liu and Liao, 1993).

7. Hunchun's important role in ocean trade with Japan goes all the way back to the Tang dynasty (618–907 CE). The Hunchun-Japan shipping route earned a reputation as the "Ocean Silk Road" or the "Japan Road." Even after Russia took over a large portion of China's northeastern territory in the late 19th century, a Sino-Russian border treaty signed in 1886 continued to allow Chinese ships to enter the Sea of Japan from Hunchun on the Tumen River. There were regular commercial vessels running between Hunchun and Posyet and Vladivostok. In 1906, for example, over 1,500 vessels passed through the Hunchun port with a total tonnage of 25,000. The Hunchun border customs established in 1909 was the very first such facility in northeastern China (Liu and Liao, 1993). China lost the shipping rights from the Hunchun port to the Sea of Japan in 1938 due to Japan's military blockade of the mouth of the Tumen River during the Russian-Japanese War.

8. *Renmin Ribao* (The People's Daily), overseas edition, January 2, 2002, p. 8.

9. *Renmin Ribao* (The People's Daily), overseas edition, November 7, 2000, p. 1.

10. The mother company of the Hunchun-based textiles/garment factory, headquartered in Seoul, went bankrupt, while the Japanese steel company pulled back from its ambitious plan. Interview with the director of the Tumen River Research Institute under the Academy of Northeast Asian Studies at Jilin University, Changchun, Jilin province, July 28, 1999.

11. *Renmin Ribao* (The People's Daily), overseas edition, January 2, 2002, p. 8.

12. Vladivostok's harbor was largely occupied with naval vessels until it was officially converted from a naval base to a civilian commercial port in 1993. Although most military vessels left afterward, a few old submarines remained in the harbor. Commercial shipping was slow to develop. Interview with the president of the Academy of Northeast Asian Studies at Jilin University, Changchun, Jilin province, July 28, 1999.

13. The administrative units bounded by the Rajin-Sonbong FETZ included seven *Lees* (the equivalent of China's towns), two industrial districts, and one *Ba* (a unit smaller than a *Lee*) under Sonbong Kun; the zone also encompassed one *Lee* and seven *Dongs* (similar to China's neighborhood wards administered by residential committees). Besides the populated coastal areas just mentioned, the Rajin-Sonbong FETZ also enveloped undeveloped and uninhabited hilly and mountainous land and small lakes at the lower reaches of the Tumen River (Zhang, 1994). About two-thirds of the approximately 150,000 people in the Rajin-Sonbong zone live in urban areas and the other third in the countryside. The main center is Rajin City, which contains the zone's main port, while Sonbong has a port that specializes in processing oil and petroleum products (United Nations Development Programme [UNDP], 2001–2003).

14. The name Sonbong means "vanguard," which refers to this place being regarded and developed as a leader in North Korea's industrialization drive a generation ago under the former Soviet model of prioritizing heavy industries (Glain, 1996).

15. According to North Korea's Law on free economic and trade zones, land rental cost in the Rajin-Sonbong FETZ ranges from a high of US$0.6 to a low of US$0.1 per sq meter. The average wage is US$0.4 per hour, which is even lower than in neighboring China (Jin, 1999).

16. The hotel/casino project, the largest in the Rajin-Sonbong FETZ, catered only to a small number of Chinese visitors from across the border. It lost more business after the Asian financial crisis, which negatively affected the Hong Kong–based Emperor Group and the supplies to the entertainment complex from China's Yanbian region. Interview with the director of Tumen River Research Institute under the Academy of Northeast Asian Studies at Jilin University, Changchun, Jilin province, July 28, 1999.

17. The bays, beaches, capes, and islands along the coast of the Rajin-Sonbong zone provide picturesque settings for swimming, boating, picnics, and seafood dinners. The bays of Rajin, Sinhae, Sonbong, and Ungsang are particularly scenic, and the beaches in Hae Sang Gum and Chujin are excellent for swimming and water sports. Access to the Rajin-Sonbong zone is relatively easy. The most convenient route from China is to travel from Hunchun over the Quanhe/Wonjong Bridge on the Tumen River into the Rajin-Sonbong zone. By air it takes one and half hours to reach Yanji from Beijing, three hours by car from there to Quanhe, and an additional one and a half hours by car from Wonjong to Rajin. International tourists do not need a visa to visit the Rajin-Sonbong zone (UNDP, 2001–2003).

18. Interview with the director of Tumen River Research Institute under the Academy of Northeast Asian Studies at Jilin University, Changchun, Jilin province, July 28, 1999.

19. The RFE consists of 10 separate administrative units, or federal subjects, which are rough equivalents to China's provinces. They accounted for 36.4 percent of the territory of the Russian Federation, 5.1 percent of its population, and 5.8 percent of its GDP in 1995. The RFE as a whole has no legal administrative status in the Russian Federation, as it was used in a system of economic planning regions of the former Soviet Union. However, the various administrative units of the RFE, or regions in a loose sense, have gradually taken on an identity of their own (Bradshaw, 1999, p. 1). ·

20. In May 1993, the former governor, Vladimir Kuznetsov, was voted out of office by local legislators who attributed such problems as crime, pollution, and soaring prices to his free-market policies. Unlike Kuznetsov, who was an intellectual from Moscow, the new governor, Yevgeny Nazdratenko, was a locally born mechanic who worked his way through the ranks to head a local mining company. His new policies aimed at fighting crime, stabilizing food supplies, and strengthening economic links with neighboring Russian regions. Despite these policy departures from his predecessor, Nazdratenko expressed his identity with regional politics and the desire to rely more on local efforts and less on help from outside, which included assistance from Moscow and Pacific links (Lilley, 1993b, p. 42). Eight years after coming into power, Nazdratenko resigned as governor of Primorskii Territory in March 2001 under Putin's persuasion and left the region in a mess, characterized by organized crime, street violence, power shortages, bankrupt factories, unpaid wages, and deepening poverty. Soon after his resignation, however, Nazdratenko was picked by Putin to be the new head of the State Fisheries Committee against the opposition of Putin's own government. Reported in *Chicago Tribune*, March 12, 2001, Section 1, p. 3.

21. *Chicago Tribune*, March 12, 2001, Section 1, p. 3.

22. *Chicago Tribune*, March 12, 2001, Section 1, p. 3.

23. The North Korean official who headed the Rajin-Sonbong FETZ was Kim Jong U. A relative of supreme leader Kim Il Sung, Kim Jong U also was chairman of the Committee for the Promotion of External Economic Cooperation and held a ministerial-level position. His four-day visit to Hong Kong was paid for by foreign companies who wanted to hear what North Korea had to offer in the Rajin-Sonbong FETZ (Clifford, 1993).

24. The Haeju District is located just north of Incheon. Under a tentative agreement with the North Korean government, Hyundai would develop the Haeju District into a special economic zone for a period of 10 years. This would involve Hyundai developing the required basic infrastructure at the site and then leasing areas in the zone to smaller South Korean and other foreign

companies. Hyundai officials claimed that 200 small and medium-sized businesses expressed interest in leasing these facilities (Flake, 1999). Unlike Rajin-Sonbong, Haeju has two distinctive comparative advantages in a much favorable geographic location and the strong backing of Hyundai and, by extension, the South Korean government. They will make Haeju more attractive than Rajin-Sonbong to small and medium-sized companies as a site for light manufacturing operations (Noland, 2000).

25. "North Korea's Kim steams into Russia," news report by Softcom Internet Communications, www/softcom.net/webnews/wed/az/Qrussia-nkorea-arrive, accessed on May 9, 2003.

26. According to local government statistics, among the overseas relatives and close social acquaintances of the over 50,000 households of ethnic Koreans, over 200 had high economic, political, and social status. Nearly 70 were entrepreneurs with over US$1 million in assets, 28 were provincial level government officials, and more than 40 were professors (Li and Wu, 1998).

27. The Korean language, like Japanese, reverses the order of verb and object that is used in Chinese. In imitating South Koreans, even some ethnic Chinese students would say "my meal finished" instead of saying "finished my meal." Interview with an ethnic Korean professor at Yanbian University, Yanji, Jilin province, July 25, 1999.

28. Interview with an ethnic Korean professor at Yanbian University, Yanji, Jilin province, July 25, 1999.

29. The ethnic Korean residents in Japan are split into the pro–North Korea and the pro–South Korea groups. The pro-North group is organized as the General Association of Korean Residents in Japan (*Chosen Soren* in Japanese, *Chochongnyon* in Korean) with an estimated membership of about 100,000 to 250,000. These Koreans, many of whom are wealthy, are reported as a major source of money flow to North Korea (Eberstadt, 1996, p. 523). These Koreans stayed behind in Japan after World War II, as Japan was very rigid in letting Koreans go home by allowing them to take only 1,000 yen each. Interview with an ethnic Korean professor at Yanbian University, Yanji, Jilin province, July 25, 1999.

30. Interview with an ethnic Korean professor at Yanbian University, Yanji, Jilin province, July 25, 1999.

31. See Shim (1999) and "North Koreans seek to improve their lot in China," *Chicago Tribune*, November 11, 2002, p. 14. This account also draws from the two-part documentary aired on the ABC News *Nightline* program on June 4 and 7, 2002.

32. See "China targets North Korean refugees," *Chicago Tribune*, July 7, 2002, p. 3; "Tumen's harsh reality," *The Standard*, March 4, 2003, p. A-22.

33. "Tumen's harsh reality," *The Standard*, March 4, 2003, p. A-22.

34. According to former prisoners in these labor camps, torture and execution were common. Accused of carrying Chinese sperm, pregnant women were forced to take injections that would lead to stillborn babies, while those babies born alive were immediately killed by prison guards. See "N. Korea killing prison babies, defectors say," *Chicago Tribune*, June 12, 2002, p. 6.

35. "China must work with South Korea to solve the refugee issue," accessed from scmp.com on February 6, 2003.

36. The Soviet authorities saw the Korean minority in the RFE as a potential fifth column after Japan's move into Manchuria. In 1937, with little advance warning, they deported 180,000 Korean residents of the Pacific coast regions to Central Asia, where many had to scratch a living on uncultivated land. In the wake of the Soviet Union's collapse, many of the 280,000 ethnic Koreans in Central Asia found they were no longer welcome under rising nationalism in the region. A civil war between former communists and an alliance of Muslims in Tajikistan drove 6,000 ethnic Korean residents into neighboring states and Russia. Under these push forces, many ethnic Koreans began to look to return to the RFE and saw new job opportunities in South Korea–invested enterprises (Lilley, 1993a).

37. In the town of Pogornichnyi in the Siberian district of Primorskii, a brawl between a gang of Chinese Koreans and their Han compatriots took place that involved 70–100 people armed with knives, clubs, and brass knuckles. The local police, which had only one Chinese-speaking officer on the 370-member force, had to call in the Chinese police from the border city of Suifenhe of Heilongjiang province for the investigation. Ethnic Chinese also were reported to be involved in the rising rate of highway robbery, extortion, and racketeering. Worse, the ethnic Chinese appeared to have enlisted strong local resentment as the Chinatown in Vladivostok was labeled a "ghetto" (Kaye, 1993). The evidence suggests scapegoating the Chinese for the region's economic woes just as the low-priced, competitive Chinese products were degraded.

38. "Korea: Russia looking to the North," *International Herald Tribune,* February 13, 2003, p. 6.

39. See Lilley, 1993a.

40. *Chicago Tribune,* March 12, 2001, Section 1, p. 3.

III

COMPARISONS, GENERALIZATIONS, AND IMPLICATIONS

7

Four Cases Across Southeast Asia

MOVING SOUTH AND WEST FROM THE Greater Tumen Subregion (GTS) in the northeastern corner of the western Pacific Rim past the Bohai/ Yellow Sea Subregion (BYSS) and the Greater Southeast China Subregion (GSCS), we can identify four transborder subregions that stretch from mainland Southeast Asia abutting southwestern China to the eastern end of Indonesia and the southern tip of the Philippines in maritime Southeast Asia (see map 1.1 in chapter 1). This chapter takes a comparative, albeit uneven, look at these four subregions as secondary cases. This comparison achieves two analytical purposes: (1) it demonstrates additional differences and similarities across a larger number of Asia-Pacific transborder subregions, and (2) it illustrates how varied presence, absence, and interactions among the key factors associated with the four lenses could account for the differences and similarities between the Southeast Asian cases and the three primary cases in East Asia. I begin with a somewhat more detailed examination of the Greater Mekong Subregion (hereafter the GMS), on which I have conducted more research than on the three maritime Southeast Asian cases.

The Greater Mekong Subregion: A Hybrid Case

Given its composition and boundary, the GMS may cross over the formal-informal divide of regional cooperation and integration. The GMS comprises Thailand, Vietnam, Lao People's Democratic Republic (hereafter Lao PDR), Myanmar (formerly Burma), Cambodia, and China's Yunnan province (see

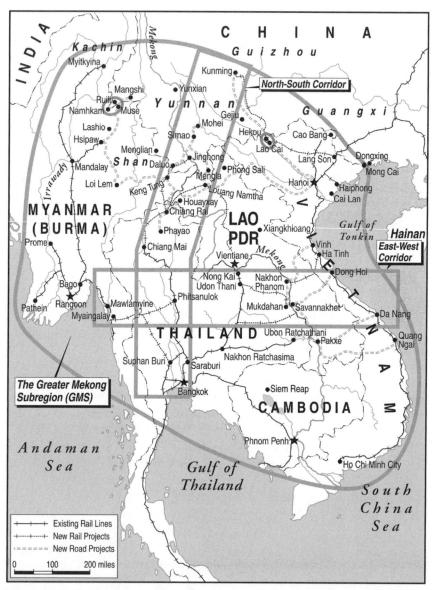

MAP 7.1
The Greater Mekong Subregion (GMS): Two Major Economic Corridors

map 7.1). The inclusion of Yunnan as a subnational administrative entity qualifies the GMS as a transborder subregion in the definition used (see chapter 2).

The overall size of the GMS and the involvement of six units (five of which are entire countries) stretch the analysis of their cross-border links to a daunting scope. Given the book's central concern with border-intensive ties among subnational or local areas, especially in China's border regions, I settle with a consistent focus on cross-border relations among selected localities in the GMS that are contiguous or adjacent to international boundaries. However, since the GMS features a formal layer of inter-state participation and the facilitating role of the Asian Development Bank (ADB), we must be aware of the economic and political relations among the GMS countries as the broader context for subregional or local cross-border dynamics.

As the three primary cases indicate, subregional economic integration has varied in the enabling effect of cross-border trade. More globally oriented trade has strengthened economic ties among the units of the GSCS and the BYSS and the latter's strong integration with the global economy. Heavy reliance on more localized border trade has created some trans-local economic links within the GTS but has failed to plug it favorably into the global economy. Similar to the GTS, the GMS provides another instructional case for examining the differential role of border trade in fostering subregional economic integration and global-(sub)regional-local ties.

Growing Trade Ties Among the GMS Countries

Inter-country and intra-subregional trade provides the starting point for examining the extent of economic integration in the GMS. According to statistics cited in Than (1997, p. 49), official trade among the six GMS countries rose from US$1.1 billion in 1985 to US$14.8 billion in 1995, with an average annual growth rate of 30 percent. The dependence of these countries on intra-subregional trade, however, varies considerably. For Cambodia and Lao PDR, 50 percent and 52.9 percent of their exports went to the other GMS countries in 1995, while 46 percent and 73.5 percent of their imports came from intra-GMS trade, respectively. While Myanmar contributed 14.5 percent to the GMS's total exports, it drew 46.8 percent of its imports from other GMS countries. On the other hand, both the export and import shares of Thailand, Vietnam, and China in intra-GMS trade were below 10 percent, with China exporting only 2.1 percent to and importing 1.5 percent from the GMS countries. Nevertheless, China's trade with the GMS countries is important for understanding the essential role of border trade in the GMS, in which Yunnan province is the only official subnational-level participant (see table 7.A in the appendix).

Intra-GMS trade between any pair of countries has been uneven, with Thailand being the increasingly dominant trade node among the five countries. Before 1990, Thailand-Cambodia trade never exceeded US$10 million a year, but rose to US$392 million in 1999. Thailand's trade with Lao PDR quadrupled from less than US$100 million annually prior to 1990 to US$441 million in 1999. Thailand-Vietnam trade surged from US$112 million in 1990 to US$903 million in 1999 (IMF, various years). During the 1960s and 1970s, Myanmar's trade with Thailand accounted for about 1 percent or less of its total trade. This share rose to 10–15 percent after Myanmar normalized border trade with Thailand in 1989 (Than, 1996). Thailand's imports from Myanmar, Lao PDR, and Vietnam grew almost 10 percent annually from 2000 to 2002 (ADB, 2004). Trade between Myanmar and Lao PDR has remained very limited due to such barriers as difficult terrain, similarity of economic and foreign trade structures, and different colonial ties. These bilateral trade ties aggregated into growing intra-GMS trade in the 1990s and beyond. (More information on the balance and content of intra-GMS trade can be found on the book's Web page.)

The Past and Present Importance of Border Trade

More than conventional international trade among the GMS countries, border trade has constituted the most visible and significant cross-border economic tie among the key border regions within the GMS. While the lack of reliable data and limited space do not permit an examination of all pairs of border trade flows, available data on Yunnan province, coupled with its shared borders with Myanmar, Lao PDR, and Vietnam, improve our understanding of border trade in the GMS.

With its advantageous location and frontier status, Yunnan province provided the historical must-go-through pathway on the "Southern Silk Road"[1] to India, Myanmar, Lao PDR, Vietnam, and Thailand dating back to China's Han dynasty around the transition from BCE to CE. During the first century, Burmese and Indian merchants traded diamonds, jade, spice, cotton, and ivory for silk from China's Sichuan province and copper, salt, herbs, and agricultural tools from central China across the Yunnan border. In the 1960s, the Yunnan–Vietnam railway carried the bulk of the Chinese goods into Vietnam in support of its war with the United States. Yunnan's active historical role in border trade and transportation, however, stagnated from the Cultural Revolution to the early 1980s, when coastal provinces and cities were heavily favored over inland border provinces. Yunnan's international trade rose from US$130 million in 1980 to nearly US$750 million in 1990 (Wang and Li, 1998).

The 1990s saw the return of Yunnan's important role in international trade, especially in border trade. Yunnan's foreign trade grew 20 percent annually and amounted to US$15 billion in 1997. Foreign trade as a share of provincial GDP rose from 1.8 percent in 1978 to 10.3 percent in 1997. Yunnan's border trade grew from a cumulative total of US$24 million during 1978–1984 to US$431 million in 1994 alone (see table 7.1), averaging an annual rate of over 30 percent. In the first six months of 2004, Yunnan province handled US$2.5 billion in border trade, a 25.4 percent rise over the same period of 2003.[2] As table 7.1 reveals, Yunnan's foreign and border trade is heavily oriented toward the three neighboring countries. Between 1991 and 1995, Myanmar, Vietnam, and Lao PDR were the first, fifth, and tenth largest markets for Yunnan's exports, absorbing 34.2 percent of its total exports. The largest importer by far, Myanmar accounted for 77 percent of Yunnan's exports to the three countries in 1999 (Zhonghua Publishing House [ZHPH], 2001). In 2002, Yunnan's trade with Myanmar reached US$407 million, which accounted for 47.2 percent of China's total trade with Myanmar.[3] Vietnam and Lao PDR raised their shares of the total trade with China from 3.5 percent and 2.5 percent in 1991 to 11.5 percent and 6.8 percent in 1995, respectively (Li and Zhao, 1997). In the first six months of 2004, Vietnam registered a growth rate of 37 percent, the highest among Yunnan's border trading partners.[4]

Until the early 1990s, Yunnan's trade with Myanmar, Lao PDR, and Vietnam had been conducted mostly through small registered border traders. The improved border transport infrastructure, coupled with tax rebates only for formal (non-border trade), enticed more of China's inland trading companies to conduct more trade with and through border traders or agents. Official reductions of export tax rebates also pushed trading companies to increase their exports before the policy became effective. These conditions contributed to the decline of border trade as a share of Yunnan's total trade through 1995 (see table 7.1).

The Geographic Focal Points of Border Trade

As table 7.2 shows, Yunnan's six border prefectures, which are geographically contiguous with the three neighboring countries, accounted for just about all the provincial border trade through 1995.[5] Dehong Minority Autonomous Prefecture had the lion's share of the total border trade due to its location advantages. Bordering on the Kachin and Shan states of Myanmar for over 500 km, Dehong is close to such important Myanmar cities as Lashio, Myitkyina, and Mandalay (see map 7.1). From the Burma Road (built as a vital supply route after Japan's 1937 invasion of eastern China) between Kunming and Mandalay at Lashio, there is a road link to India via Myitkyina, and

TABLE 7.1
Yunnan Province's Border Trade with Myanmar, Lao PDR, and Vietnam, 1989–1995 (in millions of U.S. dollars)

Year	Yunnan's Total Border Trade (1)	Yunnan's Trade with Myanmar, Lao PDR, and Vietnam (2)	Yunnan's Border Trade with Myanmar, Lao PDR, and Vietnam (3)=(5)+(6)	Border Trade as a Percentage of Total Trade (4)=(3)/(2)	Border Import from Myanmar, Lao PDR, and Vietnam (5)	Border Export to Myanmar, Lao PDR, and Vietnam (6)
1989	109	—	—	—	—	—
1990	151	141	131	92.9	43	88
1991	198	165	154	93.4	52	102
1992	274	233	228	97.8	74	154
1993	346	311	271	87.2	76	195
1994	431	431	255	59.2	110	145
1995	—	556	229	41.2	112	117

Sources: Adapted from Li and Zhao (1997), p. 185; SSB (1998), various tables; Wang and Li (1998), p. 31.

TABLE 7.2
Yunnan's Top Six Prefectures and Regions in Border Trade, 1990–1995 (in millions of U.S. dollars)

Year	Dehong Prefecture[a]	Xishuang-Banna Prefecture[b]	Baoshan Region[a]	Honghe Prefecture[c]	Lincang Region[a]	Wenshan Prefecture[c]
1990	117	—	5	—	2	—
1991	159	5	8	17	4	4
1992	207	11	18	18	8	7
1993	242	27	45	19	27	14
1994	280	52	54	43	36	23
1995	255	66	54	42	30	23
% of total[d]	60%	10%	10%	8.5%	7%	4.2%

Source: Adapted from Li and Zhao (1997), pp. 235–248.
[a]Bordering Myanmar.
[b]Bordering both Myanmar and Lao PDR.
[c]Bordering Vietnam.
[d]The figures in this row are each region's estimated share of Yunnan's total border trade.

rail and river (the Irrawaddy) connections to Yangon (Rangoon) and the Indian Ocean.

Key Chinese and Myanmar border towns are intensive spots for border trade. The end of Chinese support before the collapse of the Burmese Communist Party in 1989 facilitated the opening of more border trading posts between the two countries. The Myanmar border town of Muse became open for border trade in 1988. The Chinese border city of Ruili created the Jiagao Border Economic Development Zone in 1991. Thanks to Ruili's most active trading role, border trade accounted for half of Dehong county's revenue in the early 1990s (Kuah, 2000). On the Myanmar side, border trade not only has enlivened the town of Muse but also has revived cities away from the border. Every day in Lashio, a remote but important Shan market town 195 km away from Mandalay, approximately 300 trucks loaded with Chinese consumer goods rolled through the town and on to the booming Mandalay, which had a population of 850,000 and a newly developed upscale suburb (DeVoss, 1996).

The Yunnan–Vietnam border trade has widened the narrow borderline into a more connected transnational economic corridor. This trade has been channeled primarily through the Chinese border city of Hekou in Honghe prefecture and the Vietnamese border city of Lao Cai in Lao Cai province (see map 7.1). Although Honghe prefecture accounted for only 8.7 percent of Yunnan's total border trade (see table 7.1), its geographic importance lies in bordering Vietnam's Lao Cai and Lai Chau provinces for over 800 km. The Kunming-Haiphong Railway, which was built by the French colonialists with massive Chinese and Vietnamese labor around the turn of the twentieth century, connects Kunming through Hekou and Lao Cai to Hanoi and the port of Haiphong (see map 7.1). It provides the shortest overland route from landlocked southwestern China through northern Vietnam to maritime Southeast Asia by sea.

Like Ruili for Dehong prefecture's border trade with Myanmar, Hekou is the central hub for the Honghe prefecture's (also Yunnan's) border trade with Vietnam. From 1989, when limited trade between Yunnan and Vietnam was resumed after a bloody war, to 1995, the volume of cross-border trade at Hekou jumped from US$4 million to US$60 million (Mellor, 1996). Chinese exports through Hekou were primarily manufactured products such as cigarettes, beer, glass, TV sets, children's clothes, tires, and some heavy machinery. In the other direction came Vietnamese timber, rubber, lacquerware, leather, and agricultural products (Li and Zhao, 1997). Thanks to the booming border trade, Hekou (population 75,000) emerged from its remote and sleepy status into a lively frontier city. Along and above the muddy, potholed roads rose glass-and-steel office towers anchored by the 13-story Agricultural Bank of China building. The Vietnamese border town of Lao Cai also got a boost as a frontier trading post for northern

Vietnam, as the trade freight volume on the Hanoi–Lao Cai rail line more than doubled during 1990–1995 (Mellor, 1996).

Opportunities and Challenges Beyond Border Trade

Yunnan's border trade is primarily characterized by small-scale transactions between border residents and petty traders at about 100 border crossing points of varied administrative grades along a lengthy border.[6] Local border residents and international traders frequently cross the almost invisible and lightly guarded checkpoints to buy and sell at border trade markets that consist of rows of stalls or small storefronts. At the border trade market in Ruili, there are often close to 1,000 petty traders and dealers, including some from Myanmar, Bangladesh, India, Nepal, Pakistan, and Thailand, selling cotton, jade, bracelets, ivory items, and aquatic products such as dried fish and prawns.

In the Myanmar town of Muse, the less busy market streets are dominated by imported Chinese goods such as garments and consumer electronics, which occupy 80–90 percent of the local markets in northern Myanmar, as local products can't compete on quality or price. This Chinese advantage in border trade has contributed to a stronger Chinese influence through tourism and immigration to Myanmar's border areas. There are one-day tours by Chinese to the Myanmar towns of Muse and Namhkam, which are visited by about 200 residents from Ruili and Wanding daily. The peak periods (November through February) bring as many as 1,000 Chinese and their purchasing power across the border every day (Kuah, 2000).[7] The population of Lashio is reported to be 50 percent Chinese, while Mandalay is one-fifth Yunnanese. A network of Chinese clan and linguistic credit associations has emerged to provide capital to Chinese-owned business ventures in northern Myanmar.[8] Some Chinese farmers who were displaced by the Three Gorges Project in Hubei province and received government compensations have migrated to buy land and start businesses in Mandalay, driving out local farmers. The influx of Chinese money has spilled over into the local social and cultural realms. The visiting Chinese businessmen have become main customers of local prostitutes. The Chinese also have donated money to refurbishing local temples with a Chinese flavor, as in the use of more colorful and shining tiles.[9]

Vietnam's border trade with Yunnan also has taken on a broader scope of spatial and economic influence beyond the border zone. Chinese goods, especially cheap clothing funneled through the border, have reached and even saturated the street markets in Hanoi. Some farmers in the villages around Hanoi have gone north to purchase Chinese goods at the border and bring them back to sell at higher prices locally and in Hanoi. The resold Chinese goods are still relatively cheap and of good quality. These farmers have made money from extending the border trade into the hinterlands of northern Vietnam and the capital city of Hanoi.[10] While China-Myanmar and China–Vietnam border trade has remained fairly active, cross-border trade in other parts of the GMS has been sluggish due to economic, political, and other barriers (see the book's Web page).

The lack of true comparative advantages and natural complementarities, which has impeded integration of the GTS, has haunted economic coopera-tion in the GMS, with such undesirable consequences as unbalanced trade, protectionism, and cross-border smuggling. In spite of its less developed sta-tus in China, Yunnan province, like Jilin province in the GTS, has benefited disproportionally from border-trade surplus. The perceived threat of Yun-nan's exports has caused protective responses from the neighboring countries, such as the Vietnamese government's temporary ban on the import of 17 cat-egories of Chinese merchandise in 1992 (Zhao, 1997). This protective policy had little effect on stemming the illegal entry of Chinese goods into Vietnam via a network of smugglers who often carry 40-kilogram loads along narrow and hidden cross-border trails. Furthermore, the 150 percent import duty im-posed by the Vietnamese government failed to prevent Lao PDR and Cambo-dia from becoming other transit points for Chinese goods to be smuggled into Vietnam (Mellor, 1994). Borders in the GMS are porous to the flow of goods, legal or otherwise.

Regardless of the limitations and problems of small-scale border trade, there have been some favorable macro trends and efforts to move cross-border economic cooperation in the GMS beyond the localized exchange of raw commodities or simple goods. At the subregional level, net FDI flows from the six GMS economies to Cambodia, Lao PDR, Myanmar, Thailand, and Vietnam rose sharply from US$130 million in 2000 to about US$210 mil-lion in 2002 (ADB, 2004). In Yunnan, the Ruili and Wanding governments have encouraged foreign investors to utilize raw materials to manufacture products to meet both local and international demand (HKTDC, 1992). By 1997, imported materials for export processing (mainly jade, precious stones, and rubber) as a share of Yunnan's total border imports reached 35.5 percent (J. Wang, 1999). This integration of border trade and simple manufacturing has facilitated the evolution of Yunnan's border trade, more of which has been conducted according to such international trade practices as standard pricing, quality inspection, and transparent customs clearance, rather than through convenient arrangements. Border trade has shifted from involving primarily local commodities to broadly sourced products, as the proportion of indus-trial goods from elsewhere in China and exported through Ruili and Wanding reached almost 90 percent (ETCNCB, 1995). The evidence suggests the possi-bility of achieving broader and deeper economic cooperation in the GMS beyond just border trade. This objective has been facilitated by both inter-state cooperation at the central level and the decentralized policy-making at the subnational and local levels.

From the Outside to the Inside: The Tiered State in the GMS

What differentiates the GMS from the other cases, especially the GSCS and the BYSS, are the external institutional forces that facilitate economic cooperation and infrastructure development. While the GTS also has benefited from semi-formal inter-government ties and assistance by the UNDP, the GMS owes much of its formal existence and some of its cross-border projects to stronger inter-state relations and the backing from the ADB. This external institutional force, however, has had less impact on border trade, which has been fostered by decentralization and local autonomy. The two tiers of institutional influence deserve separate analyses.

The Inter-state Arrangements as Institutional Facilitators

The commercial links in the GMS, somewhat unlike those in the other three subregions, have been fostered by several overlapped but largely unrelated mechanisms of inter-state cooperation. The first such mechanism refers to the program of economic cooperation involving all six GMS countries (hereafter the GMS Program) that was initiated in 1992 with the assistance of the ADB (more on its role later). The GMS Program has continued officially through an annual ministerial-level Conference on Economic Cooperation in the Greater Mekong Subregion held in Hanoi, Manila, and Chiang Mai, with the twelfth meeting held most recently in Dali, Yunnan province, in September 2003. The program has focused on identifying and implementing priority projects in such sectors as transport, energy, telecommunications, environment, human resources development, trade and investment, tourism, and drug control (which was added later). In spite of the Asian financial crisis in 1997–1998, the eighth Conference on Economic Cooperation in the GMS held in 1998 reaffirmed the commitment of the six participating countries to focusing resources on priority transport projects (Y. Li, 1999). However, the GMS Program has maintained itself as an informal grouping of countries that collaborate on specific activities based on the market mechanism, rather than striving for formal, institutional integration of the EU or NAFTA brand.

The second mechanism for GMS cooperation, which dates back to the Mekong Committee formed in 1957, takes the form of the Mekong River Commission (MRC) agreement in 1995 that involves all the GMS countries[11] to different degrees. The purpose of the MRC is to explore and manage the development of the Mekong River as a shared, valuable water resource for commercial shipping and energy generation. While the MRC is an important inter-government mechanism, its influence tends to be limited due to a relatively narrow goal and lack of full participation by all GMS countries.

The third mechanism is referred to as the Golden Growth Quadrangle that consists of Yunnan, Lao PDR, Myanmar, and Thailand.[12] The aim is to formalize and develop cross-border trade, tourism, and transport links among the four geographically contiguous or adjacent countries into an economic corridor. With their shared borders and many important natural resources, the four countries of the Golden Quadrangle have developed closer border trade and investment ties since the early 1990s and become an increasingly integrated market embedded in the GMS.[13]

While the three mechanisms have created some national-level spatial and functional overlaps, they lack inherent interconnections. Collectively, however, they have created a favorable climate for closer cross-border economic cooperation.

The Role of the ADB: Holding the Purse Strings or Acting as a Broker?

The GMS Program has been most effective largely because of the substantial involvement of the ADB from the very outset. The ADB steadily increased its financial contribution and technical assistance to GMS cooperation, especially to the improvement of physical infrastructure within and across the six countries' boundaries. The ADB also has helped mobilize resources from multilateral and bilateral donor agencies and from the private sector for subregional projects. As of 2003, the ADB provided loans worth US$887 million to finance 15 completed and ongoing projects and mobilized US$302 million of co-financing.[14] The ADB also has co-sponsored investment forums to promote the GMS to private investors in such cities as Bangkok, Seoul, Tokyo, Brussels, and Frankfurt.

The ADB has characterized its multifaceted role in GMS cooperation as catalytic, demonstrational (ADB, 1996a), brokering, advising, and co-financing (ADB, 2002b). By combining these approaches, the ADB has intended to convince private sector investors and other lenders of the importance to participate in co-financing infrastructure projects. Attracting private investment for the subregional priority projects remains an ongoing challenge, given the tremendous demand for capital, technology, and management skills scattered around the vast space of several of Asia's least developed countries. While maintaining subregional infrastructure projects as a top priority, the ADB began in the late 1990s to facilitate a shift for the GMS Program to reduce nonphysical, cross-border barriers of trade and investment between countries. As the GMS Program moved into the twenty-first century, the ADB again worked with the GMS countries in developing a new strategic framework for the next 10 years. This framework has included some new or refined approaches, such as better integrating cross-border subregional projects with national development plans (e.g., linking new transborder and existing national highways into subregional corridors), addressing cross-border human resources development and labor market issues, and protecting the environment and promoting the sustainable use of shared natural resources such as water, as well as combating the cross-border spread of AIDS and drug trafficking (see ADB, 2002a, 2002b). The environmental emphasis reminds us of the UNDP-initiated multilateral effort to preserve biodiversity and international water resources in the GTS. In comparison, the ADB has played a more comprehensive and effective role in the GMS, even though both development agencies have attempted to achieve some similar objectives for the two transborder subregions.

Compared with the other three transborder subregions, the GMS exhibits a more complex, dualistic political dimension. The GMS is characterized by more formal or institutional inter-state relations and agreements, which are largely absent in the other three subregions. The GMS also is similar to the GTS in being subject to the influence from an outside international organization in the ADB, but the extent and form of that influence differs greatly between the two. Nevertheless, the GMS resembles the other three subregions in featuring an important influence of provincial or local government on cross-border economic cooperation. We now turn to using the state de-centering lens to examine the internal, vertical aspects of the states in the GMS.

Better Late Than Never: The Local Government Playing Catch-up

The relative role of the local state in the transborder subregions, critical as it is, varies by the degree and timing of the decentralization process by which state restructuring has unfolded, especially on the Chinese side of the borders. The GMS is more like the GTS than the BYSS and the GSCS concerning the involvement of the local states in facilitating cross-border links. Of the six participating states in the GMS, China, as the only one with a subnational-level involvement, deserves the closest scrutiny.

Despite the long-standing trade between the border peoples of Yunnan and the neighboring countries, China's central government imposed severe restrictions on border trade prior to 1978, based on the premise that its border regions were politically sensitive and militarily insecure. For example, the central government limited the purchase of goods by Chinese farmers across the border to 30 Chinese yuan (about US$4) at each transaction and the exchange boundary to a 10 km stretch from the border line (Kuah, 2000). This tight control and monitoring began to loosen by 1985, when the central government promulgated a policy that encouraged provincial governments and border residents to be more liberal in border trade. By 1992, the central government took the further step of handing over to the provincial government the rights to implement regulations and control over border trade. The central government also introduced guidelines for trade with Myanmar and designated Kunming, Ruili, Wanding, and Hekou as state-level open cities and towns for border trade and investment. This was similar to the policy of designating 14 open coastal cities in the mid-1980s, which contributed to the growth of the GSCS and the BYSS, and of granting the same status to several cities of Jilin province near the North Korean border in the early 1990s.

The growing power of the provincial and county governments has reinforced autonomy and targeted policy-making at the subnational levels. While Yunnan province unveiled its own policy for border trade as early as 1985, which included tax concessions and bureaucratic streamlining, the early 1990s saw the acceleration of provincial independence in formulating bolder border-trade policies. The provincial government, for example, would provide additional incentives to foreign investors in designated border towns and areas. It also simplified visa and customs procedures for those residents to cross the border as tourist-traders who could re-enter Yunnan multiple times on a daily basis (Kuah, 2000). Although getting the "green light" from the center later than the Guangdong and Fujian governments, the Yunnan provincial government has been more aggressive than Jilin province, where state-owned industries were more dominant, in pushing border trade. The active provincial government fueled strong initiatives of the local governments of Yunnan's key border cities and towns.

The Dehong county government provided the most illustrative example of effective local autonomy in line with the trickle-down of decentralized central and provincial government power. It established the Jiegao Border Economic Development District Zone in the border town of Ruili that had previously been designated by the central and provincial governments as a key outpost for border trade. The zone, which covers an area of 4 sq km and borders on Muse in Myanmar, has attracted a steady inflow of small-scale investments from Hong Kong, Thailand, and Singapore. In addition, a China-Myanmar Street was set up between Jiegao and the border to accommodate small shops and mobile daily traders (HKTDC, 1992). Other local government pro-development actions included setting up a center to provide investors and enterprises with information on border trade, and introducing favorable changes in customs inspection, taxation, border control, and customs duties. These measures spurred border trade and related activities, which contributed

to over 50 percent of provincial and local government revenues in the first half
of the 1990s (Kuah, 2000).

Political Shifts and Decentralization on the Other Sides of the Borders

State policies of Yunnan's neighboring countries toward border trade have
been similar to and yet different from those on the Chinese side. The main
similarity involves the respective national governments of Myanmar, Lao
PDR, and Vietnam granting favorable policies to the border regions and localities to encourage border trade with Yunnan. In this regard, the Myanmar
government has gone some distance, since it has a large stake in border trade
with Yunnan. The government introduced a general open policy in the late
1980s after the military junta came to power. The policy comprised a set of
new laws that encouraged border trade and foreign investment. In 1991 and
1994, Myanmar signed several agreements for promoting border trade and
technological cooperation with China, particularly Yunnan. More specifically,
the Myanmar government opened up the border towns of Muse and
Namhkam opposite the Chinese towns of Ruili and Wanding as customs
points (see map 7.1), as well as four other border towns. It began to provide
financial incentives and subsidies to large trading companies in the border region to trade with China. Through an agreement with Yunnan, Myanmar issued passes to border residents, who could use them to freely enter and exit
Yunnan's border towns (Li and Shi, 1994).

Although trailing Myanmar in border trade with China, Lao PDR implemented policies that favored its northern border provinces of Phong Saly and
Luang Aan Tha in the early 1990s. These policies permitted the provincial
governments to (1) approve small- and medium-sized investment projects;
(2) transfer the rights of land, factories, mines, and equipment if they are used
for industrial development; and (3) draw from a large fund set aside for subsidizing foreign trade (B. Yu, 1998). In November 2002, the Vietnamese government designated Lao Cai near the border with Yunnan as a "border gate"
for trade with China, with a new international trade center and preferential
tax and regulatory measures for new trading entities (Yow, 2003).

The policies of Myanmar, Lao PDR, and Vietnam were partly similar to
China's in that they involved favoring the border regions with varying degrees
of administrative and fiscal decentralization. A crucial difference, however, lies
in the degree and type of autonomy of Myanmar's local governments, some of
which are hampered by local political and military instability. For example, the
governments of Myanmar's border cities and towns were not granted the flexible and locally targeted trade and development measures of Yunnan's border
towns of Ruili and Wanding. By opening up Muse, the Myanmar government

enticed Wa and Shan guerrilla leaders to become border traders. While the Wa group and its soldiers are loyal to the military government, the insurgent army in the Shan state has continued to threaten the region's stability. The former insurgent leaders also fought over distribution rights, venture capital, and prime locations (DeVoss, 1996). Ironically, even though Myanmar's local governments near the Chinese border were not given formal autonomy and decision-making authority, there have always been de facto decentralization and local autonomy of a different kind: warlords and military leaders rule these territories tightly, with little regard for what the central government may or may not allow them to do. These unfavorable conditions severely limit the otherwise positive role of the local governments in promoting border trade.

Despite a long tradition of centralized policy-making that has favored the development of Bangkok, the Thai government has recently introduced decentralization measures such as allowing the mayors of important northern cities like Chiang Mai to be democratically elected; the persons in these positions used to be appointed by the center. While the current prime minister of Thailand (Thaksin Shinawatra) was from that region,[15] which reminds us of the personalized regional politics in the South Korean context (see chapter 5), the policy might have been intended to take greater advantage of northern Thailand's increasing opportunities for regional economic cooperation with the neighboring countries, especially China. Even without sharing a border, the Thai Investment Commission and the Kunming High-Tech Development Zone signed an agreement to set up a "China Shopping Center" and a duty-free industrial district for China-invested manufacturing ventures near the border city of Chiang Rai, close to the Myanmar and Lao borders with China (see map 7.1).[16]

The GMS exhibits the heaviest outside institutional influence from the various inter-government programs and the ADB's substantial involvement without developing institutional integration. For example, the GMS Program has helped member economies prepare for a single GMS visa system to promote tourism and reduce the direct cost of cross-border control and management (ADB, 2004). While this may be characterized as de-centering in the upward direction, de-centering in the downward direction through decentralization has played a comparatively stronger role in facilitating the spread and intensity of border trade in the GMS. In this subregion of several least developed Asian economies, the relationship between decentralization policies and border trade has favorable local benefits in the short term, while the large subregional infrastructure projects initiated and implemented under the GMS Program hold broader and longer-term potentials. Finally, regardless of the relative importance of the external/horizontal and internal/vertical relations of the states in the GMS, their impact is mediated in a subregion steeped in varied cross-border historical, cultural, and ethnic ties, which are examined via the cross-border social capital lens below.

The Revival of Border-Straddling Ethnic Ties

As the previous three chapters have demonstrated, cross-border ethnic ties, which lay dormant under inter-state hostility and border closure, have re-asserted themselves as a form of boundary-spanning social capital to facilitate economic transactions in a more open transborder context. The GMS reveals a distinctive variation of how deep-rooted and extensive cross-border ethnic ties constitute a bottom-up force in economic cooperation, irrespective of the top-down or horizontal institutional influence. The root of cross-border social capital in terms of cultural and ethnic ties in the GMS runs deep into a long history of intensive and contentious political and economic interactions.

Historical Incorporation and Trade Routes

Much of the border trade facilitated by cross-border ethnic ties takes place along Yunnan's borders with Myanmar, Lao PDR, and Vietnam and adjacent to Thailand. Although these borders marked China's shifting southern frontier in the past, they didn't fully differentiate China's economic/geographic edge to the south, whereas the northern boundary was more clearly demarcated, especially after the Great Wall was built. The recent Chinese maps show no formally delimited southern border until the Qin dynasty (ca. 220 BCE) that approximated what are today Guangxi and Yunnan provinces. Maps for the dynasties through the Tang (618–907 CE) depicted China's southern border to include what are northern Vietnam and northern Myanmar today. All these maps were intended to portray "incorporation" of Chinese areas rather than "expansion" of imperial China (G. Wade, 2000, pp. 34–35). Real history may prove otherwise, however.

According to Wade (2000), the Chinese push to the southwest, which began as early as the Qin dynasty, reached deep into the Red River Delta after defeating an indigenous resistance by the famous Tru'ng sister of Jiaozhi (now part of Vietnam) in the first century CE. During several subsequent centuries of failed Chinese invasions to incorporate Vietnam, a mixed culture of great Chinese influence and strong antagonism toward the Chinese state developed across and around this southern border. By the 1380s, the Chinese effort to control the Yunnan region, which intensified during the Tang dynasty through the invasion and incorporation of the state Nanzhao (centered at Dali in Yunnan today), led to the formal incorporation of much of Yunnan into the Chinese state. This historical evidence points to the gradual southward expansion of the Chinese polity through primarily military conquests. On the other hand, the historical relations between Yunnan and Burma, which date back to the early eleventh century, were characterized by King Anawrahta of the Pagan dynasty sending religious or peace missions over the border to stop the war waged by the Mongols (Than, 1996). So there was both a conflictual and cooperative aspect to these early cross-border relations.

Through external incorporation and local resistance and adaptation, the region that today forms the northern part of the GMS became an important trading frontier in ancient times. According to Chinese historical records, the Southern Silk Road originated as early as the Qin dynasty and prospered during the Han and Tang dynasties. In 69 CE, the Han dynasty set up a commandery at Yongchang (which is Baoshan, Yunnan, today) on the major trade route to strengthen local administration. Yongchang subsequently became a lively trading outpost where Chinese merchants from Sichuan and the central plains traded a variety of items with their Indian and Burmese counterparts. From the Song through the Qing dynasty, the trade route between Tengchong (farther west of the old Yongchang) in Yunnan and Bhamo in Burma remained very busy for cross-border trade, with long caravans of as many as hundreds of laden oxen and mules (Wang and Li, 1998). China-Burma trade amounted to about 700,000 pounds sterling in 1827. Despite a subsequent decline, this cross-border trade continued even after Burma was conquered by the British and made a province of British India in 1855 (Than, 1996).

Like Myanmar, Thailand has long historical and economic links with Yunnan, going back to the mid-1300s when the kingdom of Ayudhya was founded as a petty Tai principality and acknowledged as a vassal state by Siam, the predecessor of modern Thailand. After its inception, Siam traded actively with China. In the latter part of the eighteenth century, Siam granted Chinese merchants such privileges as traveling freely inside the country. The nineteenth and early twentieth centuries were a "golden period" for the ancient caravan trade, as 700 to 1,000 laden mules traveled between Yunnan and Chiang Mai yearly. By the 1920s, the estimated volume of Sino-Siam trade reached 35,000 tons (Berlie, 2000; Than, 1996). While Myanmar and Thailand had political, economic, and social relations from ancient times, trade between them was limited by many conflicts and didn't grow rapidly until the early 1900s. At that time, Burma imported more from Siam than from China, while exporting more to China than to Siam. Laos (now Lao PDR) existed as a number of dependent tributary states under Siam during much of the pre-colonial period. Besides sending tributes to Siam, Laos engaged in limited trade with Siam by exporting silver, gold, and wood and importing rice and salted fish (Than, 1996). The historical trade between these neighbors along the ancient routes and across porous borders has taken on a new life with the revival of entrenched cross-border ethnic ties.

The Geographic Spread of Old Cross-Border Ethnic Ties

Regardless of the early Chinese incorporation, periodic conflicts, and constant shifts of political/administrative boundaries, ancient trade routes through what is today the GMS were sustained by the participation of merchants of the same or similar ethnic origins and religious beliefs moving and living on different sides of the borders. For example, the migration of Yunnanese Muslims to mainland Southeast Asia during the eleventh through fourteenth centuries facilitated maritime and overland trade with southwestern China (Berlie, 2000). The ethnic, cultural, and religious ties not only reach far back into history but also cluster distinctively in space.

First of all, Yunnan province is home to 26 of China's 55 minorities. In 1996, the minorities accounted for 35 percent of Yunnan's total population and occupied about two-thirds of the area, much of which involves the border zones next to Myanmar, Lao PDR, and Vietnam (Li and Zhao, 1997). Ten minorities in Yunnan's border region, including the Dai, Jinpo, Miao, Yao, and Yi, have settled across borders for a long time. The Dai, who reside heavily in Xishuanbanna and Simao prefectures along the China-Myanmar and China-Lao borders, are known as the Shan, who are concentrated in the Shan state of Myanmar. The Dai also share the same ancestry with the Tai of Thailand and Lao in Lao PDR (Hsieh, 1995). The Hmong in northern Vietnam, Lao PDR, Thailand, and Myanmar originated from the large ethnic group and linguistic family of Miao-Yao. The Jinpo of Yunnan and the Kachin in the Kachin state of Myanmar belong to the same ethnic origin (Zhao, 1997). The Hani in Yunnan are known as the Akha in Myanmar and Thailand. In 1991, of Ruili's total population, the Dai accounted for 45.8 percent and the Jinpo 12.6 percent, while the Han Chinese and other minorities made up the remaining 41.6 percent (Liu and Liao, 1993). In 1991, the Shan numbered 2.2 million and accounted for 5 percent of Myanmar's total population. The Kachin were estimated to be 470,000, which made them the second largest ethnic group in the country (Li and Shi, 1994). In 1994, there were an estimated 66 million people in China, Myanmar, Thailand, and Lao PDR whose native language was Dai (Bradley, 1994, cited in Than, 1996, p. 15).

The Chinese in Yunnan and overseas Chinese in mainland Southeast Asia, especially the ethnic Chinese in Thailand, Myanmar, Lao PDR, and Cambodia have had historical and contemporary ethnic ties across the borders in today's GMS and beyond. Through early migration, descendents of Yunnanese Muslims are present in Chiang Rai and Chiang Mai in northern Thailand, and in

Kengtung and Mandalay in northern Myanmar (see map 7.1). Approximately 10 percent of Thailand's population today is ethnically Chinese, who are divided into a powerful rich elite and a "middle class" (Berlie, 2000). More specifically, the majority of the Chinese Thai trace their ancestral roots to Yunnan, Fujian, and Guangdong provinces. Many Cantonese who fled Guangdong in the 1940s to escape the Chinese civil war are heavily present in Hekou, a major border town of Yunnan facing Vietnam (Mellor, 1996). In the old "Guangdong Street" in Yangon (Rangoon), where only Cantonese settled historically, ethnic Chinese with origins in other provinces have set up businesses. This renewal of an old Chinese enclave would not have occurred if the Myanmar government had not adopted a more favorable attitude toward local Chinese in response to China's rising economic prowess.[17]

In the Lao city of Pakxé on the Mekong River where the Thai, Lao, and Cambodian borders join, Chinese from Guangdong have lived for over a century and maintained a quality Chinese school for over 80 years, which has drawn both locally born Chinese children and those of other Chinese living in the border areas of Thailand and Cambodia.[18] In Cambodia, Chinese immigrants, mostly from Chaozhou and Shantou in Guangdong province, began to settle in large numbers in the late 1900s, when there were about 130,000 Chinese. By the mid-1960s, ethnic Chinese in Cambodia reached 430,000. However, over 100,000 ethnic Chinese left for fear of persecution from the early 1970s through most of the 1980s, when different Cambodian regimes fought with Vietnamese communist forces first and the united Vietnam later. Today ethnic Chinese in Cambodia range between 300,000 and 400,000, accounting for 3.5 percent of the total population, as the second largest ethnic group behind the Khmers. Although most of the ethnic Chinese were born in Cambodia, many maintain strong ties to China, especially to their places of origin in Guangdong. Like the ethnic Chinese in Lao PDR, they often visit the southern Chinese provinces to do business or as tourists.[19]

Fostering New Transboundary Economic Links

For decades, the old ethnic ties mentioned above lay dominant in their respective local areas when wars in Indochina and lack of political trust among the countries preempted cross-border economic and cultural exchanges. Approximately 100,000 ethnic Chinese living in Hanoi were forced to return to China or go somewhere else before Vietnam's border war with China in the late 1970s.[20] The 1990s marked a new decade for the Mekong River region with the launch of the GMS Program and the opening of China's southwest. In this more open environment, ethnic identity and linguistic capacity have become favorable factors in border trade, especially in small-scale bartering and transactions at the border free markets.

Most of the Myanmar traders crossing over the border are ethnic Chinese, many of whom originated in Yunnan, and some of them left as recently as during the Cultural Revolution.[21] They used the Chinese language for communication during buying and selling, which was convenient and efficient for both parties (HKTDC, 1992). This ethnically mediated border trade bears remarkable similarity to border trade between North Koreans and Korean Chinese along the Jilin–North Korea border in the GTS. Yangon-based Henry Chai, who is ethnic Chinese, bought new Mercedes-Benz cars from Singapore and then sold them in Yunnan's border town of Ruili. Despite the official requirement for high import duties on luxury cars, Henry Chai continued to conduct his border-crossing business, knowing that local customs officials would pay little attention. Hong Feng, a China-born Thai citizen, advised the Thailand Chamber of Commerce in successfully acquiring a controlling interest in a moribund state-owned bus factory in Kunming (Mellor, 1993). In Yunnan's booming border town of Hekou, people of Cantonese origin, known for their cross-border kinship ties and entrepreneurial acumen, were the most active traders and investors (Mellor, 1996). In Lao PDR, Japanese companies such as Toyota and Yamaha set up motorcycle factories through their Thai subsidiaries, counting on the close cultural affinities between the Thais and Lao (Clewley, 1993).

Growing cross-border trade and investment has translated into new cross-border social interactions and outcomes, especially for Yunnan's border towns. In the pre-reform and pre-opening era, poverty in this remote border region forced residents in such towns as Ruili to pick tea leaves over in Myanmar to supplement their meager income. And local women often married Burmese men. In recent years, however, many of these old trends have reversed. A large number of Myanmar border residents came to work in Ruili. Many of the former local residents who had left returned and resettled. More and more Myanmar women preferred to marry men in Ruili (CCAE, 1993). This "reversal of fortune" bears remarkable similarity to the purpose and direction of people movement across the Jilin–North Korea border in the GTS and the Guangdong–Hong Kong border in the GSCS before and after reform and opening brought prosperity to China's border areas (see chapters 4 and 6).

Without the revived ethnic ties, border trade in the GMS might have been more limited, even under the favorable policies of the central and local governments involved. Cross-border ethnic Chinese ties have exerted more influence on economic activities across boundaries, whereas the historical ties between the other cross-border ethnic groups in Yunnan, Vietnam, Myanmar, and Lao PDR are less instrumental in fostering economic links across the border areas. This difference reinforces the evidence on the strong role of regionally and locally based cross-border ethnic Chinese ties in fostering trade and investment links in the GSCS and the BYSS to a lesser extent. Overall, the

GMS provides further evidence that once revitalized, cross-border ethnic bonds will widen and deepen, serving as an valuable social asset for promoting cross-border economic links.

Connecting the Corridors of Commerce

Cross-border ethnic ties go only so far in fostering economic links across the vast GMS, which, covering a land area of 2.3 million sq km with a population of almost 250 million (ADB, 2002b), is much larger than the other three transborder subregions. Other than the constraint of large geographic distances, economic cooperation and balanced development within the GMS are hampered by the lack of transport infrastructure that has stemmed cumulatively from low levels of development and the shortage of investment capital. To overcome this constraint, the GMS countries, with assistance from the ADB, have adopted a new strategy of developing economic corridors along existing and new highways, with two major north-south and east-west corridors[22] (see map 7.1). Ambitious and costly as these may be, they are critical to cross-border economic cooperation and development, given the subregion's natural endowments, geographic make-up, current transport bottlenecks, and future growth potentials.

From a Waterway to a Commercial Pathway

More so than political boundaries, a dominant natural or ecological feature often defines a geographic region, or a transborder subregion. Just as the Tumen River is the ecological glue for the three subnational areas, especially China's Jilin province and northern North Korea that make up the GTS, the Mekong River supplies rich water resources that bind the riparian GMS countries together.[23] The twelfth largest and sixth longest river in the world and the sixth largest in Asia, the Mekong ranks only behind the Yangtze River of China in flow volume. During the Vietnam War, the Mekong River was known as the world's most notorious waterway—the "Iron Curtain of Asia"—which symbolized death and division (*Asia, Inc.*, 1996). By the 1990s, the mighty Mekong emerged as a major ecological corridor for subregional economic cooperation due to renewed inter-state arrangements such as the Mekong River Commission and the GMS Program (discussed above). For goods transported from China's interior northwestern region to mainland Southeast Asia, shipping along the Mekong instead of through the southeastern ports would shorten the distance by about 3,000 km (G. Tang, 1995).

The Mekong, sometimes known as the "Danube of the Orient," appeared poised for booming commercial use. However, its shipping capacity has been limited by two factors. First, a long stretch of the Mekong is difficult to navigate. For example, the river between the China-Myanmar border down along the Thailand–Lao PDR border to Vientiane, about 1,080 km long, contains dangerous shoals and shallow beds. A segment of the river dries up for six months of the year and can't accommodate boats exceeding 200 tons, even at the highest water level for a few months (G. Tang, 1995). Second, most of the ports and docks along the Mekong, especially upstream, are relatively small and old. Resources for upgrading them are highly limited, as the upper Mekong runs through the less developed regions of four GMS countries, namely southwestern China, northern Thailand, northwestern Lao PDR, and eastern Myanmar.

To improve the difficult navigating conditions, a number of government efforts have been made in recent years (see the book's Web page). At the beginning of 2002, China, Lao PDR, Myanmar, and Thailand reached a new agreement to improve the navigating conditions of the Mekong River, with China putting up the bulk of the funds (US$5 million) and being responsible for all technical solutions and implementations. The planned projects include fixing dangerous shoals, erecting navigation marks and signs, and widening and deepening some stretches of the riverbed. These improvements are intended to ensure the smooth sailing of 100-ton boats and allow 300-ton barges to navigate, with further upgrading to be completed by 2007.[24] The central and Yunnan governments have invested heavily in upgrading such major ports as Jinghong and Simao on the segment of the Mekong called Lancang near Yunnan's border. In 1994, a major construction project began to enlarge the Jinghong port and build a new passenger dock and a freight berth, with the capacity of handling 400,000 passenger arrivals and 100,000 tons of cargo annually (Wang and Li, 1998). This investment paid off in the growing activities at Jinghong and other river ports (see table 7.B in the appendix). Despite these ambitious plans, commercial shipping on the Mekong, even at the more navigable upper reaches, has not been smooth sailing, while other contentious issues regarding the use of the water also have arisen (see the book's Web page).

When several countries have varying degrees of dependence on a major cross-border river for economic livelihood, political consultation and cooperation with one another may be more important than technical improvements such as building better ships and port upgrades. With more cooperative efforts and sustained investment for exploring the Mekong, the river is destined to become the primary and most valuable commercial pathway for linking the six countries to the outside world.

Toward a Network of Roadways

While the Mekong River provides the backbone of transportation for a riparian region, the geographic layout and preexisting transport routes make railways an important part of an expansive infrastructure network for the GMS (see the book's Web page). However, in an underdeveloped region without a crisscrossing rail network and without the resources to build one, road transport appears to be a less expensive and more effective option. But a decent road system within and across borders is not in place. The worst road conditions are found in Myanmar and Lao PDR, where trucks sometimes take 20 hours to travel less than 200 km on alternately heat-baked and monsoon-lashed dirt roads (Mellor, 1993).[25] To improve these appalling road conditions, the GMS countries, with considerable ADB assistance, have made major progress with several projects in recent years (see the book's Web page).

Arguably the most significant of these projects is the multilane cross-border highway along the East-West Economic Corridor (EWEC). Designated at the GMS Ministerial Meeting in 1998 as the first of several corridors to be completed, the EWEC land route stretches nearly 1,500 km from Mawlamyine on the Andaman Sea in Myanmar through Thailand and Lao PDR to the port city of Da Nang on the South China Sea in Vietnam (see map 7.1). The first land route to run across mainland Southeast Asia upon completion in 2006, it is expected to generate several economic and spatial benefits, including better access to raw materials, development of remote and isolated towns (e.g., Mouang Phin) in a poor landlocked country such as Lao PDR, growth of secondary cities such as Khon Kaen in Thailand, greater cross-border trade, and improved access to seaports, especially the Vietnamese city of Da Nang with its deep-water port, for people living in country interiors. Financing for completing the eastern end of this route by 2004 and a second international bridge across the Mekong at Mukdahan-Savannakhet by 2006 came from several multilateral and bilateral agencies besides the ADB (see ADB, 2002b). The Thai government has taken advantage of this corridor by promoting a program of sister border cities such as Myawaddy–Mae Sot across the Myanmar-Thai border and Savannakhet-Mukdahan along the Lao PDR–Thai border.[26]

Despite successful projects such as the EWEC, building and integrating a truly cross-border transport network to link several least developed countries in the expansive GMS is more challenging and costly than in the other three transborder subregions. It remains to be seen if all the main transport projects will be sufficiently financed and successfully completed. This tall order requires large-scale cooperation among the GMS countries and sustained assistance from the ADB. When it comes to building subregional transport projects across international borders, as opposed to promoting small-scale border trade, formal inter-governmental cooperation through the GMS Program is more important than informal transborder ties among local governments and border communities and groups.

The Challenges of Cross-Border Drug and Human Trafficking and Other Illicit Activities

Unlike the other three transborder subregions, the GMS faces a daunting challenge with cross-border drug and human trafficking. Although drug trafficking in the "Golden Triangle" (the linked border areas of Yunnan, Myanmar, and Lao PDR) was a vexing problem for years, if not decades (see Maule, 1992), it has become a more visible and damaging illicit transnational activity that could cross more borders as a result of greater flows of commerce and people in the GMS. In fact, illicit transnational activities such as drug trafficking, migrant smuggling, and toxic waste dumping have been generally on the rise in a more globalizing economy (see Friman and Andreas, 1999). What is unique about the GMS is how the national and local governments have been responding to the cross-border drug problem.

In the past, the unilateral and multilateral efforts of China (Yunnan), Myanmar, and Lao PDR to reduce cross-border drug trafficking focused exclusively on interdiction. More recently, they have begun to cooperate by aiming to eliminate the supply of illegal drugs, especially heroin, at their original sources. In this "Green Drug Reduction Project" launched in 1994, Yunnan province has taken the lead in assisting the neighboring Lao and Myanmar regions (e.g., Phong Saly, Namtha)—which are among the world's largest opium and heroin producing areas—to grow rice, sugar cane, rubber, and tea to substitute for the prevalent poppy that is used for making heroin. Yunnan has sent over 3,000 agricultural experts and technical personnel to Myanmar and Lao PDR to teach the techniques of growing the substitution products. During harvest times, Yunnan would buy back some of these agricultural products at favorable prices. Yunnan also has provided training to drug enforcement officers from northern Myanmar. Various substitution agricultural products, especially rice, have taken up 26,721 hectares of land in northern Myanmar since 1994. With the guidance of Chinese experts, rice yields in the Myanmar and Lao border areas in 2001 were reported to have quadrupled over the mid-1990s.[27]

Despite some success with this cross-border cooperation, the cross-border flow of illegal drugs has continued. In 2001 alone, Yunnan authorities made a total of 6,000 drug-related busts and raids and confiscated over 10 tons of cocaine, opium, and heroin, which accounted for 70 percent of the total volume of the interdicted illegal drugs in China. To curb this renewed inflow of drugs, the antidrug agency and border police of Yunnan have worked closely with the

Myanmar and Thai police and security forces in successfully hunting down two notorious ethnic Chinese drug lords in northern Myanmar.[28]

As the battle against the cross-border drug trafficking has been waged, human trafficking across the border areas of Yunnan province has become more active since the 1980s, when China opened up. The traffickers target young Chinese women and children from Yunnan's border villages, tricking them into prostitution or hard labor in Thailand, Malaysia, and other Southeast Asian countries through sightseeing and job offers. By 2000, a total of 1,041 women from Yunnan's border region of Menghai (total population 293,400) had crossed into Thailand and even Malaysia through Myanmar. While some of these women went of their own will, others were trafficked. Many young women from Simao in southern Yunnan, some 70 percent of them under 18, have been trafficked to Thailand and Malaysia for sexual exploitation. This human trafficking has been fueled by the low income in some of Yunnan's border villages (per capita income under US$120), the convenience in crossing the China-Myanmar border (no fences or walls), and proximity to Thailand (200 km from Yunnan by the shortest route). A few women who have returned with money they saved abroad have built shining two-story buildings in their home villages, while most of the local Dai residents continue to live in traditional black-roofed houses (see a photo on the book's Web page). Most of these trafficked women are not so lucky. A number of them, however, have been rescued from Thai brothels and repatriated back to Yunnan, with the help of Thai social workers and the Chinese embassy. Having experienced the trappings of human trafficking, the returned women feel so uprooted that they are not comfortable anymore either at home or abroad.[29]

Cross-border sex trade under lax control at the China-Myanmar and other international boundaries in the GMS also has contributed to the spread of HIV/AIDS (see ADB, 2002a). The spread of AIDS in Yunnan, which has the highest rate of HIV/AIDS in all of China's provinces, has occurred partly through truck drivers carrying commercial loads through Myanmar between Yunnan and Thailand (which has 800,000 people with HIV/AIDS, the largest of all GMS countries), where contact with the virus is most likely to originate. While most of the drivers are Han Chinese, some are Dai from Yunnan and Shan from Myanmar who are ethnically identical groups.

Although not on the scale of either narcotics or AIDS, gambling has been active on and near the China-Myanmar border. Since gambling is officially banned in China, entrepreneurs from Yunnan, mostly Han, have set up gambling dens on the Myanmar side of the border so that they are easily accessible to residents from both sides. They even managed to set up a casino on an island in the middle of a river separating China and Myanmar but not in either territory. It takes only a few minutes for gamblers to reach the island from both countries (Mackerras, 2003).

Cross-border drug and human trafficking and the spread of AIDS and gambling pose common threats to the countries in this part of the GMS by creating criminal activities, money laundering, public health hazards, and political instability and animosity. The substitution project to tackle the supply-side problem of drug production and trafficking represents a new approach that draws the expertise of Chinese rice farming to the less knowledgeable and poorer neighbors across borders. China's willingness to provide this assistance may reflect a vested self-interest in stopping illegal drugs from infiltrating its border and causing crimes and instability. The active involvement of the Chinese embassy in Thailand to repatriate young women back to Yunnan represents another effort of the state to combat human trafficking. The real challenge is for China (Yunnan province), Myanmar, and Lao PDR to cooperate at both the national and local levels to deal with their shared problems resulting from more open borders, with their policies to be better coordinated through broader transnational cooperation at the GMS level. A recent effort of this kind and scope was an official agreement signed by China, Thailand, Lao PDR, and Myanmar in October 2002 to increase joint controls against narcotics trafficking along the upper Mekong River, beginning with a joint survey of drug smuggling routes (Yow, 2003). The ADB also has lent assistance for tackling these cross-border problems by setting community-based HIV/AIDS prevention projects in Cambodia and Lao PDR and the Shifting Cultivation Stabilization Pilot Project in Lao PDR (financed for US$8.8 million) in 1999, which aimed to improve upland farm income and thereby reduce poppy cultivation (ADB, 2002b).

Combining Transborder and Transnational Subregional Cooperation

Unlike the other three transborder subregions, the GMS possesses distinctive features of small-scale, market-driven, and socially mediated cross-border economic links on the one hand, and large-scale, officially negotiated, and institutionally grounded inter-government cooperation on the other. Many centuries before politicians in distant capitals laid down arbitrarily defined modern international boundaries during and after colonial occupation and national independence, the people of this subregion had created international trade crossroads. Yunnan has always been the gateway for southwest China to access Southeast Asia and for both maritime and mainland Southeast Asia to interface with southwest China. Of the four transborder subregions, the GMS has the most countries that share common borders. It also has the largest number of ethnic groups that have straddled these borders through centuries of trade, shared (sub)cultures and languages, and intermarriages. The latent power of linked history, geographic proximity, and ethnic ties has resurfaced in recent years as the socialist economies (China, Vietnam, Lao PDR) have introduced market reforms and opening policies.

While these favorable factors came together later in the GMS than in the GSCS or the BYSS, they have begun to create a synergistic effect in strengthening cross-border links in a similar way, lending some support to the harmonious hypothesis advanced in chapter 3. First, a series of decentralization measures introduced by both the central and provincial governments boosted Yunnan's advantages in border trade with Myanmar, Lao PDR, and Vietnam. Second, the strong ethnic ties have formed new social networks that bring traders and merchants together from different sides of the borders. Again the government policy of setting up cross-border free markets has provided the convenient space for socially mediated economic transactions. Third, the improved transport infrastructure, assisted by the ADB, has strengthened the opportunistic effect of geographic proximity and more open borders. This in turn has facilitated cross-border flows of people, vehicles, and cargo.

Regarding the formal, inter-governmental dimension of the GMS, which does not exist in the GSCS and the BYSS and is only partially present but less effective in the GTS, the GMS Program has worked in ways that the informal, small-scale cross-border links cannot. The 12 ministerial Conferences on Economic Cooperation in the GMS from 1992 to 2003 facilitated a number of priority projects, especially in the transport sector. Faced with the Asian financial crisis in 1997–1998, this inter-governmental cooperative program has adopted a renewed but more efficient focus on putting limited resources into developing economic corridors, rather than activities of a broader spatial scale. Since these official cooperative projects transcend borders, they are consistent with the efforts of the various GMS countries and their local governments to open and develop the border regions and localities. The inter-state cooperation also reinforces a broad subregional identity based on a common history, shared cultural and ethnic ties, joint borders, and similar recent political transformations. These conditions and processes, however, have their own dynamics, whose importance would be missed if we looked at the GMS only from the perspective of official inter-state cooperation.

Even the best combination of formal inter-state and informal transborder cooperation may not bridge all the deep-rooted or newly emergent disparities and animosities across some of Asia's least developed borders in the GMS. In the late 1970s, the Khmer Rouge started a war with Vietnam but then was dominated by the latter throughout the 1980s. During this period, the government persecuted thousands of ethnic Vietnamese in eastern Cambodia, even though some of them were of Khmer heritage. In January 2003, some Cambodians in Phnom Penh staged a riot at the Thai embassy to vent a nationalist fervor against a rumored claim that Angkor Wat, located in the town of Siem Reap (literally meaning "defeated Thai") deep inside Cambodia (see map 7.1), actually belongs to Thailand. Built during the reign of Kong Jayavarman of the mighty Khmer empire that dominated a large area of today's GMS during the eleventh and twelfth centuries, Angkor Wat, the dominant symbol of Cambodia's national identity, is to Cambodia what Mecca is to Muslims and the Great Pyramids are to Egypt.[30] In response to the riot, the Thai government closed the border but reopened it immediately. Given its severe underdevelopment, Cambodia not only is heavily dependent on tourism revenue at Angkor Wat, which is frequented by about 10,000 Thais a year, but also has over 30,000 of its citizens working at dirty and low-paying jobs in northeastern Thailand.[31] The practical response from the Thai government to the riot reduced a potentially more damaging impact on the close economic links between Thailand and Cambodia.

No matter what traditional or modern economic, political, and cultural differences may create new border barriers, there appears to be sufficient mutual reinforcement between informal cross-border economic and social links from below and inter-government cooperation from above to facilitate economic integration and more balanced development for the GMS after peace has returned to this subregion. (See appendix table 7.C for a comparative summary of the GMS with the three previous cases.) In the remaining space of this chapter, I will take a brief look at three transborder subregions in maritime Southeast Asia to build a broader foundation for comparison and generalization.

Same Lenses but Different Cases in Southeast Asia

The similarities and differences among the four cases thus far revealed through the four analytical lenses suggest that they largely belong to a common phenomenon in East Asia and mainland Southeast Asia. The existence of three transborder subregions in maritime Southeast Asia points to a broader manifestation of this phenomenon through almost the entire Pacific Asia. Beyond the extensive geographic scope of the transborder subregions, we need to know whether and in what aspects the three cases in maritime Southeast Asia differ from the four cases just examined, especially the GMS. The three cases again are the Indonesia-Malaysia-Singapore Growth Triangle (IMS-GT), the Indonesia-Malaysia-Thailand Growth Triangle (IMT-GT), and the Brunei-Indonesia-Malaysia-Philippines East ASEAN Growth Area (BIMP-EAGA, hereafter EAGA).[32] The three cases are examined here as a set, through each of the four analytical lenses.

The Proven Argument and Evidence on Economic Complementarity

Viewed through the economic lens, the IMS-GT demonstrates the most complementary mix of resources and facilities, with the strongest and most direct global-local ties, among the three cases. Singapore's advantages include its abundant capital, well-developed financial markets, managerial and professional expertise, excellent infrastructure in sea and air transport, and advanced telecommunication facilities. In contrast, Johor of Malaysia and Riau of Indonesia have lower land and labor costs. In 1989, unskilled labor in Johor was about 40 percent of that in Singapore, while unskilled labor in Batam—the major island of Riau, only 20 km away from Singapore—was less than one-quarter of Singapore's (Chia and Lee, 1993, p. 243). This labor cost differential facilitated strong links between Singapore and Johor back in the 1970s, when Johor supplemented the growing labor shortage and rising labor cost in Singapore during its rapid export-oriented industrialization. Despite a much later start, Singapore's investment in Riau grew quickly in the late 1980s and early 1990s, from US$89 million in 1988 to US$290 million in 1991 (cited in Ho and So, 1997, p. 246). This was spurred by bilateral agreements between Singapore and Indonesia to focus on joint development of industrial parks, tourism, and real estate on Batam Island. By 1996, Batam captured over 20 percent of all foreign investment in Riau province and over 2 percent of the total in Indonesia (Peachey, Perry, and Grundy-Warr, 1998). Given a lack of comparative advantages, Johor and Riau had little economic interaction before 1993, but the shortage of labor in Johor prompted firms in the plantation sector to invest in Indonesia in the mid-1990s.

Economic complementarity in terms of differential factors of production among the three nodes of the IMS-GT not only has fostered growing internal links, especially between Singapore and Johor and Singapore and Riau, but also has created new manufacturing opportunities for Western multinational corporations. For example, Thomson Consumer Electronics (TCE) of France—one of the world's largest consumer electronics companies—reorganized its existing manufacturing facilities in the IMS-GT according to the relative advantages of the three areas. Its production facilities in Johor specialized in the final assembly of audio products and equipment, with components and parts coming from its plants in Singapore. While the R&D for both the television and audio division were kept in Singapore, the Batam plant took over the more labor-intensive operation of the subassembly of the television and tuner module. The assembled parts were then sent back to Singapore for final assembly (Fong, 1992, pp. 33–34). This restructured subregional production network is similar to that linking Hong Kong, Taiwan, and certain localities in Guangdong and Fujian provinces in the GSCS (see chapter 4). The similarity is clear evidence that Batam has become a low-cost production site for Singapore rather than living up to its marketed image of a high-tech manufacturing center and the "next Singapore" (Grundy-Warr, Peachey, and Perry, 1999). Unlike the IMS-GT's economic structure and orientation, the IMT-GT is well endowed with maritime (fishing) and mineral resources, such as tin, oil, and natural gas, especially in DI Aceh, and characterized by a heavy agricultural presence due to the shared soil systems and hot, humid climates of the three participating areas (Naseem, 1996).[33] While these factors have facilitated similar economic activities in livestock, horticulture, rubber, palm oil, and forestry, the national regions of the IMT-GT possess some complementarities that could induce synergistic growth based on manufacturing. Northern peninsular Malaysia industrialized rapidly during the 1980s and into the 1990s, and Penang has become the region's dominant manufacturing center, especially for electronics. Northern Sumatra has been the largest industrial region in Indonesia outside Java, with Medan (Indonesia's third largest city behind Jakarta and Surabaya) being its manufacturing center. Although southern Thailand is a less industrialized region of Thailand, it has gained some ground through the construction of export processing zones (EPZs) and industrial estates around Hai Yai, Pattani, Yala, and Songkhla. A general indicator of economic complementarity is the differential 1992 GDP per capita of US$1,149 for peninsular Malaysia, US$769 for southern Thailand, and US$405 for northern Sumatra (Naseem, 1996, p. 36).

More specific economic complementarities among the three members of the growth triangle also exist. The differential wages for unskilled workers ranged from US$5 per day in northern peninsular Malaysia (US$7 in Penang) to US$1.5–3.8 per day in northern Sumatra and US$4 in southern Thailand (Salleh, 1994, p. 4). Rising wages in peninsular Malaysia such as a 9 percent jump in Penang in 1995 contributed to labor shortages, which together with higher land prices accelerated industrial restructuring from the mid-1980s into the 1990s.[34] These economic changes pushed Malaysia's manufacturing and agribusiness industries to relocate over the border in northern Sumatra and southern Thailand, where industrial activities are more limited. While Malaysia's strength in rubber and palm oil production benefit its Thai and Indonesian neighbors, Malaysia could learn from the experience and expertise of the Thais in fruit crops and horticulture and of the Indonesians in timber-based production with the rich forest reserves in northern Sumatra.

Cross-border labor mobility in the IMT-GT has increased in recent years. Thai workers from as far north as Chiang Mai have traveled south to fill factory and construction jobs in northern Malaysia, earning less than Malaysians. Indonesians from northern Sumatra and Bangladeshis also have joined the temporary labor force in northern Malaysia, getting paid less than the Thais. The three border states of northern peninsular Malaysia (Kedah,

Perak, Penang) have issued a six-month informal visa (a sheet of paper with a photo) to guest workers, who can renew them upon expiration. They pay the equivalent of one U.S. dollar when passing through the Malaysian-Thai border. In the opposite direction, Malaysians often drive through the border for weekend shopping and entertainment in the Thai border towns, where goods and food are cheaper, which is similar to Hong Kong residents crossing the border to consume in Shenzhen in the GSCS (chapter 4).[35] Although the economic ties of peninsular Malaysia with southern Thailand and northern Sumatra have been growing, there has been a very weak link between southern Thailand and northern Sumatra (Tambunlertchai, 1994). This unbalanced triangle, with one of the three bilateral links being weak, resembles the IMS-GT, which features little economic interaction between Johor and Riau.

The EAGA is known for its agricultural and agro-industry activities (e.g., pineapple growing and production) but is also rich in natural resources such as oil, minerals, timber, and some of the world's best fishing grounds, and thus is suited to developing natural-resource-based manufacturing. However, it lacks the kind and level of economic complementarity of the IMS-GT, and even the IMT-GT. Despite the abundant wealth and capital of the oil-rich Brunei, the other component areas except Sabah are poor, with per capital GDP in northern Sulawesi amounting to less than US$300 (Gluckman, 1997). However, the southern Philippines have plentiful manpower and steel and cement resources that could support certain manufacturing industries. In addition, Davao is the third largest city of the Philippines. The Malaysian government has been promoting Lubuan off the coast of Borneo as a new offshore financial center since 1990. These conditions constitute some elements of economic complementarity that could foster an inflow of foreign capital and intra-EAGA economic links and growth.

Between 1990 and early 1996, 50 large banks from the West and Japan joined a dozen lenders from Singapore and Malaysia in setting up offices and branches on the island of Lubuan, with a deposit totaling US$3 billion. Lubuan also drew an influx of US$200 million from Taiwan during the China-Taiwan missile crisis (Tripathi, 1996, 1996/1997). Most of the economic activities, however, occurred in the form of more bilateral trade and investment ties among the various component areas. North Sulawesi began to purchase more cement from Davao, which in return bought asphalt from its Indonesian partner. A large construction company from East Malaysia set up a joint venture with a timber giant from eastern Indonesia (Kurus, 1997). Filipino and Indonesian workers were drawn to job opportunities and higher pay in East Malaysia. Some of them took up the heavy chore of loading and unloading trucks carrying Indonesian cocoa in the town of Tawu, Sabah (Gluckman, 1997). Another strong economic suit, tourism in the EAGA, grew rapidly during 1994-1997. In Mindanao alone, the number of hotel rooms rose by 63 percent, from 5,730 in 1994 to 9,317 by the end of 1997 (Dominguez, 2003).

Limited as they may be, economic interactions within the EAGA developed in response to limited comparative advantages and economic complementarity of the component areas before the Asian financial crisis in 1997–1998. More recent developments in the EAGA reflect the closer interaction between the central state, the local government, and the private sector, as well as the growing involvement of the ADB.

The Initiating and Reasserted Role of the State: Where Do the Other Actors Fit In?

While the three subregions vary in economic complementarity and activity, they share a common political feature of the central state pushing the project off the ground initially. This raises the critical comparative question of how the state's role in the cases here differs from that in the four previous cases. A brief answer may come from a cursory look at the level and extent of state engagement relative to the private sector in light of the view that the state should open the gate to cross-border development and then let the private sector take over (Gluckman, 1997). This argument is complicated by the question of how or whether the local government and outside institutional actors, such as the ADB, get involved.

In the case of the IMS-GT, while Singapore and Johor had largely market-driven economic links going back to the 1970s, there was a high level of interstate cooperation between them at the outset, as exemplified by the planning of several industrial estates close to Johor Bahru, the major city in Johor, for Singaporean and multinational investment (Ho and So, 1997). High-level government cooperation has been critical to launching and sustaining the development of the Singapore-Riau link through a series of investment agreements covering several geographic units and industrial sectors in Riau province.[36] The state also facilitated the establishment of a number of institutionalized inter-government organizations for overseeing various projects, such as the Coordinating Team for Riau Province Development. Most notable was the intensive development of Batam Island, which was managed as a national project with little input from regional authorities (Grundy-Warr, Peachey, and Perry, 1999). In fact, the governor of Riau province, whose capital (Pekanbaru) is on the mainland in Sumatra, was concerned about a splitting effect from the IMS-GT, which focused on the islands (primarily Batam) closest to Singapore rather than on the entire Riau province (see Ho, 1999).

The IMT-GT was conceived after extensive high-level government discussions among Malaysia, Indonesia, and Thailand. In fact, it was only after extensive feasibility studies by the ADB and other consultants requested by the three governments that the IMT-GT was formally launched at the end of 1993 (Thant, 1996).[37] All three governments had implemented policy measures bearing on the IMT-GT even prior to its formation and early development. The Thai government promoted industrial growth outside the Bangkok metropolitan region by declaring the five provinces included in the IMT-GT a large special economic zone. Export processing zones also were set up in Songkhla, Hai Yai, and other nearby areas (Naseem, 1996). During its Fifth Plan (1989–1993), the Indonesian government, for the first time, placed priority on industrial development in the province of North Sumatra (Salleh, 1994). However, a sustained focus on economic development in oil- and gas-rich Aceh province has been difficult due to the continued fighting, which started in 1976, between the Indonesian government soldiers and separatist rebels. Generally speaking, all three countries adopted policies to promote exports, attract foreign investment with financial incentives, and upgrade physical infrastructure, which contributed to the growth of the IMT-GT. Despite these facilitating state policies, the lack of opening to private sector participation from the outside has limited the growth of the IMT-GT.

The EAGA started out in 1994 as a cooperative initiative among Brunei, Indonesia, Malaysia, and the Philippines. From the very outset, the governments saw their role as providing a facilitative policy framework and building adequate physical infrastructure through a National Secretariat in each country, while letting the EAGA be market driven and private sector led. This led to the creation of the East ASEAN Business Council (EABC) in 1994 as a unified organization for the private sector dominated by small and medium-sized enterprises (SMEs) to oversee their interests and concerns. In 1996, the ADB got involved with an investigative study on the EAGA that identified major investment opportunities in agro-industry, natural-resource-based manufacturing, and tourism, as well as 150 program and project initiatives.[38] The initial role of the states manifested itself through a series of ministerial meetings, yielding 14 MOUs worth about US$200 million between Malaysian and other EAGA members. The governments of the EAGA offered investment incentives and built some industrial and transport infrastructure. The government of Indonesia extended the tax holiday to eastern Indonesia from 10 to 12 years. Brunei established the Muara Export Zone in 1994, while Sabah built the Kota Kinabalu Industrial Park. New ferry services were opened between Zamboanga City in Mindanao and Sandakan in Sabah in 1994, and later between General Santos City of Mindanao and Bitung in Sulawesi (Gluckman, 1997; Siddique, 1997).

The Asian financial crisis slowed down economic growth and private sector activities in the EAGA, which also suffered major setbacks from the natural disaster of El Niño (triggering a severe drought, forest fires, and haze and causing an estimated damage of US$9 billion), kidnapping, and ethnic violence in some parts of the subregion. Under these circumstances, the states reasserted themselves to revitalize the EAGA by calling the ASEAN Summit in 2001 to help improve the subregional investment climate, appointing the ADB as the regional development advisor to the EAGA, and by establishing the BIMP-EAGA Facilitation Center in 2003. A more centralized intra-subregional public agency, the Facilitation Center was intended to better coordinate trade and investment activities that were lacking under the decentralized structure of the National Secretariats and the EABC (Dominguez, 2003). As part of its more substantive involvement, the ADB and a consulting team, through a new large-scale study completed in November 2003, recommended a subregional cooperation strategy and program for revitalizing the EAGA. More moderate and realistic than the approximately 150 projects envisioned for the EAGA in the mid-1990s, the new proposal identified 34 projects totaling US$37 million directed at the targeted productive sectors of agribusiness and eco-tourism and the supporting sectors of trade and investment and transport, communications, and power (ADB, 2003).

Compared to some of the other transborder subregions, especially the GSCS, the three Southeast Asian growth triangles or areas feature a fairly strong role of the central state, with limited autonomy for the regional and local governments of the component areas. Some exceptions have occurred in the IMS-GT, where the state government of Johor and provincial government of Riau have gained differential autonomy in cooperating with Singapore. The lack of local autonomy in the IMT-GT may be partly attributable to the difficulty of having an unusually large number of participating institutional actors: four states in northern peninsular Malaysia, four provinces in southern Thailand, and two provinces in northern Sumatra. The central governments have sustained a strong influence on the EAGA's development largely because they are concerned about the frontier, the strategic status of the component areas, and aligning them closely with national agendas (Siddique, 1997), although local governments have become more involved recently as stakeholders. This is partly why decentralization reached the frontier border provinces of Jilin and Yunnan later than the coastal areas of China, contributing to the different timing and outcomes of the GTS and the GMS versus the GSCS and the BYSS. Since the rapid growth and integration of the GSCS and the BYSS have benefited from earlier and considerable local autonomy, primarily in China, it may be in the interest of the central governments to grant a greater degree of administrative and economic autonomy to the component areas of the IMT-GT and the EAGA.

The central state also is facing a dilemma vis-à-vis the private sector. While inter-government agreements have played a strong initial role in creating the growth triangles, that role should be limited to shortening the period over which natural integration based on economic complementarity, as perceived by the private sector, will take place (Naseem, 1996). As this balancing and sequencing of the relative role of the state versus the private sector has worked to the advantage of the GSCS and the BYSS, it has been recognized as important and beneficial by the GMS and the EAGA but has not widely occurred yet. At the same time, the central governments may be stuck with an ever present and increasing need to finance large-scale infrastructure development, harmonize investment rules, and remove other cross-border barriers such as restrictions on labor flows and immigration, actions that must be taken to induce the private sector to step up its role. In this regard, the IMT-GT and the EAGA are not that different from the cases examined earlier.

Finally, the IMT-GT and the EAGA demonstrate the complementary but seemingly indispensable role of the ADB, which has done more for the EAGA than the IMT-GT over the last decade. The national governments involved appear to have become dependent on the ADB for technical assistance and project financing, which may be unavoidable due to their development status and severe lack of resources, especially in the remote border areas. In this sense, the EAGA is similar to the GMS and the GTS but quite different from the GSCS and the BYSS.

The Latent and Still Relevant Historical and Cultural Ties

Do the important economic and political factors render the sociocultural conditions in the development of the Southeast Asian growth triangles irrelevant? Could the third analytical lens used for the earlier transborder subregions shed any light on similarities and differences across these cases? If cross-border social capital exists at all in the growth triangles, it could and should be traced to varied historic-cultural ties that once linked some of these territorial units.

Under the British colonial influence in the nineteenth century, Singapore rose as a colonial port city that not only linked Malaysian exports to the West but also helped revive the Indonesian trade, which had stagnated under the Dutch colonial system. Singapore and Malaysia shared a colonial past and sociocultural ties before they separated from each other in the mid-1960s. There were long-standing trade and family links among the component areas of the IMT-GT. The Kedah state in the northwestern corner of peninsular Malaysia was constantly involved in the fighting between Siam and Burma and was invaded and occupied by Siam in 1821. Of the population in Kedah, especially

on the island of Langkawi off the Malay mainland, a large proportion originally migrated from southern Thailand or are direct descendants of the early
immigrants. They see southern Thailand as part of their social world and
often cross the border to visit kin, shop, and participate in marital ceremonies
(Carsten, 1998). Long before Western colonial penetration, the islands that
form the parts of the EAGA today had enjoyed complex trade and cultural
links, especially between Sabah, the Sulu Archipelago, and Mindanao, all of
which were under the ancient Sulu state. After the latter vanished around
1940, Sabah was ceded to colonial Britain, which returned the territory to
Malaysia upon its independence. Because of this linked history, Sabah continues to be claimed by the Philippines. While Muslims populate much of the
EAGA (Siddique, 1997), the cities of General Santos and Davao in Mindanao
and northern Sulawesi, including the city of Bitung in Indonesia, have largely
been Christian.

In the IMS-GT, the historical, cultural, and also ethnic ties have fostered
business and other exchanges between Singapore and Johor. There is a strong
Chinese ethnic connection in Singapore-Indonesian joint ventures in Riau
(Chia and Lee, 1993), although they do not operate to the extent and depth
that tight social networks lubricate business relations in the GSCS. The historical and cultural ties have made relatively little difference to the IMT-GT
and the EAGA. In the IMT-GT, they have been overshadowed by the more
powerful economic and political constraints such as the multiple component
areas competing for the same kind of foreign investment and presenting a
challenge for decentralized cooperation and governance. In the EAGA, certain
historical baggage such as conflicting territorial claims, the lack of a common
language, and religious differences may impede economic cooperation.[39] The
overall sentiment about the areas' shared past and cultural ties has not translated into a more practical and realistic approach toward pooling resources to
increase cooperation (Siddique, 1997).

The mixed evidence suggests that unless fully revived by a favorable economic and political environment, the historical, cultural, and ethnic ties will
remain largely latent, with limited real influence on growth and integration.
In this connection, the three maritime Southeast Asian cases are quite different from the GSCS, the BYSS, and even the GMS.

Connecting Frontier Border Areas:
The Importance of Transport Infrastructure

In chapter 4 through the first half of chapter 7, we demonstrated the critical importance of cross-border transport infrastructure in the integration of
four transborder subregions, especially the cases involving frontier areas (the

GTS and the GMS), regardless of their varied economic, political, and socio-cultural characteristics. Of the three subregions in maritime Southeast Asia, the EAGA and to a lesser extent the IMT-GT contain some of the more re-mote, marginal, and underdeveloped areas and backwaters in Pacific Asia. Even the IMS-GT, labeled as a model of metropolitan spillover into the hinterlands (Chia, 1993), encompasses Indonesia's peripheral islands of Riau. In this dyad, physical infrastructure takes on a broader significance than the frequent ferry services and convenient crossings. Singapore has financed a major portion of the massive investment for building industrial infrastructure in Riau from scratch. One of the flagship projects of the industrial infrastructure was the BatamIndo Industrial Park—a joint venture between Singapore Technologies Industrial Corporation, Jurong Environmental Engineering (total share 40 percent), and Indonesian investors led by the Salim Group. From 1991, when the park was opened, to 1997, 330 of the 500 hectares reserved for development had been completed. This park attracted 85 corporate tenants, mostly American, European, and Japanese multinationals already operating in Singapore (Peachey, Perry, and Grundy-Warr, 1998). Singapore and Malaysia completed a second link across the Johor Strait by the end of 1997. On the Malaysian side, the bridge ended at Gelang Patah, which was transformed from a large plantation into a new industrial city called Nusajaya. Its proximity to Singapore, coupled with lower land and labor costs, began to lure more Singaporean companies (Tripathi, 1996/1997).

In the IMT-GT, while transport infrastructure in northern peninsular Malaysia is adequate, northern Sumatra outside Medan, especially DI Aceh, has the least developed transport infrastructure. There were no dual carriage highways. Many of the bridges were dilapidated. The railroad system was in bad shape, with some tracks in DI Aceh being abandoned (Salleh, 1994; Naseem, 1996). While the transport infrastructure in southern Thailand was underdeveloped for a long time due to the favoring of infrastructure projects in central Thailand, especially around Bangkok, a few transport projects have been initiated since the launch of the IMT-GT in 1994 to alleviate the infrastructure constraint on the Thai side of the border. The roads between Yala and Satun provinces and the Malaysian border couldn't meet the demand of commercial trucking as they passed through rugged terrain, which was worsened by only a single road leading to the crossing point.[40] This transport bottleneck received partial relief from the construction of a superhighway and high-speed train between Krabi and Khanom (the Southern Seaboard Development Project), not far from the Thai section of the IMT-GT. The main north-south railroad links southern Thailand directly to peninsular Malaysia, specifically to the port at Penang. With the rapid growth of cross-border trade between Thailand and Malaysia from US$963 million in 1991 to US$5.7 billion in 1999, the two countries in 1999 agreed to commence a container-block train service from the port of Bangkok to Klang port about 40 km west of Kuala Lumpur. The train, which carries 50 container units, covers 1,500 km in six hours and is efficiently cleared and checked at the border crossing of Padang Besar between Thailand and Malaysia.[41] While the ports on southern Thailand's east coast were inadequate,[42] southern Thailand, with airports in Hat Yai, Nakhon Si Thammarat, Pattani, and Narathiwat, has a better civil aviation infrastructure than other parts of the IMT-GT, even though there were weak commercial air links among them (Naseem, 1996).

The lack of transport infrastructure in the EAGA appears more critical in light of the distances separating the various large island regions and their national capitals. However, the island regions are geographically closer to one another than to the respective capital cities,[43] which makes it much more sensible to re-create inter-island transport links severed during the colonial period than build new ones. A few ocean links, which traditionally constituted the highway connecting the Southeast Asian islands, have been restored. They include the fast-craft ferry services for both passengers and cargo between Zamboanga (Mindanao) and the two Malaysian port cities of Lahad Datu (Sabah) and Sandakan (Sabah) connecting via the Filipino island of Tawi-Tawi, and chartered vessel services between the ports at General Santos (Mindanao) and Bitung (Sulawesi), as well as between Davao and Manado (Sulawesi) (see a map on the book's Web page). Improved overland transportation took place as Brunei, Indonesia, and Malaysia started a joint bus system across Borneo. Malaysia completed several new roads in Sabah and Sarawak by 2003 and will complete more by 2005. Indonesia has proposed several cross-border roads along and across the border between both West Kalimantan and East Kalimantan and Sarawak and Sabah to be completed by 2005 and 2007. In the air, Brunei expanded flight services to Sarawak, Labuan, and Sabah following a US$1 billion airport expansion. While small carriers have been flying between Davao and Manado and between General Santos and Manado, a new air route between Davao and Kota Kinabalu of Sabah was under discussion by the end of 2003.[44]

Despite the rapid growth of these inter-island transport links, their success may depend on a number of uncertain economic and political factors. Under less favorable economic growth and tourist activities in the EAGA, the limited travel and trade among the major islands may make regular sea and air services operate under capacity and thus lose money. This scenario could be worsened by the repetitive expansion of port facilities and the resultant competition for limited cargo and passenger flows. Politically, if the capital cities continue to channel trade through the existing main airports and seaports such as Manila, Batavia of Jakarta, and Port Klang of Malaysia, it would restrict the effectiveness of better transport links between the islands in the

EAGA (Siddique, 1997). Nevertheless, these contingencies should not dampen the critical importance of transport infrastructure for the development of the EAGA.

Shedding Light on the Harmonious Hypothesis

Thus far this book has carried out a detailed and in-depth analysis of three transborder subregions in East Asia as primary cases, examined in chapters 4 through 6, and a more truncated examination of four subregions in Southeast Asia as secondary or reference cases in this chapter. (See table 7.C in the appendix for a comparative summary of four cases along the four analytical lenses and dimensions.) Although this analytical strategy may not allow using the last four cases to directly evaluate the harmonious hypothesis (chapter 3), they shed some light on it regarding why and how it is central to explaining the variation across all Asia-Pacific transborder subregions.

First, the IMS-GT is remarkably similar to the GSCS in terms of the mix and strength of economic complementarity. This similarity, which defines the core of both transborder subregions, lies in the city-state of Singapore, serving a largely identical role as Hong Kong, in using the Johor state of Malaysia and Riau Island of Indonesia as differentially complementary sites for low-cost manufacturing. While one would quickly point out that Johor differs wildly from Taiwan in terms of size, strength, level of development, and relative weight in the respective subregions, the type and extent of Singapore's links to Johor and Riau are largely equivalent to Hong Kong and Taiwan's economic relations with the Guangdong and Fujian provinces. Although the IMS-GT had its start in the initial state-level cooperation among Singapore, Malaysia, and Indonesia—a cooperation that was absent in the GSCS—the subsequent sustained push behind growth and integration has come from the partnership between private firms and national and local government initiatives. These factors were sufficient to obviate the need for cross-border ethnic ties, which are limited anyway in the IMS-GT, and for building a new large-scale transport infrastructure given the geographic contiguity and proximity and the existing transport links among the constituent units of the IMS-GT.

Secondly, the IMT-GT and the EAGA share several important features with the GTS and the GMS, such as limited economic complementarity, relatively low levels of development, rich natural resources, and remote and frontier status. Like the GTS and the GMS, the IMT-GT and the EAGA have involved a certain degree of planning and cooperation among the national governments from the outset. Similar to the GTS and the GMS, the EAGA also has tried to improve cross-border transport infrastructure to connect the frontier cities and towns on a number of territorial units separated by bodies of water, with logistic and financial assistance from the ADB. Given this mix of potential advantages but greater constraints, the IMT-GT and the EAGA have trailed the IMS-GT with regard to the key outcomes such as growth and integration, just as development gaps separate the GTS and the GMS from the GSCS and the BYSS.

The three cases in maritime Southeast Asia collectively yield two important insights into the explanatory significance of the factors embedded in the harmonious hypothesis. For one, they reconfirm the point that any or all four sets of factors could matter to the formation and development of a transborder subregion. Moreover, the three additional cases show that the involvement of at least one highly developed economy as a central node in an economically complementary set of areas is more critical than the other factors. The latter argument underlies the foundation of the transborder subregion being based on comparative advantages and economic complementarities that are governed principally by market mechanisms and private sector activities. If this foundation is sound, the addition of any or all of the favorable political (local autonomy), sociocultural (social capital), and infrastructure (transport links) factors would only increase the chance of success cumulatively. The GSCS and the IMS-GT are convincing examples. Without this foundation, a transborder subregion is less likely to succeed, even if any or all of the other three sets of conditions are present.

If anything, the extended and cumulative comparative analysis going back to the GSCS and ending with the EAGA raises the next logical set of questions: Do the main conditions examined for the seven Asia-Pacific cases thus far exist in different regional contexts? Will they contribute to similar or different processes and outcomes of cross-border growth and cooperation, given varied contexts? These questions prompt me to push the envelope of comparative analysis beyond the Asia-Pacific cases to two other regional settings in the next chapter.

Notes

1. The main route of the "South Silk Road" originates from the capital city of Chengdu through Xichang in Sichuan province, extends southwest to Qingling (today's Dayao in Yunnan), Dabonong (today's Xiangyun in Yunnan), Yeyu (Dali in Yunnan), winds through Baoshan and Tengchong in Yunnan, and connects to Myitkyina in Myanmar before reaching into northern India (Wang and Li, 1998).

2. Reported by China's Xinhua News Agency on www.chinaview.cn, accessed on August 6, 2004. I thank Ted C. Fishman for bringing this report to my attention, which allowed me to bring the information on Yunnan's border trade up to date during the copyediting of this book.

3. Reported in *Renmin Ribao* (The People's Daily), overseas edition, December 18, 2003, p. 3.

4. China's Xinhua News Agency on www.chinaview.cn, accessed on August 6, 2004.

5. Border trade in Yunnan takes three forms: regional border trade, civilian border trade, and trade between border residents. Regional border trade refers to official border trade carried out by governmental organizations, often according to an economic plan. Civilian border trade refers to trade conducted by civilian-owned local border trade companies, which react to market demand and supply. Trade between border residents refers to dealings in government-designated markets in border counties and cities. The majority of the goods sold are mainly daily-use products (Hong Kong Trade Development Council [HKTDC], 1992, p. 15).

6. Yunnan's border with Myanmar, Lao PDR, and Vietnam stretches a total of 4,060 km, of which 1,997 km, 710 km, and 1,353 km separate the province from the three neighboring countries, respectively. Yunnan province has 17 prefectures, eight of which, with 26 counties, border Myanmar, Lao PDR, and Vietnam. Yunnan has eight state-level (first-grade) border crossings, eight provincial-level (second-grade) border crossings, and over 80 third-grade crossings with checkpoints and border street markets for border residents and petty traders (Economic and Trade Cooperation with Neighboring Countries Bureau [ETCNCB], 1995). In addition, there are hundreds of unofficial land or river border crossings between Yunnan and Myanmar (Mellor, 1993).

7. To attract more Chinese tourists over the border, the Myanmar government allowed the Chinese currency to be used officially in Myanmar beginning on July 18, 2002. Reported in *Renmin Ribao* (The People's Daily), overseas edition, July 16, 2002, p. 3.

8. See "Why China and Myanmar are drawing closer," accessed on the *South China Morning Post*'s website, scmp.com, on January 18, 2003.

9. I am thankful to Heike Löschmann for sharing these observations during our conversation in Hanoi, February 28, 2003.

10. This information was provided by a young Vietnamese clerk in a Hanoi hotel, March 1, 2003. He told me that a few of the people in his village about 40 km from Hanoi have begun to travel to the Chinese border to buy goods in bulk and bring them back for resale and have made money that way.

11. The establishment of the Mekong Committee in 1957 was initiated by the United Nations Economic Commission for Asia and the Far East (ECAFE) and four riparian countries of the Lower Mekong Basin (Cambodia, Lao PDR, Thailand, and South Vietnam), with the United States and Thailand playing chief roles in the committee. Its objective was to promote, coordinate, and supervise the use of the waterway in the Lower Mekong Basin for energy, irrigation, transportation, and fisheries. For almost two decades, the Mekong Committee carried out only a few joint projects due to political disturbances in the region. During 1978–1989, the committee was reactivated under the Interim Mekong Committee by the three founding nations, Cambodia, Lao PDR, and Vietnam, but accomplished little. The committee gained a new life in the early 1990s when China and Myanmar, the two upstream riparian states, joined as dialogue members. In 1995, the founder states signed the Mekong River Sustainable Development Cooperation Agreement, which resulted in the establishment of the Mekong River Commission to replace the old Mekong Committee. While the new agreement began to facilitate broader coordination and cooperation in the entire Mekong River Basin, it reduced the veto rights of downstream countries over the water resource projects of upstream countries. (Y. Li, 1999, pp. 25–26; Than, 1997, pp. 41–42).

12. The idea of the Golden Quadrangle originated with Thailand's proposal in 1992 to replace the notorious Golden Triangle. The rationale behind the proposal was that the geographic proximity of the four countries and the existence of old trade routes would lead to successful economic cooperation through border trade and investment among this loose grouping of four national and subnational economies. In 1999, the Chinese government lent

further support to the Golden Quadrangle by signing a new cooperation treaty with Thailand (Y. Li, 1999; Than, 1996).

13. While the old problem of opium production and peddling continued, the new problems included illegal laborers, refugees, the spread of AIDS and sexually transmitted diseases from prostitution, cross-border crimes, and pollution. For example, there were about 350,000 illegal laborers in Thailand, most of whom came from China and Myanmar (Than, 1996, p. 34).

14. Figures from the presentation by Myo Thant at the workshop on "Regional Cooperation and Cross-border Infrastructure" sponsored by the Asian Development Bank Institute, Tokyo, December 9–12, 2003.

15. I thank Heike Löschmann for sharing this information during our conversation in Hanoi, March 1, 2003.

16. Reported in *Renmin Ribao* (The People's Daily), overseas edition, April 18, 2002, p. 2.

17. Reported in *Renmin Ribao* (The People's Daily), overseas edition, November 28, 2002, p. 5.

18. *Renmin Ribao* (The People's Daily), overseas edition, November 7, 2002, p. 5.

19. See *Renmin Ribao* (The People's Daily), overseas edition, April 3, 2003, p. 5.

20. This information was shared by a local Vietnamese artist of ethnic Chinese heritage, Hanoi, Vietnam, February 28, 2003.

21. From the city of Ruili alone, over 10,000 people crossed the border into Myanmar (Burma at the time) in the Great Famine of 1958. In 1969, due to the ultra-leftist policy of politicizing the border associated with the Cultural Revolution, another 9,000 people left. The two exoduses drained half of the town's total population (Chinese Central Academy of Ethnology [CCAE], 1993).

22. The first north-south corridor runs from Kunming through Mandalay to Yangon (Rangoon). The second north-south corridor originates from Kunming and passes through Lao PDR to terminate at Bangkok. The third north-south corridor also begins at Kunming but extends through Hanoi and ends at Haiphong on Vietnam's northeastern coast. The first east-west economic corridor stretches from Yangon (Rangoon) through Bangkok and Phnom Penh to Ho Chi Minh City. The other east-west corridor runs from Moulmein (Mawlamyaing), the third largest city of Myanmar, through Phnsanulok in Thailand and Savannakhet on the Thailand–Lao PDR border to the port of Da Nang on Vietnam's east coast (Tang, Zhu, and Hu, 1999).

23. With its portion in China known as the Lancang, the Mekong River originates from the northern wing of the snowy Tanggula Mountain in the Tibetan plateau, flows down through the southern part of Qinghai province and western Yunnan, exits China at Xishuanbanna, and passes through Lao PDR, Myanmar, Thailand, Cambodia, and Vietnam before emptying into the South China Sea via a massive delta known as the Dragon's Mouth. The Mekong River is 4,880 km in total length, and 2,161 km are within China, with 1,247 km flowing through Yunnan alone. The Mekong covers a drainage area of 810,000 sq km (Wang and Li, 1998).

24. *Renmin Ribao* (The People's Daily), overseas edition, January 17, 2002, p. 4.

25. The Burma Road is a case in point. Built as a vital supply route by the Chinese after Japan's 1937 invasion of eastern China, the Burma Road links Mandalay through Maymyo, Lashio, and the border town of Muse to Kunming (see map 7.1). After winding through stands of golden teak in a series of switchbacks from Mandalay to Maymyo, the road to China gradually disintegrates into such bad shape in parts of the Shan Plateau that trucks from Muse take six days to travel the 300 km to Mandalay (DeVoss, 1996).

26. This information was provided by Damrong Saengkaweelert at the workshop on "Regional Cooperation and Cross-border Infrastructure" sponsored by the Asian Development Bank Institute, Tokyo, December 9–12, 2003.

27. Reported in *Renmin Ribao* (The People's Daily), overseas edition, March 10, 2002, p. 4; March 18, 2002, p. 4.

28. Reported in *Renmin Ribao* (The People's Daily), overseas edition, May 10, 2002, p. 1.

29. See "Calls to curb cross-border human trafficking," *The China Daily*, Hong Kong edition, December 16, 2003.

30. "Cambodia clings to Angkor for sign of national identity," *Vietnam Investment Review*, February 17–23, 2003, p. 24.

31. I would like to thank Sedara Kim from Cambodia for sharing this information and observation during our conversation in Hanoi, February 28, 2003.

32. The IMS-GT started out as a form of subregional economic cooperation proposed by Singapore's then Deputy Prime Minister Goh Chok Tong in December 1989 among Singapore, the southern Malaysian state of Johor, and the Indonesian island province of Riau, which was known as the SIJORI Growth Triangle. The SIJORI-GT eventually evolved into the broader IMS-GT through the signing of an official trilateral memorandum of understanding (MOU) in December 1994. This growth triangle had a combined area of almost 20,000 sq km, a population of about 5 million, and a total GDP of US$38.9 billion in the early 1990s (Chia and Lee, 1993, p. 239). In 1996–1997, the three participating members agreed to enlarge the IMS-GT to include West Sumatra of Indonesia and the Melaka, Negri Sembilan, and South Pahang states of Malaysia neighboring Johor. The new IMS-GT expanded the covered area from 5.1 million to about 15 million people (Tham, 1997/1998). The IMT-GT originated from high-level government discussions among the three countries on how to increase economic cooperation in the early 1990s, leading to the establishment of a growth triangle comprising the following border areas: North Sumatra and the Special Territory of Daerah Istimewa (DI) Aceh in Indonesia; the northernmost states of Kedah, Perak, Penang, and Perlis in peninsular Malaysia; and the four border provinces of Satun, Songkhla, Yala, and Narathiwat, plus Patani in southern Thailand. The three governments requested the ADB to conduct a formal feasibility study at the end of 1993, which helped launch the development of the IMT-GT. This growth triangle covered nearly 200,000 sq km and a population of over 20 million, with a combined GDP of US$12.5 billion in 1988 (Salleh, 1994, pp. 9–10). The EAGA came into being when the economic ministers of Brunei, Indonesia, Malaysia, and the Philippines signed a cooperation agreement in March 1994. This subregion links the southern Philippines (Mindanao and Palawan), East Malaysia (Sabah, Sarawak, and the Federal Territory of Labuan), eastern Indonesia (East, West, and Central Kalimantan; North, Central, South, and Southeast Sulawesi), and all of Brunei, with Maluku and Irian Jaya added in 1996. The subregion, the largest of the three in Southeast Asia, covers 1.7 million sq km (see map 1.1) and 48 million people (roughly the population of South Korea), with a combined GDP of US$54 billion (Siddique, 1997, p. 7).

33. In 1992, agriculture accounted for 25 percent of the IMT-GT's gross regional domestic product (GRDP), with the shares for the Indonesian and Thai portions higher at about one-third of GRDP, while agriculture's shares in GDP were 18 percent, 16 percent, and 13 percent for Indonesia, Malaysia, and Thailand, respectively. Even in gas-rich DI Aceh, agriculture accounted for 47 percent of the non-gas output and approximately 70 percent of total provincial employment ((Naseem, 1996, pp. 40–41).

34. For example, Penang's electronics industry grew so rapidly in the early and mid-1990s that it accounted for 60 percent of the local 492,000 workforce and half of Malaysia's total exports by 1996. U.S. PC makers Dell and Packard Bell set up huge assembly factories in Penang. While the multinational investors were attracted by the skilled labor and relatively low-cost operations (rents being one-fifth of those in Singapore and wages one-quarter), this influx of investment helped to drive up regional labor and land costs (Tripathi, 1996/1997).

35. Based on my conversations with customs officials and fellow travelers at the Malaysian-Thai border during my fieldwork trip from southern Thailand through Malaysia to Singapore during June 1999. Despite the fairly open border, I was detained for two hours for the reason of

entering Malaysia from Thailand by land alone on a PRC passport. The weekend border crossing of Malaysians into Thai border cities and towns is almost identical to Singaporeans driving across the Causeway Bay into Johor for weekend shopping and entertainment. I was caught in a long line of cars and people returning from Johor to Singapore at the Malaysian-Singapore border before I found a speedy way to pass through the checkpoint.

36. In August 1990, Singapore and Indonesia signed agreements for economic cooperation in the context of developing Riau province that focused on the promotion and protection of investments. These included (1) simplification of product distribution, payment, and delivery procedures between Singapore and Riau province, (2) joint tourism promotion and development, (3) cooperation in development and maintenance of infrastructure for joint development projects, and (4) simplification of entry and exit procedures. In June 1991, Singapore and Indonesia signed a 50-year water agreement, under which water resources in Riau would be developed to supply Singapore as well as Riau. In August 1991, Singapore and Indonesia signed a MOU through which Karium would be incorporated into joint development as a center for shipbuilding and petroleum processing and storage (Peachey, Perry, and Grundy-Warr, 1998, pp. 14–15).

37. At the request of the three governments, the ADB, together with domestic consultants from the participating countries, implemented a small-scale study in mid-1993. This led to the main IMT-GT study by a large number of international consultants, government officials, and ADB staff that covered five sectors: (1) trade, investment, and labor mobility; (2) industry and energy; (3) transportation and communications; (4) agriculture and fisheries; and (5) tourism. During the eight-month study, international consultants visited each of the IMT-GT countries twice. The findings of the study were submitted to the ADB and presented at three major conferences organized by the ADB for officials from the three participating countries (Thant, 1996).

38. Presentation by Femy Calderon (executive director of the Mindanao Economic Development Council) at the "Regional Cooperation and Cross-border Infrastructure" workshop sponsored by the Asian Development Bank Institute, Tokyo, December 9–12, 2003.

39. Territorial claims refer mostly to the Philippines' claim over Sabah, ownership dispute over the island of Sipadan-Ligitan between Indonesia and Malaysia, and the gray border area between Sarawak's Limbang district and Brunei. While English is widely used within the business community in Malaysia, Brunei, and the Philippines, a common colonial legacy, it is not in extensive use in Indonesia due to Indonesia's Dutch colonial background. Despite the similarity in the national tongues of Brunei, Indonesia, and Malaysia, English is the business language. This lack of a common language has prompted Indonesians to polish up their English and Filipinos to take crash courses in Bahasa, Indonesia. Regarding religion, Davao, North Sulawesi, and nearby South Maluku are mainly Christian, whereas most of Borneo and Western Mindanao are Muslim (Kurus, 1997).

40. While riding in a tourist van from the southern Thai city of Hat Yai to the Malaysian border in July 1999, I noticed that much of the road was a somewhat narrow and not well-paved single lane, which limited the speed of vehicle traffic, especially for commercial trucks.

41. At the Padang Besar checkpoint, only paper documents are examined; the container boxes on the train can't be opened to checks. This mutual trust dates back to a railroad trade agreement signed by Great Britain and the kingdom of Siam in 1922. Despite subsequent amendments, the original practice of having the cargo checked at the origin on one side and the other side accepting it at the border has continued to this day. Aided by this convenient border custom clearance, the container traffic at Padang Besar rose from about 6,000 TEUs in 1999 to 25,000 in 2003 (Yoshida, 2003).

42. The existing Thai ports in Narathiwat and Satun provinces could not accommodate medium- or large-sized fishing or cargo vessels. While coastal freighters and support vessels for

offshore gas fields could dock at the Songkhla port, the overall lack of facilities made it preferable to ship goods through the Penang port by rail. Since Malaysia's east coast states are not part of the IMT-GT, there are no economically viable sea links between the eastern coast of southern Thailand and the rest of the IMT-GT centered on the Strait of Malacca (Naseem, 1996, p. 46).

43. Davao is closer to Manado, Indonesia, than Manila, while Zamboanga, the Philippines, is closer to Sabah than Cebu. Yet seagoing cargoes from Kota Kinabalu, Indonesia, could only be shipped directly to Davao through Cebu or Manila, while a spice trader in Maluku, Indonesia, must send goods to neighboring Mindanao via Jakarta, due to national trade regulations and lack of intra-regional shipping links (Siddique, 1997).

44. Information from the presentation by Femy Calderon, "Regional Cooperation and Cross-border Infrastructure" workshop.

8

Variations Between the
Pacific and the Atlantic

THE EXTENDED COMPARATIVE ANALYSIS in the preceding chapter by no means exhausts the cases of transborder subregional integration, which have existed beyond the Asia-Pacific region prior to and simultaneously with the cases covered. To stretch the outer limit of the analytical framework and scope of comparison, this chapter takes a look at transborder links and dynamics in the North American and European settings. This further extension of comparative analysis aims to produce additional evidence on the varied forms and processes of transborder subregionalization to facilitate more systematic interpretation and theorizing.

The U.S.-Mexico Border: The Long and Twisted Road of Integration

An older phenomenon than the Asia-Pacific transborder subregions and growth triangles is the U.S.-Mexico border region, which provides both historical and current evidence on the general and particular characteristics of cross-border interaction and integration that pertain to the Asian cases. A defining economic feature of the U.S.-Mexico border region is the maquiladora industry, which offers the best case for examining the form and extent of the global-local economic nexus in a transborder context. However, simple and different economic links across the U.S.-Mexico border region predate the maquiladoras by almost a whole century.[1]

The Maquiladora Phenomenon and Border Cities Before and After NAFTA

The maquiladora system that began in the mid-1960s in Mexico's border areas is a form of labor-intensive assembly through which duty-free imported components are assembled into exports that are sent back to the United States. According to Sklair (1989, p. 43), the maquiladora industry experienced three phases of growth through the 1980s (the mid-1960s to 1973–1974; 1975–1982; 1982 to the late 1980s). Patricia Wilson (1992) differentiated the maquiladoras into two phases (1965–1982 and post-1982) and identified the 1990s as the beginning of new maquiladoras. The number of maquiladora plants grew from a few dozen in the mid-1960s to 1,279 at the beginning of 1988, with employment rising from about 4,000 in 1967 to approximately 350,000 in 1990 (Sklair, 1989, p. 68; Wilson, 1992, p. 43). Growth varied considerably among the Mexican border cities. The most rapid growth occurred in Ciudad Juárez (across the border from El Paso, Texas), which registered the largest number of maquiladora employees after 1970. In terms of growth rate, the maquiladora industry was the most dynamic sector of the Mexican economy from the mid-1960s to the 1990s.

The early or old maquiladoras were predominantly labor-intensive assembly operations in clothing and consumer electronics, which created a negative and yet largely accurate image of sweatshops exploiting young female workers and a lack of backward links with the domestic economy. A government decree in 1989 of granting more financial incentives to domestic suppliers and subcontractors for maquiladoras and creating new zones for maquiladoras in the interior, coupled with steady industrial upgrading after the mid-1970s, fostered the emergence of new maquiladoras at the end of 1980s and the beginning of the 1990s. They became more oriented toward less labor-intensive production in automobiles and advanced microelectronics, more involved in domestic links and subcontracting, and spatially more diffused. Skilled workers as a percentage of total maquiladora employment rose from 9 percent in 1975 to 13 percent in 1990, while the share of female workers dropped from 78 percent to 61 percent (Wilson, 1992, p. 44). The proportion of all maquiladora plants along the border declined from 88 percent in 1981 to 66 percent in 1994 (X. Chen, 1995). Although these changes might not be sufficient to alter the overall perception that the maquiladora industry relied on cheap and female labor and was heavily concentrated in the border region, they signaled another phase for maquiladoras until new developments began to occur with the onset of NAFTA.

NAFTA, which became effective on January 1, 1994, contributed significantly to the further growth of the maquiladora industry and its reconfiguration across the U.S.-Mexico border, as illustrated by the garment industry. The total number of maquiladora plants reached 3,486 in 2000 (80 percent of which were located in the northern border region of Mexico); the number of employees more than doubled from less than a half million to 1.2 million (Frey, 2003). Regarding the garment industry, the number of maquiladora plants grew from 412 in 1994 to 1,119 in 2000, while garment workers jumped from 82,500 to 286,000 (Spener, Gereffi, and Bair, 2002). By 2000, garment maquiladoras accounted for one-third of all maquiladora plants and approximately 20 percent of the entire maquiladora workforce. This simultaneous growth and restructuring was very different for the border cities of El Paso and Ciudad Juárez, as well as for the Mexican interior city of Torreón. In addition to replacing existing bilateral trade agreements and regulations such as Item 807 for in-bond assembly,[2] NAFTA, in conjunction with the devaluation of the peso at the end of 1994 and early 1995, lowered Mexican labor costs considerably by removing the 20 percent duty assessed on the value added to garments assembled in Mexico.

As the multiple effects of NAFTA gradually set in, El Paso, one of the leading apparel cities in the United States, with the nickname of "Jeans Capital of the World," saw its apparel employment decline continuously from the pre-NAFTA peak of 23,581 in 1993 to 11,851 in 2000 (Spener, 2002). While one would expect El Paso's loss to be a gain for Ciudad Juárez across the border, it didn't quite happen that way; the number of apparel maquiladora plants in the Mexican border city (fewer than 20) in 1996 remained about the same as back in 1982. This lack of cross-border manufacturing relocation, which occurred extensively in the GSCS and the IMS-GT, was attributed to the tight labor market in Ciudad Juárez due to competing maquiladoras in automotives and electronics and the higher wage level in the border region.[3] In addition, cross-border subcontracting and supplier-producer links between El Paso and Ciudad Juárez were weak and limited (van Dooren, 2002).

The boom of the Mexican apparel industry at the expense of U.S. border cities like El Paso under NAFTA has largely bypassed the border region and benefited some interior cities, especially Torreón.[4] By progressively eliminating U.S. tariffs and nonmonetary barriers to such apparel production activities as laundering, cutting, and finishing, NAFTA made it possible for these activities to be conducted in Mexico without quota restrictions, thus lowering production costs for U.S. companies. As the excellent case study of Torreón by Gereffi, Martinez, and Bair (2002) has shown, after NAFTA Mexican apparel producers became more involved in full-package production encompassing all stages and segments of apparel and delivery of finished products to U.S. retailers, as opposed to their role as mere subcontractors before NAFTA. The three scholars have argued that this spatial and organizational shift of apparel manufacturing facilitates local development in multiple ways, such as rapid job creation, higher than prevailing wages, improved working conditions, upgraded personnel, and some revival of rural communities around Torreón.

Despite originating from a different source, the direct and indirect effects of NAFTA on the apparel industry straddling the U.S.-Mexico border are similar to the spatial and organizational restructuring of some labor-intensive industries across the Hong Kong–Guangdong and the Singapore-Riau borders. One difference is that cross-border movement of apparel production has hardly stopped at the border cities but reached into the interior, whereas Hong Kong and Taiwanese manufacturing facilities were confined largely to the border cities in southeastern China and spread inland only later. More importantly is the strikingly similar challenge facing the established central nodes of these transborder subregions as they restructure global-local economic links. While Hong Kong and Singapore have tried to reinvent themselves on a larger scale, El Paso is struggling to sustain its eroding position as the support and distribution hub for North American apparel production (van Dooren, 2002) and to refashion itself as a new international center for high-fashion production of women's clothing, moving away from traditional men's denim jeans (Ortiz, 1998).

This economic restructuring has become more painful, especially for the less developed and less privileged Mexican border cities, as a result of the economic downturn that began before but worsened after the terrorist attacks of September 11, 2001. Ciudad Juárez has lost about 40,000 manufacturing jobs since 2000 and sustained high unemployment. The tough economic times have ironically contributed to the further growth of selling and buying American castoffs (used clothing, kitchen appliances, old cars) at the large number of tented markets in both El Paso and Ciudad Juárez (more in the latter). The business not only caters to the need and purchasing power of low-income Mexican residents in Ciudad Juárez, but it also draws merchants from as far as Japan who have come to pick up such special items as disco-era dresses and flashy men's suits for resale back home.[5] This border scene bears an uncanny resemblance to the activity of petty traders on the Yunnan-Myanmar and Yunnan-Vietnam borders in the GMS, even though the nature of trade and the larger contexts are different.

Politics, Culture, and Ethnicity on and Beyond the Border

While the U.S.-Mexico border bears the strong imprint of global, regional, and local economic forces that have intensified since NAFTA, the interaction between political, cultural, and ethnic factors has left lasting marks on the border and far beyond. This continues to justify using the analytical lenses of the de-centering state and cross-border social capital, albeit from a more integrated angle. The goal is to demonstrate the relative role of different-tiered states and cultural and ethnic ties in shaping and reshaping transborder economic flows and social spaces.

The early involvement of the state goes back to the Mexican government launching the Border Industrialization Program (BIP) by providing financial incentives to foreign investors to set up maquiladora plants in the mid-1960s. This role of the Mexican state continued from the 1970s into the 1980s as more targeted and favorable regulations helped broaden and deepen the maquiladora industry and its integration with the domestic economy, as discussed earlier. Since the inter-state cooperation through NAFTA led to greater binational trade and investment between the United States and Mexico, state and local governments of such Mexican border cities as Mexicali and Tijuana have become more active in promoting their sites to multinational investors from north of the border and Asia.[6] Regarding water as a transborder public good (similar to the appreciation of the Mekong River in the GMS), Governor Patricio Martinez of the border state Chihuahua, which controls the Rio Grande's main Mexican tributary, resisted President Vicente Fox's proposed solution for supplying water to Texas despite a bilateral water treaty.[7] From the U.S. side of the border, state officials of Texas, under then Governor George W. Bush, approved building a low-level nuclear waste site in the border town of Sierra Blanca, 30 km from Mexico, to store radioactive material from Texas and other states. This project provoked strong resistance from the Mexican government and border residents, who staged frequent protests in both Mexico City and along the border.[8] While state and local governments under a more decentralized political system are more autonomous than their Mexican counterparts, the U.S. government has had to step in to deal with much more important border issues, such as stopping illegal immigration and tightening border security after September 11, 2001. Only toward the end of 2002 did President Bush belatedly approve allowing Mexican trucks and buses to travel deep into the United States, even though it should have been implemented in compliance with NAFTA several years earlier.[9]

These shifting state policies before and after NAFTA and September 11 have highlighted and reinforced the formal "boundary" between the United States and Mexico as an exact geometric line separating the two nation-states. The long border, however, has always been a broad, indistinctive, and fluctuating zone that spans and overlaps both nation-states (Kearney, 1998) through historical links, cultural ties, linguistic affinity, kinship networks, and shared ethnic identity. Despite the archaeological evidence that the region known as the U.S.-Mexico border has a history of approximately 12,000 years, the present boundary separating the two nations became more or less fixed as a result of the United States acquiring Mexican territories culminating with the 1848 war with Mexico. This re-bordering was very similar to the redrawing of borders because of colonial conquests in Southeast Asia (see chapter 7). Between 1848 and 1985, the history of the border region consists of three distinct periods of fluctuating cross-border relations.[10] One could argue that the onset of NAFTA in 1994 might have ushered in a new era for the U.S.-Mexico border region characterized by stronger economic links and broader spatial extension. Culturally speaking, the region has become Mexicanized north of the border and Americanized south of the border as a result of demographic dynamics, bilingualism, and mutual cultural penetration (Fernandez, 1989). In El Paso, the largest mostly Mexican city in the United States, residents of Mexican ancestry or origin accounted for 73.4 percent of the population in the late 1990s. Over 90 percent of the Latino population in El Paso is of Mexican ancestry or origin, and two-thirds of El Paso's residents speak Spanish (Ortiz, 1998). Thousands of Mexicans regularly cross the border to visit relatives in such cities as El Paso and Houston, although this routine has become increasingly difficult since September 11, 2001. Beyond the border region, 18 million Mexican immigrants in the United States sent home an estimated US$14.5 billion in 2003, providing the country with its second largest source of foreign income, behind only oil exports and ahead of the maquiladora sector. About 18 percent of Mexicans receive money from relatives in the United States and many depend on it to help pay living costs.[11]

The extensive Mexican presence on the U.S. side of the border is sustained by constant immigration, permanent or temporary, and is characterized by a persistent national identity that permeates the border region and spreads much beyond. This is best exemplified by the more than 2 million Mexicans in the United States who return to their native towns and villages on the border and in the interior for holidays in December every year. While down somewhat in 2001 due to tightened border security in the aftermath of terrorist attacks, the numbers of returnees bounced back to close to the normal level in 2002. These returnees bring back Christmas gifts for relatives and money, spending it on parties, large private houses, and local community projects. The central state of Guanajuato around Mexico City receives nearly 200,000 annual returnees. The town of Nuevo Chupicuaro, located four hours northwest of Mexico City, swells to three times its normal size of 1,000. The town has prospered from dollars sent and brought back by those who are farm workers in California. Almost every family has a telephone. Many have built large and lavish houses (by Mexican standards), which stand vacant during the year and get occupied during December through early January every year. Some of the emigrants from this town, especially men, consider themselves nothing but Mexican, and their native town as their real home. They build beautiful houses as a symbol in their native place of the "American Dream" that they work hard for during their many years north of the border (Quinones, 1998). In 2002, the village of La Puristima in the Michoacan state welcomed back several hundred residents of Carpentersville, Aurora, and other Chicago-area communities, all returning for the inauguration of a modern hilltop church funded with $190,000 that they had sent home.[12] The deep local roots and strong national identity of these transborder workers are reflected in their practice, year in and year out, of crossing the bridge that joins economic opportunity north of the border with cultural and emotional attachments south of the border. In this sense, the border merely connects two linked and partially overlapped segments of an extended transnational social space.

The above practice represents one form of what Luin Goldring (2001) terms transmigrant-led transnationalism, which is not only kin- and family-based but also involves such broader transnational collective groups as mutual aid societies and hometown organizations. However, Goldring focused primarily on state-mediated transnationalism, which refers to the Mexican state's policies and programs for fostering closer ties between Mexicans in the United States and their localities of origin from the late 1980s on. Specific initiatives included the Program for Mexican Communities Abroad, established in 1991, and the new laws in 1998 regarding Mexican nationality.[13] In the central state of Zacatecas, the governor, the federal government, and the provincial federation of hometown clubs were all involved in implementing the program. These state policies contributed to the geographic fragmentation of transmigrant citizenship practices by pushing Mexicans in the United States to naturalize while keeping close affective ties to Mexico, to sustain investment and remittance flows to localities of origin. Moreover, due to the combined influence of state policies, the structure of hometown organizations in the United States, and Mexico's patriarchal gender relations, male transmigrants have been much more active in social citizenship practices by carrying out community projects in homelands, thus perpetuating their privileged status in the transnational social space (see Goldring, 2001, pp. 525–526).

The Mexican state has further stepped up its role in strengthening and mediating immigrants' home ties. To convey the importance attached to the Christmas homecoming in a personal way, President Fox visited the border at Nuevo Loredo in December 2002 with a public speech intended to allay the fears of returning immigrants that they would be shaken down by corrupt officers and bandits on their way home through the border. For the first time, Nuevo Laredo offered police escorts through town to returning immigrants. Mexico also established a new National Council of Mexican Communities Abroad in August 2002, headed by President Fox himself, coordinated by a Mexican living in the United States (a dual citizen), and advised by a panel of other Mexican expatriates.[14] In November 2002, an election was held in the United States for representatives on the 120-member advisory group for the presidential council. The state of Illinois selected seven members (Chicago has the second-largest population of Mexican descent in the United States). While election organizers saw the election as significant for Mexican migrants to express their needs and priorities, some Mexican American groups opposed it on the ground that the council would not have true independence from the Mexican government.[15]

This political effort to woo the larger Mexican diaspora reflects the state's persistent role in shaping the broader transnational economic and social ties to its favor, bypassing the formal U.S.-Mexico boundary. Similarly, the Chinese central government has consistently appealed to the overseas Chinese as compatriots, especially those in Hong Kong, by appointing their prominent business representatives to a national political advisory council, facilitating the goal of inducing more of their capital to places such as the PRD in Guangdong province in the prospering GSCS (see chapter 4).

A Difficult Balance: Keeping the Border Open Versus Keeping It Secure

The U.S.-Mexico border offers useful lessons for a better understanding of how geographic proximity, transport links, and macroeconomic integration constantly reshape the bridging versus the barrier effect of borders. More open and with more crossing points than any of the binational borders examined in the Asian subregions, the U.S.-Mexico border features an extremely large flow of people and vehicles, the latter of which number 94.3 million each year. These frequent crossings, however, are very uneven along the 3,200 km border that consists of diverse regions, subregions, and twin cities facing each other.[16] While Laredo–Nuevo Laredo toward the west end of the border is the most important crossing point for commerce, the El Paso–Ciudad Juárez area competes with Tijuana-Ysidro as the busiest land port, especially for human crossings. There are closer and more frequent interactions of different kinds between El Paso and Ciudad Juárez[17] than between any other pair of communities on the border. The Mexican border cities are well connected within the border zones by roads and to the distant, more central national centers, such as the capital of Mexico City, by both highways and railroads. However, the transport links between the border cities across the zones are weak and underdeveloped. Thus it is more difficult for someone in Mexicali to travel to El Paso by train or bus within Mexico than to cross over to the United States to travel to El Paso (Fernandez, 1989). The uneven transport infrastructure on either side of the border, ironically, lessens the typical "barrier effect" of borders stemming from better transport links on both sides of the border than across it (see Rietveld, 1993). In fact, the "barrier effect" across the U.S.-Mexico border has diminished considerably due to well-developed highways north of the border and through the multiple border crossings, as well as the constant and extensive transborder flows of commerce and people.

In both expected and unintended ways, this open border and fairly routinized crossing over it have encountered new "barrier effects" since NAFTA and September 11, 2001, albeit for different reasons yet with similar consequences. While NAFTA has generated much larger trade flows between the United States and Mexico, moving a lot more traded goods across the border began to strain the existing transborder transport infrastructure, which was built for an open border in a bygone era. From the mid-1990s, some freight trains at the Mexican border could be backed up all the way to Kansas, waiting to squeeze through one-track crossings. Seething, honking lines of trucks often choked tiny Texas border towns with Manhattan-style traffic jams. In San Diego, almost one million trucks passed through the Otay Mesa border crossing in 1998, whereas the number was 450,000 five years earlier. Local officials said that they would need a new freeway to relieve the traffic congestion. Not only were there not enough roads, rails, and bridges, but the existing ones were often in the wrong locations; some were mired in the traffic of busy downtowns. The border bottlenecks incurred as much as $2.5 billion in extra transport expenses a year for the United States, Canada, and Mexico combined.[18] Contributing to this woe of cross-border transportation of goods was the unilateral blocking by the United States in 1995 of the NAFTA accord for allowing Mexican trucks to cross the border and move freely on U.S. highways. While few U.S. trucking companies have managed to do more brisk cross-border transport business since NAFTA,[19] the border "barrier effect" appears to have returned under the double pressure of the much heavier flows of goods through NAFTA and the constraint of the existing cross-border transport infrastructure.

The post-9/11 security threat and the much tighter border control not only depressed the small businesses such as retailing on the border and routine crossings by longtime border residents (see chapter 1) but also slowed down the U.S.-Mexican trade, valued at US$245 billion a year, by lengthening the inspection of Mexican trucks, which numbered about 63,000 with 4.3 million crossings over the U.S. border in 2001.[20] Earlier in 2002, President Bush unveiled a 22-point border security plan for the United States and Mexico to take joint steps, including the inspection of bridges, dams, and transmissions facilities along the border, and more rigorous inspections of cargo at rail crossings and ports. In May 2002, the U.S. House of Representatives unanimously passed a border and immigration bill. A key measure of this bill was to implement a "smart border" program that relies on an electronic scanner to rapidly scan the photo and other "biometric" information (e.g., fingerprints) of a border-crossing person into the computer screen of border agents. The bill also called for extending the use of special machines that can X-ray entire tractor-trailers, showing inspectors exactly what's inside. The implementation of these measures, however, has suffered from lack of funding and person-nel.[21] In the meantime, increasingly tighter border and immigration security has halted Mexicans crossing the border for long-standing humanitarian medical care and cultural exchanges.[22] The evidence reaffirms that the state at both the central and local level is always capable of either eroding or enhanc-ing the "barrier effect" of borders, which in turn may disrupt cross-border cul-tural ties and social life. This is often done on the justification of protecting border security at the expense of other cross-border flows, legal or illegal.

A Tragic Irony: Border Protection and the Toll on Illegal Human Crossers

The beefed-up border controls by the U.S. government after September 11, 2001, were intended to increase border protection against further terrorist threats, which reflects a rational political response that any sovereign state would make based on national security. Ironically, this reassertion of border control for protection increases the risk of loss of life for illegal immigrants. While risk has always been there, more than 2,000 illegal immigrants crossing the U.S.-Mexico border have died since the U.S government escalated border controls in the mid-1990s. The issue, however, is more complex in light of the most recent statistics and real-life tragic stories. On one hand, the number of deaths of illegal immi-grants dropped to 282 in 2002 from 391 in 2001, one of the highest annual totals over the last decade. Of the 282 deaths in 2002, dehydration/sunstroke (123 cases) in the scorching Arizona desert accounted for 43.6 percent and drowning (54 cases) in the Rio Grande 19.1 percent, leading all other causes of death. The decreased number of deaths from 2001 to 2002 could be attributed to slightly fewer illegal immigrants crossing the border due to tightened border controls. But illegal immigrants have continued their attempts to cross the border, using highly risky means. For example, 11 illegal immigrants suffocated to death in a closed train car in Iowa, which occurred in June 2002 but was not discovered until October 14, 2002,[23] and 18 illegal Mexican immigrants were found dead in an abandoned trailer in Victoria, Texas, on May 14, 2003. And 2004 saw the largest wave of illegal immigration since 2001 (Bartlett and Steele, 2004).

While terrible human tragedies, these deaths will not stop hundreds of thousands of other migrants from crossing the U.S.-Mexico border to realize their dreams of finding work and making some money. Illegal immigrants are willing to pay "coyotes," or human smugglers, several thousand dollars to help them avoid U.S. Border Patrol agents by going through less guarded points of entry and resorting to more clandestine means. Human smugglers have taken advantage of the greater demand for their services by charging higher fees and finding more customers at the border. It is reported that the Wal-Mart store in Laredo, Texas, located less than one km from the borderline, has become a meeting ground where human smugglers and potential illegal immigrants make contact and prepare for the last leg of their journey into the United States. Drawing over 100,000 shoppers a day, most of them Mexicans who come over to shop on a temporary visa, the Laredo Wal-Mart is the chain's busiest store in the United States. Some of the Mexican shoppers stock up on water and sleeping bags at the store for their long journey into the interior of the United States and then try to hook up with smugglers.[24] This location, like other Texas and Arizona border towns, is a major relay point for the long trips by illegal immigrants from as far south as Central America who are bound for certain interior U.S. cities. Even if these migrants are not as poor and desperate as the illegal North Korean migrants crossing into China in the GTS (see chapter 6), their border crossing is filled with risks, not the least of which is being caught and sent back.

More recent human smuggling has involved a growing number of young children. Their parents inside the United States are willing to pay hefty fees to smugglers and take huge risks to bring these children over the border. While a few lucky ones have rejoined their parents, many have been abused by smugglers or caught by border guards and repatriated. In the first nine months of 2003, the Mexican consular authorities in the U.S. southwestern states repatriated about 9,800 unaccompanied minors under the age of 17 who were caught crossing illegally.[25] Beginning in July 2004, the U.S. and Mexican governments implemented a new, voluntary repatriation program intended to reduce the number of undocumented immigrants who die horrible deaths sneaking across the hot Arizona desert each summer. Under the program, which costs US$13 million, Mexicana Airlines runs daily flights from Tucson to Mexico City and Guadalajara to return voluntary immigrants caught crossing the border. While the U.S. Border Patrol attributed the declining number of dead immigrants to this program, others contended that there was an undercount of deaths and some Mexican immigrants were forced to take these return flights; some also argued that the program was too expensive and the money could be better spent on more effective methods.[26]

Despite the tragic fate of many illegal immigrants and new border control measures, the broader concern over the security of the U.S.-Mexico border in light of September 11 has refocused bilateral policy attention on immigration reform. Seeing the creation of the Homeland Security Department as an opportune occasion, the Mexican government has attempted to convince the United States of the importance in linking border security to a normalization of the flow of Mexican workers into the United States and granting a legal status to nearly 4 million illegals already north of the border. This was the sole purpose of President Fox's three-day visit to Arizona, New Mexico, and Texas in November 2003. However, the U.S. government has been reluctant to link

these issues because of its priority for securing the border against terrorist attacks and the persistent anti-immigrant backlash domestically. The two countries, however, have agreed to implement more initiatives under a "border
partnership" program that aims at limiting security threats while ensuring the
smooth flow of legitimate commercial and commuter traffic.[27] One would
think that this new round of border control differs from the escalation of border policing to reduce illegal immigration that started in the mid-1990s. Andreas (2000b), however, argues that the earlier escalation was more about the
state recrafting the image of the border and symbolically reaffirming the
state's territorial authority than achieving the instrumental goal of reducing
illegal border crossers. This may be even more true of the objective of the current escalation of border control, given the greater threat of terrorist attacks,
real or perceived.

The European Border Regions: Integration from Above, Below, and Outside

As we move from the U.S.-Mexico border to the European border scene of our
cross-continental comparison, we see many more borders and thus more border (sub)regions than the binational boundary that we have just left behind.
What strikes us first in a familiar fashion is whether the European Union, as a
supranational arrangement, has the same impact on various transborder subregions that NAFTA has on the U.S.-Mexico border. While this level of effect
differentiates the U.S.-Mexican and European cases from the Asian cases, the
presence of similar conditions and factors in the former, as has just been
demonstrated in the U.S.-Mexican context, justifies a final application of the
analytical lenses. To maintain a balance between being consistent with our analytical strategy and doing some justice to the more varied border regions in
Europe, the following discussion compromises by focusing on how economic,
political, cultural, and spatial forces intersect in the context of two types of
cases that reflect the most salient features of transborder subregional integration in Europe.

More Bottom-Up than Top-Down: A View of the Cores

While border regions in most European countries tend to be peripheral regions, some important border regions in the developed, western side of Europe qualify as the cores of cross-border integration relative to the increasingly important transborder developments in a number of peripheral areas
on the emerging, eastern side of the post–Cold War Europe. Transborder
subregional integration in the cores has unfolded as a largely bottom-up

process of steady cooperation among different actors at different political and spatial scales.

Transborder regionalism accelerated and spread in the 1990s, especially after the Cold War and with the official inception of the EU. This phenomenon began to scale up into super-regions that have enveloped multiple core border zones in Western Europe. One such transnational region stretches from southeastern England through northern France and the Benelux countries and down the Rhine Valley into Switzerland, and there are others like it[28] (see Church and Reid, 1996; Newhouse, 1997; Cappellin and Batey, 1993). We choose three smaller and adjacent regions for their more comparable dimensions and reference to the cases already covered in this book.

Similarities Among Three Core Cases

The first case is the Dutch-German EUREGIO, one of the oldest border regions, dating back to the simple bilateral cooperation between local municipalities of Germany on the border with central Holland in the mid-1950s. It was created in 1954 as the Rhine-Ems local government association, whose principal objective was to improve Germany's cooperation with Dutch communities. It remained active during the 1960s and 1970s through the establishment of several Councils of Governments, which consolidated their transborder activities in infrastructure and economic development into the EUREGIO-Council in 1978 (see Scott, 1998). In the early 1990s, 106 municipalities in an area of 1.9 million people on both sides of the border cooperated with one another via the Regional Association in the EUREGIO, which is organized as a parliamentary assembly and elected by the representatives of the municipalities in the Regional Associations. In 1992, the national governments of Germany and the Netherlands signed a treaty that ensured further cross-border cooperation between local authorities in the EUREGIO (van der Veen, 1993).

Located south of the Dutch-German EUREGIO, the Euregion Maas-Rhine was established in 1976 as one of about 40 Euregions (an abbreviation of European region) by the end of the 1980s. The Euregion Maas-Rhine comprises South Limburg of the Netherlands, Belgian Limburg (Flanders), the province of Liège and the German-speaking community in Belgium (Wallonia), and the Aachen region in Germany. Covering 10,475 sq km with almost 3.6 million people, the Euregion Maas-Rhine encompasses diverse cities, political units, cultures, and languages in this triangular transborder subregion.[29] While cross-border cooperation in the Euregion Maas-Rhine would take place on a regional (provincial) level, it moved down to the urban (local) level in 1989. Cross-border cooperation at both tiers of government facilitated industrial restructuring in the region, which shared a long history of industrialization based on the declining coal and iron sector, by improving the already very good cross-border infrastructure (e.g., roads, rail), attracting new firms, and establishing research institutes. The existing firms in the region had two different orientations. Small and medium-sized enterprises, more regionally oriented, regarded their customers and suppliers in the region as most important, while large enterprises operated on a global scale, with links to such multinational corporations as Ford, Volvo, and Siemens and a strong export orientation (see Corvers, Dankbaar, and Hassink, 1996). This regionalizing of the global-local economic nexus is quite different from an Asia-Pacific transborder subregion such as the GSCS, where Chinese SMEs in Guangdong and Fujian provinces are globally oriented as subcontractors, suppliers, and even joint venture partners for multinationals directly, or through Hong Kong and Taiwanese firms indirectly.

The third case is the Regio Basiliensis, a trinational coordinating and planning organization established around 1963 for the Alsace-Baden-Basel region, located farther south of the Euregion Maas-Rhine, at the intersection of France, Germany, and Switzerland. Consisting of the French region of Alsace, the western part of the German federal state of Baden-Württemberg, and the Swiss region of Basel and parts of the surrounding counties,[30] this triangle covers 10,000 sq km with about 2 million inhabitants, more or less equally divided among the three nations. The Basel region was economically prosperous as a major European railroad and highway junction and a center of chemicals, banking, and insurance industries. During the early 1980s, approximately 18,000 workers from France and 8,000 from Germany commuted to Basel every day (Briner, 1986). While the economy of the Alsace region was not as strong as that of Basel or Baden, it benefited from being contiguous with the German and Swiss border regions. Some 16,000 Alsatians commuted to work in Germany on a daily basis, while another 21,000 crossed the border to work in Switzerland. Back in the 1960s, German residents in the border towns frequently crossed over to the French side to buy cheaper cigarettes. Even those who didn't smoke went to get their shares of the quota for their friends or relatives.[31] Residents in the French border town of Strasbourg could hop on the frequent buses across the Rhine River Bridge into the neighboring German town of Kehl to buy some better and cheaper goods (Hansen, 1986). Extensive local, organizational, and individual cross-border economic links make the Alsace-Baden-Basel region similar to the other two cases as long-standing cores of the EU.

Accounting for the Similarities: History, Culture, and Local Politics

The similarly close economic integration of the three core border regions can be accounted for by two sets of factors in transborder integration that have been focused on consistently in this book. First of all, cross-border social capital is deep and extensive, as these regions have always been historically, culturally, and linguistically linked. The Dutch-German EUREGIO has been around for half a century. The Euregion Maas-Rhine not only includes the German-speaking community of Belgium but also has a largely multilingual population. The Alsace-Baden-Basel region shared cultural ties for centuries, long before the existence of France, Germany, and Switzerland as nation-states. Many people in Alsace speak a German dialect as their first language, and the French region was described as simultaneously French, Rhenish, German, and very European (Hansen, 1986). The intensified European integration in the 1990s added a stronger layer of European identity over the shared cultural and regional identities of these core transborder areas. The border town of Saverne in the Alsace region, for example, went out in a big way to project a European image and facade in the late 1990s. Compared with some of the Asia-Pacific transborder subregions and the U.S.-Mexico border region, the European border regions are just as historically, culturally, and linguistically intertwined.

The much stronger force shaping these European border regions in recent years, however, is the policies and programs of the state at the local, regional, and national level, as well as of the semi-public agencies (e.g., chambers of commerce) and increasingly the EU. For the Dutch-German border region, while the EUREGIO has no public law status or decision-making authority, it has existed as an international de facto official institution involved in the regional planning process. Working with other border region associations consisting of local municipalities, the EUREGIO has developed a Transboundary Development Program that focused on defining transboundary problems and finding problem-solving strategies. The EUREGIO also received US$13.7 million during 1990–1993 from the European Community under the INTERREG Program (Scott, 1998), which was set up after the Single European Act of 1986 to promote cross-border regional cooperation with a budget of 3 billion ECUs (European currency units, about US$3.3 billion) for 1994–1999 (Chapman, 1996). In the Euregion Maas-Rhine, the Minister of Spatial Planning of the Netherlands, Flanders, Wallonia, and North Rhine–Westphalia signed a declaration of intent in 1989 to improve the cross-border infrastructure among and around the major cities. A local-level cooperative initiative focusing on tourism and environment soon followed. In 1990, the provinces involved submitted 60 projects to the INTERREG Program for funding (Corvers, Dankbaar, and Hassink, 1996). For the Alsace-Baden-Basel region from the 1970s, a multilayered cooperative structure of national commissions, regional committees, working groups, and local planning agencies began to facilitate cross-border cooperation in infrastructure networks, university exchanges, and business ties among small and medium-sized enterprises through periodic meetings (see Briner, 1986; Funck and Kowalski, 1993).

While there are varied degrees and forms of institutionalization in cross-border cooperation across the three regions, the comparison highlights a striking political feature of European cross-border integration—the stronger role of regions and the EU than the nation-state and local government (see Chapman, 1996; Newhouse, 1997). This again confirms the merit of seeing through the prism of the de-centered state, even though the European cases differ in some ways from most Asia-Pacific cases. Instead of the central state yielding power to certain regions, which facilitated cross-border integration as in the GSCS, the Western European states took a backseat to the bottom-up initiatives of the border regions earlier on, while ceding more power to the EU more recently regarding policy-making and financial assistance for the border regions and towns. However, cross-border cooperation such as the twining of towns across the French-German border is still subject to the differential influence from France's centralized system versus Germany's federal system. In general, the core European border regions differ from the Southeast Asian growth triangles where the national governments are stronger than regional and local authorities. While the EU is similar to NAFTA in terms of being a free trade bloc, it uses its unique supranational administrative approach to promote cross-border cooperation by allocating financial resources to targeted border areas.

Strong Top-Down with Bottom-Up and Outside-In: A Look at the Peripheries

To the extent that the set of core border regions became closely integrated over time, the creation of a single borderless market by 1992 and the ratification of the Treaty on the European Union in 1993 has since reduced, if not eliminated, the traditional distinctions of Western Europe's internal frontiers. However, considering that the internal borders make up only 60 percent of the EU's land frontier of almost 10,000 km, there is a renewed significance about the borders between the EU and its neighbors in Central and Eastern Europe (Corvers, Dankbaar, and Hassink, 1996). The fall of the Berlin Wall and the break-up of Yugoslavia and the Soviet Union raised new questions about the traditional meaning and functions of the closely guarded boundary that used to separate Europe into two physically connected but politically and economically disjointed halves. The accelerated process of enlarging the EU in the second half of the 1990s, which has culminated in 10 new countries, most of which are in Central Europe, officially joining the EU in May 2004,[32] warrants a serious look at the border regions along the outer edges of the EU. This is where new dynamics have emerged to confront the old "barrier effect" of borders that once demarcated the so-called peripheral border regions, some of which cover connected parts of the old Western Europe and East-Central Europe. Three cases are used here to illustrate the scope and variation of peripheral border regions around Europe's shifting outer boundary.

The first case is the Alpe-Adria community. Dating back to the era of the Cold War and a divided Europe, the Alpe-Adria was the first officially established transborder subregion that involved both Western and Central European contiguous subnational areas. It began in 1978 when the representatives of two northeastern Italian provinces, four Austrian provinces, Bavaria of West Germany, and Slovenia and Croatia of the former Yugoslavia met in Venice to form an action association to coordinate different fields of regional development, with emphases on transport crossing points in the Alps, energy production, agriculture and forestry, and tourism. In the 1980s and through 1990, more Italian and Austrian regions, five bordering territorial units of Hungary, and a Swiss canton joined the association in succession.[33] While the Alpe-Adria working community stretches over 28,000 sq km with a combined population of 38 million people, the Italian and German regions had lopsided economic weights, with 40 percent and 29 percent of the population and 42 percent and 39 percent of the GDP, respectively. The western and developed member regions generally shared a post-industrial economy featuring advanced manufacturing and services such as finance and R&D, whereas the eastern peripheral region, especially the Hungarian areas and Croatia, was dominated by agriculture and tourism. The region as a whole focused on information exchange, cultural relations, and infrastructure coordination through most of the 1980s, but shifted toward more extensive economic cooperation toward the end of the 1980s and the beginning of the 1990s as political and economic changes in East-Central Europe brought about a closer involvement of the eastern, peripheral part of the region.

Despite the relatively brief existence of the Alpe-Adria community, a substantial portion of this region has a much longer history of close political, cultural, and economic ties going all the way back to the Habsburg dynasty in the twelfth century or earlier that ended with the fall of the Austro-Hungarian Empire in 1918.[34] Even after that and despite the treaties of Germain and Trianon banning trade between the follow-up states, Austria maintained strong ties with Hungary, Czechoslovakia, and Yugoslavia that were only interrupted by World War II. In spatial and economic terms, this region became known as a crucial part of "Middle Europe," which was defined as the European core between Germany and Russia, extending from the Baltic to the Adria regions and the Black Sea, and sharing long periods of occupation (see Steiner and Sturn, 1993). At the dawn of the twenty-first century, an important part of the

Alpe-Adria community took on the renewed significance of an older ethnic dimension that was a legacy of the early twentieth century. In 2001, the Hungarian government passed a law that would allow about 3 million ethnic Hungarians in the neighboring countries to receive health and pension benefits as well as education and travel privileges while working in Hungary.[35] This state initiative to attach some meaning to the notion of "Greater Hungary" not only antagonized Hungary's neighbors but also alarmed the EU on the eve of admitting Hungary as a new member. Hungary's assertion beyond its current political boundary has complicated and conflated Europe's eastern flank.

The second relatively peripheral case, located farther north on the EU's external boundary, refers to a set of embedded border regions that have (re)emerged and begun to blur the distinction between the core and periphery of Europe. At the most aggregate spatial scale is the Baltic region of Denmark, Germany, Poland, Lithuania, Latvia, Estonia, Finland, Russia, Sweden, and Norway, which established the representative body of the Baltic Council in March 1992. They also created the inter-governmental Council of Baltic Sea States (CBSS) and the private sector body of the Baltic Chambers of Commerce Association (BCCA) in the same year. While Michael Porter (2001) and Ketels (2002) suggested that the Baltic Rim region of neighboring nations could become a competitive geographic unit through close cooperation, this region may be unwieldy in terms of territory and population. Even on a smaller scale, a central part of the Baltic region within the north-south belt of land between Lappland County in Finland and Kaliningrad (discussed later) in the south boasts 17 million inhabitants. Cross-border economic links among these residents were lively even during the Cold War, when this set of countries was split by the Iron Curtain. High school students in Helsinki would often take a short ferry ride on a "vodka trip" to Estonia, where they could drink a lot of cheap strong liquor.[36] Beginning in the 1990s, these countries began to pursue regional cooperation that included the provision of infrastructure, economic development, human rights, the environment, and the eventual incorporation of the Baltic states into the EU (Veggeland, 1993). At a smaller, more restricted spatial level, the Barents region consisting of seven subnational administrative units (Nordland, Troms, and Finmark in Norway, Norrboten in Sweden, Lappland in Finland, and Murmansk and Archangel counties in Russia) was established in 1993 through an agreement among the four countries. Under the separate authorities of the Barents Council and the Regional Council,[37] cooperation among the subregions would focus on polar resource utilization, trade principle formulation, environmental problem-solving, and security assurance (Veggeland, 1993).

At the smallest, binational subregional level exists cooperation over the Russian-Finnish border. Despite the long history of conflict and territorial disputes between Russia and Finland,[38] strong trade ties and cross-border co-operation between the two countries existed during the Cold War and continued after the dissolution of the Soviet Union in 1991. Cross-border cooperation occurred intensively over the territory of Karelia, which was both a focal point of territorial disputes and a crucial cultural link between the two countries.[39] The most intensive and focused cross-border cooperation involved the Finnish city of Kuhmo and the Russian city of Kostamuksha from the 1970s through the early 1990s. Under a bilateral government agreement in the mid-1980s, which legitimized cities as legal actors in dealing with cross-border issues, the two cities strengthened their ties, with the establishment of a new border crossing and regular bus service (Sweedler, 1994). Despite the improved cross-border relations, some Finns still harbor a strong nationalist sentiment toward the Russians for having taken their territories. The Finnish state, on the other hand, has faced a different dilemma most recently. Having passed a law to encourage Russians and Estonians of Finnish heritage to return to Finland and receive welfare benefits, the Finnish government found some of the returnees difficult to accommodate due to their inability to speak Finnish and their drinking behavior but has not been successful in sending them back.[40]

The third peripheral border case is located north of the Alpe-Adria community and straddles Europe's external boundary. It involves new cross-border dynamics on both the western and eastern sides of Poland, which, like Hungary, entered the EU in May 2004. On the western side, Poland shares the border with the part of Germany that used to be East Germany, before Germany's unification. After 1990, regional cooperation across the German-Polish border began to increase at the encouragement of the EU and the German government. After 1991, the Dutch-German EUREGIO model was adapted to the German-Polish situation, leading to the creation of Intergovernmental Commissions and several interagency working groups at the national and regional level, which focused on spatial planning, land use coordination, and protecting environmentally sensitive areas. The EU, through the INTERREG Program, had allocated US$464 million to the German-Polish border region in the early 1990s (Scott and Collins, 1997).

The German-Polish border began to take on greater importance by the mid-1990s when Poland became one of six countries (with the Czech Republic, Cyprus, Estonia, Hungary, and Slovenia) involved in negotiations to join the EU. While all six countries, as potential (but now official) new members, were expected to become a ring of buffer zones to filter out the unwanted flow of people and goods into the EU (Jesien, 2000), the German-Polish border stood out as the key buffer for stemming the smuggling of migrants through Poland into Germany. Through a bilateral agreement, Poland began to take back those who attempted to enter Germany illegally, while Germany provided assistance to Poland to police its own long eastern border. Of course, Poland has another vested economic interest in protecting the border with Germany, which accounts for 30 percent of Poland's total foreign trade. In 1994, Germany sent US$89 million to Poland for border-control purposes. In 1999, the Polish government spent US$8.5 million to reinforce its border force, five times more than in 1998, while also spending US$24 million of EU funds on beefing up its eastern border, including the establishment of 18 new posts by the year 2002 (see Andreas, 2000b, pp. 123–124). Since the Czech Republic was joining the EU with Poland in 2004, making the border between them internal, Poland shifted some of its border control personnel from the southwest to its much longer boundary with Belarus and Ukraine.[41]

In spite of these institutional arrangements and financial assistance, it would not be easy for Poland, or in its best interest, to fully control the heavy flow of crossers, legal or illegal, over the German-Polish border. In fact, Poland has faced a major dilemma concerning its border. To keep its economy going, Poland needed to keep the border open to foreign traders and consumers. It has benefited from having a large number of small-scale, migrant traders from Germany in the west and Ukrainians, Belarussians, and Russians in the east. On the other hand, Poland has been seriously concerned about regulating the chaotic free markets at and the heavy flow of traders over its eastern border, as well as reducing illegal immigrants in the country numbering up to 200,000 in 1999 (Andreas, 2000b), all of which might threaten the eastern boundary of the EU. To circumvent the arbitrary and badly enforced laws and to circle around the corrupt economic police and customs officers, small-scale traders from eastern Poland have relied heavily on cross-border social capital in terms of ethnic ties, family links, and social networks[42] (Wallace with Shmulyar and Bedzir, 1999). With regard to achieving certain economic objectives, this is remarkably similar to how cross-border social capital operates in several Asia-Pacific transborder subregions, especially the GSCS, even though the political actors vis-à-vis the social capital users are somewhat different due to the varied contexts.

The tension between states, non-state actors, and social networks also manifests itself in the area of illegal migration across the EU's new eastern border. For example, a quarter of the 16,000 residents in the small town of Siematycze in northeastern Poland regularly take a 22-hour bus ride over the Poland-German border into Brussels, the capital of the EU, where they work illegally in wealthy households, on farms, and in construction groups. An estimated 35,000 Poles, the vast majority from northeastern Poland, live and work in Brussels on three-month tourist visas. The presence of this temporary Polish community is felt at Les Abattoirs Market, where Belgian butchers sell kielbasa and other popular Polish sausages. Ethnic food markets run by Belgians cater to the Eastern immigrants' tastes with fresh sour cream, dumplings, tea, and candies, all imported from Poland. Back home in Siemiatycze, the money made by the local long-distance commuters has turned into shiny Mercedes whizzing down the street, designer dress shops, a Levi's jeans store, a new hotel and restaurant in the town center, and even fancy two- and three-story houses in a neighborhood known as "Little Belgium." With a much easier and less risky border crossing, these illegal Polish migrant workers have brought home what many Mexican illegal workers have to their home villages in the interior of Mexico. Concerned about a large invasion of cheap labor from Eastern Europe after the addition of new member states, the EU has voted to ban labor migration from those countries for up to seven years.[43]

As the EU and its Western member states cooperate to control unwanted migration from the East, illegal migrants (both workers and asylum seekers) have turned to social networks to facilitate their movement. The most important actor of these networks is smugglers, who have become more active under more strict border control. While between 15 percent and 30 percent of the illegal migrant workers who entered Western Europe in 1993 used smugglers, half of some 300,000 people who entered the EU illegally in 1998 did so with the help of smugglers. The Czech Republic, Hungary, and Poland provided some of the transit routes for this smuggler-aided illegal immigration into the EU. Many illegal migrants, from such poor places as Albania and northern Iraq, were willing to pay several thousand dollars to smugglers (Koslowski, 2000). This type of illegal cross-border flow bears some similarities to illegal migration across the U.S.-Mexico border. Both flows may be specific to borders that divide very rich and very poor countries, as they do not exist at a large scale in the Asia-Pacific transborder subregions, except the somewhat unique phenomenon of illegal North Korean migrants over the Chinese border.

The above border regions of varied scales are largely peripheral in that they comprise mainly border zones of the post-communist countries of Central and Eastern Europe. However, with the active participation of the Scandinavian countries, the Baltic Sea region might be emerging as a potential European core. This process has gained momentum from the involvement of Mecklenburg-Vorpommern, eastern Germany's northernmost state, as the corner stone for the region. This German state not only has surging biotech and medical ventures, vast agricultural tracts, and huge tourism potential, but it also has six important ports, including Germany's largest port of Rostock on the Baltic Sea.[44] At a more trivial economic level, the liquor stores in the city of Rostock have been doing brisk business, attracting a steady influx of Swedes, who come via ferry to buy large quantities of alcohol.[45] Despite the increasing cooperation between the old West and East and cross-border links between the old West and new East, tensions and challenges have continued to crop up along the EU's external frontier, given its visa restrictions on non-EU nations. This is exemplified by the predicament in resolving the visa issue for residents in the Russian territorial enclave of Kaliningrad as recently as 2002.[46] If the border-crossing issue is not satisfactorily resolved, Kaliningrad will be a non-EU enclave stuck on the northern border of the EU following the entry of its neighbors Poland and Lithuania into the EU. The Russian enclave's illegal smuggling ties with Poland will continue to pose a threat to the latter's border from the north, while Poland has tried to firm up its eastern frontier with Belarus and Ukraine.

Forces Incorporating the Periphery: EU Enlargement and Responsive State Policies

In general, regarding the second set of European border regions, which are more peripheral to Europe due to their locations and compositions, cross-border links and cooperation are determined primarily by the strong role of the EU in shaping the incorporation of selected Central and Eastern Europe countries from the top down. This downward pressure stems from the central principle embodied in the Schengen Agreement[47] that stipulates both open and free internal borders and a common external frontier for members of the union. This principle is a key to the process of EU enlargement by which the new East-Central European countries are admitted through applications and negotiations. More importantly, these candidate countries must live up to this principle, especially the more difficult stipulation of making the new common external border safe and secure.

To pave the way for joining the EU, Poland and other states responded to the top-down political pressure by adopting a variety of necessary border control measures, with guidance and assistance from the EU itself and the existing members such as Germany that share borders with them. The responsive state policies reflect the interdependence and mutual blending between the EU as a supranational organization and the states that belong to it as subordinate members. On one hand, creating a hard external frontier requires the EU to take on state-like functions and assume state-like roles (Snyder, 2000). On the other hand, the member states, especially the candidate states, are willing to transfer some of the policy-making regarding border control up to the EU. While this could be seen as the states "losing control," they may end up increasing their capacities through a redeployment of resources for other purposes (Koslowski, 2000). With this much give-and-take or trade-offs in sovereignty versus capacity, the real distinction between the independent sovereignty and autonomy of the member states and the "pooled sovereignty" of the EU has become increasingly blurred, just like the internal borders between the member states. With regard to safeguarding the newly emerged external boundary of the EU, the relative importance and influence of state policy-making and the EU-wide policies also have become more intertwined.

Insights for the Asia-Pacific Cases

What have we learned from taking a comparative detour through the U.S.-Mexico border region and several European border regions? What insights have we gained along the way that bear on the harmonious hypothesis about how transborder subregions form and evolve and on the central argument about the bridging versus barrier role of borders? On the surface, it would seem that the non-Asia-Pacific cases are less relevant because they belong to the category of formal regional integration characterized as inter-state-led and rule-based, whereas the Asia-Pacific cases are largely informal and driven by market activities and supplementary state action (see chapter 2). While this is true at the most aggregate level, the non-Asia-Pacific cases offer comparative evidence and insights as they have been examined at levels and scales beneath the supranational structures like the EU and NAFTA. Several significant insights can be derived from the transnational, national, and local levels.

First of all, there is no doubt that the EU and NAFTA constitute two different transnational contexts for links and activities across the European regions and the U.S.-Mexico border region and thus exert strong influence on these flows and activities. As an economic and political union, the EU has had a greater impact on the border regions than NAFTA as a free-trade agreement has affected the U.S.-Mexico border region. The broader and stronger role of the EU, however, has varied between the core versus peripheral border regions. For the well-developed core cases, such as the Alsace-Baden-Basel region, the EU has merely reinforced its long-standing connections with a more European identity. Regarding the more peripheral borders with greater economic disparities between both sides, such as the German-Polish border, the EU has exerted a strong top-down pressure, as it has in strengthening the control over the German-Polish border as a condition for Poland to join the EU. In comparison, NAFTA has had a broad economic impact on the U.S.-Mexico border in terms of facilitating greater bilateral trade and cross-border commerce without necessarily and significantly changing the border cities, which shared close economic and social links for a long time. The comparative evidence suggests that there are different limits to how strongly formal inter-state arrangements such as the EU or NAFTA can determine cross-border links and integration at the (sub)regional or local level considering the shifting yet still strong role of the nation-state.

Both the U.S.-Mexico and European cases, in their different ways, have demonstrated the role of the nation-state in affecting border regions and local-level cross-border flows, either in conjunction with the EU and NAFTA or in little connection with them. In the European setting, several states agreed to establish the representative body of the Baltic Council to facilitate subnational cross-border cooperation, which had little to do with the agenda of the EU. On the other hand, the German and Polish governments' close and specific cooperation to beef up the controls over their shared border and Poland's eastern border had everything to do with the principle and interests of the EU as a supranational institution. In the case of the U.S.-Mexico border region, the U.S. government unilaterally elevated border control to fend off further terrorist threats after September 11, even if it interfered with cross-border economic, social, and transport links and activities, including raising the risk for illegal migrants to cross the border. This tightened border control harkens back to the escalation of border policing to reduce illegal immigrant and drug smuggling in the mid-1990s. If that early policy was seen more as a symbolic representation of state authority to mark and maintain the borderline than achieving its intended practical objectives (Andreas, 2000b), the recent round of border policing asserts the state's power to restrengthen the "barrier" role of the U.S.-Mexico border, which has become quite an open "bridge" for free movement of goods and people between the two countries. In complementary ways, the European and the U.S.-Mexico cases reinforce what we have uncovered about the more complex and double-edged role of the nation-state in stemming the illegal flow of North Korean food migrants and political refugees in the GTS and drug trafficking across the Yunnan-Myanmar border in the GMS.

The comparative analysis beneath both the EU-NAFTA and nation-state layers has revealed an even richer picture of the relative roles of regional and local governments, non-state actors, and social networks in helping determine the form, scale, and outcomes of cross-border links and integration. In the European border regions, especially the core regions, regional and local governments have developed partnerships with business associations to coordinate spatial planning and economic development. In some of Europe's peripheral border regions, cross-border trade has benefited from active ethnic and social network ties. Across the U.S.-Mexico border region, the hometown organizations of Mexican migrants in the United States, coupled with their extended social networks of relatives and friends, play very important roles in sustaining strong cross-border links in terms of money and people flows, even though these social networks, which also involve smugglers, could induce some illegal migrants to risk their lives in crossing the border. Other than the overarching, supranational influence of NAFTA and the EU, some of the political and sociocultural dynamics in the U.S.-Mexico and European border regions are broadly similar to those in the Asia-Pacific context. In this sense, the non-Asia-Pacific cases confirm the crucial importance of emphasizing and integrating some factors suggested by the harmonious hypothesis in chapter 3, even if they do not provide a direct test on the hypothesis.

Notes

1. As early as the second half of the nineteenth century, there was widespread smuggling of cheaper U.S. goods to the Mexican side of the border, where daily necessities were expensive due to high protective tariffs. From the 1860s to the 1930s, the Mexican government allowed the establishment of Free Zones along much of the border belt to provide duty-free imports of raw materials and industrial goods from the United States, in order to stop smuggling and to facilitate the supply of products not available locally or too expensive to import from the interior. Following the first large wave of Mexican workers entering the United States to pick cotton and build railroads during the 1910s–1930s, many more crossed the border under a bilateral agreement signed in 1944, which permitted the hiring of Mexican workers (*braceros*) by U.S. employers during WWII. In 1961, Mexican President Lopez Mateos launched the ambitious *Programa Nacional Fronterizo* (PRONAF) to accelerate economic development in the border cities. However, the program largely failed, as its import substitution approach didn't create competitive Mexican factories producing for the border market. With the dismantling of the *braceros* program by the U.S. government in December 1964, creating more pressure on jobs in the border region, the Mexican government under President Diaz Ordaz unveiled the Border Industrialization Program (BIP) consisting of highly labor-intensive assembly plants. Under the BIP, foreign and Mexican investors could import duty free the inputs and equipment for assembly so long as they would reexport the products with the purchase of a bond. The plants under the BIP were referred to as maquiladoras. Spanish in origin, *maquiladora* refers to the amount of corn paid by farmer to a miller to grind corn. A maquiladora plant is the miller that uses the inputs provided by the corporate client (the farmer) to return the output (assembled products) to the client. (See Fernandez, 1989, p. 69; Sklair, 1989, pp. 25–29; Wilson, 1992, pp. 36–37).

2. NAFTA superseded previous trade agreements between the United States and Mexico, including the Multifiber Agreements and regulations pertaining to in-bond assembly under Item 807. Item 807 of the U.S. Tariff Schedules, in effect since September 1962, allowed fabricated components made in the United States to be reimported duty free if they were assembled abroad into either intermediate or final goods (Wilson, 1992, p. 38). Item 807 is more relevant to the maquiladoras than Item 806, which applied to metal articles only. But the U.S. imports from Mexico under both 806 and 807, most of which were from the maquiladoras, constituted around 50 percent of total U.S. 806 and 807 imports through the end of the 1980s (Sklair, 1989, p. 12).

3. The rapid establishment of new production facilities and the expansion of existing ones in Mexico's border region after NAFTA helped create 115,000 jobs in 1997, bringing the total number of jobs in border factories to nearly one million. France's Thomson SA is a good example. In 1998, it added 1,200 employees to its newest television assembly plant in Ciudad Juárez, which partly replaced the output of the 1,000 workers at its Bloomington, Indiana, facility. Before April 1, 1998, the Bloomington factory completed the sophisticated circuitry work on the television chassis assembled at the Juárez plant, which took over the work. By completing the production in Ciudad Juárez, Thomson could build a television set in four hours instead of two weeks. The

much lower labor cost in Mexico, coupled with the elimination of shipping components across the border increased Thomson's competitiveness, as the price of a TV set dropped from US$800 to US$200 over the 1990s. The relocation of more sophisticated and higher value-added work to Ciudad Juárez required Thomson to provide continuous training and to reduce the high turnover rate that is typical of maquiladora factory jobs. See "High-tech jobs transfer to Mexico with surprising speed," *Wall Street Journal*, April 9, 1998, p. A18.

4. A dynamic industrial center of 500,000 people, Torreón is located in the northern Mexican state of Coahuila and about four hours by car from the Texas portion of the U.S. border (Gereffi, Martinez, and Bair, 2002).

5. The flourishing free market for used goods on both sides of the U.S.-Mexico border is based on and sustained by the castoffs of the consumer-driven U.S. society, especially discarded old clothing, which amounts to about US$2 billion annually. El Paso–based Midwest Textiles Co. buys semi-trailer loads of used clothing every day and wraps them in 900-pound bundles to be sold in Latin America, Mexico, and other parts of the world. In Ciudad Juárez, a pair of broken-in Levi's fetches US$10, and a nice pair of 1980s-era Nike shoes can be found for US$20. These prices are attractive to thousands of local buyers, particularly to laid-off maquiladora workers who can no longer afford to buy new items at local malls. See "America's castoffs are border boom," *Chicago Tribune*, December 4, 2002, pp. 1, 30.

6. Under NAFTA, for example, Mexico's exports to the United States and Canada grew from US$45 billion to US$133 billion, while its foreign direct investment (FDI) rose from US$4.4 billion to US$11.6 billion. See "North America doesn't need borders," *Wall Street Journal*, August 29, 2000, p. A26. The flow of FDI into Mexico's northwest state of Baja California, which administers the border cities of Tijuana and Mexicali, was estimated to be US$1.6 billion in 1998, nearly twice the amount of the previous year, and almost 80 percent of it came from Asia. A lot of this investment was made by South Korean and Japanese companies through their North American subsidiaries based in the United States. "Asian firms plunge into Mexico on NAFTA's promise," *Wall Street Journal*, August 14, 1998, p. A13.

7. The Water Treaty of 1944 gave the United States rights to 431 million cubic meters of Rio Grande water every year. In exchange, the United States agreed to send Mexico four times as much water from the Colorado River farther west for use in arid Baja California. During a decade-long drought that lasted into mid-2002, Texas farmers were mad because Mexico did not meet its obligations under the treaty. Some of the farmers blocked the Pharr-Reynosa International Bridge near the Texas border city of McAllen to protest water shortages and policies that favored Mexican farmers on the other side of the border. While officials from both national governments tried to find a solution, including conservation and improvements in irrigation technology, the Chihuahua state officials insisted that local Mexican farmers also suffered from the drought and should have priority over the water. "Texans burn as Mexico comes up dry," *Chicago Tribune*, June 7, 2002, p. 3.

8. See "A nuclear waste dump becomes a border issue," *Chicago Tribune*, October 19, 1998, p. 6.

9. While this implementation was delayed due to safety concerns and the pressure of U.S. trucking and labor unions, it was postponed further because of growing concerns over border security after the terrorist attacks of September 11, 2001. Even after President Bush's approval, it would still take a long time and increased personnel of the Transportation Department to actually make it happen for Mexican trucks to travel on interior U.S. highways. See "Bush opens truck access from Mexico," *Chicago Tribune*, November 28, 2002, p. 3.

10. The first period (1848–1900) was characterized by confrontation between the socioeconomic system set up by the Spaniards and new and stronger forces of development of the Anglo settlement north of the border. By the end of the nineteenth century, the Southwest was formally

and substantively incorporated into the U.S. culture and society. During the second period (1900–1945), the Southwest region grew rapidly through the development of agriculture, especially large irrigation projects and the emergence of border towns and commerce. The Mexican Revolution of 1910 temporarily destabilized cross-border economic relations and triggered the beginning of northward migration from Mexico into the United States. The third period (1945–1985) saw even greater economic and geographic changes along the border, as border cities had become relatively large urban centers and sites for clusters of maquiladora factories, and northward migration streams had turned into steady flows (Fernandez, 1989, pp. 14–16).

11. A survey found that on average, a Mexican immigrant sends about US$190 home each time, several times a year. See "Emigrants aid those who want to stay," *Chicago Tribune*, November 23, 2003, p. 4.

12. Aside from the church, money made in the Chicago area paid for two municipal water pumps, the sewer system, and an upgraded cemetery. "Visiting home is gift enough," *Chicago Tribune*, December 26, 2002, pp. 1, 28.

13. One of the main goals of the Program for Mexican Communities Abroad (PCME in Spanish) was to encourage Mexicans and people of Mexican origin to maintain social and cultural ties with Mexico, reinforcing national identity. Built on the existing hometown clubs and their members' interest in projects to improve their hometowns, the PCME created a matching funds program in 1993 that matches two dollars to every one dollar raised by the hometown clubs. The new state laws approved in 1996 and effective in 1998 established that there would be no loss of Mexican nationality for nationals who had obtained another citizenship, and they permitted the recovery of Mexican nationality by the foreign-born children of Mexicans living abroad. While these measures aimed to grant a largely symbolic form of membership in the nation that would affirm Mexican identity and nationalism, they didn't grant formal political citizenship (see Goldring, 2001, pp. 515–516).

14. This agency was set up after an earlier presidential office for Mexican expatriates, headed by a Texas-born literature professor (Juan Hernandez), was abolished in July 2002. It was reported that Hernandez, who lobbied hard to improve undocumented immigrants' access to education and health care in the United States and to make it easier and cheaper for them to wire money back home, lost a power struggle with the foreign minister of Mexico. The reaction of various Mexican American groups to the new council was mixed. See "Mexico plans agency to aid expatriates," *Chicago Tribune*, August 7, 2002, p. 4.

15. See "Migrants get say in Mexico," *Chicago Tribune*, November 24, 2002, p. 1.

16. It has been generally recognized that the U.S.-Mexico border comprises three, if not more, distinctive zones. While the west and east ends of the border are anchored by Brownsville-Matamoros and San Diego–Tijuana complexes, El Paso and Ciudad Juárez mark the central region. In addition, there are subregions that vary considerably by population size, economic base, and income level. For example, there were over one million people living in the extreme southern region of Texas known as the Lower Rio Grande Valley and the northeastern Mexican border region of Tamaulipas. The key economic activities in this border region are tourism, agriculture, and import and export with Mexico through the port of Brownsville. The income and rate of unemployment on both sides of the border were higher than the respective national averages (see Fernandez, 1989, pp. 37–40).

17. Although the two cities have been so integrated for so long, they used to operate on different times. El Paso historically was on Mountain Standard Time, one hour behind Ciudad Juárez, which was on Central Standard Time. The problem used to correct itself from April to October, when the United States moved one hour ahead with Daylight Saving Time. Nevertheless, the lack of time harmony created considerable scheduling difficulty and inconvenience. For example, plant managers on the U.S. side had to rise at 5:30 A.M. to beat the traffic to Ciudad

Juárez, where it was already half past six. In 1998, the two neighboring cities decided to set their clocks to the same hour. "Mexico city won't spring forward so Texas neighbor can catch up, " *Wall Street Journal*, September 3, 1998, p. B1.

18. See "NAFTA reality check: Trucks, trains, ships face costly delays," *Wall Street Journal*, June 3, 1998, pp. A1, A10; "U.S. border towns suffer from post-NAFTA syndrome, " *Wall Street Journal*, August 28, 1998, p. B1.

19. Without the free entrance and movement of Mexican trucks in the United States and U.S. trucks driving freely within Mexico, U.S.-based trucks would typically hand their trailer loads off at border-town interchange points; drayage companies would pull the trailers across the border to a pickup point just inside Mexico, and Mexican freight haulers would take over for the final leg of the southward run. Similar procedures are used for trucks heading north from Mexico. However, Celadon, a relatively small trucking company based in Indianapolis, Indiana, was quite successful and efficient in moving manufactured components (e.g., axles, auto hoods) from such heartland industrial centers as Detroit and Chicago to auto plants south of the border through Loredo, Texas. Its revenue more than doubled from 1994 to 1998. Celadon's rare success had a lot to do with its ability to cultivate solid affiliations with a number of Mexican trucking companies. Having pioneered the practice of sending company-owned trailers into Mexico, it allows nearly 2,000 of its roughly 6,000 trailers in Mexico on any given day. See "Celadon prospers as its trucks cruise the NAFTA trail," *Wall Street Journal*, June 23, 1998, p. B4.

20. "Bush opens truck access from Mexico," *Chicago Tribune*, November 28, 2002, p. 3.

21. See "House OKs bill on border security," *Chicago Tribune*, May 9, 2002, pp. 1, 26.

22. Citing security concerns over terrorism, U.S. immigration officials insisted that all foreigners have valid passports and U.S. visas, which created insurmountable barriers for poor Mexicans who couldn't afford the high passport and visa fees. As a result, a group of Mexican children were denied entry into the United States for scheduled surgeries to correct disfiguring medical conditions at Otay Mesa, California. For the first time in memory, the upcoming Christmas parade in the border town of Calexico would not include hundreds of children from its Mexican sister city, Mexicali. See "Security fears put border life on hold," *Chicago Tribune*, December 8, 2002, pp. 1, 11.

23. "Mexico hoping Iowa deaths spur U.S. policy review," *Chicago Tribune*, October 20, 2002, pp. 1, 17.

24. "Wares, 'coyotes' await at border Wal-Mart," *Chicago Tribune*, January 20, 2003, p. 11.

25. "Border net snares the very young," *International Herald Tribune*, November 4, 2003.

26. See "Millions spent to return immigrants to Mexico," *Chicago Tribune*, August 29, 2004, p. 6.

27. See "Immigration reform pushed," *Chicago Tribune*, April 25, 2003, p. 4; "In Arizona, Fox campaigns for legal border crossings," *Chicago Tribune*, November 5, 2003, p. 4.

28. A second super-region arches from the Veneto in Italy, west through Lombardy and the Piedmont into the Rhone-Alps, across France's Mediterranean coast and hinterlands, and into Catalonia, Spain. Another potential region extends from Ireland through Wales and Brittany across the sea into Galicia and Portugal, while still another would resemble the former Hanseatic League, which would be built around the original Nordic and Baltic membership (Newhouse, 1997, pp. 69–70).

29. In addition to the five regions, the Maas-Rhine includes five major cities: Maastricht and Heerlen in the Netherlands, Hasselt and Liège in Belgium, and Aachen in Germany; four regional authorities: Province of Limburg (the Netherlands), Provinces of Limburg and Liège (Belgium), and Regierungsbezirk Köln of Germany; four cultures: Dutch, Flemish, Walloon, and German; and three languages: Dutch/Flemish, French, and German (see Corvers, Dankbaar, and Hassink, 1996, p. 184).

30. To be more exact, the Swiss portion of the region includes two demicantons (Basel-Town and Basel-Country), as well as seven districts of four adjacent cantons. The French portion embraces the Territory of Belfort and the Department of Haut-Rhin, while the German portion includes one urban district—Stadtkreis Freiburg—and two rural districts—Landkreis Lorrach and Landkreis Emmendingen, and the western parts of Landkreis Breisgau-Hochschwarzwald and Landkreis Waldshut (Briner, 1986, p. 46).

31. My thanks to Dr. Christian Wagner from Germany for sharing his personal experience and observation when he was a youth living in a German town bordering France in the Alsace-Baden-Basel region.

32. At the European Union Summit in Copenhagen in December 2002, the EU agreed to invite Poland, Hungary, the Czech Republic, Slovakia, Lithuania, Estonia, Latvia, Slovenia, and the Mediterranean island nations of Cyprus and Malta to join the EU in 2004, and they did in May 2004. The talks for Turkey's accession into the EU would begin no later than 2003, while the EU would provide financial assistance to Bulgaria and Romania to make needed reforms before they could be considered for membership by 2007. "Turkey left out of EU festivities," *Chicago Tribune,* December 14, 2002, p. 1.

33. The two founding Italian regions were Friuli–Venezla Giulia and Veneto, while the original four Austrian provinces were Carinthia, Styria, Upper Austria, and Salzburg. In 1981, the Italian region of Trebtubi–Alto Adige joined, as did Lombardy in 1985 and the Austrian Burgenland in 1987. The five Hungarian territorial units that joined during 1986–1989 were Gyôr-Moson-Sopron, Vas, Zala, Somogy, and Baranya counties. In 1990, the Swiss Ticino canton was also admitted (Horváth, 1993, p. 159).

34. The Habsburg or Hapsburg family, which can be traced to the tenth century, originally held lands in Alsace and in northwest Switzerland. Otto (1111) took the name Hapsburg from a castle near Aargau, Switzerland, when he was designated count. The election (1273) of Count Rudolf IV as Rudolf I, king of the Germans, provoked war with King Ottocar II of Bohemia. Ottocar's defeat and death at the Marchfeld (1278) confirmed Hapsburg possession of Austria, Carniola, and Styria. Possession of these dominions marked the rise of the Hapsburgs to European significance. The Hapsburg lands were reunited under Maximilian I at the end of the fifteenth century. In the meantime, Tyrol (1363), northeast Istria (1374), and Trieste (1382) were added to the Hapsburg domain. Albert V of Austria, married to a daughter of Holy Roman Emperor Sigismund, succeeded him as king of Bohemia and Hungary. The Spanish and Austrian branches of the dynasty cooperated in the Thirty Years War (1618–1648) and opposed the French in the Third Dutch War (1672–1678) and in the War of the Grand Alliance (1688–1697). The division of the family holdings, the acquisition of the royal crowns of Bohemia and Hungary, and the wars against the Turks in the seventeenth century—these factors transformed the dynasty into a polyglot monarchy, interested more in extending the family power in the Balkans than in purely German affairs. Giving up the Austrian Netherlands, the Hapsburgs regained Dalmatia, Istria, and Tyrol. They were compensated with Salzburg and in Northern Italy with Lombardy and Venetia, which, with Tuscany, Modena, and Parma, made the Italian peninsula virtually a Hapsburg appendage. In the nineteenth century, the Hapsburg position was challenged in Germany by Prussia, in Italy by Sardinia, and in the Balkans by Russia. During the Revolution of 1848, Francis's son Ferdinand abdicated in favor of his nephew Francis Joseph, whose long rule (1848–1916) saw Austria lose (1859) its dominance in Italy and surrender (1866) leadership in Germany to Prussia. In 1867, the Hapsburg lands were reorganized as the Austro-Hungarian Monarchy. The assassination of heir apparent Francis Ferdinand precipitated World War I; the death (1916) of Francis Joseph left his grandnephew, Emperor Charles I, to witness the defeat of Austria-Hungary, which was dissolved immediately after Charles's abdication in 1918. This historical account of the Habsburg dynasty was taken from www.factmonster.com/ce6/history/A0822669.html, accessed on December 19, 2002.

35. Hungary had its border redrawn as a result of the Treaty of Trianon in 1920, which led to the relocation of millions of ethnic Hungarians into bordering countries. Ethnic Hungarians represented Europe's second-largest minority population, behind Russians scattered in the former Soviet republics after the country's break-up in 1991. Today, there are about 1.6 million ethnic Hungarians in Romania, 567,000 in Slovakia, 345,000 in the former Yugoslavia, 163,000 in Ukraine, 33,000 in Austria, 22,000 in Croatia, and about 8,000 in Slovenia. "Hungary has ethnic goulash in the making," *Chicago Tribune,* May 10, 2001, p. 3.

36. I thank Turo-Kimmo Lehtonen at the University of Helsinki in Finland for sharing this information during my visit to Helsinki in November 2003.

37. The Barents Council is made up of representatives from Norway, Sweden, Finland, Iceland, Denmark, and Russia, while the Regional Council consists of actors from the seven regions involved. The Barents Council represents a top-down approach instigated by the Norwegian government; the Regional Council's task is to promote horizontal cooperation through mobilizing private and public investments and stimulating local actors to play active roles (Veggeland, 1993, pp. 43–44).

38. From 1155 to 1809, Finland was part of Sweden, and the border between Finland and Russia separated the Russian and Swedish empires. However, as a result of the war between Sweden and Russia during the Napoleonic Wars in the early 1800s, Finland became a grand duchy under the Russian czar, but it gradually developed its national economic and political system with a fair degree of autonomy. In 1917, Finland declared independence from Russia during the Russian Revolution and normalized its relations with Russia in 1920 through the Treaty of Tartu. Since the southeast boundary of Finland was just 32 km from Leningrad after its independence, Stalin demanded certain Finnish territories, which led to the Winter War of 1939–1940, followed by another war that ended in 1944. Finland lost a total of 100,000 lives, and 50,000 were permanently injured. As a result of these wars, Finland ceded considerable territory to the Soviet Union, especially in the south, including the important Baltic port city of Vyborg. The present Russian-Finnish border was set by the Treaty of Paris in 1947 and remains at the same position today, even though a new bilateral treaty signed in 1992 nullified all previous treaties (see Sweedler, 1994, pp. 4–5).

39. A large part of what is now Russian Karelia was part of Finland before World War II, and in language and culture Karelia is much closer to Finland than to Russia. Of the 850,000 people in the Russian Republic of Karelia, which became an autonomous republic after 1991, 15 percent are Finns and Karelians. Although the non-Russian minority in Russian Karelia raised the issue of sovereignty from Russia in 1992, it didn't amount to anything, since Finns had little interest in regaining lost territory in Karelia and the Finnish minority was already Slavicised. However, Finland began to assist developing Finnish culture in Karelia by funding schools and providing books in Finno-Ugric languages (see Sweedler, 1994, pp. 5–6).

40. I thank Dr. Stephen Rose for sharing this information during my visit to Helsinki in November 2003.

41. I would like to thank Rebekah Sundin for sharing this information with me.

42. Surveys during 1993–1996 showed that 73 percent of small traders in Poland used co-nationals or co-ethnics (e.g., Ukrainians in Poland) in their journeys across the border to trade, 31 percent used relatives as part of their trading activities, while 73 percent used "friends" or "contacts" in their social networks to facilitate their cross-border trade (Wallace with Shmulyar and Bedzir, 1999).

43. See "Crossing borders: Poles' 22-hour commute pays off—illegally—in EU," *Christian Science Monitor,* December 9, 2003, pp. 9, 12.

44. See "Scandinavia helps shape Mecklenburg-Vorpommern into linchpin of Baltic Sea region," Industrial Investment Council, Germany, December, 1999, p. 3.

45. I thank Dr. Christian Wagner from Germany for this information.

46. Located on the Baltic Sea between Lithuania and Poland, Kaliningrad was a free-standing Russian province (oblast) about 322 km west of Russia's border with Belarus. Although Lithuania and Poland allowed Kaliningrad's 947,000 residents to travel in and out of the province freely after the collapse of the Soviet Union in 1991, they would have to require Russians in Kaliningrad to obtain visas as a requirement for joining the EU. The Russian government reacted angrily to the idea of visas, citing the division of Russian sovereignty and the concern that the visa requirements would further isolate the Kaliningrad enclave, which was plagued by a host of social ills, such as organized crime and an increase in the rate of AIDS cases. As a compromise, the Lithuanian government proposed issuing Kaliningrad residents transit visa cards with magnetic strips that would reduce border crossing to simple card swipes, taking about 30 seconds. The Kaliningrad dispute threatened to sour the improving relations between the EU and Russia, which was recognized as a free-market economy and a partner of NATO in the spring of 2002. See "EU visa restrictions test relations with Russia," *Chicago Tribune*, August 11, 2002, p. 4.

47. The purpose of the original Schengen Agreement—signed by Belgium, France, West Germany, Luxembourg, the Netherlands, Portugal, and Spain on June 14, 1985 in the village of Schengen, on the borders of Luxembourg, France, and West Germany—was not to create an external border, but to gradually remove all border controls at internal land, sea, and airport frontiers among themselves. Italy (1990), Greece (1992), and Austria (1995) also signed the Schengen Agreement. Denmark, Finland, and Sweden acceded to the Convention Implementing the Schengen Agreement, but it didn't come into force for the three Nordic countries until March 25, 2001. Norway and Iceland—neither members of the EU—also have fully implemented the Schengen regime since March 25, 2001. As of this writing, the enlarged Schengen zone includes the 15 countries mentioned above, where the holder of a uniform visa is entitled to stay for a maximum of 90 days per six-month period during the visa's period of validity once checks at common borders are completely abolished. This up-to-date information was compiled from two websites: www.auswaertiges-amt.de/www/en/willkommen/einreisebestimmungen/schengen_html and http://europa.eu.int/en/agenda/schengen.html, accessed on August 26, 2004.

9

Re-bordering Transnational Spaces

Theoretical Contributions and Practical Challenges

THIS LAST CHAPTER TAKES ON THE CHALLENGE of bringing the far-reaching comparison of transborder subregions on three continents to a focal conclusion with theoretical and practical implications. We examined three transborder subregions on the western Pacific Rim in great detail (chapters 4–6). This was followed by a comparative, albeit more truncated, analysis of four Southeast Asian transborder subregions, with more attention devoted to the GMS (chapter 7). Then the comparative analysis moved across the Pacific to the U.S.-Mexico border region before crossing the Atlantic to several European border regions (chapter 8). Unfortunately, space constraint prevents the comparative analysis from reaching the African continent (see Asiwaju, 1994; Cheater, 1998; Driessen, 1992; Callaghy, Kassimir, and Latham, 2001; Lundin and Söderbaum, 2002, for recent studies of African cases; also see Parsa and Keivani, 2002, for a cross-border region in the Middle East). Because the Zambia-Malawi-Mozambique Growth Triangle (ZMM-GT), established in 2000 and championed by the UNDP Zambia with assistance from the African Development Bank, is similar to the IMT-GT,[1] studying the ZMM-GT case[2] would have yielded additional evidence and insights. Nevertheless, the combination of three primary cases in East Asia and a number of secondary cases in Southeast Asia and elsewhere has provided a broad empirical ground on which to draw analytical and theoretical conclusions about transborder subregional integration, especially in the Asia-Pacific context. This final task will be made easier by having applied four analytical lenses consistently throughout the preceding case chapters.

A World of Transborder Subregions:
The New Reality and Analytical Significance

What would the Asia-Pacific region be like if the western Pacific Rim were spatially reconfigured around the seven transborder subregions (see map 1.1 in chapter 1) instead of the current nation-states? What would Europe look like if we remapped the continent, whose geopolitical boundaries were already redrawn in 1989, in terms of the six border regions and others like them under the significantly enlarged EU in 2004? Such questions force us to update how we view the world and the future in two significant ways. First of all, these transborder subregions, covering huge territories and millions of people of diverse but linked histories and cultural and ethnic ties, carry significant spatial and demographic weights in the world. In fact, most of the cases examined in this book approach or exceed the upper limit of what Kenichi Ohmae (1995) called "region-states," which tend to have 5–20 million people. Second, even though the existence of transborder subregions does not mean the formal, de jure redrawing of state boundaries, it may signal a real, de facto reconfiguration of functional zones of extensive economic and human flows that slice through state boundaries. Let's briefly reiterate the growing salience of borders and border (sub)regions.

Out of the Shadow: De-bordering and Re-bordering Revisited

Borders have always been important throughout world history and politics. Some of the great ancient battles were fought over disputed border territories and led to subsequent re-bordering of tribes, empires, and states. Borders have gained greater symbolic and functional importance in the era of the modern state because they not only represent the limit of national sovereignty but also demarcate political boundaries. In economic terms, however, borders and border regions have fared less well. They tend to occupy a peripheral or marginal position relative to the central regions of a country. They tend to be economically disadvantaged; the national government neglects them because they are geographically distant, and they receive limited development resources because they are vulnerable military frontiers. This irony of borders and border regions in the modern era may account for why they have not often appeared on the radar screen of mainstream social science analysis. Borders and border regions don't grab our attention unless they erupt as hot spots of large-scale military conflicts or real wars. Few of us would have known anything about the Turkish-Iraqi border region, which suffered economic devastation from 15 years of bloody fighting between the Turkish army and the

Kurdish separatists until 1999, if there had not been massive and frequent press coverage of the recent U.S.-led war against Iraq and its ramifications.[3] To some extent, the relative obscurity of borders and border regions might have left the study of them to a small number of anthropologists and regional scientists. Empirically, these scholars tend to take a localized ethnographic approach in focusing on the cultural and spatial features of specific borders and border zones, which characterizes much of the traditional borderlands literature mentioned in chapter 3 (see Donnan and Wilson, 1994; Driessen, 1992; Lecker, 1991; Wilson and Donnan, 1998b).

What has happened that attaches renewed significance to borders and makes border regions emerge from the large political and economic shadows of capital cities and economic centers? Small border cities have not entered the glamorous terrain of research on world and global cities since the second half of the 1980s (see Robinson, 2002). The most myopic view on the emerged importance of borders and border zones and cities would zero in on the terrorist attacks of September 11, 2001, and the policy responses of the United States and the international community that put national borders in the limelight. A slightly longer perspective would probably focus on the fall of the Berlin Wall in 1989 and the disintegration of the Soviet Union in 1991, which removed the most striking physical and institutional symbols of the Iron Curtain that had separated the West and the East by what seemed an insurmountable barrier. Covering a longer time horizon, this book's in-depth, comparative analysis has focused on the emergence and development of the Asia-Pacific transborder subregions over the past two decades. More importantly, this book has shown that some of the forces that facilitated the rise of the Asia-Pacific transborder subregions were embedded in a much earlier history and became more visible and active only recently. Because of these old and new conditions, borders and border regions have undergone dramatic changes and even complete transformations. They have arisen from the geographic margins and scholarly backstage to demand our central attention.

Chapter 1 characterizes the new dynamics of borders and border regions as a simultaneously de-bordering and re-bordering process, which is a more realistic conceptualization than the image of an emergent "borderless world" (see Ohmae, 1990). The merit of my perspective rests on two distinctive but connected dimensions of change. First, borders have clearly become more permeable than ever before by letting through greater and more intensive flows of goods, people, and information. There is so much permeability over borders now that they have lost much of their barrier effect, which represents a sort of de-bordering. Secondly, links and flows over porous borders have begun to spread so far beyond the immediate border zones that broader transborder subregions have formed. In this sense, borders may be shifting and extending the border region from either or both sides of the boundary line. While the Guangdong–Hong Kong border moving north is an example of widening border zones (chapter 4), the more diffused links of Mexican immigrants over the U.S.-Mexico border have created a much larger transnational economic and social space (chapter 8). This amounts to an extended re-bordering without resetting a sharp borderline. Taking into account the U.S. government's tightening of border control after September 11, we may be witnessing a new and different kind of re-bordering that features escalated state controls over very open borders. Both de-bordering and some re-bordering imply a reduced or disappeared barrier effect of borders and an enhanced bridging role. Other kinds of re-bordering, however, may involve states restoring some barrier effects of borders, intentionally or otherwise, although they are unlikely to completely reverse the inevitable long-term trend toward de-bordering. This is a brief echo of the central argument laid out in chapter 1.

Another Look at the Transborder Subregion as a Unit of Action and Analysis

What does de-bordering and re-bordering really lead to? This dynamic process reminds us of the four types of borderlands described by Oscar Martínez (1994): alienation, coexistence, interdependence, and integration. Martínez focused more on differentiating distinctive borderlands in terms of political and economic contact and interface rather than specifying conditions under which alienated borders evolve through coexistence and interdependence to integrated ones. While I could have attempted fitting each of the cases to any of the four types, it would be mechanically narrow. This book instead set out to examine transborder subregions as a new transnational space created by how the de-bordering and re-bordering process is shaped by a multiplicity of macro-, mezzo-, and micro-level forces. In other words, instead of seeing transborder subregions as merely conventional borderlands straddling two countries, I treat them as a broader transnational spatial entity with economic, political, and sociocultural dimensions.

Even as I try to distinguish transborder subregions from the object of study in the borderlands literature, I reemphasize region as a unit of analysis for understanding the complexity of globalization, national development, and local dynamics (see Amin, 1999; Grabher, 1993; Oman, 1994; Scott, 1995). Those scholars, however, have focused on domestic regions such as industrial districts or formal transitional regional structures like the EU or NAFTA. Although these regional units are relevant to and actually enter the analysis of transborder subregions here, the latter are a distinctive phenomenon of the last two decades or so that deserve the kind of treatment in this book.

In the most important sense that transborder subregions are more than borderlands, the former have emerged as a major transnational terrain for the convergence and interaction among economic, political, social, and infrastructure factors, which either didn't exist until more recently or used to lay dormant or operate in isolation. While borderlands allow ethnographically oriented scholars to obtain distinctive and concrete views of social, cultural, and political identities at the most tangible interface of nation-states (Donnan and Wilson, 1994), transborder subregions examined in this book have provided us with a broad vista to search for structural explanations for the varied attributes and outcomes of integration across the cases. Furthermore, they offer rich evidence from which we could extract insights into the major theoretical debates today. In the section below, a number of theoretical contributions from the cases are highlighted to clarify, advance, and perhaps reshape arguments about globalization and localization, the changing state, the role of social capital, and geographic proximity, which have been employed as analytical lenses, albeit unevenly, for the cases in chapters 4 through 8.

Transborder Subregions and Globalization: Mediating the Uneven Impact

The systematic comparative study of transborder subregions here contributes new conceptual nuance and empirical insights to the literature on the economic process and impact of globalization. In setting up the analytical framework for the Asia-Pacific transborder subregions, we acknowledged the relevance of the argument by Rosenau (1997) about the integrating impact of globalization and the fragmenting impact of localization (see chapter 3). Seeing this double, simultaneous impact dialectically, Yeung (2000, p. 403) suggests that globalization leads to both spatial integration (a result of globalized economic activities) and spatial disintegration (an outcome of localization of these activities) due to the persistence of geographic differences. This perspective emphasizes a bifurcating tendency toward global economic integration at a grand scale accompanied by diverse national- and local-scale activities, without identifying specific intermediate structures or mechanisms that connect or mediate economic globalization and localization. Scholars paying explicit attention to regionalization as part of and in relation to globalization tend to focus on formal regional blocs (e.g., the EU, NAFTA) as politically motivated initiatives (see Oman, 1994) or on cultural trends and practices (see Berger and Huntington, 2002).

Transborder subregions are a tiered in-between spatial entity that mediates global and local economic processes and activities by connecting them in some cases, isolating them in others, and even reconfiguring them under certain circumstances. They are capable of this varied role because they involve diverse sets of subnational border areas of comparative economic advantages and disadvantages that create different mixes and levels of complementarity or lack of it. In addition, the subnational border areas of a transborder subregion may be asymmetrical to and different from one another in relation to the national economies of which they are a part. In the GSCS, for example, although Hong Kong is a very small and "independent" part of China, it exerts a disproportionately larger influence on Guangdong province, especially the Pearl River Delta (PRD). The IMS-GT is similar in terms of Singapore stacking up against the national economies of Malaysia and Indonesia relative to the neighboring Johor state and Riau province. Finally, the subnational areas of a transborder subregion vary in terms of when, how soon, and how extensively they are exposed to the impact of economic globalization.

Given these various conditions, transborder subregions operate on different economic logics that interface with the global economy in varied ways. At one extreme, the GSCS is highly globalized through a subregionalized division of labor among three complementary economies and full integration into the global manufacturing and export loops of such industries as electronics and toys. It can be concluded that the GSCS embodies a full-fledged global-(sub)regional-local economic nexus where direct and indirect links between the global and many local economies are embedded in a transborder subregional system. At the other end are the GTS, the GMS, the EAGA, and activities across some Central and East European borders, which are hardly globalized in that they feature primarily localized economic activities such as simple manufacturing and petty trade across borders, for reasons discussed in earlier chapters. For these cases, the transborder subregional frame serves as a weak middle link or a light "filter" between the global economy and the many local economies. In between these two types are cases like the BYSS and the IMT-GT that have a varied mix of orientation and connections to the global, national, and local economies. For these cases, the transborder subregional structure provides a wider conduit that facilitates the flows and links between the global economy and various local economies. As a whole set, these eclectic cases provide a full range of possible interfaces and mutual responses between local economies, transborder subregional economies, and the global economy.

Transborder Subregions and the State: Re-scaling the De-centered Power

Building on the above argument that transborder subregions mediate the uneven impact of economic globalization in different ways, this section stakes out a follow-up claim that transborder subregions play a central role in re-scaling the de-centered state and its power. This claim dovetails with the more prevalent view in the globalization-state debate that globalization contributes to a weakening or erosion of the state without sliding to the extreme position of the "dying state" (see Clark, 1999, chaps. 2 and 3, for a sophisticated rendition of this debate). Transborder subregions allow us to deepen the argument about the impact of globalization on the state via an intermediate or bridging logic that globalization reconfigures political space by challenging the state's bounded sovereignty defined by borders (Jarvis and Paolini, 1995).

In proffering the de-centered state as an analytical lens for transborder subregions in chapter 3, I stated that state power that is normally exercised by and from the political center has become more scattered and diffused among the multilayered units inside and outside a transborder subregion, such as regional/local governments and supranational organizations. This new spatial milieu must be recognized as more complex and more compromising for central state power than what Jarvis and Paolini (1995, p. 15) described as an environment of competing forces, both local and global, that leads to interactive compromise and adjustment between them and the state. Transborder subregions re-scale the weakened power of a de-centered state both vertically and horizontally. While some power is scaled down and takes root at the local level, some is scaled up and exercised permanently at the level of the EU or NAFTA. In Southeast Asia where ASEAN/AFTA was evolving toward a formalized political/economic bloc, the growth triangles might either distract or be inconsistent with the larger agenda of ASEAN-wide economic cooperation (Abonyi, 1994). In a horizontal sense, the direct and routinized trans-local interaction among more autonomous local governments in a transborder subregion has relocated state power out of the internal political space and re-embedded it inside a transnational space.

The simultaneous or sequential de-centering and re-scaling of the state in the transborder subregional context is real and pronounced but by no means powerful enough to deplete all central state power. In fact, the twin force of de-centering and re-scaling not only has further blurred the internal (national) and the external (international) domains of the state but also rebalanced the whole range of roles still played by the state. This point converges with the argument by Clark (1999) that the internal/external dichotomy of the state is misconceived and misplaced because the state's chosen policies and internal transformations are part and parcel of globalization, instead of being just a stand-alone victim of the latter. The supporting evidence has come out clearly from the GSCS context in which the mutually reinforcing policies of China's central, provincial, and municipal governments to target overseas Chinese investors are instrumental in globalizing the Guangdong–Hong Kong and Fujian-Taiwan borders and beyond. The U.S. government's measures to balance border security and free flow of commerce over the Canadian and Mexican borders after September 11, 2001, illustrate the realigned power of the state and its intention to reconcile seemingly linked international goals of promoting free trade and fighting terrorism with the domestic concern over border security. This balancing act is further complicated by the U.S. government having to deal with the implications of local civilian groups in the state of Arizona policing the border with Mexico to reduce both illegal immigrants and a potential terrorist threat.[4] The manifestations and ramifications of de-centered and re-scaled state power in transborder subregions appear endlessly consequential.

Transborder Subregions and Social Capital: Gluing Border-Spanning Worlds

As state sovereignty and power is compromised through de-centering and re-scaling in transborder subregions, cross-border social and cultural ties play a more active role in shaping the contour of this transnational space. These ties, aggregated into and operating as a form of social capital, are not a passive derivative of the de-centered state. Quite the opposite. These ties, based on early human settlements, trade routes, migration patterns, ethnicity, religion, and language, existed long before the beginning of modern states and their political and physical boundaries. While there is neither a need nor space here to rehash the familiar lack of correspondence between nation and state in the modern nation-state (see Wilson and Donnan, 1998a), it is instructive to mention the distinction drawn by Kearney (1998, p. 118) between boundaries as legal spatial delimitations of nations and borders as geographic and cultural zones or spaces that vary independently of formal boundaries. This necessary distinction sharpens our argument that transborder subregions are wider and deeper geographic and cultural zones where rich social capital has been cumulated and interacts with economic and political forces to either glue together or fragment communities and regions sharing or adjacent to international boundaries.

One powerful element of cross-border social capital is ethnic identity, which entails links that have exerted differential influence on the transborder subregions compared in this book. Cross-border ethnic ties have deep and persistent roots in history that linger on today; they also carry cultural and linguistic continuities that stretch beyond border zones. This is characterized by Fernand Braudel as "the amazing permanence of cultural frontiers and cultural zones in the face of all the cross-fertilization in the world" (Braudel,

1976, cited by Wilson and Donnan, 1998a, p. 11). The enduring and resilient cross-border ethnic ties were often suppressed by the priorities of state-building and border control. They have, however, resurfaced in different forms over the past two decades as state policies and inter-state relations have changed, especially with the end of the Cold War. In the Balkans, the old ethnic boundaries, which used to circumscribe regions within the state of the former Yugoslavia, have reconstituted state borders (Thuen, 1999; also see Roudometof, 2001). This exemplifies the fragmenting impact of resurgent ethnic movements on geopolitical borders in the post-Cold War era.

As shown in the early chapters of this book, cross-border ethnic ties in the Asia-Pacific transborder subregions, blended with other social and cultural elements into a form of social capital, tend to glue together economic activities across borders, even though this influence is much stronger in the GSCS and across the U.S.-Mexico border than in the other cases. This gluing effect was seen as realistic in the idea of (re)creating a functional Baltic region based on network ties among cities and towns that once were controlled by the Hanseatic League (Veggeland, 1993). While much of the empirical analysis focused on the casual influence of cross-border social capital, we are better off here stressing that transborder subregions allow us to see the formation of social capital at an aggregate spatial scale. Instead of operating from its typical locus between individuals, groups, and organizations, cross-border social capital resides within a range of ties among multiple actors and units across international boundaries and holds these ties together with sustaining power. Studying social capital in transborder subregions creates a broader vantage point from which to appreciate how social capital is formed and exerts diverse but real consequences at both micro and macro levels.

Transborder Subregions and Geographic Proximity: Constructing Crucial and Close Links

If cross-border social capital is capable of weakening the barrier effect of state borders on economic flows, geographic contiguity and proximity that link different border areas into a transborder subregion create a double-edged sword with regard to the relative role of borders as bridges or barriers. Border zones are connected by a fairly short distance, usually shorter than that which separates border zones from national centers or core areas. While this facilitates close and intensive interactions, control over international boundaries and the lack of cross-border transport links relative to those on either side of a border (Rietveld, 1993) reinforce the barrier effect that otherwise might be reduced by short distance. Therefore, transborder subregions shed some light on the seemingly ironic phenomenon of the declining significance of distance in the age of globalization and advanced communications technology and the critical importance for building cross-border transport links to enhance the natural advantages of geographic proximity.

Parallel to the strong globalist thesis that globalization leads to "the end of the state" is the equally strong claim of "the end of geography" under conditions of globalization (see O'Brien, 1992). Without going that far, much of the globalization literature with a spatial tilt has echoed the gist of this argument with repeated reference to the declining significance of physical distance in an integrated world economy that is increasingly coordinated from a few key nodes through advanced telecommunications technology (see Graham and Marvin, 1996). While this is true of more and more economic activities, especially in the global financial industry, it does not apply to the transborder subregions where distance remains functionally important but not in the conventional sense. Low transportation costs are usually associated with a short distance between any two or more physical locations within a national economic space, but cities and towns on different sides of an international boundary may not obtain this benefit of geographic proximity. They are generally faced with an underdeveloped cross-border transport infrastructure for a variety of reasons, including border control, lack of investment, incompatible roads and rails on different sides of borders, and even natural barriers such as mountains and rivers. The lack of good cross-border transport links imposes a strong constraint on a transborder subregion, which has a great demand for efficient transport links that are capable of generating externalities from geographic proximity and intensive and frequent cross-border flow of economic activities. The need for constructing cross-border transport infrastructure is greater than what short physical distance seems to call for.

The transborder subregions in this study have offered varied evidence on the critical balance of supply of and demand for cross-border transport links in light of some facilitating or compromising circumstances. In the GSCS, the development of crisscrossing highways, railroads, and bridges appears to have kept up with the rapid economic growth on both sides of the Guangdong–Hong Kong border, to meet the rising demand for timely border crossings by business commuters and freight trucks. The absence of direct flights between Taiwan and mainland China, however, has added transport costs that would otherwise be unnecessary due to the short cross-strait distance (see chapter 4). In the GTS, while there is a great need to expand and upgrade cross-border transport infrastructure to stimulate economic growth in a backward frontier transnational subregion, the lack of large-scale external investment due to political instability in North Korea and limited economic opportunities restricts resources that might otherwise be used for constructing transport infrastructure. The long-term need to preserve the natural ecological environment and shared water use in the Tumen River and Mekong River basins also may tamper with the supply-demand equation of developing cross-border transport and energy infrastructure (see chapters 6 and 7). Even as the EU began to admit and integrate its Eastern neighbors, an existing member, Austria, demanded restrictions to stop trucks from the East with a different environmental standard polluting its Alpine highways.[5] As these cases illustrate, despite the short distance that links border areas into a transborder subregion, cross-border transport links are crucial, but they may not be put in place due to economic, political, and environmental constraints.

Positions and Connections in Layered Asian Regionalism: Competition or Cooperation?

If we add up the geographic and demographic coverage of all seven transborder subregions (see map 1.1), we can almost imagine a reconfigured Asia-Pacific region in which the bulk of the population and territory falls into the boundaries of the transborder subregions, even though they are not as fixed as the state borders. This is clearly significant in spatial terms, as it has added a distinctive layer of geographic links above and below almost all the major Asia-Pacific countries and across and through their crucial land and sea boundaries. The greater significance of this transborder subregional phenomenon, however, lies in a set of economic, political, social, and transport relations that stem from yet spread beyond geographic proximity and natural territorial links. Given these varied and uneven links, there arise two interrelated questions. The first is how the transborder subregions, or their constituent units more precisely, are positioned and connected relative to one another and how they are linked to key cities or nodes outside their boundaries. The second question is how the transborder subregions or their component areas fit with and relate to other layers and forms of regional structures or arrangements. Let me suggest how the questions may be addressed.

Regarding the first question, while we have stressed the distinctive geographic position and physical boundaries of the units that make up the transborder subregions, there are crossover ties and spillover influence between some pairs of these subregions. For example, South Korean companies have invested heavily in both the Yanbian region of Jilin province in the GTS and the coastal region of Shandong province that belongs to the BYSS. Comparative advantages, ethnic identity and ties, and geographic proximity figure differently in the South Korean investors' links to different destinations within and between the two separate, albeit adjacent, transborder subregions (see chapters 5 and 6). In the GMS, some of the historical ethnic Chinese ties through Yunnan province originated from the earlier cross-border migration of people from certain parts of Guangdong province, which also maintains strong commercial links to the GMS (see chapter 7). Regarding the economic and physical links of the transborder subregions beyond their boundaries, especially to other dominant cities, the major ports of South Korea and Japan have developed close and frequent shipping links to Shanghai (see map 5.1). Increasingly, investment from high-tech Taiwanese companies, especially in semiconductors, have overstepped the boundary of the GSCS to concentrate and cluster in the Shanghai region (see chapter 4), halfway between the GSCS and the BYSS (see map 1.1).

The informal boundaries of the transborder subregions are sufficiently porous to allow cross-border links to extend or spill. When two transborder subregions are geographically closer like the BYSS and GTS, they are more likely to have a neighboring effect on each other. Secondly, some of the major constituent units, such as Guangdong province in the GSCS, extend more links and thus exert more influence within and between the transborder subregions due to historical, economic, and cultural conditions. Some powerful cities in these transborder subregions—Hong Kong, Taipei, Singapore, and Seoul, for example—serve the different nodal functions for their respective subregional hinterlands, so to speak. However, since most of the local-level units in the transborder subregions are smaller and less influential border cities and towns, other dominant cities in the Asia-Pacific region can draw multiple links their way, even though they are not located within the boundary of any transborder subregion. Shanghai is the most illustrative example. It has emerged as a central economic and transport node between the GSCS to the south and the BYSS in the north, given its comparative and competitive advantages in size, centralized location on China's coast, rapid economic growth, and rising global city status (X. Chen, forthcoming).

Although the question about the interface and relationship between the transborder subregions and other regional groupings is beyond this study, a few brief observations could be made here. The transborder subregions are hardly connected with Asia-Pacific Economic Cooperation (APEC), which was established in 1989 by 12 countries, or economies, on both sides of the Pacific Ocean to facilitate the liberalization of trade and investment through cooperation and consultation.[6] If APEC really opposes the idea of an inward-looking trading bloc and instead pursues global free trade, as its leaders have emphasized since their 1995 Osaka Declaration (Economic Committee of APEC, 1997), this spirit would be compatible with the open nature of the transborder subregions. Given the very loose alliance among whole economies as members of APEC, it is difficult to imagine that it will ever have any direct relationship with the subnational units that make up the transborder subregions. At a lower level, there appear to be some connections and mutual influences between the ASEAN/AFTA[7] and the transborder subregions, particularly the Southeast Asian growth triangles. These connections, however, may be uncertain but certainly not inconsequential. To the extent that the growth triangles are driven by market and private sector dynamics, they are largely consistent with the open- and free-trade orientation of ASEAN/ AFTA. More specifically, if the growth triangles truly induce links of complementary activities across borders, they help promote intra-ASEAN integration and even accelerate certain elements of AFTA's implementation. On the other hand, too much focus on the growth triangles may distract from or be inconsistent with the larger agenda of ASEAN-wide economic cooperation and integration (Abonyi, 1994). Empirical analysis of how these relations may play out is beyond this study.

Other recent developments in regional alliances have rendered all seven transborder subregions more relevant entities in the growing layers of Asian regionalism. The most important and influential of the new initiatives was the first ASEAN+3 (China, Japan, South Korea) summit held in December 1997 as a mechanism of annual dialogue among these countries, which subsequently led to ministerial meetings and official cooperation in currency swaps to avoid future financial turmoil like the Asian financial crisis.[8] ASEAN+3 (13 countries altogether) include all those involved in the seven transborder subregions, except the Russian Federation, North Korea, and Taiwan. Although the geographic overlap between ASEAN+3 and the parts of the transborder subregions in the countries involved is substantial (all constituent units of the GMS are included in ASEAN+3), it remains to be seen if the more formal cooperative activities of ASEAN+3 will be compatible with the informal cross-border trade and investment flows within the transborder subregions.

Also complicating the transborder subregions is the accelerated formulation and implementation of primarily bilateral preferential trade agreements (PTAs) or simply bilateral trade agreements (BTAs) between western Pacific Rim countries, with more than 40 of them either proposed or implemented between 1999 and 2003, with Singapore leading the region in concluding such deals (ADB, 2004). While Japan and China have been the newest entrants into signing or negotiating bilateral or plurilateral PTAs, Japan and South Korea began negotiations in 2002 to sign a free trade agreement (FTA). China has proposed to implement a PTA with ASEAN in the form of a free trade zone (FTZ) by 2020 (see below). While the PTAs have the advantage of being negotiated speedily, exposing protected sectors gradually to international competition, producing deeper economic integration, and serving as testing grounds for collaboration, they tend to discriminate among non-members and exporters, and they exclude smaller, less developed countries, which are regarded as insignificant markets (Ravenhill, 2003). Despite their recency, the PTAs involving pairs or groups of countries have direct geographic coverage of the transborder subregions and may carry economic implications for some of them. If an FTA between Japan and South Korea comes into existence, it will have a direct and immediate impact on the BYSS by possibly rebalancing the direction and volume of trade flows across the Yellow Sea at the possible expense of China's Bohai rim region.

Since the transborder subregions consisting of primarily subnational and local units are distinctly different from the formal inter-state arrangements such as ASEAN+3 or PTAs, they could develop complementary and cooperative relations with the latter without having to compete or being suppressed. The largely market-coordinated transborder subregions with limited but varied levels of state involvement are generally consistent with the objectives and practices of APEC, AFTA, ASEAN+3, and PTAs to liberalize trade and promote investment. If the developing relations between the transborder subregions and the formal groupings turn out to be cooperative, it may foster positive competition that already exists or is likely to arise between the transborder subregions, especially involving the latter's most important city-level units. This competition pertains to attracting foreign investment and establishing or consolidating hub status and role, as demonstrated in the BYSS (see chapter 5), or exerting greater influence on hinterlands, as in the GSCS and the IMS-GT (chapters 4 and 7). The relative weight of cooperation and competition within and between the transborder subregions and their interface with the more formal Asia-Pacific regional and bilateral arrangements calls for the kind of extensive comparative research in this book.

The Rise of China Through the Mosaic of Transborder Subregions

While the complicating influence of formal trade initiatives on the transborder subregions is inherently limited by involving entire national economies, the rise of China's economy over the past two decades figures more prominently in setting the parameters and contours of the Asia-Pacific transborder subregions. A few statistics illustrate China's growing competitive advantage in relation to the major national economies involved in the transborder subregions. As Japan's consumption of East and Southeast Asia's total exports declined from 20 percent around 1990 to only 10 percent in 2002, China's imports from the region grew from 6.8 percent in 1990 to 15 percent in 2002. China also absorbed 85 percent of the Asia-Pacific region's total FDI in 1999, up from 24 percent in the early 1980s. China's share of the region's electronics exports rose from 14.3 percent in 1997 to 30 percent in 2002, while Singapore's share dropped from 19.3 percent to 9.8 percent, and Malaysia, Taiwan, and Thailand also lost shares (Hale and Hale, 2003, pp. 44–46). With its huge reserve pool of labor and thus cost advantages in labor-intensive production, China is in a position to further increase exports of such labor-intensive exports as textiles and clothing after the end of the Multi-Fiber Agreement (MFA) in 2005 (ADB, 2004). China's gains at the expense of the other major Asian economies have begun to realign their relative positions and connections in the regional hierarchy of economic power and competitiveness.

The looming presence of China as an economic giant in the Asia-Pacific is only magnified by the horizontal spread of its involvement in and influence on the region as a whole and the transborder subregions in particular. China has a 22,000 km land border and 18,000 km sea border with 15 Asian countries. Although the 12 frontiers inherited by China in 1949 all had historical disputes, China has signed frontier agreements with most of the neighboring countries and finished delimitating 20,222 km of the land border, 90 percent of the total length. China also has made progress in settling disputed sea borders in the South China Sea (see Fu, 2003, p. 304).[9] Due to its sheer geographic size and location, China has more physical presence in and near the seven transborder subregions than any other country involved in the Pacific Rim. China's land and sea borders wind through four of the transborder subregions (see map 1.1), while many of its frontier border towns and major port cities occupy important spots within these transborder subregions (see the maps for chapters 4–7). It is also clear that China has more of its subnational and local areas participating in the four transborder subregions than the other countries or economies either in whole (e.g., Taiwan) or in part (e.g., the RFE).

Interestingly enough, in some specific Chinese cities and areas in some of the transborder subregions we find powerful drivers for and external links to China's rapidly growing economic might in the Asia-Pacific region and beyond. The PRD in Guangdong province boasts Asia's, if not the world's, densest concentration of export-oriented manufacturing of computers, footwear, and furniture. This extreme clustering would not have occurred without the cross-border relocation of Taiwan and Hong Kong investment in these industries creating the GSCS. Producing 62 percent of the world's keyboards, 61 percent of the world's motherboards, 54 percent of the world's monitors, and 25 percent of the world's desktop PCs (Hale and Hale, 2003), Taiwanese companies now make the bulk of these peripherals and desktop PCs in the PRD, especially in the city of Dongguan (see chapter 4). The PRD has become a core of China's growing function as a hub for assembling and processing components and intermediate inputs from the rest of Asia into manufactured exports. This is reflected in the re-export share of Singapore's exports to China growing from 25 percent in 1995 to 53 percent in 2002 (Hale and Hale, 2003). Across the Pacific, China has recently overtaken Mexico as the second-largest trading partner of the United States, behind only Canada, despite the stronger cross-border economic integration under NAFTA (see chapter 8). With its labor only a quarter to a third of and its electricity half of the costs in Mexico (Hale and Hale, 2003), China has become more attractive to labor-intensive global manufacturing than the maquiladora sector in northern Mexico. However, by keeping its labor costs so low, China has recently run into an unintended problem with labor-intensive manufacturing. The main manufacturing cities in the PRD in Guangdong province have begun to experience a shortage of workers, especially young female workers in mostly small and medium-sized processing or assembling factories. This new phenomenon may be partly attributed to the stagnation of the average wage, which stayed at a little less than US$100 a month from the early 1990s to 2004.[10] If spreading and lasting, this problem could dampen the rapid growth and prosperity of the GSCS.

Through and from the less developed but strategically located GMS, China has been reaching out to make its presence felt in Southeast Asia. China has reached an agreement with ASEAN to join AFTA, with Yunnan province being the leading edge to connect with the planned establishment of the ASEAN Economic Community (AEC) by 2020 (ADB, 2004). Besides discussing with ASEAN the creation of an FTZ of 1.7 billion people with a nominal GDP of over US$2 trillion, the Yunnan government proposed to ASEAN officials in October 2002 that Yunnan be made a demonstration zone for the future ASEAN-China FTZ, with Kunming as a financial and information center covering south China and all of ASEAN (Yow, 2003). If and when the planned FTZ and Yunnan and Kunming's roles materialize, Yunnan province will benefit greatly from greater trade and investment flows through its borders with the ASEAN countries of Vietnam, Lao PDR, and Myanmar and the rest of ASEAN via Thailand. China's heavy presence in mainland Southeast Asia has come from beyond Yunnan. Concerned about a recent decline in grain yields and her future food security, China has turned to its southwestern neighboring countries to import rice—a traditional staple. Such is the demand that Thai farmers report entire crops being bought long before harvests. Vietnamese authorities blame cross-border food-smuggling for a record 20 percent increase in the price of rice. In one novel experiment, the Chongqing municipal government near Yunnan is leasing land in Lao PDR to grow food for its huge urban population.[11] These new developments are contingent on building a more extensive and efficient transport infrastructure to create an integrated system of air, rail, road, and water links to mainland and maritime Southeast Asia (see chapter 7). From maritime Southeast Asia, the renewed development plan of the EAGA calls for making commercial links with China in response to the latter's rapid growth and growing influence in the region (ADB, 2003). History has ironically come full circle, as China had already developed long-distance commercial links with the Sulu Islands as far back as the fourteenth century (Ptak, 1999). The active and deep involvement of China's many land and sea border cities in the four transborder subregions and their expanding links to the others may produce centrifugal and dislocating forces that weaken the economic, cultural, spatial, and even political aspects of national integrity. However, one could argue that the extensive and diverse economic, cultural, and transport links from and through the transborder subregions along and beyond China's boundary have facilitated its rise as a fast-growing economic power in the Asia-Pacific region.

Transborder Subregions as New Transnational Spaces: The Challenges to Governance

China's active participation in several transborder subregions has helped turn them into new transnational spaces that pose governance challenges of varied kinds and scales. The first such challenge may concern the more conventional role of Asian states in responding to the looming presence of China at their doorstep or in their vicinity. These responses may be limited due to the rapidity with which China has risen and its powerful influence. At the inter-state level, how other Asian states respond to China may have more to do with how China manages its trade and investment links with the region. It is at the transborder subregional level that other Asian states may have more flexibility and even leverage in dealing with China because it is their subnational and local governments and economies that engage in cross-border interactions with China's provincial and local economies of considerably varied strengths and external links within and across the subregions.

Besides the striking "China factor," broader economic, political, and spatial dynamics, reinforced by revived sociocultural links, have shaped the transborder subregions into new transnational spaces. This becomes clear as we evaluate other governance challenges. One obvious challenge of transborder subregions to governance is their fairly large size. Although smaller than such supranational blocs of entire countries as the EU or ASEAN, most of the transborder subregions have larger populations and territories than some medium-sized countries. The demographic and geographic span of transborder subregions calls for a long and wide reach of any potential governance structure. The related but much more difficult challenge to governance posed by the transborder subregions derives from the structural and spatial aspects of their composition. To reiterate, transborder subregions consist of a multiplicity of subnational areas and localities on or adjacent to one or more international boundaries. This structure not only includes units from incompatible economic and political systems but also heterogeneous cultural and ethnic groups, as well as diverse transboundary ecological conditions. Moreover, the transnational space of a transborder subregion spans one or more interfaces of bounded national spaces. The Baltic Rim region consisting of entire proximate nations (see chapter 8) might enhance governance by creating and improving regional institutions such as sharing best practices in government operations and setting up a regional development bank and dispute resolution mechanisms (Porter, 2001). The internal heterogeneity, coupled with a sort of in-between status across tiered levels, makes transborder subregions doubly difficult to govern with any conventional authority structure or administrative mechanism.

The transborder subregions have emerged in a new world order in which conventional governance is becoming less effective anyway. It is pertinent here to refer to Rosenau's (1997) conception of the turbulent, postinternational world, which is no longer based on a system of sovereign states, each enjoying exclusive control over a defined territory with no authority above it (see Mansbach, 2000, p. 12). If this represents a shift from a "state-centric" to a "multi-centric" world, characterized by more blurring and nesting between the internal and external realms of the state (see Sassen, 1999), transborder subregions contribute more complexity to it with linked units both above and below the state, as well as transcending it. Transborder subregions do more than just complicate the conventional state structure and inter-state relations. Transborder subregions change how parts of the existing system are configured, creating a new whole that is more important than the sum of its parts, and that may need to be governed as such.

In the political sense, various national, regional, and local governments not only struggle to redefine their vertical relations within national boundaries but also how they interact with their counterparts across borders. While this redefinition is keyed to the national state's delicate balancing act of redistributing power versus autonomy across vertical and horizontal administrative hierarchies, national states increasingly have to contend with the growing influence from supranational organizations (e.g., the EU) that have begun to bypass national governments to work directly with regional and local authorities in cross-border economic cooperation. The state at different levels of a transborder subregion must learn to deal with the more assertive private sector and ethnic interests, as well as more active non-government or quasi-government organizations involved in cross-border coordination and cooperation.

The diverse evidence from our cases points to some possible ways in which these governing challenges may be met, at least on a temporary, trial-and-error basis. In the GSCS, economic complementarity and autonomous and market-oriented local governments in Guangdong and Fujian provinces, reinforced by lubricating cross-border social capital, have led to rapid growth and some shared prosperity. To sustain this growth, the provincial and municipal governments have begun to work more closely with the government of the Hong Kong Special Administration Region on such old and new issues as further improving cross-border transport infrastructure, more effective handling of recently lengthened border crossing hours and controlling illegal crossings over the more porous border, and better coordination in dealing with SARS after learning the lessons and mistakes in the outbreak early in 2003 (see chapter 4). While the GSCS represents more decentralized governance, the GMS features more conventional, centralized governance in the form of regularly scheduled multilateral conferences involving national ministries for enhancing cross-border cooperation. This style of governance was also reflected in the earlier establishment of specialized multi-government agencies such as the Mekong Water Commission. At the same time, the persistent, if not worsening, problems of illegal migration, drug and human trafficking, and spillover industrial pollution across the Jilin–North Korea, Yunnan-Myanmar, and U.S.-Mexico borders call for greater and more targeted cooperation among GMS-level policy-makers, the national governments involved, and local authorities (see chapters 6–8).

Regarding the IMS-GT in Southeast Asia, under the official agreement between Singapore and Indonesia's national governments, there was a layered governance structure of a high-level coordinating committee involving different ministries and the Riau governor and a lower-level ad hoc coordination board consisting of the regional development agency of Riau province and Singapore's central agency of Economic Development Board (see chapter 7). In the European context, even as the EU has begun to exert greater top-down influence on border regions through targeted financial assistance, bodies of authority involving regional and local government planning or other agencies across borders, especially in long-established border regions, continue to have the primary governing role in promoting cross-border cooperation (see chapter 8).

As these experiences indicate, there is no single, standard response to the governing challenges created by transborder subregions. These challenges will only become stronger and thus demand more effective responses as the transborder subregions continue to proliferate, and the economic and cultural interactions within them widen and deepen. More importantly, if border-bending forces continue to escalate, and if accelerated regionalization of varied forms and scopes moves us to a more region-centric world, transborder subregions are likely to become more visible organizing units and transnational spaces of denser and more extensive economic, political, and cultural activities. The challenges to governance then will be more daunting. We will be better prepared to cope with these challenges if we can incrementally improve our understanding of transborder subregions by sustaining the systematic and comparative study of their multiple dimensions and implications.

Notes

1. I thank Mr. Heim Yee Leong from Malaysia for sharing this information.

2. Asia Policy Research Company Limited in Bangkok, Thailand. carried out a recent study on this growth triangle. See www.asiapolicyresearch.com/APRSelectedProjects.htm.

3. "Prospect of war worries 'risky region,'" *Chicago Tribune*, March 19, 2003, p. 5.

4. In Nogales, Arizona, the newly formed Civil Homeland Defense group of several hundred border town residents began to conduct armed patrols of the border in December 2002. While the group cited its concerns about the federal government's border control not doing a sufficiently good job as the reason for taking this action, a newly elected Democratic Congressman from Arizona, Raul Grijalva, asked the U.S. Border Patrol to keep close tabs on this group for fear that innocent people might get shot. In the meantime, local organizations aiding immigrants called these patrols dangerous and a throwback to the Old West, when armed posses carried out vigilante justice across the southwestern United States. See "Armed civilians form border control," *Chicago Tribune*, December 29, 2002, pp. 1, 18.

5. See "Turkey must wait, EU says," *Chicago Tribune*, December 13, 2002, p. 3.

6. Proposed by Australian Prime Minister Hawke in 1989, Asia-Pacific Economic Cooperation (APEC) was established as an intergovernmental consultative forum within the region. Current members are Australia, Brunei, Canada, Chile, China, Hong Kong, Indonesia, Japan, Malaysia, Mexico, New Zealand, Papua New Guinea, Peru, the Philippines, Russia, Singapore, South Korea, Taiwan, Thailand, the United States, and Vietnam. India and North Korea have expressed interest in joining APEC.

7. The Association of Southeast Asian Nations (ASEAN) grew out of the Association of Southeast Asia (ASA), which was formed in 1961 and consisted of Malaya (before the founding of Malaysia), the Philippines, and Thailand. ASEAN was formed on August 8, 1967, with the addition of Indonesia and Singapore to the original ASA. Brunei joined ASEAN as the sixth member on January 8, 1984. Vietnam joined on July 28, 1995, Lao PDR and Myanmar on July 23, 1997, and Cambodia on April 30, 1999. With these accessions, ASEAN has 10 member countries. In 1992, the ASEAN members agreed to set up the ASEAN Free Trade Area (AFTA) within 15 years, aiming to reduce tariffs for most manufactured goods to 5 percent or less by 2003 for members, and for Vietnam by 2008. In 1994, ASEAN decided to reduce the implementation period of AFTA from 15 to 10 years, or by January 1, 2003. This decision led to the 1995 Protocol to amend the 1992 Agreement (Economic Committee of APEC, 1997).

8. The ASEAN+3 summit subsequently produced a historic regional financial mechanism, the Chiang Mai Initiative (CMI), which was intended to reduce a recurrence of future financial turmoil like the Asian financial crisis triggered by the fall of the Thai baht in 1997. At the ministerial meeting of the ASEAN+3 in May 2000, the participants agreed to use the CMI to expand the ASEAN currency swap as well as existing bilateral currency swaps (Ahn, 2003, p. 4).

9. In 2000, China signed with Vietnam the "Agreement Between the People's Republic of China and the Socialist Republic of Vietnam on the Delimitation of the Territorial Sea, the Exclusive Economic Zone and the Continental Shelf of the Beihu Bay." In November 2002, China

signed with ASEAN the "Declaration of the Conduct of Parties in the South China Sea" (Fu, 2003).

10. While US$100 a month might appear relatively high by Chinese standards in the early 1990s, especially given that the majority of factory workers in the PRD were from rural areas in inland China, this wage fell behind the rapidly rising cost of living and faster wage increases in other professions in the PRD cities. A recent survey in eight PRD cities reported that while 80 percent of the labor shortage was for young female workers age 18–25, there was an unfulfilled need for some technical workers. Some of this labor shortage in the PRD might also be accounted for by more workers migrating to the Yangtze River Delta (YRD) around Shanghai to seek higher wages offered by more capital and technology-intensive manufacturing there. See *Renmin Ribao* (The People's Daily), overseas edition, August 16, 2004, p. 12.

11. See Jonathan Watts, "China's farmers cannot feed hungry cities: No longer self-sufficient in food, the country today increasingly has to buy abroad, raising global prices," *The Guardian*, Thursday, August 26, 2004, from www.guardian.co.uk/china/story/0,7369,1290852,00.html. I thank Kim Scipes for bringing this report to my attention.

Appendix

TABLE 4.A

Trade Between Mainland China and Taiwan via Hong Kong, 1979–2002 (in millions of U.S. dollars)

Year	Taiwan's Transit Trade to China Via Hong Kong (1)[a]	Taiwan's Exports to Hong Kong (F.O.B.) (2)[b]	Hong Kong's Imports from Taiwan (C.I.F) (3)[a]	Estimated Taiwan's Total Exports to China (4)=(1)+Difference between (2) and (3)[c]	Taiwan's Imports from China via Hong Kong (5)[b]	Estimated Total Trade Between Taiwan and China (6)=(4)+(5)
1979	22	—	—	—	56	78
1980	235	—	—	—	76	311
1981	384	1,897	1,896	385	75	460
1982	195	1,565	1,570	195	84	279
1983	158	1,644	1,600	201	90	291
1984	426	2,087	2,218	426	128	553
1985	987	2,540	2,682	987	116	1,103
1986	811	2,921	3,073	811	144	956
1987	1,227	4,123	4,275	1,227	289	1,515
1988	2,242	5,587	5,682	2,242	479	2,721
1989	2,897	7,042	6,607	3,332	587	3,919

Year	(1)	(2)	(3)	(4)	(5)	(6)
1990	3,278	8,556	7,440	4,395	765	5,160
1991	4,667	12,431	9,605	7,494	1,126	8,619
1992	6,288	15,416	11,156	10,548	1,119	11,667
1993	7,585	18,455	12,047	13,993	1,104	15,097
1994	8,517	21,263	13,758	16,023	1,859	17,881
1995	9,883	26,124	16,573	19,434	3,091	22,525
1996	9,718	26,805	15,795	20,727	3,060	23,787
1997	9,715	28,708	15,968	22,455	3,915	26,371
1998	8,364	24,820	13,343	19,841	4,111	23,951
1999	8,175	26,013	12,875	21,313	4,522	25,835
2000	9,593	31,336	15,920	25,010	6,223	31,233
2001	8,812	26,961	13,837	21,946	5,902	27,848
2002	10,312	30,845	14,860	29,465	7,948	37,413

Source: Mainland Affairs Council (2003), June, table 6.

[a](1) and (3) are based on Hong Kong customs statistics.
[b](2) and (5) are based on Taiwan customs statistics.
[c]A negative figure between (2) and (3) is treated as zero.
F.O.B. stands for free on board (i.e., price on departure).
C.I.F. stands for cost, insurance, and freight (i.e., price on arrival).

TABLE 4.B

Remittance and Communications Across the Taiwan Strait, 1989–2002

Year	Taiwan's Indirect Individual Remittance to Mainland China[a]	Taiwan's Indirect Business Remittance to Mainland China[a]	Mainland China's Indirect Remittance to Taiwan[a]	Indirect Letter Delivery Between Taiwan and Mainland China[b]	Mainland China's Telephone Calls to Taiwan[c]	Taiwan's Telephone Calls to Mainland China[c]
1989	—	—	—	**4,684**	**768**	**730**
	15,815	—	—	6,127	2,939	3,074
1990	19	—	—	**5,663**	**4,409**	**4,422**
	57,706	—	—	7,586	16,397	13,999
1991	82	—	—	**6,128**	**8,026**	**8,719**
	90,290	—	—	9,042	26,257	26,990
1992	204	—	—	**6,561**	**14,306**	**16,204**
	73,665	**505**	**809**	11,661	47,071	50,272
1993	238	16	26	**7,104**	**21,169**	**26,790**
	99,665	**2,521**	**2,342**	10,298	67,247	81,145
1994	350	100	89	**6,887**	**26,974**	**34,192**
				12,225	82,246	105,996

Year						
1995	**104,326**	**3,954**	**1,143**	**6,714**	**36,286**	**41,519**
	391	152	78	10,944	102,223	133,796
1996	**107,996**	**9,442**	**1,673**	**6,533**	**42,956**	**53,541**
	379	282	94	11,510	115,163	168,740
1997	**113,349**	**8,195**	**3,076**	**6,018**	**56,653**	**69,078**
	425	33	208	10,284	151,720	198,069
1998	**103,967**	**10,196**	**4,839**	**5,752**	**69,203**	**79,952**
	351	378	293	8,930	180,643	236,141
1999	**122,180**	**11,129**	**8,013**	**5,032**	**82,295**	**96,033**
	365	477	509	8,492	214,145	286,034
2000	**142,666**	**18,301**	**20,790**	**5,410**	**95,049**	**111,604**
	511	698	770	9,338	241,113	342,988
2001	**172,572**	**26,880**	**34,470**	**5,004**	**102,206**	**133,657**
	678	1,013	1,250	8,396	294,392	435,029
2002	**234,946**	**56,121**	**48,397**	**9,224**	**101,213**	**137,003**
	941	1,579	2,250	7,046	318,870	453,180

Source: Mainland Affairs Council (2003), June, tables 14–18.

[a] The number of remittance is in bold; the amount of remittance (in millions of U.S. dollars) is below the bolded number.

[b] The number of letters (in thousands) from Taiwan to China is in bold; the number of letters from China to Taiwan is below the bolded number.

[c] The number of calls is in bold; the total number of calling minutes (in thousands) is below.

TABLE 4.C
Number of Visitors Across the Taiwan Strait, 1988–2002

Year	Cumulative Taiwanese Visitors to the Mainland (Number of Person-Trips)	Cumulative Mainland Visitors to Taiwan (Number of Person-Trips)
1988	437,700	381
1989	978,700	5,219
1990	1,926,700	12,379
1991	2,783,332	23,813
1992	4,191,102	36,947
1993	5,718,071	55,290
1994	7,108,286	78,852
1995	8,640,595	121,486
1996	10,374,492	179,496
1997	12,492,068	251,842
1998	14,666,670	342,468
1999	17,251,318	449,167
2000	20,359,968	966,292
2001	23,801,968	700,280
2002	26,993,368	828,235

Source: Bureau of Entry and Exit, National Police Administration, Ministry of Interior, Taiwan, February 2003.

TABLE 5.A
Trade Between China, South Korea, and Japan, 1978–2000 (millions of U.S. dollars in current price)

Year	China's Trade with S. Korea (1)	Percent of China's Total Trade (2)	Percent of S. Korea's Total Trade (3)	China's Trade with Japan (4)	Percent of China's Total Trade (5)	S. Korea's Trade with Japan (6)	Percent of S. Korea's Total Trade (7)
1978	—	—	—	4,824	23.4	8,686	31.4
1979	19	0.06	0.05	6,708	22.9	9,559	27.0
1980	188	0.5	0.5	9,201	24.1	8,433	21.2
1981	353	0.8	0.7	9,978	22.7	9,035	19.1
1982	129	0.3	0.3	8,761	21.1	8,139	17.7
1983	134	0.3	0.3	9,077	20.8	9,413	18.6
1984	462	0.9	0.8	12,728	23.8	11,416	19.1
1985	1,100	1.6	1.8	16,434	23.6	11,303	18.4
1986	1,282	1.7	1.9	17,217	23.3	15,891	23.0
1987	1,679	2.0	1.9	16,472	19.9	21,517	24.4
1988	3,100	3.0	2.8	19,429	18.9	27,269	24.2
1989	3,200	2.9	2.6	18,897	16.9	29,422	23.7
1990	3,800	3.3	0.5	16,550	14.3	29,242	21.7
1991	4,500	3.3	2.1	20,283	15.0	32,469	21.2
1992	5,028	3.0	3.2	25,361	15.3	29,382	18.6
1993	8,211	4.2	5.0	39,065	20.0	30,934	18.7
1994	11,721	5.0	5.9	47,906	20.2	37,885	19.1
1995	16,983	6.0	6.5	57,471	20.5	48,621	18.7
1996	19,981	6.9	7.1	60,067	20.7	45,349	16.1
1997	24,045	7.4	8.6	60,813	18.7	40,703	14.5
1998	21,287	6.6	9.4	58,025	17.9	29,355	13.0
1999	25,036	7.0	10.1	66,167	18.4	39,355	15.8
2000	34,500	7.3	10.4	83,166	17.5	51,157	15.3

Sources: Adapted from X. Chen (1998), table 9.1, p. 191; calculated from SSB (1999), pp. 19, 94; and adapted from IMF (various years).

TABLE 5.B

Passenger Liner Routes Between the Major Cities in the BYSS and Beyond, 1992–1998 (passengers in thousands)

Route	1992	1993	1994	1995	1996	1997	1998	Launch Date	Nautical Miles[b]
Incheon-Weihai	65	64	80	112	117	107	112	9/1990	238
Incheon-Tianjin	35	39	61	33	32	36	29	12/1991	460
Incheon-Qingdao	—	10	31	20	22	28	31	5/1993	338
Incheon-Dalian	—	—	—	10	63	63	42	10/1995	292
Incheon-Dandong	—	—	—	—	—	—	17	7/1998	300
Incheon-Shanghai	—	—	—	—	—	—	—	7/1998	500
Pusan-Yantai	—	—	4	—	8	11	9	5/1994	525
Kunsan-Yantai	—	—	—	—	9	13	8	6/1996	325
Kunsan-Shanghai	—	—	—	—	—	—	—	1996	450
Mokpo-Lianyungang	—	—	—	—	—	—	—	10/1997	380
								9/1973,	
Pusan-Shimonoseki	74	—	—	—	99	99	90	4/1998	125
Pusan-Fukuoka		97	130	150	186	186	198	2/1990	110
Incheon-Yingkou[a]									500
Pusan-Shanghai[a]									500
Cheju-do-Shanghai[a]									300

Sources: Adapted from Kim (2000), table 4.12, p. 78; Ministry of Maritime Affairs and Fisheries (1999); the City of Incheon's website, www.metro.incheon.kr/.
[a]Possible routes that have been discussed but not opened yet.
[b]The distances between the first four routes were adapted from the website www.metro.inchon.kr/, but the other distances were measured off a map and thus only approximate the true sailing distances.

TABLE 6.A
Trade Between China, the Former Soviet Union (Russia), and North Korea, 1977–1999 (millions of U.S. dollars in current price)

Year	China's Trade with Russia[a] (1)	Percent of China's Total Trade (2)	China's Trade with North Korea (3)	Percent of China's Total Trade (4)	North Korea's Trade with Russia[a] (5)	Percent of North Korea's Total Trade (6)
1977	329	2.2	374	2.5	—	—
1978	437	2.1	454	2.2	—	—
1979	493	1.9	647	2.2	—	—
1980	492	1.3	678	1.8	—	—
1981	225	0.6	480	1.2	—	—
1982	276	0.7	545	1.4	—	—
1983	674	1.7	493	1.2	—	—
1984	1,183	2.4	500	1.0	—	—
1985	1,881	3.1	473	0.8	—	—
1986	2,640	4.4	509	0.8	1,800	—
1987	2,519	3.4	513	0.8	2,000	—
1988	3,258	3.6	579	0.6	2,650	—
1989	3,997	4.5	563	0.6	2,400	—
1990	4,370	3.8	483	0.5	2,620	55.2
1991	3,904	2.9	610	0.5	367	13.6
1992	5,862	3.5	697	0.4	340	12.8
1993	7,673	3.9	900	0.5	234	8.9
1994	5,077	2.1	624	0.3	97	4.3
1995	5,463	1.9	550	0.2	91	4.5
1996	6,846	2.4	566	0.2	75	3.8
1997	6,120	1.9	656	0.2	78	3.0
1998	5,480	1.7	413	0.1	65	—
1999	5,720	1.6	370	0.1	100	—

Sources: Adapted from X. Chen (1998), table 9.1; Fukagawa (1997), table 3.6; and calculated from Goto (1999), figure 1; SSB (2000), table 17.7; Winder (2000), figure 2; and Wishnick (2002), table 5.1.

[a] Data before 1991 pertained to the former Soviet Union.

TABLE 6.B

Overland Border Crossings at the Yanbian Ethnic Korean Autonomous Prefecture, Jilin Province, China

Name	Location	Opposite Crossings[a]	Grade[b]	Road Types	Access and Functions	Open Date
Changlingzi	Changlingzi, Hunchun City	Kraskino, Primorskii Krai	1	Railroad, Railroad	Jilin's only border crossing with the RFE	1991
Quanhe	Jingxin Town, Hunchun City	Yuanding *Lee*, Hamgyong-Bukdo, N. Korea	1	Road only	The only crossing to the Rajin-Songong FETZ	1936, 1995
Shatuozi	Sanjiazi Town, Hunchun City	Liuduo *Lee*, Hamyong-Bukdo	2	Road only	Local crossing to N. Korea	1929
Tumen	Tumen City	Namyang, Hamyong-Bukdo	1	Railroad, Road	Important crossing for international trade and transshipping trade with N. Korea	1933
Sanhe	Sanhe Town, Longjing City	Huining *Kun*, Hamyong-Bukdo	1	Road only	A short-cut crossing to Chongjin port	1930
Kaishantun	Kaishantun Town, Longjing City	Sanfengli *dong*, Hamyong-Bukdo	1	Railroad, Road	An important crossing to N. Korea	1923
Nanping	Dehua Town, Helong City	Qixinli *dong*, Hamyong-Bukdo	1	Road only	Local crossing to N. Korea	1929
Guchengli	Chongshan Town, Helong City	Sechon, Yangkang-Do	2	Road only	Local crossing to N. Korea	1929
Shuangmu-feng	Hepingyingzi Township, Antu County	Sanchiyuan, Yangkang-Do	Business	Road only	Local crossing to N. Korea; primarily for transporting lumber	—

Source: Adapted from C. Chen (1998), p. 2.

[a]Except for Kraskino, all crossings are on the North Korean side of the borders.

[b]Designated by the Chinese government; 1 denotes a higher grade and hence larger and more important crossing than 2. Business crossing is a special type of crossing.

TABLE 6.C
Import and Export Volumes Through Land Border Crossings at the Yanbian Ethnic Korean Autonomous Prefecture, Jilin Province, China, 1993–1996 (in tons)

Crossing	1993			1994			1995			1996		
	Import	Export	Total	Import	Export	Total	Import	Export	Total	Import	Export	Total
Changlingzi	65,308	10,929	76,237	16,532	15,552	32,084	3,983	7,504	11,487	3,004	4,139	7,143
Shatuozi	40,161	7,676	47,837	17,308	8,478	25,786	2,469	4,181	6,650	1,940	3,020	4,960
Quanhe	—	—	—	—	—	—	—	—	—	8,741	15,032	23,773
Tumen	217,588	287,588	505,176	144,200	100,497	244,697	186,769	186,269	373,038	32,240	40,204	72,444
Kaishantun	13,302	14,406	27,708	11,508	11,548	23,056	2,420	1,200	3,620	3,310	3,310	6,620
Nanping	14,104	1,143	15,247	15,795	12,112	27,907	4,130	2,496	6,626	16,666	6,911	26,277
Guchengli	13,905	965	14,870	12,762	473	13,235	8,872	1,172	10,040	14,042	1,000	15,024
All Crossings	364,368	322,707	687,075	218,105	148,660	366,765	208,643	202,822	411,465	79,943	73,616	153,559

Source: Adapted from C. Chen (1998), p. 7.

TABLE 7.A
China's Trade with Vietnam, Myanmar, Lao PDR, Thailand, and Cambodia, 1978–2001 (millions of U.S. dollars in current price)

Year	China's Trade with Vietnam (1)	China's Trade with Myanmar (2)	China's Trade with Lao PDR (3)	China's Trade with Thailand (4)	China's Trade with Cambodia (5)
1978	57	—	—	145	—
1979	—	—	—	295	—
1980	—	—	—	452	—
1981	—	52	10	382	1
1982	—	47	7	515	4
1983	—	48	5	330	1
1984	—	45	5	439	—
1985	—	80	11	379	2
1986	—	95	10	446	—
1987	—	164	16	706	—
1988	—	270	21	1,145	—
1989	8	314	14	1,256	3
1990	3	372	20	1,240	3
1991	32	392	13	1,270	2
1992	179	390	32	1,318	13
1993	400	490	41	1,351	21
1994	533	512	40	2,023	36
1995	1,054	768	54	3,363	58
1996	1,150	658	31	3,149	70
1997	1,436	643	29	3,507	123
1998	1,241	595	26	3,593	162
1999	1,318	508	32	4,216	160
2000	2,466	621	41	6,624	224
2001	2,815	632	62	7,050	240

Sources: Adapted from IMF (various years) and Xu (2002), p. 24.

TABLE 7.B

Cross-Border Flows Through the Major River Ports and Overland Crossings of Yunnan Province, 1993–1997

Ports or Crossings	Year	People (Number)	Vehicle (Number)	Cargo (Ton)	Cargo Value (US$10,000)
Jinghong Port (Bordering Myanmar)	1993	6,850	140	1,260	2.3
	1994	26,000	444	11,760	4.9
	1995	6,951	410	12,329	504.9
	1996	25,600	3,209	33,100	1,136.3
	1997	11,275	1,454	32,550	1,208.9
Simao Port (Bordering Myanmar, Lao PDR, and Vietnam)	1993	1,990	35	700	0.4
	1994	3,800	681	1,850	0.4
	1995	1,404	268	20,551	494.1
	1996	6,100	159	10,300	606.6
	1997	680	306	15,283	147.8
Mohan Crossing (Bordering Lao PDR)	1993	98,000	16,780	10,780	1,251.7
	1994	196,800	48,819	20,997	1,538.7
	1995	144,500	12,374	69,538	3,407.0
	1996	114,400	3,364	32,800	1,545.0
	1997	90,770	7,756	19,410	1,287.3
Daluo Crossing (Bordering Myanmar)	1993	260,000	44,087	79,205	1,508.3
	1994	350,000	53,719	91,730	1,827.7
	1995	396,800	71,565	96,540	1,961.6
	1996	2,050,000	137,008	57,800	1,152.9
	1997	2,040,912	132,166	21,320	682.5
Menglian Crossing (Bordering Myanmar)	1993	15,700	9,876	9,730	231.3
	1994	184,100	1,306	35,200	287.8
	1995	117,878	11,981	16,041	1,095.3
	1996	322,700	34,070	25,000	552.3
	1997	185,522	32,008	22,177	336.6

Source: Adapted from Wang and Li (1998), p. 38.

TABLE 7.C
An Analytical Summary of Four Asia-Pacific Transborder Subregions

Primary Analytic Factors	Greater Southeast China Subregion (GSCS)	Bohai/Yellow Sea Subregion (BYSS)	Greater Tumen Subregion (GTS)	Greater Mekong Subregion (GMS)
Comparative Advantage and Economic Complementarity	Strongest, but weakening slightly	Strong and sustaining (esp. Shandong–S. Korea)	Weak, but with some potential to grow	Weak, but growing
Local Government Autonomy	Greatest (for cities in Guangdong and Fujian)	Great (Shandong); Growing (S. Korea, Japan)	Strong (Jilin); Less strong (RFE); Hardly any (N. Korea)	Strong (Yunnan); Limited (Myanmar, Vietnam, Lao PDR)
Cross-Border Ethnic Ties and Social Networks	Strongest, densest, and most facilitating	Limited, but facilitating (Shandong–S. Korea)	Fairly extensive and facilitating (Jilin–N. Korea)	Extensive and uneven, but facilitating (Yunnan–Myanmar-Vietnam)
Cross-Border Transport Infrastructure	Well developed (despite no direct cross-strait links)	Very well developed	Moderate and uneven with uncertain demand	Rapidly developing with greater potential

Main Processes and Outcomes	GSCS	BYSS	GTS	GMS
Degree of Integration	Tightest (economic, heavily cultural)	Tight (economic)	Increasing slowly, but uneven (economic)	Increasing faster, but uneven (economic and partially political)
Growth and Wealth Creation	Most rapid and sustained	Quite rapid (esp. Shandong, China)	Relatively slow (worst for N. Korea)	Slow, but catching up quickly (esp. Yunnan and Vietnam)
Symmetry and Distribution of Benefits	Largely symmetrical; mutually beneficial	Somewhat asymmetrical, but mutually beneficial	Largely asymmetrical (most benefit for Jilin, China)	Asymmetrical and uneven benefits (mostly for Yunnan, and Vietnam)
Prospect	Continued economic prosperity (despite Taiwan–China tension)	Steady growth and greater cooperation	Continued barriers to prosperity (primarily N. Korea's future)	Great potential for growth and cooperation

Source: Developed by the author.

References

Publications in English

Abonyi, George. 1994. "The institutional challenges of growth triangles in Southeast Asia." Paper presented at the Fourth Southeast Asia Roundtable on Economic Development, Kuala Lumpur, Malaysia, June 27–28.

Agnew, John, and Stuart Corbridge. 1995. *Mastering Space: Hegemony, Territory and International Political Economy* (New York: Routledge).

Ahn, Choong-yong. 2003. "The newly emerging economic order in Northeast Asia and a vision of Korea as a business hub." Pp. 1–28 in Korea Economic Institute (Ed.), *Raising the Bar: Korea as a Global Economic Player* (Washington, DC: Korea Economic Institute of America).

Amin, Ash. 1999. "An institutional perspective on regional economic development." *International Journal of Urban and Regional Research*, Vol. 23, No. 2, pp. 365–378.

Amin, Ash, and Nigel Thrift. 1994. "Living in the global." Pp. 1–22 in Ash Amin and Nigel Thrift (Eds.), *Globalization, Institutions, and Regional Development in Europe* (London: Oxford University Press).

Amsden, Alice H. 1989. *Asia's Next Giant: South Korea and Late Industrialization* (New York: Oxford University Press).

Andreas, Peter. 2000a. "Introduction: The wall after the wall." Pp. 1–11 in Peter Andreas and Timothy Snyder (Eds.), *The Wall around the West: State Borders and Immigration Controls in North America and Europe* (Lanham, MD: Rowman & Littlefield).

———. 2000b. *Border Games: Policing the U.S.-Mexico Divide* (Ithaca: Cornell University Press).

Arrighi, Giovanni. 1998. "Globalization and the rise of East Asia: Lessons from the past, prospects for the future." *International Sociology*, Vol. 13, No. 1, pp. 59–77.

Asia, Inc. 1996. "The Mekong: Corridor of Commerce." Special map attached to the February 1996 issue of the *Asia Inc.* magazine, Hong Kong.

Asia Monitor Resource Center. 1995. "Conditions of workers in the shoe industry of China." Reported by Asia Monitor Resource Center, November.

———. 1997. "Working conditions in sports shoe factories in China: Case studies." Joint report by Asia Monitor Resource Center, Hong Kong Christian Industrial Committee Christian Aid (HK), Hong Kong, August.

Asian Development Bank (ADB). 1996a. *Economic Cooperation in the Greater Mekong Subregion: An Overview* (Manila: ADB).

———. 1996b. *Economic Cooperation in the Greater Mekong Subregion: Facing the Challenges* (Manila: ADB).

———. 2002a. *Building on Success: A Strategic Framework for the Greater Mekong Subregion Economic Cooperation Program* (Manila: ADB).

———. 2002b. *Connecting Nations Linking People* (Manila: ADB).

———. 2003. *Prioritizing Strategic Directions for BIMP-EAGA*, A Report for ADB, Manila, November.

———. 2004. *The Mekong Region: Economic Overview*, accessed on the ADB's Web site (www.adb.org/Documents/Reports), August.

Asiwaju, Anthony I. 1994. "Borders and borderlands as linchpins for regional integration in Africa: Lessons of the European experience." Pp. 57–75 in Clive H. Schofield (Ed.), *Global Boundaries* (New York: Routledge).

Axline, W. Andrew. 1994. "Comparative case studies of regional cooperation among developing countries." Pp. 7–33 in W. Andrew Axline (Ed.), *The Political Economy of Regional Cooperation* (London: Pinter).

Babson, Bradley O. 2002. "Inter-Korean economic relations in a regional context." Pp. 12–20 in Korean Economic Institute (Ed.), *Cooperation and Reform on Korean Peninsula* (Washington, DC: Korean Economic Institute of America).

Bartlett, Donald L., and James S. Steele. 2004. "Who left the door open?" *Time* (September 20), pp. 51–66.

Berger, Peter L., and Samuel P. Huntington (Eds.). 2002. *Many Globalizations: Cultural Diversity in the Contemporary World* (Oxford: Oxford University Press).

Berger, Suzanne, and Richard K. Lester (Eds.). 1997. *Made by Hong Kong* (Hong Kong: Oxford University Press).

Berlie, Jean. 2000. "Cross-border links between Muslims in Yunnan and northern Thailand: Identity and economic networks." Pp. 222–235 in Grant Evans, Christopher Hutton, and Kuah Khun Eng (Eds.), *Where China Meets Southeast Asia: Social and Cultural Change in the Border Regions* (Bangkok: Institute of Southeast Asian Studies).

Blake, Gerald H. 1994. "Preface." Pp. xii–xvii in Clive H. Schofield (Ed.), *Global Boundaries* (New York: Routledge).

Block, Fred L. 1987. *Revising State Theory: Essays in Politics and Post-Industrialism* (Philadelphia: Temple University Press).

Blunden, Caroline, and Mark Elvin. 1983. *Cultural Atlas of China* (Oxford: Phaidon).

Bradshaw, Michael. 1999. "Economic crisis in the Russian Far East." Paper presented at the American Association of Geographers, Hawaii, March.

Brimble, Peter, and David Oldfield. 1999. "Regional economic development areas in Asia: Trade, FDI, and a new framework for analysis." Background paper, Brooker Group [now Asia Policy Research Company Limited], Bangkok, Thailand, November.

Briner, Hans J. 1986. "Regional planning and transfrontier cooperation: The Regio Basiliensis." Pp. 45–53 in *Across Boundaries: Transborder Interaction in Comparative Perspective* (El Paso: Texas Western Press).

Bufon, Milan. 1994. "Local aspects of transborder cooperation: A case study in the Italo-Slovene border landscape." Pp. 19–29 in Werner A. Gallusser (Ed.), *Political Boundaries and Coexistence* (Berlin: Peter Lang).

Bunker, Stephen G. 1989. "Staples, links, and poles in the construction of regional development theories." *Sociological Forum*, Vol. 4, No. 4, pp. 589–610.

Callaghy, Thomas, Ronald Kassimir, and Robert Latham (Eds.). 2001. *Intervention and Transnationalism in Africa: Global-Local Networks of Power* (Cambridge: Cambridge University Press).

Cambodian Development Research Institute (CDRI). 2002. *Understanding Decentralization in Cambodia: A Research Framework to Support the Process of Devolution and Decentralization in Cambodia* (Phnom Penh: Prepared by PADRIGU Consultants for and edited by CDRI, August).

Cappellin, R., and P. W. Batey (Eds.). 1993. *Regional Networks, Border Regions and European Integration* (London: Pion Limited).

Carsten, Janet. 1998. "Borders, boundaries, tradition and state on the Malaysian periphery." Pp. 215–236 in Thomas M. Wilson and Hastings Donnan (Eds.), *Border Identities: Nation and State at International Frontiers* (Cambridge: Cambridge University Press).

Chan, Ming K. 1995. "All in the family: The Hong Kong–Guangdong link in historical perspective." Pp. 31–63 in Reginald Yin-Wang Kwok and Alvin Y. So (Eds.), *The Hong Kong–Guangdong Link: Partnership in Flux* (Armonk, NY: M. E. Sharpe).

Chapman, Keith, and David Walker. 1987. *Industrial Location: Principles and Policies* (London: Basil Blackwell).

Chapman, Michael. 1996. "The role of the European Union in local economic development." Pp. 139–157 in Christophe Demazière and Patricia A. Wilson (Eds.), *Local Economic Development in Europe and Americas* (London: Mansell).

Cheater, A. P. 1998. "Transcending the state? Gender and borderline constructions of citizenship in Zimbabwe." Pp. 191–214 in Thomas M. Wilson and Hastings Donnan (Eds.), *Border Identities: Nation and State at International Frontiers* (Cambridge: Cambridge University Press).

Chen, Edward K. Y., and C. H. Kwan (Eds.). 1997. *Asia's Borderless Economy: The Emergence of Subregional Economic Zones* (St. Leonards, Australia: Allen and Unwin).

Chen, Xiangming. 1991. "China's city hierarchy, urban policy and spatial development in the 1980s." *Urban Studies*, Vol. 28, No. 3, pp. 341–367.

———. 1993. "The changing role of Shenzhen in China's national and regional development in the 1980s." Pp. 251–279 in George T. Yu (Ed.), *China in Transition: Economic, Political and Social Developments* (Lanham, MD: University Press of America).

———. 1994a. "The new spatial division of labor and commodity chains in the greater south China economic region." Pp. 165–186 in Gary Gereffi and Miguel Korzeniewicz (Eds.), *Commodity Chains and Global Capitalism* (Westport, CT: Greenwood Press).

———. 1994b. "The changing roles of free economic zones in development: A comparative analysis of capitalist and socialist cases in East Asia." *Studies in Comparative International Development*, Vol. 29, No. 3, pp. 3–25.

———. 1995. "The evolution of free economic zones and the recent development of cross-national growth zones." *International Journal of Urban and Regional Research*, Vol. 19, No. 4, pp. 593–621.

———. 1996. "Taiwan investments in China and Southeast Asia: 'Go west but also go south.'" *Asian Survey*, Vol. 36, No. 5, pp. 447–467.

———. 1998. "China's growing integration with the Asia-Pacific economy." Pp. 89–119 in Arif Dirlik (Ed.), *What Is in a Rim? Critical Perspectives on the Pacific Region Idea* (Lanham, MD: Rowman & Littlefield).

———. 1999a. "Business over politics." *China Business Review*, Vol. 26, No. 2 (March–April), pp. 8–14.

———. 1999b. "Networking, downloading, upgrading, and competing: The economic triangle of China, Hong Kong, and Taiwan, 1980–2000." Unpublished manuscript.

———. 2000a. "Regional integration, networked production, and technological competition: The 'Greater China' economic circle through and beyond 1997." Pp. 454–471 in Pedro Conceição, David V. Gibson, Manuel V. Heitor, and Syed Shariq (Eds.), *Science, Technology and Innovation Policy: Opportunities and Challenges for the Knowledge Economy* (Westport, CT: Quorum Books).

———. 2000b. "The geoeconomic reconfiguration of the semiperiphery: The Asian-Pacific transborder regions in the world system." Pp. 185–201 in Georgi M. Derlugian and Scott L. Greer (Eds.), *Questioning Geopolitics: Political Projects in a Changing World-System* (Westport, CT: Greenwood Press).

———. 2000c. "Both glue and lubricant: Transnational ethnic social capital as a source of Asia-Pacific subregionalism." *Policy Sciences*, Vol. 33, Nos. 3–4, pp. 268–297.

———. 2001. "From regional integration to export competition? The evolution of the Chinese economic triangle." Pp. 23–42 in Alvin Y. So, Nan Lin, and Dudley Poston (Eds.), *The Chinese Triangle of Mainland, Taiwan, and Hong Kong: Comparative Institutional Analyses* (Westport, CT: Greenwood Press).

———. (Forthcoming) "Global cities West and East: Shanghai in comparative perspective." In Xiangming Chen (Ed.), *Local Transformations in Global Cities: Shanghai in Comparative Perspective*.

Chen, Yu-chiu. 1997. "The Macau nexus." *Topics*, Vol. 27, No. 3 (March), pp. 39–41.

Chia, Siou Yue. 1993. "Motivating forces in subregional economic zones." (Honolulu: Pacific Forum/CSIS Occasional Papers, December).

Chia, Siow Yue, and Lee Tsao Yuan. 1993. "Subregional economic zones: A new motive force in Asia-Pacific development." Pp. 225–269 in C. Fred Bergsten and Marcus Noland (Eds.), *Pacific Dynamism and the International Economic System* (Washington, DC: Institute for International Economics).

China Shipping Gazette. 2003. "World's 10 busiest port cities." February 14, p. 1. (The *China Shipping Gazette* is a main shipping trade journal.)

Christaller, Walter. 1972. "How I discovered the theory of central place: A report about the origin of central places." Pp. 601–610 in Paul Ward English and Robert C. Mayfield (Eds.), *Man, Space, and Environment* (New York: Oxford University Press).

Chu, Yun-han. 1997. "Cross-strait dilemma," *Free China Review* (June), pp. 42–46.

Chua, Amy. 2003. *World on Fire: How Exporting Free Market Democracy Breeds Ethnic Hatred and Global Instability* (New York: Doubleday).

Chung, Chin. 1997. "Division of labor across the Taiwan Strait: Macro overview and analysis of the electronics industry." Pp. 164–209 in Barry Naughton (Ed.), *The China Circle: Economics and Electronics in the PRC, Taiwan, and Hong Kong* (Washington, DC: Brookings Institution Press).

Church, Andrew and Peter Reid. 1996. "Urban power, networks and competition: The example of cross-border cooperation." *Urban Studies*, Vol. 33, No. 8, pp. 1297–1318.

Clark, Ian. 1999. *Globalization and International Relations Theory* (Oxford: Oxford University Press).

Clewley, John. 1993. "Laos: New routes to riches." *Asia, Inc.*, Vol. 2, No. 6 (June), pp. 40–45.

Clifford, Mark. 1993. "Send money: North Korea appeals for investment in free-trade zone." *Far Eastern Economic Review* (September 30), p. 72.

Coleman, James. 1988. "Social capital in the creation of human capital." *American Journal of Sociology*, Vol. 94, pp. S95–S120.

———. 1990. *Foundations of Social Theory* (Cambridge, MA: Belknap Press of Harvard University Press).

Cooper, Frederick. 2001. "Networks, moral discourse, and history." Pp. 23–46 in Thomas M. Callaghy, Ronald Kassimir, and Robert Latham (Eds.), *Intervention and Transnationalism in Africa: Global-Local Networks of Power* (Cambridge: Cambridge University Press).

Corvers, Fabienne, Ben Dankbaar, and Robert Hassink. 1996. "Euregions: Springboard to regional development? Innovation policy and cross-border cooperation in the Euregion Mass-Rhine." Pp. 175–199 in Christophe Demazière and Patricia A. Wilson (Eds.), *Local Economic Development in Europe and Americas* (London: Mansell).

Crispin, Shawn W., Margot Cohen, and Bertil Lintner. 2000. "Choke point." *Far Eastern Economic Review* (December 12), pp. 22–24.

Cumings, Bruce. 1998. "The northeast Asian political economy." Pp. 99–141 in Arif Dirlik (Ed.), *What Is in a Rim? Critical Perspectives on the Pacific Region Idea* (Lanham, MD: Rowman & Littlefield).

DeVoss, David. 1996. "Making money in Mandalay." *Asia, Inc.*, Vol. 5, No. 2 (February), pp. 8–10.

Diamond, Jared. 1999. *Guns, Germs, and Steel: The Fates of Human Societies* (New York: W. W. Norton).

Dicken, Peter, Philip F. Kelly, Kris Olds, and Henry Wai-Chung Yeung. 2001. "Chains and networks, territories and scales: Towards a relational framework for analyzing the global economy." *Global Networks*, Vol. 1, No. 2, pp. 89–112.

Dirlik, Arif. 1998. "Introduction: Pacific contradictions." Pp. 3–13 in Arif Dirlik (Ed.), *What Is in a Rim? Critical Perspectives on the Pacific Region Idea* (Lanham, MD: Rowman & Littlefield).

DK Publishing. 1997. *World Atlas: The Atlas for the 21st Century* (London and New York: DK Publishing).

Dominguez, Paul G. 2003. "BIMP-EAGA: Sustainable economic development through public-private sector partnership." Paper presented at the Regional Cooperation and Cross-border Infrastructure workshop sponsored by the Asian Development Bank Institute, Tokyo, December 9–12.

Donnan, Hastings, and Thomas M. Wilson (Eds.). 1994. *Border Approaches: Anthropological Perspectives on Frontiers* (Lanham, MD: University Press of America).

Douglass, Mike. 1995. "Global interdependence and urbanization: Planning for the Bangkok mega-urban region." Pp. 45–77 in T. G. McGee and Ira M. Robinson (Eds.), *The Mega-Urban Regions of Southeast Asia* (Vancouver: University of British Columbia Press).

Driessen, Henk. 1992. *On the Spanish-Moroccan Frontier: A Study in Ritual, Power and Ethnicity* (New York: Berg).

Drover, Glenn, Graham Johnson, and Julia Tao Lai Po-Wah (Eds.). 2001. *Regionalism and Subregionalism in East Asia: The Dynamics of China* (Huntington, NY: Nova Science Publishers).

Duara, Prasenjit. 1997. "Nationalists among Transnationals: Overseas Chinese and the Idea of China, 1900–1911." Pp. 39–60 in Aihwa Ong and Donald M. Nonini (Eds.), *Ungrounded Empires: The Cultural Politics of Modern Chinese Transnationalism.* (New York: Routledge).

Duchacek, Ivo D. 1986. "International competence of subnational governments: Borderlands and beyond." Pp. 11–28 in Oscar J. Martinez (Ed.), *Across Boundaries: Transborder Interaction in Comparative Perspective* (El Paso: Texas Western Press).

Duncan, Otis Dudley, Ray P. Cuzzort, and Beverly Duncan. 1961. *Statistical Geography: Problems in Analyzing Areal Data* (Glencoe, IL: Free Press).

Eberstadt, Nicholas. 1996. "Financial transfers from Japan to North Korea: Estimating the unreported flows." *Asian Survey*, Vol. 36, No. 5 (May), pp. 523–542.

Economic Committee of APEC (Asia-Pacific Economic Cooperation). 1997. *The Impact of Subregionalism on APEC*. Mimeo (November).

Edwards, Mike. 1997. "Boom times on the gold coast of China." *National Geographic* (March), pp. 6–29.

Enright, Michael J., Edith E. Scott, and David Dodwell. 1997. *The Hong Kong Advantage* (Hong Kong: Oxford University Press).

Evans, Peter B. 1995. *Embedded Autonomy: States and Industrial Transformation* (Princeton, NJ: Princeton University Press).

Evans, Peter B., Dietrich Rueschemeyer, and Theda Skocpol (Eds.). 1985. *Bringing the State Back In* (New York: Cambridge University Press).

Flake, L. Gordon. 1999. "Inter-Korean economic relations under the 'Sunshine Policy.'" *Korea's Economy 1999*, Vol. 15, pp. 100–106.

Fernandez, Raul A. 1989. *The Mexican-American Border Region: Issues and Trends* (Notre Dame, IN: University of Notre Dame Press).

Fong, Khai Seck. 1992. "Electronic manufacturing in the Singapore-Johor-Riau growth triangle: A study of the strategic FTT and implications for Singapore." Master's thesis submitted to the School of Postgraduate Management Studies, National University of Singapore.

Frank, Andre Gunder. 1998. *ReORIENT: Global Economy in the Asian Age* (Berkeley: University of California Press).

Frankel, Jeffrey A. 1993. "Is Japan creating a yen bloc in East Asia and the Pacific?" Pp. 53–87 in Jeffrey A. Frankel and Miles Kahler (Eds.), *Regionalism and Rivalry: Japan and the United States in Pacific Asia* (Chicago: University of Chicago Press).

Frey, R. Scott. 2003. "The transfer of core-based hazardous production processes to the export processing zones of the periphery: The maquiladora centers of northern Mexico." *Journal of World-Systems Research*, Vol. 9, No. 2, pp. 327–354.

Friedmann, John. 1986. "The world city hypothesis." *Development and Change*, Vol. 17, No. 1, pp. 69–84.

Friman, H. Richard, and Peter Andreas. 1999. "Introduction: International relations and the illicit global economy." Pp. 1–23 in H. Richard Friman and Peter Andreas (Eds.), *The Illicit Global Economy and State Power* (Lanham, MD: Rowman & Littlefield).

Fu, Ying. 2003. "China and Asia in a new era." *China: An International Journal*, Vol. 1, No. 2, pp. 304–312.

Fukagawa, Yukiko. 1997. "The Northeast Asian economic zone: Potential for the latecomer." Pp. 59–88 in Edward K. Y. Chen and C. H. Kwan (Eds.), *Asia's Borderless Economy: The Emergence of Subregional Economic Zones* (St. Leonards, Australia: Allen and Unwin).

Fuller, Graham E. 1997. "Redrawing the world's borders." *World Policy Journal*, Vol. 14, No. 1, pp. 11–21.

Funck, R. H., and J. S. Kowalski. 1993. "Transnational networks and cooperation in the new Europe: Experiences and prospects in the upper Rhine area and recommendations for Eastern Europe." Pp. 205–214 in R. Cappellin and P. W. Batey (Eds.), *Regional Networks, Border Regions and European Integration* (London: Pion Limited).

Gallusser, Werner A. 1994. "Borders as necessities and challenges: Human geographic insights paving the way to a new border awareness." Pp. 381–389 in Werner A. Gallusser (Ed.), *Political Boundaries and Coexistence* (Berlin: Peter Lang).

Gereffi, Gary. 1994. "The organization of buyer-driven global commodity chains: How U.S. retailers shape overseas production networks." Pp. 95–122 in Gary Gereffi and Miguel Korzeniewicz (Eds.), *Commodity Chains and Global Capitalism* (Westport, CT: Greenwood Press).

———. 1996. "Commodity chains and regional divisions of labor in East Asia." *Journal of Asian Business*, Vol. 12, No. 1, pp. 75–112.

———. 1999. "International trade and industrial upgrading in the apparel commodity chain." *Journal of International Economics*, Vol. 48, No. 1, pp. 37–70.

Gereffi, Gary, Martha Martinez, and Jennifer Bair. 2002. "Torreón: The new blue jeans capital of the world." Pp. 203–223 in Gary Gereffi, David Spener, and Jennifer Bair (Eds.), *Free Trade and Uneven Development: The North American Apparel Industry After NAFTA* (Philadelphia: Temple University Press).

Gilpin, Robert. 1987. *The Political Economy of International Relations* (Princeton, NJ: Princeton University Press).

Glasmeier, Amy. 1994. "Flexible districts, flexible regions? The institutional and cultural limits to districts in an era of globalization and technological paradigm shift." Pp. 118–146 in Ash Amin and Nigel Thrift (Eds.), *Globalization, Institutions, and Regional Development in Europe* (Oxford: Oxford University Press).

Glain, Steve. 1996. "A North Korean port, now seeking business, may play crucial role." *Wall Street Journal*, September 18, pp. A1, A10.

Gluckman, Ron. 1997. "The last frontier." *Asia, Inc.* Vol. 6, No. 4 (April), pp. 38–43.

Goldring, Luin. 2001. "The gender and geography of citizenship in Mexico-U.S. transnational space." *Identities*, Vol. 7, No. 4, pp. 501–537.

Goto, Fujio. 1999. "North Korea will reinforce connections with the South." *Korea's Economy 1999*, Vol. 15, pp. 87–93.

Grabher, Gernot. 1993. "The weakness of strong ties: The lock-in of regional development in the Ruhr area." Pp. 255–277 in Gernot Grabher (Ed.), *The Embedded Firm: On the Socioeconomics of Industrial Networks* (New York: Routledge).

Graham, Stephen, and Simon Marvin. 1996. *Telecommunications and the City: Electronic Spaces, Urban Places* (Oxford: Routledge).

Grundy-Warr, Carl, Karen Peachey, and Martin Perry. 1999. "Fragmented integration in the Singapore-Indonesian border zone: Southeast Asia's 'growth triangle' against the global economy." *International Journal of Urban and Regional Research*, Vol. 23, No. 2, pp. 304–328.

Hale, David, and Lyric Hughes Hale. 2003. "China takes off." *Foreign Affairs*, Vol. 82, No. 6 (November/December), pp. 35–53.

Hamashita, Takeshi. 1997. "The intra-regional system in East Asia in modern times." Pp. 113–135 in Peter J. Katzenstein and Takashi Shiraishi (Eds.), *Network Power: Japan and Asia* (Ithaca, NY: Cornell University Press).

Hannon, Brent. 2002. "Kinmen: Now the target is tourism." *Topics*, Vol. 32, No. 10 (December), pp. 63–66.

Hansen, Niles. 1986. "Border region development and cooperation: Western Europe and the U.S.-Mexico borderlands in comparative perspective." Pp. 31–44 in *Across Boundaries: Transborder Interaction in Comparative Perspective* (El Paso: Texas Western Press).

Harding, Harry. 1993. "The concept of 'Greater China': Themes, variations and reservations," *China Quarterly*, No. 136 (December), pp. 660–686.

Hatch, Walter, and Kozo Yamamura. 1996. *Asia in Japan's Embrace: Building a Regional Production Alliance* (New York: Cambridge University Press).

Henderson, Jeffrey, and Richard P. Appelbaum. 1992. "Situating the state in the East Asian development process." Pp.1–26 in Richard P. Appelbaum and Jeffrey Henderson (Eds.), *States and Development in the Asian Pacific Rim* (Newbury Park, CA: Sage).

Ho, K. C. 1999. "Transborder regional governance and planning: The case of Singapore and its neighbors." Pp. 81–100 in John Friedmann (Ed.), *Urban and Regional Governance in the Asia Pacific* (Vancouver: University of British Columbia Press).

Ho, K. C., and Alvin Y. So. 1997. "Semi-periphery and borderland integration: Singapore and Hong Kong experiences." *Political Geography*, Vol. 16, No. 3, pp. 241–259.

Hong Kong Trade Development Council (HKTDC). 1992. *Market Report on Yunnan Province.* (Research Department, HKTDC, December).

———. 1997. *Hong Kong Trader* (January), pp. 1–8.

———. 1998. *Hong Kong Trader* (June), pp. 1–8.

———. 1999. *Hong Kong Trader*, Services Supplement: Transportation (August), pp. 1–4.

———. 2000. *Hong Kong Trader* (October), pp. 1–8.

———. 2001. *Hong Kong Trader* (February), pp. 1–8.

Hoover, Edgar M. 1968. *The Location of Economic Activity* (New York: McGraw-Hill).

Hopkins, Terrence K., and Immanuel Wallerstein. 1986. "Commodity chains in the world economy prior to 1800." *Review*, Vol. 10 (Summer), pp. 157–170.

Horváth, G. 1993. "Restructuring and interregional cooperation in Central Europe: The case of Hungary." Pp. 157–176 in R. Cappellin and P. W. Batey (Eds.), *Regional Networks, Border Regions and European Integration* (London: Pion Limited).

Hsieh, Shih-chung. 1995. "On the dynamics of Tai/Dai-Lue ethnicity: An ethnohistorical analysis." Pp. 301–328 in Steven Harrell (Ed.), *Cultural Encounters on China's Ethnic Frontiers* (Seattle: University of Washington Press).

Hsing, You-tien. 1997. "Building *guanxi* across the straits: Taiwanese capital and local Chinese bureaucrats." Pp. 143–164 in Aihwa Ong and Donald M. Nonini (Eds.), *Ungrounded Empires: The Cultural Politics of Modern Chinese Transnationalism* (New York: Routledge).

———. 1998. *Making Capitalism in China: The Taiwan Connection* (New York: Oxford University Press).

Hunter, Jason. 1998. "Tumen River Area Development Program and transboundary water pollution." Talk given at the Woodrow Wilson Center, Environmental Change and Security Project, on www.nautilus.org/papers/hunter_tumen.html, accessed on January 23, 2003.

Hutton, Christopher. 2000. "Cross-border categories: Ethnic Chinese and the Sino-Vietnamese border at Mong Cai." Pp. 154–276 in Grant Evans, Christopher Hutton, and Kuah Khun Eng (Eds.), *Where China Meets Southeast Asia: Social and Cultural change in the Border Regions* (Bangkok: Institute of Southeast Asian Studies).

Incheon International Airport (IIA). 2001. "A New Hub for Asia," original source *Korean Trade and Investment*, Vol. 19, No. 2 (March–April), IIA News 39, on www.airport.or.kr/Eng/helper/news_list, accessed on April 13, 2003.

———. 2002. "China tops Japan in number of flights from Korea," original source: *Korean Herald* (August 26), IIA News 55, www.airport.or.kr/Eng/helper/news_list, accessed on April 13, 2003.

International Monetary Fund (IMF). *Direction of Trade Statistics* (Washington, DC: various years).

Jarvis, Anthony P., and Albert J. Paolini. 1995. "Locating the state." Pp. 3–19 in Joseph A. Camilleri, Anthony P. Jarvis, and Albert J. Paolini (Eds.), *The State in Transition: Reimagining Political Space* (Boulder, CO: Lynne Rienner).

Jesien, Leszek. 2000. "Border controls and the politics of EU enlargement." Pp. 185–201 in Peter Andreas and Timothy Snyder (Eds.), *The Wall Around the West: State Borders and Immigration Controls in North America and Europe* (Lanham, MD: Rowman & Littlefield).

Jiang, Zaihuan. 1999. "The Tumen programme: China's perspective." Presentation at the Ninth Northeast Asia Economic Forum, Tianjin, China, October 27, accessed from the UNDP Tumen Secretariat's website, www.tumenprogramme.org/tumen/publications/speeches/Tianjin/jiangzaihuan, January 30, 2003.

Johnson, Chalmers. 1982. *MITI and the Japanese Miracle* (Stanford, CA: Stanford University Press).

Jordan, Amos A., and Jane Khanna. 1995. "Economic interdependence and challenges to the nation-state: The emergence of natural economic territories in the Asia-Pacific." *Journal of International Affairs*, Vol. 48, No. 2, pp. 433–462.

Kasarda, John D. (Forthcoming). "Aviation infrastructure, competitiveness, and aerotropolis development in the global economy: Operational implications for Shanghai and China." In Xiangming Chen (Ed.), *Local Transformations in Global Cities: Shanghai in Comparative Perspective*.

Katzenstein, Peter J. 1997. "Introduction: Asian regionalism in comparative perspective." Pp. 1–44 in Peter J. Katzenstein and Takashi Shiraishi (Eds.), *Network Power: Japan and Asia* (Ithaca, NY: Cornell University Press).

Kaye, Lincoln. 1992a. "Casualty of history." *Far Eastern Economic Review* (January 16), pp. 19–20.

———. 1992b. "The Russians are back." *Far Eastern Economic Review* (January 16), p.20.

———. 1993. "Creative tensions: Cross-border contacts bring growth and friction." *Far Eastern Economic Review* (January 7), pp. 16–17.

Kearney, Michael. 1998. "Transnationalism in California and Mexico at the end of empire." Pp. 117–141 in Thomas M. Wilson and Hastings Donnan (Eds.), *Border Identities: Nation and State at International Frontiers* (Cambridge: Cambridge University Press).

Ketels, Christian H. M. 2002. "Cross-national regions and competitiveness: BCCA and the Baltic Rim agenda." A revised paper from a speech given at the tenth anniversary ceremony of the BCCA, Rostock, Germany, June 3, accessed from www.isc.hbs.edu/pdf/BCCA_Paper_CK_2002.06.03.pdf.

Kim, Eun Mee, and Sukyoung Suh. 1999. "State and business in transition, again: Development state in crisis and corporate restructuring in Korea." Paper presented at the American Sociological Association annual meeting, Chicago, August 6–10.

Kim, Samuel S., and Tai Hwan Lee. 2002. "Chinese-North Korean relations: Managing asymmetrical interdependence." Pp. 109–137 in Samuel S. Kim and Tai Hwan Lee (Eds.), *North Korea and Northeast Asia* (Lanhan, MD: Rowman & Littlefield).

Kim, Si Joong. 1995. "Korean direct investment in China: Perspectives of Korean investors." Pp. 199–216 in Sumner J. La Croix, Michael Plummer, and Keun Lee (Eds.), *Emerging Patterns of East Asian Investment in China: From Korea, Taiwan, and Hong Kong* (Armonk, NY: M. E. Sharpe).

Kim, Won Bae. 1990. "The future of coastal development in the Yellow Sea rimlands." Reprints of the East-West Population Institute, No. 276, Honolulu, Hawaii.

———. 1994. "Sino-Russian relations and Chinese workers in the Russian Far East: A porous border." *Asian Survey*, Vol. 34, No. 12, pp. 1064–1076.

———. 1995. "Migration." In Mark J. Valencia (Ed.), *The Russian Far East in Transition: Opportunities for Regional Economic Cooperation* (Boulder, CO: Westview Press).

———. (Ed.). 2000. *Inter-City Networking Strategy in the Yellow Sea Sub-Region* (Seoul: Korea Research Institute for Human Settlement).

———. (Forthcoming). "Seoul: From national capital to regional city or global city?" In Xiangming Chen (Ed.), *Local Transformations in Global Cities: Shanghai in Comparative Perspective.*

Kim, Won Bae, and Young Sub Kwon. 1998. *Prospects for Sino-Korean Economic Cooperation and Collaborative Development of the Coastal Areas of Shandong and West Korea* (in Korean) (Seoul: Korea Research Institute for Human Settlement).

Kloos, Peter. 2000. "The dialectics of globalization and localization." Pp. 281–297 in Don Kalb, Marco van der Land, Richard Staring, and Bart van Steenbergen (Eds.), *The Ends of Globalization: Bringing Society Back In* (Lanham, MD: Rowman & Littlefield).

Kohan, John. 1993. "Far east, far off, far out." *Time* (August 16), p. 21.

Konrad, Victor. 1991. "Common edges: An introduction to the borderlands anthropology." Pp. vii–xviii in Robert Lecker (Ed.), *Borderlands: Essays in Canadian-American Relations* (Toronto: ECW Press).

Korea Foreign Trade Association (KOFTA). 1997. "Local governments given green light." *Trade Tower* (Newsletter), No. 28 (June); taken from www.kita.or.kr/tradetower/.

Koslowski, Rey. 2000. "The mobility money can buy: Human smuggling and border control in the European Union." Pp. 203–218 in Peter Andreas and Timothy Snyder (Eds.), *The Wall Around the West: State Borders and Immigration Controls in North America and Europe* (Lanham, MD: Rowman & Littlefield).

Krasner, Stephen D. 1999. "Globalization and sovereignty." Pp. 34–52 in David A. Smith, Dorothy J. Solinger, and Steven C. Topik (Eds.), *States and Sovereignty in the Global Economy* (London: Routledge).

Kuah, Khun Eng. 2000. "Negotiating central, provincial, and county policies: Border trading in southern China." Pp. 72–97 in Grant Evans, Christopher Hutton, and Kuah Khun Eng (Eds.), *Where China Meets Southeast Asia: Social and Cultural Change in the Border Regions* (Bangkok: Institute of Southeast Asian Studies).

Kuo, Chen-Tian. 1995. *Global Competition and Industrial Growth in Taiwan and the Philippines* (Pittsburgh, PA: University of Pittsburgh Press).

Kurus, Bilson. 1997. "The East ASEAN growth area: Prospects and challenges." Pp. 17–30 in Mohd. Yaakub Hj. Johari, Bilson Kurus, and Janiah Zaini (Eds.), *BIMP-EAGA Integration: Issues and Challenges* (Sabah: Institute for Development Studies).

Kwok, Reginald Yin-Wang, and Alvin Y. So (Eds.). 1995. *The Hong Kong–Guangdong Link: Partnership in Flux* (Armonk, NY: M. E. Sharpe).

Kyushu Economy International (KEI). 2002a. Kyushu-Asia Internationalization Report 2002, prepared by Kyushu Bureau of Economy, Trade, and Industry, Ministry of Economy, Trade, and Industry (September), downloaded from www.kyushu-kei.org/english/info.html on April 10, 2003.

———. 2002b. "Business environment Kyushu," Data on Kyushu, accessed from www.kyushu kei.org/english/info.html on April 10, 2003.

Kyushu International Information Promotion Council (KIIPC). 2000. *Business Info Kyushu*, Quarterly Newsletter, No. 4 (Autumn), pp. 1–6.

Larkin, John. 2000. "Flight of fancy." *Far Eastern Economic Review* (October 19), pp. 38–40.

Lawrance, Anthony. 2002. "Smooth running: A survey of the high-tech sector." *Topics*, Vol. 32, No. 3 (April), pp. 45–55.

Lawrence, Susan V. 1999. "Cross-border disappointment." *Far Eastern Economic Review* (April 29), pp. 12–13.

Lecker, Robert (Ed.). 1991. *Borderlands: Essays in Canadian-American Relations* (Toronto: ECW Press).

Lee, Ching Kwan. 1998. *Gender and the South China Miracle: Two Worlds of Factory Women* (Berkeley: University of California Press).

Lee, Hong Yung. 1995. "China and South Korea in a new triangle." Pp. 179–197 in Sumner J. La Croix, Michael Plummer, and Keun Lee (Eds.), *Emerging Patterns of East Asian Investment in China: From Korea, Taiwan, and Hong Kong* (Armonk, NY: M. E. Sharpe).

Lee, Karen Eggleton. 1995. "Making toys in China: Case Study of a Sino-Korean joint venture." Pp. 239–258 in Sumner J. La Croix, Michael Plummer, and Keun Lee (Eds.), *Emerging Patterns of East Asian Investment in China: From Korea, Taiwan, and Hong Kong* (Armonk, NY: M. E. Sharpe).

Lee, Tsao Yuan (Ed.). 1991. *Growth Triangle: The Johor-Singapore-Riau Experience* (Singapore: Institute of Southeast Asian Studies).

Leung, Chi Kin. 1993. "Personal contacts, subcontracting linkages, and development in the Hong Kong–Zhujiang delta region." *Annals of the Association of American Geographers*, Vol. 83, No. 2, pp. 272–302.

Lewis, Martin, and Kären Wigen. 1997. *The Myth of Continents: A Critique of Metageography* (Berkeley: University of California Press).

Liao, Darlene M. 1999. "Leader of the pack." *China Business Review*, Vol. 26, No. 6 (November–December), pp. 28–36.

Lilley, Jeffrey. 1993a. "Pacific reunion." *Far Eastern Economic Review* (March 11), pp. 26–27.

———. 1993b. "New man at the helm." *Far Eastern Economic Review* (July 8), pp. 43–44.

Lin, George C. S. 1997. *Red Capitalism in Southern China: Growth and Development of the Pearl River Delta* (Vancouver: University of British Columbia Press).

Lin, Nan. 2001. *Social Capital: A Theory of Social Structure and Action* (Cambridge: Cambridge University Press).

Lintner, Bertil, and Rodney Tasker. 1999. "Shot in the foot." *Far Eastern Economic Review* (October 28), p. 24.

Loo, Becky P. Y. 1997. "Post-reform development in the Zhujiang Delta: Growing equality or polarization?" *Asian Geographer*, Vol. 16, Nos. 1–2, pp. 115–145.

Lösch, August. 1954. *The Economics of Location* (New Haven, CT: Yale University Press).

Lundin, Iraê. Baptista and Fredrik Söderbaum. 2002. "The construction of cross-border regions in southern Africa: The case of the Maputo corridor." Pp. 241–262 in Perkmann, Markus and

Ngai-Ling Sum (Eds.), 2002. *Globalization, Regionalization and Cross-Border Regions* (Basingstoke, UK: Macmillan/Palgrave).

Mackerras, Colin. 2003. *China's Ethnic Minorities and Globalization* (New York: RoutledgeCurzon).

Macleod, Scott, and T. G. McGee. 1995. "The Singapore-Johor-Riau growth triangle: An emerging extended metropolitan region." Pp. 417–464 in Fu-chen Lo and Yue-man Yeung (Eds.), *Emerging World Cities in Pacific Asia* (Tokyo: United Nations University Press).

Magretta, Joan. 1998. "Fast, global, and entrepreneurial: Supply chain management, Hong Kong style, an interview with Victor Fung." *Harvard Business Review* (September–October), pp. 103–114.

Mainland Affairs Council. 1998. *Monthly Statistics of Cross-Strait Economic Activities*, No. 65 (January), pp. 1–68.

———. 2000. *Monthly Statistics of Cross-Strait Economic Activities*, No. 92 (April), pp. 1–68.

———. 2002. *Monthly Statistics of Cross-Strait Economic Activities*, No. 124 (December), www.chinabiz.org.tw/maz/Eco-Month/, Table 21.

———. 2004. "Three mini-links: Ships and passengers," Department of Economic Affairs, www.mac.gov.tw/english/english/csexchan/3link9211.htm, January.

Manezhev, S. 1993. "Free economic zones in the context of economic changes in Russia." *Europe-Asia Studies*, Vol., 45, No. 4, pp. 609–625.

Mansbach, Richard W. 2000. "Changing understandings of global politics: Preinternationalism, internationalism, and postinternationalism." Pp. 7–23 in Heidi H. Hobbs (Ed.), *Pondering Postinternationalism: A Paradigm for the Twenty-First Century* (Albany: State University of New York Press).

Martin, Michael F. 2000. "Whither Hong Kong?" *China Business Review*, Vol. 27, No. 4 (July–August), pp. 16–20, 51.

Martínez, Oscar J., (Ed.). 1986. *Across Borders: Transborder Interaction in Comparative Perspective* (El Paso: Texas Western Press).

———. 1994. "The dynamics of border interaction: New approaches to border analysis." Pp. 1–15 in Clive H. Schofield (Ed.), *Global Boundaries* (New York: Routledge).

Marton, Andrew, Terry McGee, and Donald G. Peterson. 1995. "Northeast Asian economic cooperation and the Tumen River Area Development Project." *Pacific Affairs*, Vol. 68, No. 1, pp. 9–33.

Matich, Mat. 2000a. "The endangered territory." *Topics*, Vol. 30, No. 6 (August), pp. 48–53.

———. 2000b. "Missing links." *Topics*, Vol. 30, No. 9 (November), pp. 32–39.

Mattli, Walter. 1999. *The Logic of Regional Integration: Europe and Beyond* (New York: Cambridge University Press).

Maule, Robert B. 1992. "The opium question in the federated Shan states, 1931–36: British policy discussions and scandal." *Journal of Southeast Asian Studies*, Vol. 23, No. 1 (March), pp. 14–36.

McEvedy, Colin. 1998. *The Penguin Historical Atlas of the Pacific* (London: Penguin).

McGee, Terry G. 1995. "Metrofitting the emerging mega-urban regions of ASEAN: An overview." Pp. 3–26 in T. G. McGee and Ira M. Robinson (Eds.), *The Mega-Urban Regions of Southeast Asia* (Vancouver: University of British Columbia Press).

McMichael, Philip. 1996. "Globalization: Myth and realities." *Rural Sociology*, Vol. 61, No. 1, pp. 25–55.

Mellor, William. 1993. "A border bonanza." *Asia, Inc.*, Vol. 2, No. 11 (November), pp. 38–46.

——. 1994. "Indochina: Battlefields into marketplaces." *Asia, Inc.*, Vol. 3, No. 2 (February), pp. 46–53.

——. 1996. "Railroad to riches." *Asia, Inc.*, Vol. 5, No. 2 (February), pp. 30–35.

Ministry of Finance and Economy of South Korea. 1998. *South Korean Direct Investment in China* (various tables in mimeo), supplied by Dr. Lim Jung Keun in Seoul.

Ministry of Maritime Affairs and Fisheries of South Korea. 1999. *Official Agreements on Maritime Transport Between the Government of the Republic of Korea and the Government of the People's Republic of China* (in mimeo), supplied by Jung Hong in Seoul.

Mitchell, Gay. 1997. "Opening address." In European Commission (Ed.), *Review of Inter-Regional Cooperation*. Proceedings of the Conference on Inter-Regional Cooperation for European Development: An Evaluation for Future Policy.

Mitchell, Mark. 2000. "Married to the Mainland." *Far Eastern Economic Review* (October 19), pp. 24–25.

Montgomery, John D. 2000. "Social capital as a policy resource." *Policy Sciences*, Vol. 33, Nos. 3–4, pp. 227–243.

Morrison, Charles E., Akira Kojima, and Hanns W. Maull. 1997. *Community-Building with Pacific Asia* (New York: Trilateral Commission).

Naseem, Syed. 1996. "The IMT-GT area: Problems and potentials." Pp. 28–68 in Myo Thant and Min Tang (Eds.), *Indonesia-Malaysia-Thailand Growth Triangle: Theory to Practice* (Manila: Asian Development Bank).

Naughton, Barry (Ed.). 1997a. *The China Circle: Economics and Electronics in the PRC, Taiwan, and Hong Kong* (Washington, DC: Brookings Institution Press).

——. 1997b. "The emergence of the China circle." Pp. 3–37 in Barry Naughton (Ed.), *The China Circle: Economics and Electronics in the PRC, Taiwan, and Hong Kong* (Washington, DC: Brookings Institution Press).

Neace, M. B. 1999. "Entrepreneurs in emerging economies: Creating trust, social capital, and civil society." *Annals of the American Academy of Political and Social Science*, Vol. 565, pp. 148–161.

Newhouse, John. 1997. "Europe's rising regionalism." *Foreign Affairs*, Vol. 76, No. 1 (January/February), pp. 67–84.

Noland, Marcus. 1996. "The North Korean economy." *Joint U.S.-Korea Academic Studies*, Vol. 6, pp. 127–178.

——. 2000. "Economic integration between North and South Korea." *Korea's Economy 2000*, Vol. 16, pp. 67–70.

O'Brien, Richard. 1992. *Global Financial Integration: The End of Geography* (London: Royal Institute of International Affairs).

Ohmae, Kenichi. 1990. *The Borderless World* (New York: HarperCollins).

——. 1995. *The End of the Nation State: The Rise of Regional Economies* (New York: Free Press).

Oi, Jean C. 1995. "The role of the local state in China's transitional economy." *China Quarterly*, Vol. 144, pp. 1132–1149.

Oman, Charles. 1994. *Globalization and Regionalization: The Challenge for Developing Countries* (Paris: Development Centre of the OECD).

Ortiz, Victor M. 1998. "NAFTA and emergency subjects in the border city of El Paso." *Dialectical Anthropology*, Vol. 23, pp. 31–54.

Orum, Anthony M., and Xiangming Chen. 2003. *The World of Cities: Places in Historical and Comparative Perspective* (Oxford: Blackwell).

Overholt, William H. 1993. *The Rise of China* (New York: W. W. Norton).

Paisley, Ed, and Jeff Lilley. 1993. "Bear necessities." *Far Eastern Economic Review* (July 8), pp. 40–41.

Park, Sam Ock. 1998. "Globalization in Korea: Dream and reality." *GeoJournal*, Vol. 45, No. 1–2, pp. 123–128.

Parsa, Ali, and Ramin Keivani. 2002. "The Hormuz corridor: Building a cross-border region between Iran and the UAE." Pp. 183–207 in Saskia Sassen (Ed.), *Global Networks Linked Cities* (London: Routledge).

Parsonage, James. 1992. "Southeast Asia's 'growth triangle': A subregional response to a global transformation." *International Journal of Urban and Regional Research*, Vol. 16, No. 2, pp. 307–317.

Pauly, Louis W. 1995. "Capital mobility, state autonomy and political legitimacy." *Journal of International Affairs*, Vol. 48, No. 2, pp. 369–388.

Peachey, Karen, Martin Perry, and Carl Grundy-Warr. 1998. "The Riau Islands and Economic Cooperation in the Singapore-Indonesia Border Zone." *Boundary and Territory Briefing*, Vol. 2, No. 3, pp. 1–59.

Perkmann, Markus, and Ngai-Ling Sum (Eds.). 2002. *Globalization, Regionalization and Cross-Border Regions* (Basingstoke, UK: Macmillan/Palgrave).

Perroux, François. 1950. "Economic space: Theory and applications." *Quarterly Journal of Economics*, Vol. 64, pp. 89–104.

Philpott, Daniel. 1995. "Sovereignty: An introduction and brief history." *Journal of International Affairs*, Vol. 48, No. 2, pp. 353–368.

Piore, Michael J., and Charles F. Sabel. 1984. *The Second Industrial Divide: Possibilities for Prosperity* (New York: Basic Books).

Porter, Michael E. 2000. "Location, competition and economic development: Local clusters in a global economy." *Economic Development Quarterly*, Vol. 14, No. 1 (February), pp. 15–34.

———. 2001. "The Baltic Rim regional agenda." Presentation at the Baltic Development Forum annual meeting, St. Petersburg, Russia, September 25, accessed from www.isc.hbs.edu/balticproject.pdf.

Portes, Alejandro. 1998. "Social capital: Its origins and applications in modern sociology." *Annual Review of Sociology*, Vol. 24, pp. 1–24.

Ptak, Roderich (Ed.). 1998. *China and the Asian Seas: Trade, Travel, and Visions of the Other (1400–1750)* (London: Ashgate).

———. 1999. *China's Seaborne Trade with South and Southeast Asia (1200–1750)* (London: Ashgate).

Putnam, Robert. 1998. "Foreword." *Housing Policy Debate*, Vol. 9, pp. v–viii.

Quinones, Sam. 1998. "No se puede volver a casa." *Hemisphere* (December), pp. 94–103.

Ratti, R. 1993. "How can existing barrier and border effects be overcome? A theoretical approach." Pp. 60–69 in R. Cappellin and P. W. Batey (Eds.), *Regional Networks, Border Regions and European Integration* (London: Pion).

Ravenhill, John. 2003. "The move to preferential trade in the western Pacific rim." *Asia-Pacific Issues*, No. 69, pp. 1–7.

Reif, Rafael, and Charles G. Sodini. 1997. "The Hong Kong electronics industry." Pp. 186–215 in Suzanne Berger and Richard Lester (Eds.), *Made by Hong Kong* (Hong Kong: Oxford University Press).

Reno, William. 2001. "How sovereignty matters: International markets and the political economy of local politics in weak states." Pp. 197–215 in Thomas M. Callaghy, Ronald Kassimir, and Robert Latham (Eds.), *Intervention and Transnationalism in Africa: Global-Local Networks of Power* (Cambridge: Cambridge University Press).

Rietveld, P. 1993. "Transport and communication barriers in Europe." Pp. 47–59 in R. Cappellin and P. W. Batey (Eds.), *Regional Networks, Border Regions and European Integration* (London: Pion).

Rimmer, Peter J. 1996. "International transport and communications interactions between Pacific Asia's emerging world cities." Pp. 48–97 in Fu-chen Lo and Yue-man Yeung (Eds.), *Emerging World Cities in Pacific Asia* (Tokyo: United Nations University Press).

Robinson, Jennifer. 2002. "Global and world cities: A view from off the map." *International Journal of Urban and Regional Research*, Vol. 26, No. 3, pp. 531–554.

Rosenau, James N. 1997. *Along the Domestic-Foreign Frontier: Exploring Governance in a Turbulent World* (New York: Cambridge University Press).

Roudometof, Victor. 2001. *Nationalism, Globalization, and Orthodoxy: The Social Origins of Ethnic Conflict in the Balkans* (Westport, CT: Greenwood Press).

Rozman, Gilbert. 1997. "Troubled choices for the Russian Far East: Decentralization, open regionalism, and internationalism." *Journal of East Asian Affairs*, Vol. 11, No. 2, pp. 537–569.

———. 1998a. "Northeast China: Waiting for regionalism." *Problems of Post-Communism*, Vol. 45, No. 4, pp. 3–13.

———. 1998b. "Sino-Russian relations in the 1990s: A balance sheet." *Post-Soviet Affairs*, Vol. 14, No. 2, pp. 93–113.

———. 1999. "Backdoor Japan: The search for a way out via regionalism and decentralization." *Journal of Japanese Studies*, Vol. 25, No. 1, pp. 3–31.

———. 2002. "Decentralization in East Asia: A reassessment of its background and potential." Unpublished manuscript.

Ruggie, John Gerald. 1993. "Territoriality and beyond: Problematizing modernity in international relations." *International Organization*, Vol. 47, pp. 139–174.

Sabel, Charles F. 1994. "Flexible specialization and the re-emergence of regional economies." In Ash Amin (Ed.), *Post-Fordism: A Reader* (London: Blackwell).

Salleh, Ismail Muhd. 1994. "Opportunities and challenge in industrial development." Paper presented at the Yayasan Indonesia Forum, Jakarta.

Sandhu, Harpal. 2003. "A doomed reform: North Korea flirts with the free market." *Harvard International Review* (Spring), pp. 36–39.

Sassen, Saskia. 1994. *Cities in a World Economy* (Thousand Oaks, CA: Pine Forge Press).

———. 1996. *Losing Control? Sovereignty in an Age of Globalization* (New York: Columbia University Press).

———. 1997. "The spatial organization of information industries: Implications for the role of the state." Pp. 33–52 in James H. Mittelman (Ed.), *Globalization: Critical Reflections* (Boulder, CO: Lynne Rienner).

———. 1999. "Embedding the global in the national: Implications for the role of the state." Pp. 158–171 in David A. Smith, Dorothy J. Solinger, and Steven C. Topik (Eds.), *States and Sovereignty in the Global Economy* (London: Routledge).

———. 2001. *The Global City: New York, London, Tokyo*, 2nd ed. (Princeton, NJ: Princeton University Press).

Scalapino, Robert A. 1995. "Natural economic territories in East Asia—Present trends and future prospects." Pp. 99–109 in Korean Economic Institute of America (Ed.), *Economic Cooperation and Challenges in the Pacific* (Washington, DC: Korean Economic Institute of America).

Scott, Allan J. 1995. "The Geographic foundations of industrial performance." *Competition and Change*, Vol. 1, No. 1, pp. 51–66.

Scott, James Wesley. 1998. "The institutionalization of transboundary cooperation in Europe: Recent development on the Dutch-German border." *Journal of Borderlands Studies*, Vol. 8, No. 1, pp. 39–65.

Scott, James Wesley, and Kimberly Collins. 1997. "Inducing transboundary regionalism in asymmetric situations: The case of the German-Polish border." *Journal of Borderlands Studies*, Vol. 12, Nos. 1–2, pp. 97–121.

Selden, Mark. 1997. "China, Japan, and the regional political economy of East Asia, 1945–1995." Pp. 306–340 in Peter J. Katzenstein and Takashi Shiraishi (Eds.), *Network Power: Japan and Asia* (Ithaca, NY: Cornell University Press).

Serageldin, Ismail, and Christiaan Grootaert. 2000. "Defining social capital: An integrating view," Pp. 40–58 in Partha Dasgupta and Ismail Serageldin (Eds.), *Social Capital: A Multifaceted Perspective* (Washington, DC: World Bank).

Shambaugh, David (Ed.). 1995. *Greater China: The Next Superpower?* (London: Oxford University Press).

Shapiro, Don. 2002. "Working on cross-strait connections." *Topics*, Vol. 32, No. 8 (October), pp. 19–28.

Shieh, Samuel. 1997. "Hong Kong will remain Taiwan-China intermediary," *Asian Business* (June–July), pp. 36–38.

Shim, Jae Hoon. 1999. "A crack in the wall." *Far Eastern Economic Review* (April 29), pp. 10–12.

Shiode, Hirokasu. 1994. "Tumen River Area Development Programme: The North Korean perspective." Pp. 277–304 in Myo Thant, Min Tang, and Hiroshi Kakazu (Eds.), *Growth Triangles in Asia: A New Approach to Regional Economic Cooperation* (Oxford: Oxford University Press).

Shirk, Susan L. 1993. *The Political Logic of Economic Reform in China* (Berkeley: University of California Press),

Siddique, Sharon. 1997. "Southeast Asia's last frontier: The East ASEAN growth area." *AsiaInsights*, Vol. 1, No. 4 (October), pp. 3–8.

Silk, Mitchell A. 1990. "Silent partners." *China Business Review*, Vol. 17, No. 5 (September–October), pp. 32–40.

Sklair, Leslie. 1989. *Assembling for Development: The Maquila Industry in Mexico and the United States* (Boston: Unwin Hyman).

Smart, Alan. 1993. "The political economy of rent-seeking in a Chinese factory town." *Anthropology of Work Review*, Vol. 14, Nos. 2–3, pp. 15–19.

———. 2000. "The emergence of local capitalisms in China: Overseas Chinese investment and patterns of development." Pp. 65–95 in Si-ming Li and Wing-shing Tang (Eds.), *China's Regions, Polity, and Economy: A Study of Spatial Transformation in the Post-Reform Era* (Hong Kong: Chinese University Press).

Smart, Alan, and Josephine Smart. 1998. "Transnational social networks and negotiated identities in interactions between Hong Kong and China." Pp. 103–129 in Michael Peter Smith and Luis Eduardo Guarnizo (Eds.), *Transnationalism from Below* (New Brunswick, NJ: Transaction).

Smart, Josephine, and Alan Smart. 1991. "Personal relations and divergent economies: A case study of Hong Kong investment in South China." *International Journal of Urban and Regional Research*, Vol. 15, pp. 216–233.

———. 1993. "Obligation and control: Employment of kin in capitalist labor management in China." *Critique of Anthropology*, Vol. 13, No. 1, pp. 7–31.

Snyder, Timothy. 2000. "Conclusion: The wall around the West." Pp. 219–227 in Peter Andreas and Timothy Snyder (Eds.), *The Wall Around the West: State Borders and Immigration Controls in North America and Europe* (Lanham, MD: Rowman & Littlefield).

So, Alvin Y. 2003. "Introduction: Rethinking the Chinese developmental miracle." Pp. 3–26 in Alvin Y. So (Ed.), *China's Developmental Miracle: Origins, Transformations, and Challenges* (Armonk, NY: M. E. Sharpe).

Spener, David. 2002. "The unraveling seam: NAFTA and the decline of the apparel industry in El Paso, Texas." Pp. 139–160 in Gary Gereffi, David Spener, and Jennifer Bair (Eds.), *Free Trade and Uneven Development: The North American Apparel Industry After NAFTA* (Philadelphia: Temple University Press).

Spener, David, Gary Gereffi, and Jennifer Bair. 2002. "Introduction: The apparel industry and North American economic integration." Pp. 3–22 in Gary Gereffi, David Spener, and Jennifer Bair (Eds.), *Free Trade and Uneven Development: The North American Apparel Industry After NAFTA* (Philadelphia: Temple University Press).

Spruyt, Hendrik. 1994. *The Sovereign State and Its Competitors: An Analysis of Systems Change* (Princeton, NJ: Princeton University Press).

Steiner, M., and D. Sturn. 1993. "Interregional cooperation and the transborder activities in a Middle European context," Pp. 177–190 in R. Cappellin and P. W. Batey (Eds.), *Regional Networks, Border Regions and European Integration* (London: Pion Limited).

Stiglitz, Joseph E. 2000. "Formal and informal institutions." Pp. 59–68 in Partha Dasgupta and Ismail Serageldin (Eds.), *Social Capital: A Multifaceted Perspective* (Washington, DC: World Bank)

Storper, Michael, and Bennett Harrison. 1991. "Flexibility, hierarchy and regional development: The changing structure of industrial production systems and their forms of governance in the 1990s." *Research Policy*, Vol. 20, pp. 407–422.

Strange, Susan. 1997. "The erosion of the state." *Current History* (November), pp. 365–369.

Sung, Yun-Wing. 1997. "Hong Kong and the economic integration of the China circle." Pp. 41–80 in Barry Naughton (Ed.), *The China Circle: Economics and Electronics in the PRC, Taiwan, and Hong Kong* (Washington, DC: Brookings Institution Press).

Sweedler, Alan. 1994. "Conflict and cooperation in border regions: An examination of the Russian-Finnish border." *Journal of Borderlands Studies*, Vol. 9, No. 1, pp. 1–13.

Tambunlertchai, Somsak. 1994. "Northern growth triangle and ASEAN industrial cooperation." Paper presented at the Yayasan Indonesia Forum, Jakarta.

Tham, Kum Yew. 1997/1998. "A case study of a European multinational corporation operating in the Indonesia-Malaysia-Singapore growth triangle." Master's thesis submitted to the Graduate School of Business, National University of Singapore.

Than, Mya. 1996. "The golden quadrangle of mainland Southeast Asia: A Myanmar perspective." ISEAS Working Papers, Economics and Finance No. 5, Institute of Southeast Asian Studies, Singapore.

———. 1997. "Economic cooperation in the Greater Mekong Subregion." *Asia-Pacific Economic Literature*, Vol. 11, No. 2, pp. 40–57.

Thant, Myo. 1996. "Overview." Pp. 1–27 in Myo Thant and Min Tang (Eds.), *Indonesia-Malaysia-Thailand Growth Triangle: Theory to Practice* (Manila: Asian Development Bank).

Thant, Myo, Min Tang, and Hiroshi Kakazu (Eds.). 1998. *Growth Triangles in Asia: A New Approach to Regional Economic Cooperation*, 2nd ed. (Oxford, UK: Oxford University Press).

Thuen, Trond. 1999. "The significance of borders in the East European transition." *International Journal of Urban and Regional Research*, Vol. 23, No. 4, pp. 738–750.

Tripathi, Salil. 1996. "Island dreams." *Asia, Inc.*, Vol. 5, No. 7 (July), pp. 28–29.

———. 1996/1997. "The Peninsular paws back." *Asia, Inc.*, Vol. 5, No. 12/Vol. 6, No. 1 (December/January), pp. 51–55.

Turner, Jonathan H. 2000. "The formation of social capital." Pp. 94–146 in Partha Dasgupta and Ismail Serageldin (Eds.), *Social Capital: A Multifaceted Perspective* (Washington, DC: World Bank).

Turner, Mark. 1995. "Subregional economic zones, politics and development: The Philippine involvement in the East ASEAN growth area (EAGA)." *Pacific Review*, Vol. 8, No. 4, pp. 637–648.

Underdown, Michael. 1997. "Behind the scenes: The real story of the Tumen River area development programme." Paper presented to the Department of Government and Public Administration, University of Sydney, August 12.

Underwood, Laurie. 2000. "Go slow no more?" *Topics*, Vol. 30, No. 9 (November), pp. 18–28.

United Nations Development Programme (UNDP). 2001–2003. "Tourism in the Rajin-Sonbong zone, DPRK: A land of many surprises." UNDP Tumen Secretariat's website, www.tumenprogramme.org/tumen/sectors/tourismrason, accessed on January 30, 2003.

———. Global Environment Facility (UNDP/GEF). 2003. "TumenNET Strategic Action Programme: Eco-regional cooperation on biodiversity conservation and protection of international waters in Northeast Asia," Regional Strategic Action Programme report, October 2002, www.tumennet.org/publication/publication.html, accessed on April 22.

Valencia, Mark J. (Ed.). 1995. *The Russian Far East in Transition: Opportunities for Regional Economic Cooperation* (Boulder, CO: Westview Press).

van der Veen, A. 1993. "Theory and practice of cross-border cooperation of local governments: The case of EUREGIO between Germany and the Netherlands." Pp. 89–95 in R. Cappellin and P. W. Batey (Eds.), *Regional Networks, Border Regions, and European Integration* (London: Pion Limited).

van Dooren, Robine. 2002. "TexMex: Linkages in a binational garment district? The garment industries in El Paso and Ciudad Juárez." Pp. 161–180 in Gary Gereffi, David Spener, and Jennifer Bair (Eds.), *Free Trade and Uneven Development: The North American Apparel Industry After NAFTA* (Philadelphia: Temple University Press).

Veggeland, V. 1993. "The border region challenge facing Norden: Appyling new regional concepts." Pp. 31–46 in R. Cappellin and P. W. Batey (Eds.), *Regional Networks, Border Regions, and European Integration* (London: Pion Limited).

Wade, Geoff. 2000. "The southern Chinese borders in history." Pp. 28–50 in Grant Evans, Christopher Hutton, and Kuah Khun Eng (Eds.), *Where China Meets Southeast Asia: Social and Cultural Change in the Border Regions* (Bangkok: Institute of Southeast Asian Studies).

Wade, Robert. 1990. *Governing the Market: Economic Theory and the Role of Government in East Asian Industrialization* (Princeton, NJ: Princeton University Press).

Walker, Andrew. 2000. "Regional trade in northwestern Laos: An assessment of the golden quadrangle." Pp. 122–144 in Grant Evans, Christopher Hutton, and Kuah Khun Eng (Eds.), *Where*

China Meets Southeast Asia: Social and Cultural Change in the Border Regions (Bangkok: Institute of Southeast Asian Studies).

Wallace, Claire, in association with Oksana Shmulyar and Vasil Bedzir. 1999. "Investing in social capital: The case of small-scale, cross-border traders in post-Communist Central Europe." *International Journal of Urban and Regional Research*, Vol. 23, No. 4, pp. 751–770.

Wank, David L. 1995. "Bureaucratic patronage and private business: Changing networks of power in urban China." Pp. 153–183 in Andrew G. Walder (Ed.), *The Waning of the Communist State: Economic Origins of Political Decline in China and Hungary* (Berkeley: University of California Press).

———. 1998. "Embedding greater China: Kin, friends, and ancestors in overseas Chinese investment networks." Presented at the International Conference on City, State and Region in a Global Order: Toward the 21st Century, Hiroshima University, Hiroshima, Japan, December 19–20.

———. 1999. *Commodifying Communism: Business, Trust, and Politics in a Chinese City* (Cambridge: Cambridge University Press).

Warner, Mildred. 1999. "Social capital construction and the role of the local state." *Rural Sociology*, Vol. 64, pp. 373–393.

Weber, Alfred. 1929. *Theory of Location of Industries* (Chicago: University of Chicago Press).

Wessel, Karin. 1997. "Basic features of economic and regional development in South Korea." Pp. 60–140 in Ludwig H. Schätzl, Karin Wessel, and Yong-Woo Lee (Eds.), *Regional Development and Decentralization Policy in South Korea* (Singapore: Institute of Southeast Asian Studies).

Williams, James H., David von Hippel, and Peter Hayes. 2000. *Fuel and Famine: Rural Energy Crisis in the Democratic People's Republic of Korea*, Policy Paper 46 (San Diego: Institute on Global Conflict and Cooperation, University of California).

Wilson, Andrew. 1996. "A place in the Pacific sun." *Asia, Inc.*, Vol. 6, No. 10 (October), pp. 10–12.

Wilson, Patricia A. 1992. *Exports and Local Development: Mexico's New Maquiladoras* (Austin: University of Texas Press).

———. 1996. "Future directions in local economic development." Pp. 311–320 in Christophe Demazière and Patricia A. Wilson (Eds.), *Local Economic Development in Europe and Americas* (London: Mansell).

Wilson, Thomas M., and Hastings Donnan. 1998a. "Nation, state and identity at international borders." Pp. 1–30 in Thomas M. Wilson and Hastings Donnan (Eds.), *Border Identities: Nation and State at International Frontiers* (Cambridge: Cambridge University Press).

——— (Eds.). 1998b. *Border Identities: Nation and State at International Frontiers* (Cambridge: Cambridge University Press).

Winder, Joseph A. B. 2000. "The economic dynamics of the Korean peninsula peace process." Pp. 95–109 in Korean Economic Institute of America (Ed.), *The Two Koreas in 2000: Sustaining Recovery and Seeking Reconciliation* (Washington, DC: Korean Economic Institute of America).

Wishnick, Elizabeth. 2002. "Russian-North Korean relations: A new era?" Pp. 139–162 in Samuel S. Kim and Tai Hwan Lee (Eds.), *North Korea and Northeast Asia* (Lanhan, MD: Rowman & Littlefield).

Wong, Christine. 1991. "Central-local relations in an era of fiscal decline: The paradox of fiscal decentralization in post-Mao China." *China Quarterly*, Vol. 128, pp. 691–715.

Woolcock, Michael. 1998. "Social capital and economic development: Toward a theoretical synthesis and policy framework." *Theory and Society*, Vol. 27, pp. 151–208.

Wu, Fulong. 2003. "The (post-)socialist entrepreneurial city as a state project: Shanghai's re-globalization in question." *Urban Studies*, Vol. 40, No. 9 (August), pp. 1673–1698.

Yeh, Anthony Gar-on, Yok-shiu F. Lee, Tunney Lee, and Nien Dak Sze (Eds.). 2002. *Building a Competitive Pearl River Delta Region* (Hong Kong: Center of Urban Planning and Environmental Management, University of Hong Kong).

Yeung, Henry Wai-chung. 2000. "The Dynamics of Asian Business Systems in a Globalizing Era." *Review of International Political Economy*, Vol. 7, No. 3, pp. 399–433.

Ying, Iris. 2001. "Business in the Tumen region from the private sector perspective: Legal and institutional barriers." UNDP Tumen Secretariat's website, www.tumenprogramme.org/tumen/, accessed January 30, 2003.

Yoshida, Tsuneaki. 2003. "Evolution of regional infrastructure development." Paper presented at the Regional Cooperation and Cross-border Infrastructure workshop sponsored by the Asian Development Bank Institute, Tokyo, December 9–12.

Yow, Cheun Hoe. 2003. "China-ASEAN relations, October 2002 to June 2003: Chronology of events." *China: An International Journal*, Vol. 1, No. 2, pp. 354–362.

Yun, Ken. 1989. "Crossing the Yellow Sea." *China Business Review* (January/February), pp. 38–42.

Zayonchkovskaya, Zhanna. N.d. "The migration situation on the Russian-Chinese border." Unpublished manuscript.

Zhao, Guangzhi. 1997. "From border trade to economic regionalism: Yunnan province and the upper Mekong corridor in the 1990s." *Journal of Chinese Political Science*, Vol. 3, No. 1 (Summer), pp. 27–63.

Zipf, George K. 1941. *National Unity and Disunity: The Nation as a Bio-social Organism* (Bloomington, IN: Principia Press).

Publications in Chinese

China Bohai Region Economic Research Association (CBRERA). 1991. *A Guide to Economic Development and Cooperation in China's Bohai Coastal Region* (Beijing: CITIC Publishing House).

Chinese Central Academy of Ethnology (CCAE). 1993. *Zhongguo Yanbian Kaifang Chengshi Touzi Maoyi Zhinan* (An Investment and Trade Guide for China's Border Open Cities) (Beijing: Chinese Central Academy of Ethnology Publishing House).

Chen, Cai. 1998. "Yanbian diqu wuliu xianzhuang yu yuce" (The current state and forecast of goods flows in the Yanbian region). *Dongbei Ya Luntan* (Northeast Asia Forum), Vol. 2, pp. 1–10.

Chen, Cai, and Sibao Ding. 1999. "Dongbei diqu bianjing kouan jingji fazhan xianzhuang de diancha yu fenxi" (An analysis of current economic development at the border posts in northeast China). *Dongbei Ya Luntan* (Northeast Asia Forum), Vol. 2, pp. 49–53.

Chen, Shumei. 2000. "Surpassing Shenzhen and catching up with Shanghai: The miracle of Taiwan businesses in Dongguan." *Sinorama Magazine* (February), pp. 1–12. (from magazines .sinanet.com/sinorama/contents).

Ding, Shicheng. 1992. "Lianheguo kaifa jihuashu tumenjiang diqu kaifa xiangmu shuping" (An appraisal of the Tumen River regional development projects of the UNDP). *Dongbei Ya Luntan* (Northeast Asia Forum), Vol. 1, pp. 54–58.

Ding, Sibao. 1993. "Guoji hezhuo tiaojian xia tumenjiang diqu kaifa gangyiao yanjiu" (A study of the Tumen River region development plan under international cooperation). *Dongbei Ya Yanjiu* (Northeast Asian Studies), Vol. 3, pp. 12–29.

Duan, Jiao. 1999. "You xianggang dao gangzhu duhuiqu" (From Hong Kong to a Hong Kong–Pearl River Delta metropolitan region). *Tequ Jingji yu Gang-Ao-Tai Jingji* (Special Zone Economy and Hong Kong, Macau, and Taiwan Economies), No. 5, pp. 27–35.

Economic and Trade Cooperation with Neighboring Countries Bureau (ETCNCB). 1995. *Zhongguo Yunnan Bianmao* (Frontier Trade in Yunnan, China), summary statistics.

Fu, Yanni. 1998. "Ershiyi shiji jilinsheng yu zhoubian guojia jingmao hezhuo zhanwang" (The prospect for economic and trade cooperation between Jilin province and the neighboring countries). Pp. 407–418 in Zhongshu Liu and Shengjin Wang (Eds.), *Dongbei Ya Dique Heping Yu Fazhan Yanjiu* (Research on Peace and Development in Northeast Asia) (Jilin: Jilin University Press).

Han, Zenglin. 1995. "Shilun bohai diqu gangkou yunshu tixi de jianshe yu buju" (The construction and distribution of the harbor system of the Bohai region). *Jingji Dili* (Economic Geography), Vol. 15, No. 1, pp. 79–84.

Huang, Zhi-Lian. 1993. "The historical background of the Chinese economic cooperation system." In William T. Liu (Ed.), *The Chinese Economic Cooperation System* (Hong Kong: Joint Publishing).

Hsuen, Chun-tu, and Nanchuan Lu (Eds.). 1999. *Zhonger Jingmao Guangxi* (Economic and Trade Relations Between China and Russia) (Beijing: China Social Science Press).

Jin, Xingre. 1999. "Luojin—xianfeng jingji maoyi diqu waiguo touzi guanxifa zhidu de jianli yu tedian" (The establishment and characteristics of the foreign investment relations laws in the Rajin-Sonbong free economic and trade zone). *Dongbei Ya Luntan* (Northeast Asia Forum), Vol. 1, pp. 32–34.

Kao, Charles H. C., Joseph S. Lee, and Chu-Chia Steve Lin. 1992. *An Empirical Study of Taiwan Investment on Mainland China* (Taipei: Commonwealth Publishing).

Kao, Charles H. C., Chu-Chia Steve Lin, Cher Hsu, and Wennie Lin. 1995. *The Taiwan Investment Experience in Mainland China: A First-Hand Report* (Taipei: Commonwealth Publishing).

Li, Fuxin. 1996. "Hanguo xibu kaifa jihua ji dui wuoguo jingji keneng changsheng de yinxiang" (South Korea's west coast development plan and its possible impact on China's economy). *Dongbei Ya Luntan* (Northeast Asia Forum), Vol. 1, pp. 46–49.

Li, Jie, and Yunzhong Zhao. 1997. *Yunnan Waixiangxin Jingji* (Yunnan's Outward-Oriented Economy) (Dehong, Yunnan: Dehong Ethnology Press).

Li, Wei, Yianming Zhu, and Yan He (Eds.). 1997. *Tumenjiang Diqu Ziyuan Kaifa, Jianshe Buju yu Huanjin Zhengzhi Yanjiu* (A Study on Resource Exploration, Construction Patterns and Environmental Treatment in the Tumen River Region) (Beijing: Science Press).

Li, Wen, and Yingji Jin. 1999. "Huan huanghai quyu jingji hezuo fangxin weiai" (The continued vitality of economic cooperation among the Yellow Sea rim). *Dangdai Yatai* (Contemporary Asia-Pacific), Vol. 6, pp. 26–33.

Li, Yigan. 1999. "Daxinan lianhe canyu lancangjiang—meigonghe ciquyu hezuo kaifa de jiyu yi tiaozhan" (The opportunity and challenges for the joint participation of the Greater Southwest in the Lancang River—Mekong River Subregional Cooperation and Development). Pp. 23–37 in Yigan Li and Mu Qin (Eds.), *Daxinan Lianhe Canyu Lancangjiang—Meigonghe Ciquyu Hezuo Kaifa Yanjiu* (Research on the Participation of the Greater Southwest in the

Lancang River—Mekong River Subregional Cooperation and Development) (Kunming, Yunnan).

Li, Yingwu, and Guilan Wu. 1998. "Zhongguo chaoxianzu zai dongbeiya heping yu fazhan zhong de zuoyong" (The role of ethnic Korean Chinese in the peace and development of Northeast Asia). Pp. 55–66 in Zhongshu Liu and Shengjin Wang (Eds.), *Dongbei Ya Dique Heping Yu Fazhan Yanjiu* (Research on Peace and Development in Northeast Asia) (Jilin: Jilin University Press).

Li, Yun, and Xuehua Liu. 1999. "Kunming zhi Mangu guoji gonglu Laowuo jingneiduan diaocha baogao" (An investigative report on the Lao portion of the Kunming-Bangkok international road). Pp. 178–182 in Yigan Li and Mu Qin (Eds.), *Daxinan Lianhe Canyu Lancangjiang—Meigonghe Ciquyu Hezuo Kaifa Yanjiu* (Research on the Participation of the Greater Southwest in the Lancang River—Mekong River Subregional Cooperation and Development) (Kunming, Yunnan).

Li, Zhuqing, and Tongyang Shi. 1994. *Shaoshu Minzu Diqu Bianjing Maoyi Yanjiu* (Research on Border Trade in National Minority Regions) (Beijing: China Ethnology University Press).

Liu, Baorong, and Jiasheng Liao. 1993. *Zhongguo Yanbian Kaifang yu Zhoubian Guojia Shichang* (China's Opening Borders and the Neighboring Countries' Markets) (Beijing: Legal Press).

Liu, Qingquan (Trans.). 1995. "Erluosi yuandong duiwai maoyi de jigou" (The structure of the Russian Far East's foreign trade). *Xiboliya Yanjiu* (Siberian Studies), Vol. 22, pp. 45–56.

Liu, Ta, and Xiaohung Hou. 1994. "Shandong bandao chengshi miji didai de jueqi" (The rise of the dense metropolitan belt on the Shandong peninsula). *Jingji Dili* (Economic Geography) Vol. 14, No. 1, pp. 59–64.

Liu, Yinhua, and Shuren Yuan. 1997. "Buke xiaoshi de chaoxian ziyou jingji maoyiqu" (The North Korean free economic and trade zone that cannot be ignored). *Dongbei Ya Luntan.* (Northeast Asia Studies), Vol. 3, pp. 69–72.

Long, Yongshu (Ed.). 1998. *Haixia Liangan Jingmao Hezhuo Guanxi Yanjiu* (A Study of the Economic and Trade Cooperative Relations Across the Taiwan Strait) (Beijing: Economic Management Press).

Peng, San, and Dongling Yan (Eds.). 1994. *Zhong Han Jingmao Hezhuo Zhinan* (A Guide to Economic and Trade Cooperation between China and South Korea) (Tianjin: Tianjin People's Press).

Rao, Mei-Jiao. 1994. "The reorientation of Hong Kong's manufacturing system and the thinking on Hong Kong–southern China economic integration." Pp. 201–219 in Rao Mei-Jiao (Ed.), *The Economic Cooperation of the Chinese Areas* (Hong Kong: World Wide Publications).

Ren, Yanqiu. 1994. "Haiwai dui tumenjiang diqu kaifa de fangxiang" (The oversea reaction to Tumen River regional development). *Dongbei Ya Yanjiu* (Northeast Asian Studies), Vol. 14 (Supplemental Issue), pp. 57–64.

Shenzhen Statistical and Information Bureau (SSIB). 2000. *Shenzhen Tongji Shouce 2000* (Shenzhen Statistical Handbook) (Shenzhen, mimeo).

Shi, Zhenkuan, and Wensheng Yu. 1995. "Jilin sheng tong chaoxian bianjin maoyi ji difang yihuo maoyi de taishi fenxi" (A current analysis of border trade between Jilin province and North Korea and local bartering trade). *Dongbei Ya Luntan* (Northeast Asia Forum), Vol. 1, pp. 52–55.

Song, Xiaolu. 1998. "Zhonger maoyi kunjing zhongde tansuo—kuaguo zhixiao" (Exploring the difficulty of China-Russian trade: Cross-national direct sales). *Dongbei Ya Luntan* (Northeast Asia Forum), Vol. 3, pp. 71–75.

State Statistical Bureau (SSB). 1991. *Fujian Tongji Nianjian 1991* (Fujian Statistical Yearbook 1991) (Beijing: China Statistics Press).

———. 1992. *China Foreign Economic Statistics 1979–1991* (Beijing: China Statistical Information and Consultancy Service Center).

———. 1994. *China's Bohai Coastal Region: A Golden Area of Northeast Asia* (Beijing: China Statistics Press).

———. 1996. *Zhongguo Tongji Nianjian 1996* (China Statistical Yearbook 1996) (Beijing: China Statistics Press).

———. 1997. *Liaoning Tongji Nianjian 1997* (Liaoning Statistical Yearbook 1997) (Beijing: China Statistics Press).

———. 1998. *Yunnan Tongji Nianjian 1998* (Yunnan Statistical Yearbook 1998) (Beijing: China Statistics Press).

———. 1999. *China Foreign Economic Statistical Yearbook 1998* (Beijing: China Statistics Press).

———. 2000. *Zhongguo Tongji Nianjian 2000* (China Statistical Yearbook 2000) (Beijing: China Statistics Press).

Sui, Yinghui. 1997. "Shandongsheng yu hanguo jingji jishu hezuo de zhengce xuanze" (Policy choices for the economic and technological cooperation between Shandong province and South Korea). *Dongbei Ya Luntan* (Northeast Asia Forum), Vol. 2, pp. 66–68.

Tang, Chengcheng. 1999. "Dui xishuanbanna fazhan Lancangjiang—Meigonghe hangyun de sikao" (Some thoughts on shipping on the Lancang-Mekong River for xishuanbanna). Pp. 192–196 in Yigan Li and Mu Qin (Eds.), *Daxinan Lianhe Canyu Lancangjiang–Meigonghe Ciquyu Hezuo Kaifa Yanjiu* (Research on the Participation of the Greater Southwest in the Lancang River–Mekong River Subregional Cooperation and Development) (Kunming, Yunnan).

Tang, Guohui. 1995. *Yunnan Yanbian Kaifang: Zhanglue he Cuoshe Yanjiu* (Yunnan's Border Opening: A Study of Strategy and Measures) (Kunming: Yunnan University Press).

Tang, Guohui, Yongming Zhu, and Songhui Hu. 1999. "Cujing jingji zoulang jiegui canyu da meigonghe ciquyu jingji hezhuo" (Facilitating the connection of economic corridors and the participation in economic cooperation of the GMS). Pp. 94–104 in Yigan Li and Mu Qin (Eds.), *Daxinan Lianhe Canyu Lancangjiang–Meigonghe Ciquyu Hezuo Kaifa Yanjiu* (Research on the Participation of the Greater Southwest in the Lancang River–Mekong River Subregional Cooperation and Development) (Kunming, Yunnan).

Wang, Fengsheng. 2003. "Lianan gaokeji chanyie jinghe celue zhi tangtao" (An exploration of competitive and cooperative strategies for high- and scientific-technology industries across the Taiwan Strait). *Xiandaihua Yanjiu* (Modernization Studies), Vol. 33 (January), pp. 1–22.

Wang, Jian. 1999. "Guanyu kuoda wuosheng yu zhoubian guojia bianjing miaoyi wenti de yanjiu" (Research on expanding our province's border trade with the neighboring countries). Pp. 286–292 in Yigan Li and Mu Qin (Eds.), *Daxinan Lianhe Canyu Lancangjiang–Meigonghe Ciquyu Hezuo Kaifa Yanjiu* (Research on the Participation of the Greater Southwest in the Lancang River–Mekong River Subregional Cooperation and Development) (Kunming, Yunnan).

Wang, Rong, and Ping Li. 1998. "Lancangjiang xiayou diqu kouan jianshe guihua yanjiu baogao" (A research report on the construction and planning for the crossings at the lower reach of the Lancang River). *Jingji Luntan* (Economic Forum), Vol. 107 (Special Issue), pp. 24–50.

Wang, Shengjin, and Donghui Zhang. 1998. "Lun difang chengshi difang zhengfu zai dongbeiya diqu jingji hezhuo zhongde diwei he zuoyong" (The status and role of localities and local governments in the regional economic cooperation of Northeast Asia). *Dongbei Ya Luntan* (Northeast Asia Forum), Vol. 4, pp. 24–28.

Wang, Shuhua, Pingyu Zhang, and Liping Yang. 1995. "Huan bohai binhai didai dazhong chengshi de fazhan" (The development of large and medium-sized cities in and around the Bohai region). *Dili Kexue* (Scientia Geographica Sinica), Vol. 15, No. 1 (February), pp. 14–22.

Xu, Ningning. 2002. *Laizi Dongnanya de Shanji Baogao* (A Commercial Report from Southeast Asia) (Beijing: Huaxia Publishing House).

Ye, Baoming, Qingshan Yang, and Lihua Sun. 1993. "Hunchun fangchuan jiangang wenti chutan" (A preliminary exploration of building a port at fangchuan, Hunchun). *Dili Kexue* (Scientia Geographica Sinica), Vol. 13, No. 2 (May), pp. 177–184.

Yu, Bindiao. 1998. "Guoji difang hezuo" (International local cooperation). In Zhongshu Liu and Shengjin Wang (Eds.), *Dongbei Ya Dique Heping Yu Fazhan Yanjiu* (Research on Peace and Development in Northeast Asia) (Jilin: Jilin University Press).

Yu, Guozheng. 1994. "Guanyu jianli tumenjiang sanjaozhou kuaguo jingji tequ de zhonghe yanjiu baogao" (An integrated research report on the establishment of a cross-national special economic zone in the Tumen River delta). *Dongbei Ya Yanjiu* (Northeast Asian Studies), Vol. 14 (Supplemental Issue), pp. 12–29.

Zang, Shengyuan. 1999. "A special plan: Taiwan's economic miracle on the shore of the Pearl River" (in Chinese). *Global Views Magazine* (September), pp. 1–18 ; downloaded from magazines.sinanet.com/globalview/contents.

Zhang, Shihe. 1997. "Chaoxian luojin-xianfeng ziyou jingjiqu de kaifa yu dongbeiya quyu guoji hezuo he fazhan" (The development of North Korea's Rajin-Sonbong free economic and trade zone and international cooperation and development in the Northeast Asian region). *Dongbei Ya Luntan* (Northeast Asia Forum), Vol. 1, pp. 72–77.

Zhang, Ying. 1994. "Chaoxian luojin-xianfeng ziyou jingjiqu jiben qingkuang ji fazhan qianjing" (The basic conditions and development prospect of North Korea's Rajin-Sonbong free economic and trade zone). *Dongbei Ya Yanjiu* (Northeast Asia Studies), Vol. 14 (Supplemental Issue), pp. 39–45.

Zhonghua Publishing House (ZHPH). 2001. *Yunnan Tongji Nianjian 2000* (Yunnan Statistical Yearbook 2000) (Beijing: Zhonghua Publishing House).

Index

About the Author

Xiangming Chen is professor of sociology and adjunct professor of political science, University of Illinois at Chicago, as well as a research fellow with the IC² Institute, University of Texas at Austin. He has been conducting comparative and transnational research on the multiple facets of global-local relations in the urban and regional contexts of China and Asia, with a recent focus on the rise of Shanghai and its surrounding region. He is co-author (with Anthony M. Orum) of *The World of Cities: Places in Comparative and Historical Perspective* (2003) and has published in a number of leading social science and urban studies journals.